Teaching through Text

Reading and Writing in the Content Areas

Michael C. McKenna

University of Virginia

Richard D. Robinson

University of Missouri–Columbia

Boston   New York   San Francisco
Mexico City   Montreal   Toronto   London   Madrid   Munich   Paris
Hong Kong   Singapore   Tokyo   Cape Town   Sydney

Executive Editor: *Aurora Martínez Ramos*
Editorial Assistant: *Kara Kikel*
Executive Marketing Manager: *Krista Clark*
Production Editor: *Cynthia Parsons*
Editorial Production Service: *NK Graphics*
Composition Buyer: *Linda Cox*
Manufacturing Buyer: *Megan Cochran*
Electronic Composition: *NK Graphics*
Interior Design: *NK Graphics*
Cover Administrator: *Linda Knowles*
Cover Designer: *Elena Sidorova*

For related titles and support materials, visit our online catalog at www.pearsonhighered.com.

Between the time website information is gathered and then published, it is not unusual for some sites to have closed. Also, the transcription of URLs can result in typographical errors. The publisher would appreciate notification where these errors occur so that they may be corrected in subsequent editions.

Library of Congress Cataloging-in-Publication Data

McKenna, Michael C.
  Teaching through text : reading and writing in the content areas / Michael C. McKenna, Richard D. Robinson.
     p.   cm.
  Includes bibliographical references and index.
  ISBN-13: 978-0-13-207472-8
  ISBN-10: 0-13-207472-9
  1. Language arts (Secondary)—United States.   2. Language arts—Correlation with content subjects—United States.   I. Robinson, Richard David, 1940–   II. Title.
  LB1631.M395 2009
  428.4'3—dc22

                              2008035788

Printed in the United States of America

10 9 8 7 6 5 4 3   BR 12 11 10

Allyn & Bacon
is an imprint of

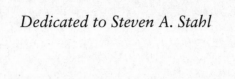

Dedicated to Steven A. Stahl

SECTION 2

PREREADING STRATEGIES 57

SECTION 3

STRATEGIES FOR GUIDED READING 99

SECTION 4

POSTREADING STRATEGIES   147

SECTION 5

MORE WAYS TO FACILITATE LEARNING THROUGH TEXT   189

Guiding Philosophy

Teaching through Text embodies certain beliefs about teachers and about learning through text. This book inevitably reflects these beliefs, which we regard as mainstream views based defensibly on available research and informed opinion. Specifically, we contend that

- The most effective content area teachers know their materials and their students and purposefully acquire information on both;
- An important (and virtually unassailable) priority of most content area teachers is the acquisition of content;
- Content literacy techniques must therefore be included only insofar as they are likely to enhance such learning (rather than merely improve general reading skills);
- The best learners from text actively engage in a process of constructing, verifying, and extending meaning as they read;
- Content area teachers are ideally placed to maximize such interaction between their students and their materials; and
- This result is most likely to be achieved when both reading and writing (the two domains of literacy) are integrated.

Our goal was to produce a book that provides a wide variety of suggestions for instructional practice that is consistent with these beliefs. We have tried very hard to include only those recommendations that have been validated through research and that teachers tend to regard as practical. This task has not been easy because of the multitude of ideas now in the literature. Rather than offer a comprehensive review of these ideas, we have sifted through them in a search for those that have proved both practical and effective.

Organization of the Book

This text is organized into five sections, each containing two or more chapters. Section One provides background in literacy and addresses second language and cultural challenges. Section Two takes a closer look at planning, focusing on activities that might precede a reading assignment, such as introducing vocabulary. Section Three presents ways of guiding students' reading in order to ensure that what they derive from an assignment corresponds with teacher expectations. Section Four discusses methods of following up assigned reading in such a way that learning is reinforced and extended. Section Five provides more techniques for helping students use literacy for developing an understanding of course content and for enhancing their attitude toward content literacy.

Each chapter begins with an organizing diagram that visually summarizes the chapter's main components. Chapter content is summarized verbally at the end of the chapter. Students are encouraged to become more active readers by means of sections titled "Getting Involved," which follow the summary of each chapter. Here, activities are suggested for applying chapter content and for making it specific to the student's teaching area.

We have attempted by several means to make the ideas presented in this book thoroughly understandable and enjoyable. One is the inclusion of numerous graphic aids, including diagrams, charts, definitions, and illustrations. We also use the unique device of the "concept bridge," indicated by the bridge symbol, that links key ideas across the book. Another feature, perhaps also unique to this text, is the integration of quotations from noted writers who, throughout the years, have addressed the very topics we examine.

If we have succeeded in creating a tool for moving content area teachers to consider, actively and openly, both the problems and the potential of using literacy in their classrooms, then the labors of constructing this book will have been rewarded.

M. C. McK.
R. D. R.

Teaching and Learning through Text

Never before have educators so actively discussed and so extensively researched the development of literacy. Reading and writing are no longer isolated issues but touch all areas of learning, including content subjects. The goal of this section is to provide the groundwork you will need to understand exactly how literacy can enhance (or limit) your students' learning.

Chapter 1 defines literacy and describes its relationship to the oral language processes of speaking and listening. We then introduce four important aspects of literacy, one of which is its potential in content area classrooms. This fourth aspect we call *content literacy*.

Chapter 2 describes reading and writing as language processes. We examine how an individual's purposes and background greatly influence what is learned through reading. We then look at writing as a process guided by intentions, a process of great usefulness as a means of refining and clarifying what we know about a subject.

Chapter 3 compares ways of gathering information about the needs of students. We look at three areas: (1) the reading ability of students, (2) the demands of reading materials, and (3) the suitability of instructional practices.

Chapter 4 discusses the challenges teachers face in meeting the educational needs of a diverse classroom. Students have always varied, of course, but demographic trends have created a much richer variety, influencing what students believe and how they learn. This chapter describes important dimensions of present-day diversity and offers practical suggestions for appropriate planning.

CHAPTER 1

The Importance of Literacy in Content Areas

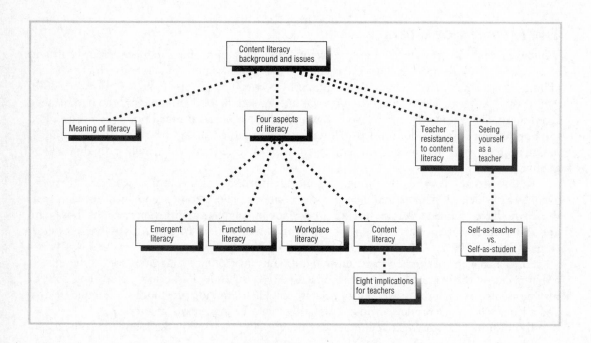

*The mass of every people must be barbarous
where there is no printing.*

—Samuel Johnson

Why should content area teachers be concerned with literacy? In the words of one teacher, "Isn't it enough to know about my teaching speciality without having to worry about reading and writing as well?" This important question will be addressed in various ways throughout this book.

This chapter is devoted to the term *literacy* and its implications for how students acquire content knowledge and skills. We begin with a discussion of what it means to be a literate person, because your eventual answer to this question (and it is *you* who must answer it!) will determine in large part your decisions concerning the role of literacy in your classes.

Objectives

After reading this chapter you should be able to

1. discuss whether content area teachers should be "teachers of reading," noting the principal reasons for and against this position;
2. define the various aspects of literacy, including emergent, functional, workplace, and content literacy;
3. describe how content literacy facilitates greater content achievement;
4. note some of the false assumptions many teachers have about reading and writing in the content fields; and
5. develop the beginnings of a philosophy toward content literacy in regard to the eventual role it will play in your own teaching.

The Meaning of Literacy

While we might all agree on the importance of being literate, defining *literacy* is a difficult and divisive task. Past definitions have often entailed the measurement of a few narrowly selected abilities (Maclachan & Cloonan, 2003; Mikulecky & Kirkley, 1998; Stephens & Brown, 2000). At one time, a literate person was one who was able to sign his or her name, or who had reached a certain grade level in school, or who had scored above a predetermined point on a test. Often the application of these definitions of literacy was handled in an arbitrary and prejudicial manner, as with the infamous "literacy tests" that once determined which individuals were qualified to vote.

Today, literacy is typically thought of in much broader terms and is seen as one of the avenues by which individuals interact in social contexts. The literate are defined not simply as those who have attained a certain level of proficiency in language ability, but rather as those who are able to use written materials effectively in the environment in which they live and work (Kaestle et al., 2001).

For the concept of literacy to be meaningful, you must think of it in relation to the unique requirements of the context in which it is to be used (Heath, 2000; Parkinson, 2000). This context may be as large as a nation or as small as a classroom. Each situation presents unique requirements, and adequate language proficiency in one situation might be inadequate in another.

To illustrate just how relative literacy can be, consider yourself in the following contexts:

- Your friend, a biology major, is hospitalized and asks you to summarize some assigned readings. As you begin, you encounter sentences like this one: "The endosteum is the vascular connective tissue lining the marrow cavities of bones."
- After driving across the border into Mexico, you see a sign containing the single word *Alto*. Luckily, it is printed on a red octagonal background.
- You buy an unassembled CD rack and encounter instructions like this: "Fasten flange G to tie-rod Q using hex nut R and a socket wrench."
- You read an e-mail message that contains the following:
  To: mmckenna@virginia.edu
  Message-id: <01HVGZIZ04K28XCNEN@asu.edu>
  Content-transfer-encoding: 7BIT

Of course, it is possible that your personal background makes one or more of these contexts no problem at all. You may actually be a biology major, for example, or you may speak Spanish. Chances are, however, that some of the situations presented difficulties precisely because you lacked the literacy skills required. This is a humbling realization, but it underscores how the same person can be literate in some contexts yet virtually illiterate in others.

We can define literacy in either broad or narrow terms. For example, Farris, Fuhler, & Walther (2004) take a narrow and traditional approach. To them, literacy is "the ability to read and understand what others have written, along with the ability to write as a means of recording information and for communicating with others" (p. 5). This definition is useful for most purposes, but a broader conception of literacy helps us appreciate how reading and writing are just two of many symbol systems through which we interpret and convey information. We now speak of *multiple literacies,* an idea that includes digital icons, the visual arts, music, drama, and even dance (Richards & McKenna, 2003).

Whether you are literate may change with the situation in which you find yourself. Can you navigate through a complex Web site? Can you "read" the tone of voice used by an actor? Can you integrate visual aids with accompanying text? Beginning with the work of Gray (1969) and extending through periodic national assessments of reading, literacy has come to mean a person's performance in relation to the need to use literacy skills in a particular social setting (Ash, 1998; Cairney, 2000; Strong, 1998; Venezky, 1995).

Four Aspects of Literacy

Recent research has led to a new appreciation for the complexity of literacy processes. One important consequence has been an abandonment of the notion that literacy is a single state or set of skills. In this section, we develop this notion by discussing four diverse aspects of literacy: emergent, functional, workplace, and content literacy. It will become clear that these aspects, while distinct in many respects, are nevertheless highly interconnected and interdependent.

Emergent Literacy

An outmoded view of learning to read and write holds that a child begins to acquire these abilities only upon entry into the formal settings of school instruction. The kindergarten teacher's job was to prepare children for actual literacy instruction (to begin in first grade) by undertaking an extensive regimen of "readiness" training.

A view that squares more accurately with the results of research (Duke, 2003; Morris et al., 2003; Roskos & Christie, 2002; Roskos, Christie, & Richgels, 2003) is that literate behavior and experiences begin long before schooling and that there is really no magic moment in the life of a child at which readiness for instruction occurs. Literacy acquisition is now seen instead as a gradual process that begins in the home. Literate behavior has been observed to emerge slowly in young children, a process described by Tompkins (2003) as follows:

> Children's introduction to written language begins before they come to school. Parents and other caregivers read to young children, and children observe adults reading. They learn to read signs and other environmental print in their community. Children experiment with writing and have their parents write for them. They also observe adults writing. When young children come to kindergarten, their knowledge about written language expands quickly as they participate in meaningful, functional, and genuine experiences with reading and writing. (p. 111)

The task of primary teachers is now increasingly perceived as a matter of building on this groundwork. In short, their job is to take children at their individual points of development and help literacy continue to emerge.

Functional Literacy

The notion of functional literacy is one of the most complex, dynamic, and elusive concepts encountered by educators. One reason for this difficulty is the political significance of the term. When functional literacy is defined broadly, large numbers of people are classified as illiterate; narrower definitions result in rosier pictures (Thompkins & Binder, 2003). In general, the term denotes the ability to use reading and writing to function adequately in one's environment, including in one's job; functional literacy includes the more specific concept of workplace literacy, which we will discuss presently. Because functional literacy varies with an individual's environment (including the demands of employment), no single level of literacy can possibly suffice to make everyone functional—unless, of course, we use the highest standard of proficiency for all individuals.

In one popular though misguided conceptualization, functional literacy has been separated from workplace demands, so that the functionally literate person is sometimes seen as one who is able to read a newspaper, street signs, and other "public" information and write a check or fill out an application when the need arises. It is difficult, however, to see how persons who are able to do these things and who are yet unequal to the literacy demands of their jobs can possibly be regarded as functionally literate.

Muller and Murtagh (2002) described functional literacy in the following manner:

> [Functional] literacy is more than the ability to read, write, and do arithmetic. It comprises other skills needed for an individual's full autonomy and capacity to function effectively in a given society. It can range from reading instructions for fertilizers, or medical prescriptions, knowing which bus to catch, keeping accounts for small business, or operating a computer. (p. 4)

Such a description serves to make clear how functional literacy has at last come to be viewed as a concept relative not just to everyday uses of print but to the demands of the workplace as well.

Workplace Literacy

In recent years, literacy demands in the workplace have drawn increased attention. At one time, the assumption was that traditional education would provide the necessary language abilities for most jobs, but this belief has changed as the realities of occupational demands have changed. The need for increasingly higher levels of literacy in particular jobs, as well as the general shift from industrial to service occupations, has made workplace literacy a growing concern (Caselton, 2002; Hemming et al., 2002; Payne, 2002; Sticht, 2002).

In the past, a prospective office worker needed to know only basic keyboarding skills. In today's world, however, this level of literacy knowledge is not sufficient in most business settings. Skills in word processing, for example, and technical reading are necessary for all but the most elementary office positions. By 1990, approximately 70 percent of American jobs required some degree of literacy (Howie, 1990). This figure is now undoubtedly higher. In contrast with literacy needs in the past, workplace literacy today requires individuals who can apply general learning strategies in a wide variety of situations.

How do workers acquire these skills? While some skills are developed on the job, the foundations of literacy ability are formed in school, and in numerous ways the foundation may be a weak one. Reading and writing have traditionally been taught in academic settings primarily as a means of acquiring and transmitting information via print. This policy is defensible, as far as it goes, but it stops short of what many students will need in the workplace. Increasingly, literacy instruction has been moved from the academic setting to the workplace (Craig, 2001; Darvin, 2001; Scholtz & Prinsloo, 2001). Students have been graded on what they are able to remember from a reading assignment rather than on how they can apply this knowledge. Formal writing instruction tends to be limited in scope, receiving far less attention than reading. Yet the literacy demands of today's workplace go far beyond the simple ability to read and recall specific information and to convey it to others through writing. Workers must be skilled in knowing how to set their own specific purposes for reading and how to choose reading strategies for achieving these purposes. In writing, they must often be able to analyze, synthesize, predict, and persuade rather than simply inform.

In many ways, the content classroom is comparable to the workplace: It places specific literacy demands on students as they attempt to accomplish the day-to-day tasks of the course. What has been called workplace literacy in the industrial world has a counterpart in the world of education. We call this counterpart *content literacy*.

Content Literacy

We define content literacy as *the ability to use reading and writing for the acquisition of new content in a given discipline* (McKenna & Robinson, 1990). Such ability includes three principal cognitive components: (1) general literacy skills, (2) prior knowledge of content, and (3) content-specific literacy skills (such as map reading in the social studies). (See Figure 1.1.) The first two of

FIGURE 1.1

Cognitive components of content literacy

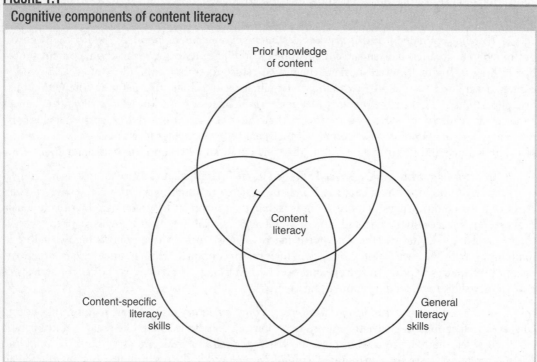

these—overall literacy ability and content knowledge—are clearly the two factors with the greatest influence on learning through text (Perfetti, 2003).

Obvious connections exist between the content area classroom and the workplace. Both require knowledge in specific areas, and both make special demands on participants that may change dramatically as they move to a new setting. Further, both may involve highly specialized literacy requirements germane to that setting and to few others. However, content literacy differs considerably from workplace literacy in purpose; it is primarily a tool for learning, not for job performance.

The potential of writing for the purpose of learning has only recently been realized. Researchers now recognize that both reading and writing are constructive processes in which information is organized and accommodated into memory structures. Accordingly, the writing-to-learn movement stresses that writing, like reading, is a means of clarifying, refining, and extending one's internalization of content (Aulls, 2003; Furr, 2003; Graham, 2003; Perry et al., 2003; Schmoker, 2007). Writing, like reading, becomes a tool for acquiring content.

The Implications of Content Literacy

The concept of content literacy has a number of important implications for content area teachers, and we believe that these implications lead to a single, inescapable conclusion: By engaging students in appropriate content literacy activities, teachers can optimize learning. We recently suggested the following specific implications (McKenna & Robinson, 1990):

1. *Content literacy is not the same as content knowledge.* The term *literacy* is often used to mean "having knowledge" of a particular area. A person who is computer literate, for example, is assumed to know about computers. Unfortunately, this kind of usage gets us dangerously far from reading and writing. The term *content literacy* is not merely a synonym for content knowledge. Instead, it represents skills needed to acquire knowledge of content. Nor is content literacy a prerequisite for content knowledge, for one can certainly acquire knowledge of content without recourse to reading or writing. On the other hand, content knowledge *is* a prerequisite for content literacy. In a cyclical pattern, the more prior knowledge one possesses, the more such knowledge will facilitate reading and writing as activities that lead to the integration of still more knowledge,

and so forth. In short, the more you know about a given area, the easier it is to learn new material in the same area.

2. *Teaching content automatically makes students more content literate.* Whether they know it or not, content area teachers enhance their students' ability to read and write about content simply by teaching it. Ironically, even those teachers who refuse to embrace the ideas of "reading in the content areas" and "writing to learn" improve their students' ability to read and write within their disciplines whenever their instruction is successful. Enchanced prior knowledge always enhances subsequent reading and writing germane to that knowledge. Unfortunately, many teachers, by providing high-quality direct instruction, set the stage for even greater levels of content acquisition (through reading and writing) but never realize this potential with appropriate assignments.

3. *Content literacy is content specific.* To be literate in mathematics, for example, is not a matter of merely "knowing" mathematics. It is being able to read and write about the subject as an effective means of knowing still more about it. While the general ability to read and write obviously bears on one's success in reading and writing about a specific subject, prior knowledge of the specific topics involved is a vital variable of content literacy. Thus, an individual who is highly literate in math may have a far lower level of literacy in history or economics. This circumstance is largely the result of differences in prior knowledge and occurs even though the individual brings the same general literacy skills to all reading and writing tasks.

4. *In content literacy, reading and writing are complementary tasks.* While reading and writing can serve well enough as alternative means of enhancing content learning, the greatest gains can be expected when the two are used in tandem. When printed materials are assigned to be read and when written responses are also required, students are placed in the position first of constructing an internal representation of the content they encounter in print and then of refining that representation through such processes as synthesis, evaluation, and summarization.

5. *Content literacy is germane to all subject areas, not just those that rely heavily on printed materials.* Teachers of subjects such as art, music, physical education, and others that tend to involve little use of prose materials have frequently objected that content area reading coursework, now compulsory in nearly every state (Come, McKenna, & Robinson, 1996), does not apply to their instructional situations. Certain states have in fact excluded such groups from these course requirements. The notion of content literacy, however, suggests that students' understanding of the content presented in all subjects could be substantially enhanced through appropriate writing assignments. While the primary presentation may comprise lecture and demonstration rather than reading, and while the principal domain involved may be psychomotor rather than cognitive, content learning nevertheless invariably includes the understanding of key concepts and their interrelationships. Such understanding can always be fostered through writing.

6. *Content literacy does not require content area teachers to instruct students in the mechanics of writing.* A long-standing misinterpretation that has hampered the effort to encourage content area reading techniques is that such techniques call for subject matter specialists to teach the minutiae of decoding—to master a new and very different curriculum, in other words, and, worse, to take class time away from subject matter instruction. This false notion has lingered tenaciously despite widespread efforts to overcome it. We need to make clear, then, in elaborating the idea of content literacy (which embraces writing as well as reading), that the concept includes no responsibility for developing the mechanical skills of writing. As Myers (1984) put it, "Writing to learn is not learning to write" (p. 7). Mechanical problems severe enough to distort meaning may require a teacher's attention, especially in subjects like mathematics, in which precise usage is an absolute necessity (Orr, 1987), but the focus should be meaning, not mechanics.

7. *Content literacy is relative to the tasks expected of students.* The literacy requirements of a classroom, like those of a workplace or of an entire culture, readily define who is literate and who is not (Guthrie, 1983; Hadaway & Young, 1994; Moje, 1993; Rafferty, 1992; Wedman & Robinson, 1990; Williams, 2007). In an effort to reduce or eliminate the "illiterate" subpopulation in their classes, teachers all too frequently resort to slashing literacy requirements. Reading assignments may be circumvented or minimized, while writing may never be seriously considered. Students consequently meet the literacy demands of the instructional setting—so that all are technically "literate"—but the opportunity to enhance content learning through reading

and writing is lost. Students at even a rudimentary level of general literacy are equipped to advance their understanding through literacy activities. This is possible whenever (1) reading materials are commensurate with ability (or steps are taken to facilitate comprehension of more difficult material) and (2) writing assignments are within the range of student sophistication.

8. *Content literacy has the potential to maximize content acquisition.* While reading content materials may introduce new ideas into a student's knowledge base, and while writing about content may help the student organize and store that information more effectively, some argue that similar results may also be accomplished without reliance on reading and writing. Instructors may indeed "spoon-feed" new content in carefully organized curricular designs using direct oral instruction. This argument has been strong enough to persuade some teachers to avoid literacy activities altogether. There are, however, at least four good reasons for not depending exclusively on direct instruction.

- The products of literacy activities will never precisely match those of oral instruction. They therefore serve to complement such instruction and broaden student perspectives.

- Individualized extension is made possible through such activities as a natural follow-up to direct instruction. Students are in a position to pursue content on their own, following in some measure their personal predilections, needs, and interests.

- Present-day models of explicit instruction incorporate practice phases that follow up the presentation of content for the purpose of reinforcing it (e.g., Rosenshine, 1986). Such practice could certainly incorporate literacy activities, which seem ideally suited to these models.

- Students who have received opportunities to become content literate will be better able to use content literacy as a means of extending their knowledge of a discipline even after they have completed a given course.

Teacher Resistance to Content Literacy

Even though research has shown the effectiveness of many content area teaching techniques that involve reading (Alvermann & Phelps, 2004; Harvey & Goudvis, 2007; Vacca & Vacca, 2004) and writing (Thorp, 2002; Walley & Kommer, 2000), teachers of content subjects frequently do not employ them. In a recent national survey, for example, Irvin and Connors (1989) found that no more than 14 percent of the respondents employed such techniques as an important part of their programs. If content literacy strategies are effective at increasing content learning, why do teachers resist their use? Stewart and O'Brien (1989) have observed that teachers offer numerous answers to this question, though three reasons stand out.

First, many teachers feel inadequate to handle reading problems in their classrooms. Certainly students who are experiencing severe reading difficulties present special problems that may exceed the expertise of most subject matter specialists. These individuals are relatively few in number, however, and strategies for meeting their needs are readily available and will be discussed at various points throughout this text. Moreover, content literacy strategies are designed to assist *all* students, the poorest readers included, by facilitating their use of text during reading and by extending and organizing their thinking through writing (e.g., Prentice & Cousin, 1993). The techniques involved are remarkably simple. No specialized training in teaching the skills of word recognition and comprehension is needed.

Second, teachers often feel that literacy activities infringe on subject matter time. We are not in any way suggesting that a portion of the daily instructional time in content classes be set aside for general reading development. The literacy activities recommended in this book require no "time-out" from content instruction. Instead they involve rearranging (rather than shortening) discussion time and merging reading and writing with content acquisition. It is important to remember that the point of the strategies discussed in this book is to increase content learning, not to improve reading and writing ability (though this may follow as a by-product).

Last, many teachers deny the need for content area reading and writing techniques. As we have mentioned, some have eliminated this need by reducing the literacy requirements of their courses, creating an atmosphere in which writing and reading have no place. While literacy may not be a liability in such classrooms, neither will it be an asset. Other teachers find that the majority of their students are capable of mastering the material assigned when they apply themselves. While this may be true as far as it goes, there are three problems with such a view: (1) It wastes students' time as they struggle unnecessarily with difficult material; (2) it dampens their attitude toward the subject matter; and (3) it results in inferior comprehension even though they have "read" the material.

Seeing Yourself as a Teacher

Teaching is possibly the only profession with which newcomers have great familiarity before they are trained. You may never have taught, but you have watched others do so for literally thousands of hours. In your many experiences as a student, you have had a chance to evaluate numerous teaching practices, primarily in terms of the effects they may have had on your own learning.

Now, as you are introduced to teaching methods that you may not have experienced as a student, it will probably seem natural to think back to your own days as a student in middle- and secondary-level classrooms. Diane Holt-Reynolds (1991, 1992) found that preservice teachers tend to evaluate the usefulness of a new method by imagining themselves as a student in a class where the method is practiced. They then attempt to project how they might have reacted to the method. If they suspect that their experience would not have been a productive one, they reject the new method as unsuitable to their future instructional practice. In other words, undergraduates tend to make a distinction between *self-as-teacher* and *self-as-student*. Because they lack actual classroom experience on which to base their judgments, any proposed new method is put to the only test available to them: their experience as students. The result is a kind of dialogue between self-as-teacher and self-as-student.

Holt-Reynolds (1991) describes the process this way:

> Almost simultaneously switching roles, they imagined participating in the activity themselves as a student. If Self-As-Student reacted to the imaginary scenario in ways that Self-As-Teacher has already decided are valuable, then these preservice teachers report making favorable decisions about that activity. If, however, Self-As-Student reacted in ways that Self-As-Teacher already sees as undesirable, the preservice teacher made a negative decision. (n.p.)

A difficulty with this very natural process is that preservice teachers' observations of the teachers they themselves have had (numerous as the observations were) have revealed little about how those teachers thought and planned. Nor does this process account for the variety of students a teacher is likely to encounter in a typical classroom. Moreover, it relies on vague and distant impressions made long ago and fails to provide any basis for comparing the methods actually experienced with those a teacher *might* have used but did not.

Our wish is to make you aware, at this early point, of the tendency to use your own background in classrooms (self-as-student) to judge the worth of instructional techniques to your teaching (to self-as-teacher). We hope that by becoming aware of the process and its limitations you can defer final judgment until you try a technique for yourself and witness its actual effects on your own students (see Figure 1.2).

Teachers, who educate children, deserve more honor than parents, who merely gave them birth; for the latter provide mere life, while the former ensure a good life.
ARISTOTLE

NET Worth

Reading Teacher Listserv

Joining the Reading Teacher listserv puts you in contact with hundreds of reading educators across the country. All you need is an e-mail address. You can pose questions about materials, methods, and specific kids. Or you can just "lurk," reading the messages posted by others. The RT list was the brainchild of Don Leu at the University of Connecticut but is now housed at the headquarters of the International Reading Association. Instructions for subscribing can be found at this site:

www.reading.org/resources/community/discussions_rt_about.html

You can subscribe to a digest form if you find that receiving ten to fifteen messages per day (the average) is too much. It's also easy to unsubscribe if you decide that the RT list is not for you.

NET Worth

Literacy-Related Organizations

International Reading Association. Provides information about literacy publications, conferences, and projects.

> **www.reading.org**

National Council of Teachers of English. Site contains ideas for teaching English, Literacy, and Language Arts for P–16 teachers. Also contains information on books and journals and NCTE news.

> **www.ncte.org**

American Library Association. Contains links to many author sites and book awards.

> **www.ala.org**

Children's Book Council. The CBC site contains links for teachers, parents, and authors in their quest to encourage children to read.

> **www.cbcbooks.org**

FIGURE 1.2

Seeing yourself as a teacher

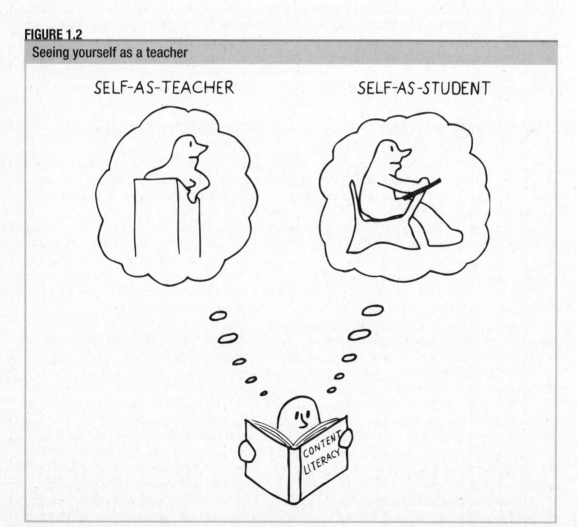

Source: Courtesy Christopher Wagner

NET Worth

Educational Research at Your Fingertips

Do you have a question about education that research can answer? These sites can help.

ERIC Database. Housed at the U.S. Department of Education.

www.eric.ed.gov

ERIC Digests. Extensive ERIC digest system providing nutshell research summaries on many topics. Also housed at the U.S. Department of Education.

www.ericdigests.org

Research Reports from the National Research and Development Centers. Makes available hundreds of reports from the twelve federal research and development centers. Reports are in full text and/or PDF format.

research.cse.ucla.edu

We close this chapter with a request and a challenge. If you are skeptical about the potential of literacy activities to improve learning in your classes, we ask that you keep an open mind as you read on and that you carefully consider our previous discussion of how content teachers often rationalize their way out of literacy activities. Should you still be skeptical at the conclusion of the course, we challenge you to give the techniques presented a fair trial in the classroom. Conduct an action research study in which comparable classes are exposed to the same unit with and without the use of literacy activities. Use your own unit test, or some similar performance measure, as the yardstick by which you compare the classes. We're confident your own evidence will satisfy your doubts.

SUMMARY

Literacy is a concept that has changed considerably over the years. A recent insight has been that the question of whether an individual is literate is relative to the demands of the individual's environment (classroom, workplace, society, etc.). To some extent, classroom teachers control whether students are literate through the assignments they make.

Four aspects of literacy are important. Emergent literacy is the developing ability among young children to read and write. Functional literacy is the ability to function within one's environment insofar as reading and writing are concerned. While this concept was once limited to "public" tasks, such as reading signs and completing forms, it now embraces demands of the workplace as well. Workplace literacy is therefore a *part* of functional literacy—the part that concerns an individual's ability to use reading and writing successfully on the job.

Content literacy is the ability to use reading and writing to acquire new content within a given subject area. It requires general literacy skills, skills related to reading and writing in the specific area of study, and existing content knowledge within that area.

This definition of content literacy has important implications for teachers. It suggests that knowing content is not the same as being able to read and write about it. Instead, content knowledge is one requirement of content literacy. This means that by teaching content, teachers automatically make students more content literate simply by adding to their knowledge base. It also means that content literacy is not a general skill, because specific knowledge within the area of study is needed. The content literate student is one who can add new knowledge through reading and refine and reorganize that knowledge through writing. These processes are not limited to certain subjects; they pertain to all areas. Because learning content is the only relevant goal of literacy activities, teachers do not have to be concerned with the fine points of teaching writing. Rather, by establishing reasonable literacy demands, teachers can extend students' understanding of new materials without presenting tasks that are beyond their abilities.

Even though the methods for using and developing content literacy have an extensive research base, teachers have often resisted using them. They have argued that they lack the training to contend with students who have special needs, that literacy activities infringe on time needed to teach content, and that such activities are not really needed to teach content. The idea of content literacy and its implications refute these arguments. Literacy activities within content classrooms tend to maximize and reinforce learning when they are appropriately matched to student abilities.

Books are the carriers of civilization. Without books, history is silent, literature dumb, science crippled, thought at a standstill.

BARBARA TUCHMAN

Getting Involved

1. A colleague tells you that she plans to revise her science course so that reading and writing are not required except for objective tests. She will rely on lecture, demonstrations, and discussion to convey content. She estimates impressive savings for the district in textbook purchases, and she looks forward to fewer papers to grade and no interference with instruction caused by reading problems. Do you think her plan is likely to result in acceptable learning? Would you support her in her efforts? Suppose the idea began to catch on among teachers in other content areas. Would you support a district policy that severely limits reading and writing in all subjects but language arts? Defend your position.

2. In the 1985 movie *Teachers*, starring Nick Nolte, a social studies instructor made the following complaint to a colleague in the lounge:

> "I signed a contract to teach social studies, not reading. I don't see why I should have to spend my time dealing with students who can't read the text. I'm a history teacher, not a reading teacher."
> Her friend looked at her thoughtfully.
> "But you are a teacher, aren't you?" he asked.

The woman had nothing to say. How would you have responded? Does being a teacher imply a duty to do whatever may be needed to ensure learning?

CHAPTER 2

Literacy Processes

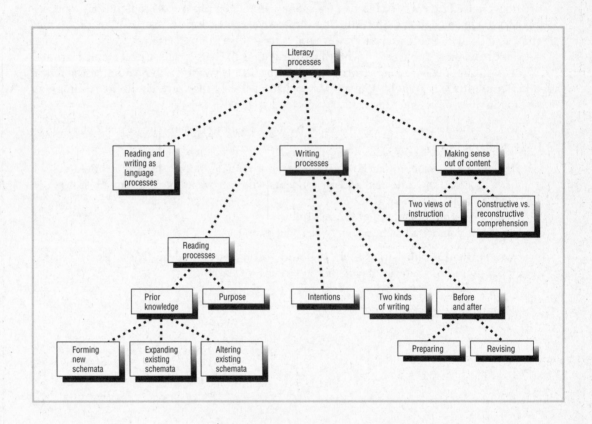

*There is in writing the constant joy of
sudden discovery, happy accident.*

—H. L. Mencken

It is probably natural to think of reading and writing as two vastly different processes, linked only by a mutual dependence on printed language. Yet we now know that writing and reading share numerous similarities. For the purposes of this text, the most important of these common traits is the potential of each process to enhance learning. To better understand this potential, it is necessary to appreciate in general terms how the two processes work.

Objectives

Your study of this chapter should enable you to

1. relate reading and writing to their oral language counterparts;

2. describe the sequence of key events in the process of written communication;

3. explain the role and purpose of prior knowledge in reading and the role of intention in writing; and

4. list important similarities shared by reading and writing and explain their implications for content instruction.

Reading and Writing as Language Processes

Imagine a world without language. To convey even the simplest thoughts would require the use of gestures, facial expressions, drawings, physical objects, and other contrivances. Even then, precise communication would seldom be assured, while expressing—or even thinking about—abstract ideas would be extremely difficult. Assume, for example, that as a cave dweller in prelinguistic antiquity you happen to shatter a stone chisel while working. In examining the broken fragments, it might occur to you that each fragment could be broken in turn into still smaller fragments, and so on. You wonder if there is some limit beyond which the fragments cannot under any circumstances be further subdivided. How would you communicate this thought to a friend? You could show your friend the pieces and break one of them a second time, gesticulating and pantomiming and perhaps painting wordless diagrams on the wall of your cave, but these efforts would in no way guarantee that you would be understood.

If, however, you had developed a collection of spoken sounds to symbolize concepts and a system of rules for combining those sounds as a means of expressing ideas, your task would be much simpler. These acoustic symbols are, of course, *words,* while the set of all available spoken words is called the *lexicon.* The rules for combining words are together referred to as *grammar,* or *syntax.* Thus, the lexicon and syntax are the two primary components of any language.

So far we have been discussing oral language. Consider now a second set of symbols, this time visual, designed to represent spoken words. These visual symbols (written words) can be combined largely according to the grammatical rules governing oral language, though written communication has nuances all its own. Historically, two principal methods have been used to represent spoken words with visual symbols. One method is to use letters to symbolize the smallest, most basic speech sounds, called *phonemes.* The advantages of this approach are that the letters are interchangeable and that relatively few are needed to depict virtually any word. Written languages formulated through this method are described as *alphabetic.* These include most Western languages, including English. Certain other languages, such as Chinese, employ an *ideographic* method, in which a unique symbol is used to represent an entire word. While in some cases complex ideographs can be constructed from simpler forms, component speech sounds are not symbolically represented. Thus, thousands of individual symbols must be learned by the language user. Because there is little relationship between print and sound, the same visual word may have entirely different pronunciations in two localities. Thus, speakers of the Mandarin and Cantonese dialects of Chinese cannot converse with one another even though they read and write the same language!

Whatever the method of visually symbolizing spoken language, the result is a second system of symbols (written ones) superimposed on the first. Reading and writing are therefore the more recent counterparts of the much older processes of speaking and listening (Aulls, 2003; Hartley, 2007; Perry et al., 2003).

Because communication involves the transmission of ideas and feelings from one individual to another, a complete model of the process, as it relates to literacy, must begin in the mind of the writer and end in that of the reader. As Figure 2.1 shows, this process starts with the thoughts a writer may wish to convey. These intentions tend to be somewhat fluid and independent of language until they are given linguistic form. This process, whether oral or written, is sometimes

FIGURE 2.1

Transformations of meaning from writing to reading

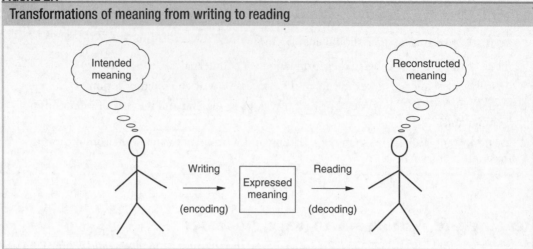

described as *encoding,* because the language itself is made up of arbitrary, cipherlike symbols that differ from one language to the next. Because the reader cannot directly access the writer's thoughts, the written product must be used in an effort to reconstruct those thoughts. The success of this effort depends on the reader's ability to *decode* the printed symbols. The degree to which the ideas the writer initially intended to convey were eventually reconstructed in the reader's mind is the degree to which communication was successful.

It is important to make clear that this model sidesteps some of the other reasons an individual might choose to write: to evoke an emotion in the reader, to persuade or move the reader to action, to mislead or distract the reader, and so on (see Smith, 2004, for a discussion). The purpose of informing the reader is, however, the chief reason writers write in content subjects and the chief reason their writing is assigned to students. Depicting the reading and writing processes from an information-processing perspective is therefore well suited to the topics we will explore in the coming chapters.

The Reading Process

What happens when we read? This "simple" question has intrigued researchers for decades and has yet to be satisfactorily answered. A good starting point is to note that fluent, mature reading is the last of several stages through which children pass as their ability develops. Several researchers have studied these stages in detail (e.g., Chall, 1983/1996; Ehri & Wilce, 1985; Freedman & Carver, 2007; Kucer & Tuten, 2003; Perfetti, 2003; Stanovich, 2000). Figure 2.2 summarizes the five stages identified by Chall. Even though our primary concern is with the third stage, Reading for Learning, it is important to recognize that children reach this stage only after successfully traversing the two stages that come before. A student with significant decoding problems, for example, will have grave

FIGURE 2.2

Chall's stages of reading development

Approximate grades and ages

Stage 1	Initial Reading or Decoding	1–2	6–7 years
Stage 2	Confirmation, Fluency	2–3	7–8 years
Stage 3	Reading for Learning	4–8	9–14 years
Stage 4	Multiple Viewpoints	9–12	14–18 years
Stage 5	Construction, Reconstruction: A World View	College	19+ years

Source: From *Stages of Reading Development* by J. Chall, 1983, New York: McGraw-Hill.

difficulties with content area reading assignments. Unfortunately, mismatches of this sort are not uncommon, and from time to time we will suggest strategies for accommodating the needs of such students.

Let's return now to the mature reading process. For our purposes, we will not be concerned with a detailed description of the subprocesses that underlie reading. We can, however, offer the following capsule description based on the conclusions that reading researchers have reached:

1. Reading is an interactive process in which a reader's prior knowledge of the subject and purpose for reading operate to influence what is learned from text.
2. The visual structure of printed words and the system by which letters represent the sounds of speech together define subprocesses used to identify words.
3. These word-identification processes are applied rapidly by fluent readers, but they may hamper readers with problems.
4. As visual word forms are associated with word meanings, a mental reconstruction of overall textual meaning is created. This reconstruction is subject to continual change and expansion as the reader progresses.
5. In the end, the nearer the reconstructed meaning is to the writer's originally intended meaning, the more successful the act of communication will be.
6. The reader's purpose may deliberately limit the scope of the reconstruction, however, as when one reads an article for its main points or consults an encyclopedia for a specific fact.

Based on this nutshell description of the process, we will define reading as *the reconstruction in the mind of meaning encoded in print*. From the perspective of the content teacher, two points are important to note. First, it is not the content specialist's role to *teach* the process we have outlined here but to facilitate students' attempts to use that process to learn through written materials. Second, the best way to achieve this facilitation is to focus on two factors in the reading process that are most easily influenced by the teacher who assigns the materials: (1) the prior knowledge of the students and (2) the purposes for which the students will read. In the chapters that follow, we will present many techniques for addressing these two factors. For now, let's examine the role each of these factors plays in the process of reading.

The Role of Prior Knowledge

Figure 2.3 presents a passage selected to demonstrate exactly how limiting prior knowledge can be when it is not adequate for making sense of new information. Read the passage now if you have not already done so. Did you become vaguely (perhaps openly) frustrated as you read? We suspect you may have, even though you knew it was part of a planned demonstration. Imagine the plight of your students when unplanned shortcomings in prior knowledge make the material they must read just as frustrating. Especially ironic is the fact that limitations in prior knowledge are often easily overcome if an instructor is aware they exist and takes a few simple steps to address them. How much better your comprehension would have been a moment ago, for example, had we bothered to provide you in advance with the simple fact that the passage deals with a cricket match!

Let's look a little farther into how prior knowledge can wield such power over comprehension. It is helpful to think of the underlying knowledge needed to comprehend what we read as being stored in interconnected categories within memory. These categories are called *schemata* (plural of *schema*). Think of a schema as all you know about a given concept. You have a schema

Knowledge is the true organ of sight, not the eyes.

PANCHATANTRA
(fifth century)

FIGURE 2.3

An example of how limited prior knowledge can hinder comprehension

Left-arm fast bowlers Ashish Nehra and Irfan Pathan skittled the top order, and off-spinner Harbhajan Singh took three crucial wickets as India toppled the home team by 23 runs. Vaughan and Ashley Giles (39) shared a determined stand of 92 for the seventh wicket, but England was bowled out for 181 with 10 balls to spare.

Source: From *Slam! Sports,* an online Canadian publication, September 8, 2004. Available at http://slam.canoe.ca.

for "contracts," for example, that may differ considerably from the extensive schema for this same concept that exists in the mind of an attorney. In the same way, the schemata for "contracts" that individual students might bring to the reading of a business law chapter are likely to vary considerably from one student to the next.

Schemata are not stored in isolation but are connected by intricate networks of associations (Fuhler, 2003; Heffernan, 2003; Lieven et al., 2003; McKenzie & Danielson, 2003). As you read, various schemata are "activated," and those portions of your prior knowledge are brought to bear on the task of bringing meaning to the print before you. Connections among schemata are also activated as you attempt to reconstruct the author's expressed meaning.

Comprehending what we read is thus highly dependent on prior knowledge. As Pearson and Johnson (1978) put it, "*Comprehension is building bridges between the new and the known*" (p. 24, original emphasis). As Gunning (2007) described it more recently, "Comprehension is a constructive, interactive process involving three factors—the reader, the text, and the context in which the text is read" (p. 266).

When a student's existing knowledge of the content to be covered by a reading assignment is scant, comprehension is poor. Accordingly, some of the techniques we shall introduce involve building background knowledge before students begin to read. This effort entails a rearrangement of discussion time and takes nothing from the presentation of content. Rather, it is merely an alternative way of introducing the content, and it pays tangible dividends in student understanding.

As the reader progresses through print, schemata for the concepts discussed by the writer will be changed in one or more of three basic ways. New schemata may be formed, or existing schemata may be expanded or fundamentally altered.

Formation of New Schemata.   The introduction of new concepts is a frequent occurrence in content learning and calls for the establishment of new schemata. This involves forming associations with existing schemata so that the new knowledge is meaningfully linked to the old.

Consider the language arts student who has just read a selection on haiku, complete with definition, examples, writing guidelines, and so on. Let us assume that the reading serves to introduce the concept of haiku for the first time. The student will already possess knowledge structures relevant to the creation of a new schema for this type of poetry. Figure 2.4(a) depicts how a portion of these structures might be diagrammed prior to the student's exposure to the new concept. Poetic genres already familiar to the student are stored in association with the general concept of poetry, which is in turn related to the larger notion of written forms, and so forth. Figure 2.4(b) illustrates how the memory structures might look after the new concept has been learned. The learning has not involved the alteration of existing schemata, other than by the addition of a new schema for haiku. This new schema fits conveniently into what the student already knows.

Expansion of Existing Schemata.   You may have had occasion as a high school biology student to dissect a frog. Your laboratory manual and the actual experience itself doubtless served to introduce many new facts about frogs, facts that greatly complemented your prior knowledge. These new facts are not likely to have contradicted any of the assumptions you may previously have made: that frogs are usually green; that they have a certain size and shape, webbed feet, slick skin, and so forth. Rather, the new information tended to amplify, extend, and supplement what you already knew. You were not compelled to "unlearn" anything in order to make room for the new facts. Piaget (1952) described the process by which existing schemata are extended in this fashion as *assimilation*. This is likely to occur whenever one's background knowledge is relatively broad so that new information fits rather well into existing cognitive structures. In such cases, the new information is largely congruent with the old.

Alteration of Existing Schemata.   What happens when new facts are encountered that do not square with what an individual believes to be true? One of two things can occur: The person can either reject the information or accommodate it by altering prior knowledge accordingly. Piaget's notion of *accommodation* (like that of assimilation) was not limited to reading but extended to all learning situations. Imagine, for example, that you were told something shocking about a close friend, someone you'd known for years. You might question your source, dismissing the new information as false because it was so out of character for your friend. If you were to accept

FIGURE 2.4

Example of the assimilation of a new schema

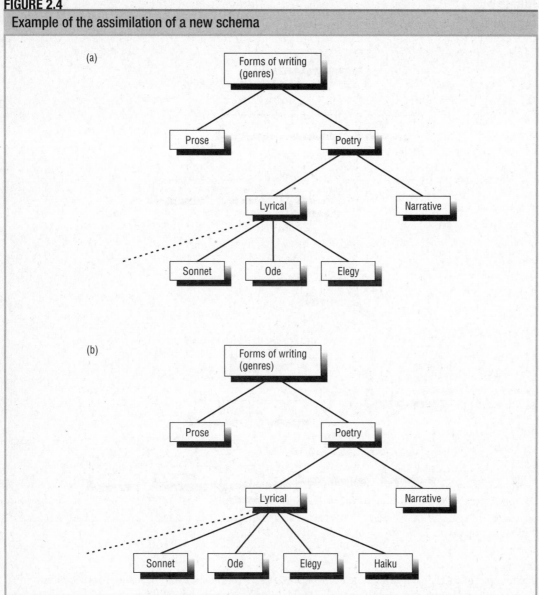

the new information, however, it would not be possible to maintain an unaltered schema of your friend. The new fact would need to be accommodated by changing the way you think about your friend. "Well," you might conclude, "this adds a whole new dimension to my friend's character."

In the circumstances of reading, comparable events occur. Let's return to our business law student, who may read the following definition in a textbook: "A contract is a promise, or a set of promises, for the breach of which the law prescribes a remedy." Like so many technical vocabulary terms, the word *contract* has many meanings beyond the precise usage of the text, and some of these may be known to the reader in advance. A portion of a typical student's schema for contracts might be diagrammed as shown in Figure 2.5(a). Here the concept of contracts has been stored in association with the broader notion of documents. It is also stored with numerous examples, personal experiences, and so on, all of which might comprise a typical individual's nontechnical knowledge of contracts. The new information, however, suggests that contracts are incorrectly classed as documents, for in fact many enforceable contracts are oral in nature. Further reading and discussion might leave the student's schemata in the substantially altered condition approximated by Figure 2.5(b). As we will see in later chapters, new ideas that require us to "unlearn" some of our previous beliefs are among the most difficult to teach. Yet, despite students' unwillingness to

FIGURE 2.5

Example of how new information may be accommodated into memory structures

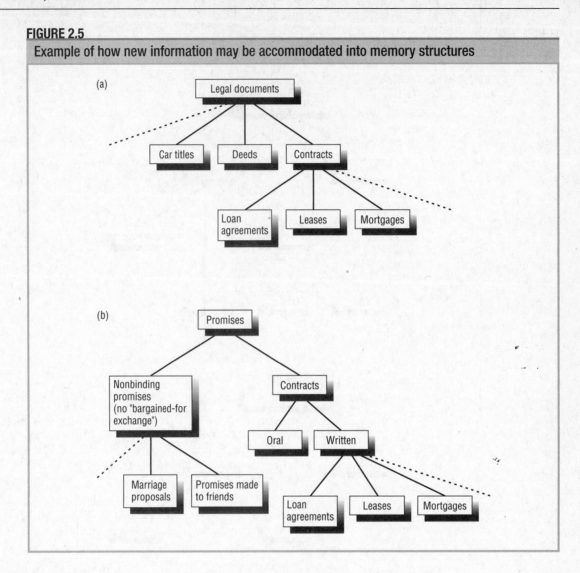

accept new ideas that might change their beliefs or schemata, the content teacher is often in an ideal position to challenge accepted ideas (Fly, 1994; Menke & Pressley, 1994).

The Role of Purpose in Reading

As we read, it is vital that relevant schemata be activated, or "switched on," so that new information can be integrated with existing knowledge. Assume, for example, that a friend has agreed to meet you for lunch but that the place and time have not been decided. You then receive the following note from your friend:

> Meat me at the Union around 12. If that's not good, call me before 10.

Books must be read as deliberately and reservedly as they were written.

HENRY DAVID THOREAU

As you begin to read, your focus is limited to certain elements in the message according to your purposes for reading. Overall, you expect your friend to specify the time and place of your meeting. In the first sentence, you look for and find these facts. While the number 12 can have many meanings, your purpose and prior knowledge assist you in knowing precisely what meaning to give it. Likewise, the Union may contain a myriad of shops, meeting rooms, commons, and so forth, but you automatically limit the meaning of the term Union to eating areas. Because the time and place are both specified in the first sentence, you create a new expectation with regard to the second sentence and a refined purpose for reading it. You may suspect that it probably conveys some further specification or clarification.

In the course of reading, your purposes have caused appropriate schemata to come into play. (Note that this is usually an unconscious process.) At the broadest level, you have a schema for notes, and perhaps even for those written by your friend. Your schemata for lunch and Union are also helpful. The former, in fact, prevented you from even considering that 12 might have meant midnight! At the lowest, most local levels, your expectations also shaped what you consciously attended to in terms of individual words and letters. Even though you are likely to have processed every letter of every word (Adams, 1990), your purposes for reading helped determine what information you eventually considered, interpreted, and remembered (Ivey, 2006; Linderholm & van den Broek, 2002). For example, you probably noticed the spelling error in the first word of the message but were quickly able to determine that it was an error.

The Writing Process

Think back to a recent writing task: a letter to a relative, an essay exam question, or a memo to a colleague. It is likely that you began with relatively general ideas about what you wished to convey through writing. Even if you had a wealth of information from which to choose, as might have been the case with an exam question, it is highly unlikely that this information existed in a form anything like complete sentences ready for transcription. Rather, your task was one of selecting, organizing, and finally encoding your thoughts into coherent prose form. Your own experiences may cause you to empathize with Johnson's comment on just how laborious this process can be when it is done well. However, the benefits of writing more than justify the effort required, for the writer's thoughts are clarified, extended, and reorganized in ways only writing can accomplish.

Composition is, for the most part, an effort of slow diligence, to which the mind is dragged by necessity or resolution.
SAMUEL JOHNSON

The Role of Intentions in Writing

Although we think of writing chiefly as a means by which one individual communicates with another, it is also a process by which writers communicate with themselves. As you rely on your overall (global) intentions to help you compose the first sentence of a paragraph, the ensuing sentence will depend not only on the global intentions with which you began but also on what you expressed in the preceding sentence. In this way, global intentions help shape "local" intentions as each new sentence is written (Smith, 2004).

The writer's relationship to print is an interactive one. Intentions (from global to local) help in formulating sentences, but their very formulation causes changes in the writer's thinking. Ideas become crystallized in print, "visible" in a sense, encoded for close inspection, not only by the reader but by the writer as well. The act of committing ideas to print tends to refine and revise one's own intentions in writing.

Let's compare this process with that of reading. While reading each new sentence, we alter slightly the overall reconstruction of meaning that is mentally forming. While writing, we also alter, with each new sentence, our inner conceptualization of the content. This happens because writing forces us to clarify and organize our own thinking before we can put it into words (encode it) for others. For this reason, reading and writing are remarkably similar as ways of enhancing our understanding.

It is true that writing is a slower and less fluent process. Writing, it has been said, "because its very slowness makes it more deliberately self-conscious, enhances our sense of details and choices" (Connolly, 1989, p. 10). Nevertheless, the similarities are striking. For both the reader and the writer, meaning is constructed through processes in which printed language is used as the primary tool (Squire, 1983).

The emerging view that writing, like reading, is a constructive process has long been realized by skilled writers, as E. M. Forster's remark suggests. This view has a major implication for teaching content, one we have already stressed in Chapter 1: Writing can be utilized as a means through which students can clarify, analyze, and integrate their own thoughts about, and knowledge of, subject matter (Myers, 1984). A colleague of ours recently confided that the experience of writing a textbook on the teaching of reading helped him clarify his own thinking on the subject. While we may tend to regard the knowledge possessed by authorities as being at all times precisely organized and articulated, this is simply not the case. For novice and expert alike, writing is a wonderfully illuminating experience!

How can I know what I think till I see what I say?
E. M. FORSTER

Two Kinds of Writing

Britton and his colleagues (Britton, Burgess, Martin, McLeod, & Rosen, 1975) offered a distinction between *transactional* writing, which targets a particular readership and is undertaken to inform, persuade, or instruct, and *expressive* writing, which amounts to "thinking on paper" and is intended for the writer's own use. The notes one makes prior to formulating the actual sentences of connected discourse are apt to be expressive in nature. They tend to be "messy, exploratory" (Rose, 1989, p. 16). The notes might be as thoroughly delineated as a formal outline or as cryptic as a mere word or phrase used to capture a complex idea, depending on the experience and sophistication of the writer. Each kind of writing is useful in content classes. Here are some examples of writing activities we will revisit in coming chapters.

Transactional Writing	*Expressive Writing*
essay	personal journal
summary	learning log
encyclopedia entry	class notes
letter	answers to questions

Expressive writing is often an end in itself. We might take notes, for example, and never take the time to develop them further. On the other hand, expressive writing sometimes leads to transactional writing, as when notes are used to compose an essay or summary.

Both kinds of writing are effective means of enhancing content learning, and we emphasize that both have a place in content classrooms. Of course, we are very much aware of the concerns of content teachers. It is one thing to note that essay writing leads to high levels of content understanding (Vacca & Linek, 1992), but such activities must be balanced with the time they require. Throughout this text, we will offer a number of ways in which both kinds of writing can be incorporated into content classrooms, and our aim will be to provide for a realistic balance between means and ends.

Before and After Writing

Transactional writing, although time-consuming, holds great potential for deepening content understanding. We now place the process of transactional writing in a larger context if we are to appreciate its potential for content instruction. Current recommendations suggest more than a single step in the process of writing (Moore, 2004). Although such models differ as to the number and nature of steps, all include (1) planning activities carried out in advance of writing and (2) revising activities undertaken afterward.

Bad authors are those who write with reference to an inner context which the reader cannot know.
ALBERT CAMUS

Preparing to Write. The famous psychologist B. F. Skinner (1981) recommended that the pre-prose stage be extended as long as possible, both because the writer's thoughts tend to remain fluid and because once the effort is expended to compose sentences and paragraphs there is a powerful resistance to dismantling them, even when the need to do so becomes clear. Despite these reasons, there is usually an impatient rush to get past the planning phase and on to the writing itself. Students must be cautioned to be deliberate in their planning, which, when done properly, actually tends to reduce the time spent "writing."

Nothing you write, if you hope to be good, will ever come out as you first hoped.
LILLIAN HELLMAN

The sense of readership needed for transactional writing is vital to good planning and is frequently ignored by students. After all, they know they are writing for the teacher, whose knowledge base is assumed to be extensive enough for accurate interpretation of anything they might say. The result can be highly assumptive, "inconsiderate" writing that fails to express ideas adequately (even for a teacher!). The observation of the French novelist Albert Camus is an insightful one. It suggests that students, from the planning stage on, be encouraged to monitor their writing carefully to avoid assumptions about knowledge the reader may not possess. An increasingly popular way to provide such encouragement is to arrange for situations in which students write not for the teacher alone but for other students, whose prior knowledge of a topic may be minimal.

Revising What Is Written. Capable writers are rarely satisfied with first drafts. Revision represents a second chance to bring expressed meaning into closer alignment with the writer's intentions. The need for targeting a specific readership is never more important than when revising, for the writer now becomes a reader—not in the ordinary sense but with the purpose of role-playing the sort of reader eventually targeted. Sentences are reconsidered in the complete context of the draft; awkward expressions are corrected; prose rhythms are tested; mechanics are mended.

Most models of process writing now make an important distinction between revising and editing. *Revising* entails conceptual changes that involve organization and expression. *Editing* entails the finer points of usage, grammar, and punctuation. Although in practice the two are often intermingled, revising should *generally* precede editing so that conceptual thinking is not sidetracked by a concern over minutiae. Both revising and editing have long been a problem for content area applications because of the time they require. Word processing, however, offers a means of speeding up both processes and of helping students devote more of their concentration to content (Cochran-Smith, 1991). We will revisit word-processing applications in later chapters.

Making Sense Out of Content

Consider the following two statements about how students acquire knowledge. Which one is closer to your own perspective?

1. The student's mind is like a vessel, to be filled by the teacher with specific knowledge.
2. The student constructs an individual representation of knowledge by interacting with the world.

These statements represent markedly different views of how knowledge develops. The first suggests that the process is a passive one and that the result is the "transmission" of knowledge, more or less intact, from teacher to learner. The second suggests that knowledge building is an active process that results in a unique conceptualization of content in the mind of each student. Our experience is that many content specialists prefer the former view. Research, on the other hand, very clearly supports the latter.

The result, however, is not a hopeless impasse. While different, the two viewpoints are not contradictory. A teacher may engage students in active encounters with content and nevertheless ensure that particular concepts, ideas, and skills have in fact been the result of such encounters. Students will construct their own ideas about content, to be sure, but teachers can guide the process so that the result, while unique to each student, nevertheless meets desirable curricular standards.

What we hope to show in this text is that reading and writing are tools a student can use in the process of constructing content knowledge. In the case of reading, the student attempts to *reconstruct* what an author intends, of course, but this is not the same as transmitting the author's message unaltered into the reader's preexisting memory and beliefs. The student does not stop at reconstructing what one author intends but uses the experience to further *construct* a more global knowledge of content. Our point is that while many educators tend to view the two statements above as offering an either-or choice, there is in fact a middle ground that we believe offers the best results.

SUMMARY

Language consists primarily of symbols (written and oral) and rules for combining those symbols into meaningful relationships. Most languages have both oral and written forms, and most written forms are alphabetic. In alphabetic languages, a small number of letters are used to represent basic speech sounds. Written language developed after oral language and involves a second system of symbols (visual) that overlies the first (acoustic).

Writing is a language process by which one attempts to "construct" with words a document that conveys an intended message. A mental construction of the message also occurs during writing as the writer's own thoughts are sharpened and clarified. Reading is a process by which one attempts to mentally "reconstruct" such a message from its printed representation. The extent to which the reconstructed message matches the one originally intended by the writer is the extent to which communication occurs.

In reading, new information encountered in print is integrated into existing knowledge structures called *schemata* (plural of *schema*). Schemata are best described as categories of knowledge corresponding to concepts. Schemata are interconnected in memory by associational links. As one reads, new schemata might be formed, or existing schemata might be expanded or altered. Because new information is always learned in relation to previous knowledge, it is important for a reader to have certain purposes and expectations about what a reading selection contains so that appropriate prior knowledge can be brought to bear.

Whereas reading is guided by what one seeks and expects, writing is guided by what one intends. Intentions guide the writer's choice of words, sentence structures, organizational patterns, and so on. Writing is now recognized as a powerful learning tool by virtue of its help in clarifying, refining, and organizing what one knows about a topic. Prior to writing, it is important to make brief notes as one examines one's own prior knowledge. It is vital at this point not to worry about forming complete sentences and paragraphs. In this way, thoughts remain fluid longer as one actively considers, manipulates, and rearranges them. After writing, it is important to revise. The object is for the writer to role-play the targeted reader and to read for the purpose of determining whether the intended meaning has been successfully incorporated into print.

Getting Involved

1. Imagine yourself in an airplane heading due south over downtown Detroit. If you continued on this course, what is the first foreign country over which you would pass? A group of our students produced such well-reasoned guesses as Mexico, Cuba, Guatemala, and so on. They were wrong. The correct answer is Canada, because an arm of Ontario extends just to the south of Detroit. If this fact surprised you as much as it did our students, you have just experienced an alteration in your geographical schemata as the new information was accommodated. Unusual facts, and their resulting accommodation, can be interest-arousing as well as instructional. Can you think of such a fact in your own subject area that might be used to evoke surprise and encourage student engagement at the beginning of a lesson?

2. Consider the concept of books. In memory, you already have an extensive schema for books, and this schema involves many meaningful associations with other concepts. For example, what concept would include books as an example? That is to say, a book is a type of what? By the same token, name a specific kind of book—a member of the category called "books." Figure 2.6 shows how these relationships can be diagrammed to produce a depiction of part of your schema for books. Note that, similar to the examples of Figures 2.4 and 2.5, larger concepts appear higher in the diagram.

FIGURE 2.6

Diagramming the concept of books as it relates to larger and smaller concepts

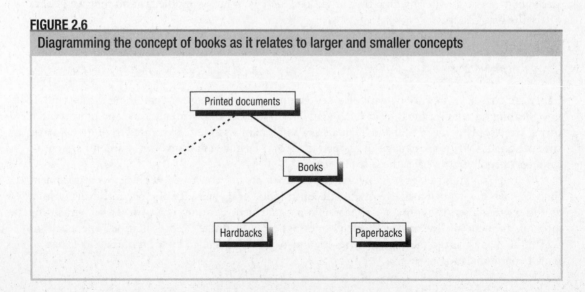

FIGURE 2.7

A schema for books that includes e-books

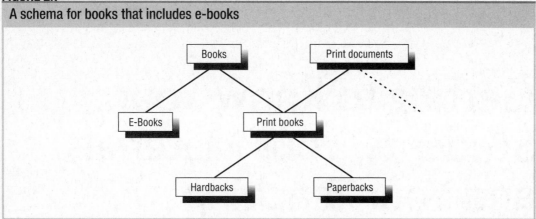

But wait! What about electronic books (e-books)? Hasn't technology forced us to change our ideas about what makes a book a book? Where do e-books fit into our schema? Do we need to change the way we conceptualize books, perhaps along the lines of Figure 2.7?

Can you think of another example of how you have had to change a knowledge structure in this way because of developments in the world around you? How might you diagram the change?

Do you think constructing and discussing such diagrams with students as they encounter new vocabulary might be productive?

3. In the meantime, free-associate from the concept of books. Make a mental list of ten other words suggested by the word *book*. In so doing, you've exposed more of your vast schema for books and, we suspect, demonstrated that it includes much more than the simple category memberships outlined in Figure 2.6. Now imagine having gone through a similar process for each of the ten related concepts you listed. If you continued in this way, you would soon have included thousands of concepts arranged in a vast network of hubs and spokes, similar to a highway map. And, as with a map, it would be possible to "travel" from any given concept to any other concept by means of associative links. Conceptualizing memory in this way suggests that new concepts are best learned when key associations with known concepts are emphasized. Think of a technical term from your own discipline. What concepts do you suppose might have been previously taught that your students should associate with the new term? Do you think a review of these prior concepts would be helpful before introducing the new one?

CHAPTER 3

Getting to Know Your Students, Your Materials, and Your Teaching

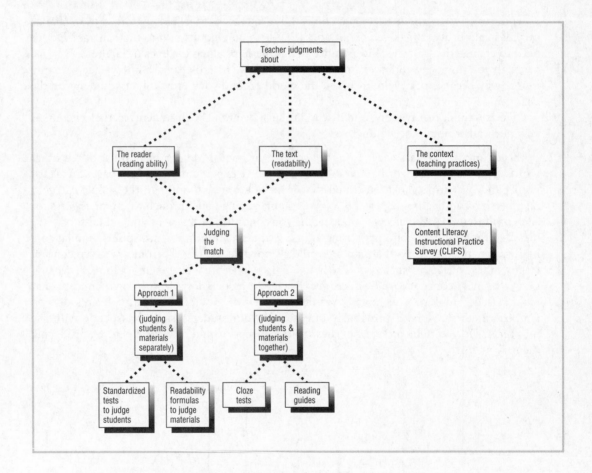

We can attempt nothing great, but from a sense of the difficulties we have to encounter.

—William Hazlitt

Have you ever been asked to perform a task that was too difficult? It might have involved solving a math problem, taking part in a sport, attempting an advanced musical piece, or responding to an essay exam question. It might also have involved reading an especially difficult book. You may still recall feelings of anxiety, frustration, and failure as you attempted the task. Depending on a host of factors—the assistance and encouragement you may have received, your determination, and the amount of time available to you—you might eventually have succeeded in performing the task.

When teachers in content subjects ask their students to read specific materials or to undertake written work, some of these students may feel a similar kind of frustration. Unfortunately, even experienced teachers often do little to assist students in contending with challenging materials (Menke & Davey, 1994). This book offers a variety of techniques aimed at minimizing such frustration. Some of the techniques are devoted to helping all students learn through reading and writing, and some are designed to help special learners. Before teachers can knowledgeably choose among such techniques, however, they must know something about the reading and writing abilities of their students. They must judge whether these abilities are equal to the demands that planned literacy activities are likely to involve. In this chapter we offer relatively quick, informal methods of gathering such information.

Objectives

When you finish reading this chapter, you should be able to

1. describe the three dimensions of assessment necessary for content literacy-based instruction;
2. define independent, instructional, and frustration reading levels;
3. identify the strengths and limitations of readability formulas;
4. apply the Raygor readability formula (1977) to a prose selection;
5. state the guidelines for constructing cloze tests;
6. interpret cloze scores in terms of approximate reading levels;
7. describe the components of a content literacy inventory;
8. interpret the results of such an inventory; and
9. describe an approach to assessing your own teaching and the literacy demands it places on your students.

Three Dimensions of Classroom Assessment

Historically, a common assumption among teachers has been that if a student experiences problems, the source of the difficulty must lie within the student. This deficit model is now being replaced with a more realistic view: that problems can sometimes be traced to the match between a given student and the materials and methods used for instruction. Lipson and Wixson (2003) speak of the need to assess not only the reader but the text and context as well. Kinney and Harry (1991) have recommended extending this three-dimensional approach to assessment to content classrooms as well as the reading clinic.

This idea is consistent with the notion discussed in Chapter 1 that the adequacy of a student's literacy skills is relative to the literacy demands made by a particular class. In this chapter we present ways of acquiring information about all three dimensions of your students' literacy performance: student ability, instructional materials, and teaching methods. The remaining chapters describe ways of achieving a balance among the three dimensions so that content literacy becomes a powerful asset.

What Is Reading Ability?

A reading clinician typically devotes many pages to describing the reading ability of a given student, especially a student with problems. Such a description entails a report of the many subskills that underlie reading ability, as well as other factors bearing on school performance. While debate continues over how best to teach reading, few experts would deny that reading ability involves the capacity to coordinate a number of mental processes that enable the reader to form a reasonable idea of the meaning represented by print. A description of these processes is beyond the scope of this book, but we must nevertheless consider the sorts of behaviors we would accept as evidence of reading ability. Which of the following, for example, would you be inclined to accept?

1. Ability to answer questions after reading
2. Ability to summarize what has been read
3. Ability to decide which of two statements is aligned with an author's views
4. Ability to guess missing words periodically deleted from a passage
5. Ability to choose from among several pictures the one that best represents the content of a selection
6. Ability to "retell" the information or events of the selection
7. Ability to apply the information contained in a selection to some new problem or situation

All of these tasks have been used as yardsticks of a reader's ability to comprehend. While they differ in what they demand, all appear to tap comprehension in some manner. Moreover, all can be quantified, if desired, so that reading ability can be described in numerical terms. Just as a coach might describe an athlete's sprinting ability by referring to average speed in the hundred-meter dash, a teacher might gauge a student's reading ability in terms of the percentage of questions answered, the thoroughness of a retelling, or the number of key points contained in a written summary.

This process is not as simple as it sounds, however. Let's consider just a few of the factors that might influence your own performance on a test about this textbook. To begin with, if this is the first reading-related course you've taken, you're not likely to do as well as the student who has had prior coursework in reading. The effects of background knowledge on reading comprehension are enormous. Second, assume that your instructor has given you highly detailed objective tests on Chapters 1 and 2 and then, without warning, asks for a written summary and critique of Chapter 3. Your expectations would have ill prepared you for such a task. Third, consider two classmates of equivalent background who differ in terms of their motivation to learn from this book. Would you predict higher comprehension scores for the more highly motivated student? You should. Our point is that reading ability is not easy to measure because a host of factors affect it. Even under the best of circumstances, reading ability cannot be reduced to a single number or test score. Scores can help us gain rather crude impressions of reading ability, but we must resist the notion that they represent precise measurements.

Even though we must face severe limitations in measuring reading ability, we can still make some fairly accurate quantitative statements about it. We know that reading ability typically increases with a student's age, as the student becomes more skilled and acquires more and more knowledge of the world to bring to bear while reading. When we say that reading ability increases, we are actually suggesting a numerical scale, or continuum, beginning at zero (no ability whatever) and progressing upward. We can describe points on this scale in various ways. Figure 3.1(a) is perhaps the simplest system, characterizing ability as

FIGURE 3.1

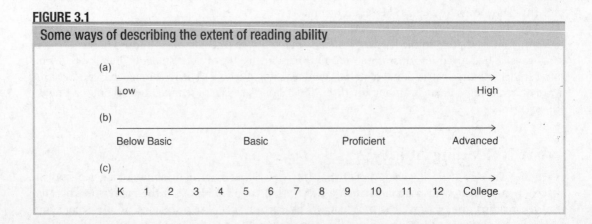

Some ways of describing the extent of reading ability

(a)

Low   High

(b)

Below Basic   Basic   Proficient   Advanced

(c)

K   1   2   3   4   5   6   7   8   9   10   11   12   College

FIGURE 3.2

Definitions of terms used by the National Assessment of Educational Progress to describe reading ability

GRADE 8

Basic

Eighth-grade students performing at the Basic level should demonstrate a literal understanding of what they read and be able to make some interpretations. When reading text appropriate to eighth grade, they should be able to identify specific aspects of the text that reflect the overall meaning, extend the ideas in the text by making simple inferences, recognize and relate interpretations and connections among ideas in the text to personal experience, and draw conclusions based on the text.

Proficient

Eighth-grade students performing at the Proficient level should be able to show an overall understanding of the text, including inferential as well as literal information. When reading text appropriate to eighth grade, they should be able to extend the ideas in the text by making clear inferences from it, by drawing conclusions, and by making connections to their own experiences—including other reading experiences. Proficient eighth graders should be able to identify some of the devices authors use in composing text.

Advanced

Eighth-grade students performing at the Advanced level should be able to describe the more abstract themes and ideas of the overall text. When reading text appropriate to eighth grade, they should be able to analyze both meaning and form and support their analyses explicitly with examples from the text; they should be able to extend text information by relating it to their experiences and to world events. At this level, student responses should be thorough, thoughtful, and extensive.

Source: National Center for Educational Statistics (2004). Available at http://nces.ed.gov/nationsreportcard/reading/achieveall.asp.

ranging from low to high. This approach is hard to fault in general, but unless we carefully define these terms, the system is not very useful. Figure 3.1(b) uses terms adopted by the National Assessment of Educational Progress (NAEP) to describe reading ability as it relates to students at the fourth, eighth, and twelfth grades. The NAEP terms are defined in Figure 3.2. Such terms make it possible to place readers of different ages on the same continuum. Perhaps the most common way of demarcating the scale of reading ability is by using grade levels, as in Figure 3.1(c), where the 3 represents the ability of the average third grader, and so on.

Of course, all of these approaches can be applied to writing ability as well. One of the scoring rubrics used in the NAEP writing assessment appears in Figure 3.3. It has more performance levels than the reading framework.

Many teachers have trouble thinking about reading ability in grade-level terms because of difficulties inherent in the grade-equivalent scores produced by standardized tests. Indeed, these difficulties are so grave that in 1980 the International Reading Association formally condemned the use of such scores. We wish to make clear, however, that the scale depicted in Figure 3.1(c) is an abstract assessment and merely portrays the typical progression of overall ability as students move through school. Figure 3.1(c) has nothing to do with grade-equivalent scores, which amount to crude estimates of a given student's position on the scale. We stress that such a position can *never* be determined precisely. However, the notion of a grade-level continuum has been a useful one in conceptualizing what is meant by reading ability.

FIGURE 3.3

Rubric used by the National Assessment of Educational Progress to evaluate informative writing at Grade 8

6 Excellent Response
- Develops and shapes information with well-chosen details across the response.
- Is well organized with strong transitions.
- Sustains variety in sentence structure and exhibits good word choice.
- Errors in grammar, spelling, and punctuation are few and do not interfere with understanding.

5 Skillful Response
- Develops and shapes information with details in parts of the response.
- Is clearly organized, but may lack some transitions and/or have occasional lapses in continuity.
- Exhibits some variety in sentence structure and some good word choices.
- Errors in grammar, spelling, and punctuation do not interfere with understanding.

4 Sufficient Response
- Develops information with some details.
- Organized with ideas that are generally related, but has few or no transitions.
- Exhibits control over sentence boundaries and sentence structure, but sentences and word choice may be simple and unvaried.
- Errors in grammar, spelling, and punctuation do not interfere with understanding.

3 Uneven Response (may be characterized by one or more of the following)
- Presents some clear information, but is list-like, undeveloped, or repetitive OR offers no more than a well-written beginning.
- Is unevenly organized; the response may be disjointed.
- Exhibits uneven control over sentence boundaries and sentence structure; may have some inaccurate word choices.
- Errors in grammar, spelling, and punctuation sometimes interfere with understanding.

2 Insufficient Response (may be characterized by one or more of the following)
- Presents fragmented information OR may be very repetitive OR may be very undeveloped.
- Is very disorganized; thoughts are tenuously connected OR the response is too brief to detect organization.
- Minimal control over sentence boundaries and sentence structure; word choice may often be inaccurate.
- Errors in grammar or usage (such as missing words or incorrect word use or word order), spelling, and punctuation interfere with understanding in much of the response.

1 Unsatisfactory Response (may be characterized by one or more of the following)
- Attempts to respond to task, but provides little or no coherent information; may only paraphrase the task.
- Has no apparent organization OR consists of a single statement.
- Minimal or no control over sentence boundaries and sentence structure; word choice may be inaccurate in much or all of the response.
- A multiplicity of errors in grammar or usage (such as missing words or incorrect word use or word order), spelling, and punctuation severely impedes understanding across the response.

Source: National Center for Educational Statistics (2004). Available at http://nces.ed.gov/nationsreportcard/writing/scale.asp.

NET Worth

Read more about the National Assessment of Educational Progress. Find information about the NAEP as well as useful research summaries through the USDE's National Center for Education Statistics.

http://nces.ed.gov/pubsearch

Levels of Reading Ability

Our grade-level depiction of reading ability is helpful in making an important point. To suggest that, given accurate measurements, a student can be placed at a particular point along the scale is actually an oversimplification. Reading specialists work under the useful assumption that individuals typically possess not one level of reading ability but three! (See Figure 3.4.)

At the *independent* level, materials are easily understood by the reader without outside assistance. For example, a popular novel you might read for pleasure is likely to be at this level. At the *instructional* level, materials are more difficult; the help of a teacher may be needed for the reader to comprehend them adequately. Reading is challenging but not prohibitive. At the *frustration* level, as the phrase suggests, materials are apt to be so trying that the reader gives up. Even the help of an instructor cannot make the reading sufficiently comprehensible.

It is important to realize that these levels differ from one individual to another. The novel that might fall at your independent level would frustrate a young child. It is also important to note that our caution about measurement applies here also. Although we can speak about John's independent level or Susan's instructional level in the abstract, these levels cannot be precisely measured, only estimated.

The definitions provided in Figure 3.4 are conventional ways of dealing with the fact that John might have, for example, more than a single independent level. After all, if he can read third-grade materials independently, he can read comparable materials of second- or first-grade difficulty. To avoid confusion, the independent level is therefore taken to be the *highest* level of independent performance. Likewise, the frustration level is assumed to be the *lowest* level at which comprehension breaks down and frustration occurs. We assume that still more difficult materials would have a similar effect. We have depicted this relationship for a particular, hypothetical child in Figure 3.5. Between the independent level of third grade and the frustration level of sixth lie two instructional levels (fourth and fifth grades), sometimes called the *instructional range*.

FIGURE 3.4

Definitions of the three levels of reading ability

Independent Level	The highest level at which there is good comprehension without assistance
Instructional Level	Any level at which there is good comprehension as long as assistance is available
Frustration Level	The lowest level at which comprehension is inadequate even when assistance is available

FIGURE 3.5

Depiction of the three levels of reading ability

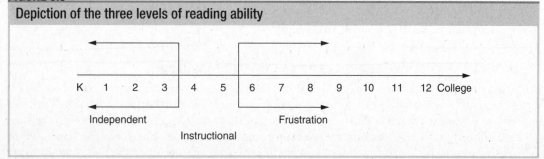

FIGURE 3.6

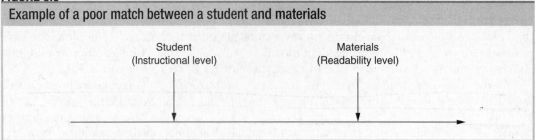

Example of a poor match between a student and materials

Reading Ability and Readability

We have spoken not only of placing *students,* theoretically, on a grade-level continuum, but also of placing *materials* on the same scale. The more difficult the reading, the higher the placement. The same continuum can thus serve as a frame of reference (though an admittedly imperfect one) for placing students *and* materials. When grade-level designations are applied to students, we speak of *reading ability;* when they are applied to materials, we speak of *readability.*

We use the term to refer to the overall difficulty level of a book (or some other unit of text) and admit that the choice of terms is unfortunate. This is because the word *readable* is also used to denote such ideas as how legible the print is or how enjoyable the writing proves to be (Fry, 1998, 2002; Hoke, 1999; Klare, 1988). For our purposes, however, the term refers in a general way to difficulty and can be thought of as synonymous with *comprehensibility* or *understandability* (terms that are more cumbersome but less ambiguous).

An advantage of using the same scale to characterize both students and materials is that it enables us to judge whether the two are suitably matched. When the reading ability of a student falls significantly below the readability of the materials the student is asked to read, as in Figure 3.6, the match is clearly unsuitable, and the results can be disastrous. Again, remember that our placement of materials and students along the continuum is theoretical. Precise measurements of this kind are not possible. Moreover, we confess to oversimplifying the notion of readability for purposes of our illustration. (Some of the factors that affect readability lie within the *reader.*) However, Figure 3.6 is a defensible depiction for our purposes and makes clear the need to determine whether the match between students and reading materials is viable. We now examine ways teachers can make such a determination.

Judging the Match Between Students and Materials

Let's consider Mr. Ross, a tenth-grade biology teacher who will use a textbook adopted by his school district. He is free to modify or even abandon the text if he chooses, but he lacks the funds to use an alternative text. Mr. Ross must determine whether his class will be able to read the typical assignments he plans to make from the book. In the process, he will identify those students who are likely to have substantial problems with the text.

Mr. Ross has two choices: (1) He can estimate the students' reading ability and the readability of the text and then compare the two measures, or (2) he can construct a brief reading and writing task based on the text itself and judge the students' success with this task. Each of these approaches has distinct advantages and drawbacks. Keep in mind that the two approaches are not mutually exclusive. It is possible to do both!

Approach 1: Assessing Students and Materials Separately

Mr. Ross can evaluate his students and his text independently by examining test scores on file for his pupils and by applying any of several common measures of readability to his book. The chief advantage of this approach is that it can be accomplished outside of class, even before the start of the school year. The disadvantages, however, are formidable. The measures available to Mr. Ross are relatively crude estimates of the information he needs. Moreover, he can never really be certain about the suitability of the text until his students actually begin to interact with it. Below, we look briefly at the measures Mr. Ross would use in this approach.

Standardized Tests.   In most U.S. schools, standardized tests are administered once a year. These measurements are designed to assess groups rather than individual students, and yet because of their availability teachers often attempt to use such tests in making tentative decisions about their students. Up to a point this practice can be beneficial, but we stress the word *tentative*. The following guidelines will help you arrive at reasonable conclusions about the reading ability of your students based on standardized tests.

1. Refer only to the reading comprehension subtest.
2. Ignore all norms but the percentile rank. (Ignore in particular the grade-equivalent score.)
3. Tentatively classify students as average, above average, or below average using the following guide:

> 0–22 below average
> 23–39 borderline
> 40–59 average
> 60–76 borderline
> 77–99 above average

When Mr. Ross finds that Richard has scored at the 47th percentile rank on a standardized subtest of reading comprehension, he can reasonably assume that Richard's reading ability is roughly commensurate with his grade level. Because Richard is a sophomore, his ability level is likely to be near tenth grade. This, however, is as far as Mr. Ross can proceed in translating Richard's score into a grade level. If the score were higher—perhaps in at least the 80th percentile rank—Mr. Ross could say only that Richard's ability level is probably higher than tenth grade.

If these restrictions seem overly prohibitive, remember that they are based on sound psychometric principles. Remember, too, that the test has already been given. Mr. Ross need only consult a roster of results (usually generated by a computer) in order to make these tentative judgments about his students.

Measures of Readability.   Mr. Ross's next step would be to estimate the text's level of difficulty. Think for a moment about what makes a reading selection easy or difficult. As we noted earlier, some of the factors we might list lie within the reader rather than the selection (the familiarity of the topic, for example). If we limit ourselves to the writing itself, the factors we might list would include at least the following (Miller & McKenna, 1989):

> Sentence length
> Vocabulary
> Grammatical complexity
> Organization
> Cohesion
> Abstractness
> Clarity
> Assumptions about prior knowledge

Attempting to arrive at an overall estimate of difficulty level by considering these factors is not an easy task. As you might expect, some teachers are better than others at doing so (Frager, 1984). In an effort to make the process of estimating readability more systematic, researchers have offered several methods. The oldest involves the use of numeric formulas that account for a few of the factors just mentioned. A second approach involves comparing a selection with a sequence of passages of progressive difficulty (Singer, 1975). The third and newest alternative entails structured (though subjective) considerations of numerous textual factors (Binkley, 1988; Zakaluk & Samuels, 1988). Currently, we believe that formulas offer teachers the most practical alternative, one that will result in defensible estimates of text difficulty (Fry, 1989).

Readability formulas typically account for only the first two of the eight factors listed previously: sentence length and vocabulary. This is a severe limitation indeed, and yet formulas succeed in predicting a remarkable amount of the variance in student comprehension performance on different prose materials. Although there are newer formulas that attempt to account for more factors, they are quite time-consuming (unless computerized). Our experience is that teachers may be willing to apply a formula only if it is sufficiently simple to use. We will consider only one such formula, the readability estimate developed by Raygor (1977).

Raygor's formula has the advantages of being extremely quick to administer and of correlating well with more complex formulas, as well as with student performance measures. The steps in using the formula and its accompanying chart appear in Figure 3.7. As you can see, the formula requires first computing the average length of sentences in three representative selections of 100 words each and next determining the proportion of words with six or more letters in these selections. These two numbers are then used to plot a point on the graph. For most selections the point will fall in one of the numbered sections. The number is the grade-level estimate.

Let's assume that Mr. Ross applies the Raygor formula to his textbook and produces a twelfth-grade estimate. Comparing this estimate with Richard's tenth-grade reading ability level might lead Mr. Ross to predict that Richard will have difficulties with the book. This may be the case, but there are two problems with Mr. Ross's reasoning. One is that both the estimate of Richard's ability and the estimate of the book's readability are highly suspect. Either or both may be off the mark. The other is that the difference between grade levels in the secondary years is smaller than that at the elementary level. No one, for example, could fail to note the difference between first- and second-grade materials, but the difference between eleventh- and twelfth-grade materials is quite small.

What we are suggesting is that in order to predict serious difficulty, it is necessary to identify a large difference between our estimate of (1) a student's reading level and (2) the readability of assigned materials. If Richard's percentile rank on the standardized test were below the average for tenth graders, and if the Raygor formula had placed the text at the college level, Mr. Ross would have had a better foundation for his fears. Because of the availability of standardized test results and the quickness of applying the Raygor formula, Approach 1 can be useful in obtaining an "early warning" about those students most likely to have difficulty.

Approach 2: Assessing Students and Materials Together

Knowledge must come through action; you can have no test which is not fanciful, save by trial.
SOPHOCLES

In this section we examine the second approach to judging the match between assigned materials and student ability. This approach involves constructing a short exercise over a brief portion of the material in order to appraise student performance. A disadvantage of this approach is that it requires class time. However, because the time is spent on materials the instructor has decided to assign anyway, few teachers object to such assessment. Moreover, basing reading evaluation on the materials to be read can lead to far more accurate predictions than those arrived at through Approach 1.

There are two principal methods of constructing such exercises: the cloze test and the content literacy inventory—two vastly different techniques that yield surprisingly similar information.

Cloze Testing. The cloze procedure has been used for four decades to assess reading comprehension, and it is extraordinarily well researched (Kolic-Vehovec & Bajsanski, 2007; McKenna & Robinson, 1980). In a cloze test, some of the words in a passage are replaced with blanks. The student is asked to infer them—to "close" the gaps—on the basis of context.

Many cloze formats have been used, but nearly all the extensive research studies done to determine scoring guidelines have used the same format. It is therefore essential to follow these same guidelines when constructing your own cloze tests. These guidelines are summarized by McKenna and Stahl (2003, p. 172):

- Start with a passage of about 300 words. Shorter passages may be used, but reliability could be jeopardized.
- Choose any word as the first to be deleted, but leave a sentence or two intact at the beginning of the test.
- Thereafter, mark every fifth word, until 50 have been marked.

FIGURE 3.7

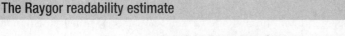

The Raygor readability estimate

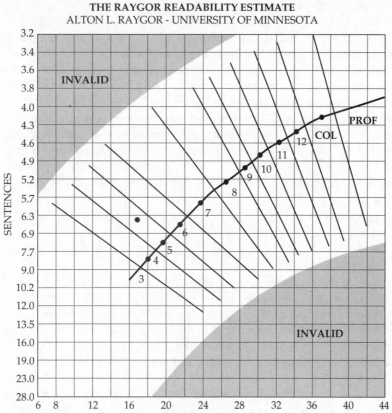

THE RAYGOR READABILITY ESTIMATE
ALTON L. RAYGOR - UNIVERSITY OF MINNESOTA

Directions:

Count out three 100-word passages at the beginning, middle, and end of a selection or book. Count out proper nouns, but not numerals.

1. Count sentences in each passage, estimating to nearest tenth.
2. Count words with six or more letters.
3. Average the sentence length and word length over the three samples and plot the average on the graph.

Example:

	Sentences	6+ Words
A	6.0	15
B	6.8	19
C	6.4	17
Total	19.2	51
Average	6.4	17

Note mark on graph. Grade level is about 5.

Source: From "The Raygor Readability Estimate: A Quick and Easy Way to Determine Difficulty" (p. 261) by Alton Raygor, in *Reading Theory, Research, and Practice: Twenty-Sixth Yearbook of the National Reading Conference* by P. D. Pearson (Ed.), 1977, Clemson, SC: National Reading Conference. Copyright © 1977 by the National Reading Conference Inc. Reprinted by permission of the National Reading Conference.

- Word-process the test so that the words you've marked are replaced by blanks.
- The blanks must be of equal length.
- For younger students, leave blanks of around 15 spaces to give students room to write.
- For older students, you may wish to number the blanks so that students can write their answers on a separate sheet.

Surprisingly, the point in the text at which the passage is selected makes little difference. Cloze items are not very dependent on preceding material. Try to choose a passage that is (1) largely typical of the material presented in the text and (2) relatively free of non-English inclusions, such as formulas and equations.

In administering the test, acquaint students in advance with the idea of a cloze exercise. Examples should be provided and thoroughly discussed. Inform students that a good score is much lower than one that would be considered good on more traditional tests. Also, make it clear that scores will not affect their grades. The testing itself is untimed.

Scoring is simple: Correct answers must be the exact words deleted, with the exception of minor misspellings. Resist the temptation to give credit for synonyms and other reasonable responses. Otherwise, scoring becomes subjective and time-consuming, and results can no longer be evaluated on the basis of research—all of which has credited verbatim responses only. Moreover, studies have clearly shown that counting synonyms adds nothing to the discriminating power of the test (Henk, 1981; McKenna, 1976; Miller & Coleman, 1967) and increases the subjectivity of scoring (Henk & Selders, 1984). The scoring guide established through criterion studies is as follows:

Independent level	60 percent or higher
Instructional level	40 to 59 percent
Frustration level	39 percent or lower

These guidelines should not be applied too rigorously. Scores in the vicinity of 40 percent or 60 percent should be regarded as borderline. As a general rule, however, these criteria are quite useful and have shown remarkable stability across populations. Investigations of upper-elementary students have resulted in similar findings (Bormuth, 1967; Clariana, 1991; Rankin & Culhane, 1969), as have studies of high school students (Peterson, Paradis, & Peters, 1973), vocational-technical and college students (Peterson, Peters, & Paradis, 1972), and reading-disabled students (Peterson & Carroll, 1974).

An example of a cloze test appears in Figure 3.8. If you are unfamiliar with the technique, we suggest you try your hand at cloze completion. Check your answers at the end of the chapter (see Figure 3.10, page 42.)

Reading Guides.   An alternative to cloze testing is the reading guide, a teacher-made device intended primarily to help students locate, consider, and write about important information in assigned reading materials. A reading guide typically consists of a few photocopied pages containing questions to answer, charts and diagrams to complete, and other tasks to undertake while reading. Using a guide is an "open book" experience, during which students go back and forth from the text to the guide. To help students keep their place, teachers often incorporate page numbers and subheadings into each guide. No two guides are alike, and there is no best way to construct one. The key is to direct students to information the teacher feels is important.

In Chapter 8, we will examine in detail how to construct reading guides and use them in content area instruction. We preview them here because guides can provide valuable assessment information about how well students can comprehend assigned materials. A reading guide requires students to write. This writing—whether it involves answers to questions, charts, diagrams, paragraphs, or other forms—provides evidence of how well the students comprehend. This evidence can be very useful at the beginning of a new school year. A teacher who asks students to open their books to a particular passage and complete a guide as they read will readily discern which students will be likely to find the material too difficult as the year progresses.

Judging the Context of Instruction

Knowing the match between the reading ability of students and the readability of materials is an important first step. There is another dimension to students' literacy performance in content classes, however. This is the context in which literacy is used. Context is often broadly defined to include socioeconomic background, cultural considerations, and similar factors (Lipson & Wixson, 2003; Rowsell & Pahl, 2007). Our approach is narrower, however. We limit our discussion of context to

FIGURE 3.8

Sample cloze test

The term *hurricane* has its origin in the indigenous religions of old civilizations. The Mayan storm god was named *Hunraken*. A _____ considered evil by the _____ people of the Caribbean _____ called *Huracan*. Hurricanes may _____ be considered evil but _____ are one of nature's _____ powerful storms. Their potential _____ loss of life and _____ of property is tremendous. _____ in hurricane-prone areas _____ to be prepared for _____ and tropical storms. Even _____ areas, well away from _____ coastline, can experience destructive _____, tornadoes, and floods from _____ storms and hurricanes.

Tropical _____ and tropical storms, while _____ less dangerous than hurricanes, _____ can be deadly. The _____ of tropical depressions and _____ storms are usually not _____ greatest threat. Heavy rains, _____, and severe weather, such _____ tornadoes, create the greatest _____ from tropical storms and _____.

On average, each year, _____ tropical storms, six of _____ become hurricanes, develop in _____ Atlantic Ocean, Caribbean Sea, _____ Gulf of Mexico. In _____ typical three-year span, _____ U.S. coastline is struck _____ average five times by _____, two of which will _____ designated as major hurricanes.

_____ cyclones are sometimes steered _____ weak and erratic winds, _____ forecasting a challenge. Warnings _____ from the National Oceanic _____ Atmospheric Administration's (NOAA) National _____ Center continue to improve _____ have greatly diminished hurricane _____ in the United States. _____ improved warnings, property damage _____ to increase due to _____ population on our coastlines. _____ agencies, such as the _____ Emergency Management Agency (FEMA), _____ organizations such as the _____ Red Cross, have combined _____ state and local agencies, rescue and relief organizations, the private sector, and the news media to improve preparedness efforts.

The *Saffir-Simpson Hurricane Scale* is a 1 to 5 rating based on the hurricane's intensity. This scale estimates potential property damage.

Source: U.S. Department of Commerce (2001). *Hurricanes—Unleashing Nature's Fury*. Available at http://hurricanes.noaa.gov.

the instructional methods a teacher uses and to the literacy demands that these methods make on students.

This idea may suggest a kind of assessment quite new to you, for it requires taking stock of your own instructional practice. This is not an empty exercise in matters that are self-evident. Many teachers fail to reflect adequately on the effects their day-to-day classroom behaviors may have on student performance. To assist you, we have constructed a self-administered survey, the Content Literacy Instructional Practice Survey (CLIPS), which appears in Figure 3.9. If you have not yet begun to teach, you can still take the survey on the basis of your intentions as a future teacher.

The survey touches on many issues that we examine in detail later in this book. We encourage you to respond to all the items, however, and to return to the survey at the conclusion of the course. At that time, you may discover areas in which your philosophy has changed.

Note that there is no provision for arriving at a total score. Each aspect of your teaching practice is considered independently, and the result is not a number but a profile you can use to modify your instruction, if need be, in order to achieve a better balance among the three dimensions—students, materials, and methods. In short, the survey allows you to become a little more reflective about your teaching and the extent to which it influences your students' ability to use reading and writing to learn content.

As a brief example, let's assume that Mr. Ross responds to the survey and that his profile reveals the following traits. We note first that his reading assignments are made daily and over a semester will include his entire biology text. His average daily reading assignment is more

[Reading] is a means whereby we may learn not only to understand ourselves and the world about us but whereby we may find our place in the world.

ELIZABETH NETERER

FIGURE 3.9

Self-assess your own teaching

CONTENT LITERACY INSTRUCTIONAL PRACTICE SURVEY (CLIPS)

Frequency of Reading (Check one.)

_____ No reading

_____ Occasional reading (much reliance on lecture, demonstration)

_____ Frequent reading (most textbook chapters assigned)

_____ Daily or near-daily reading (all or nearly all textbook chapters assigned)

Amount of Reading (Check one.)

_____ No reading

_____ Average less than 10 pages per week (per course or subject)

_____ Average between 10 and 30 pages per week

_____ Average between 30 and 50 pages per week

_____ Average over 50 pages per week

Frequency of Writing (Check one.)

_____ No writing

_____ Occasional writing (once a week or less per course or subject)

_____ Frequent writing (more than once a week per course or subject)

_____ Daily or near-daily writing

Amount of Writing (Check one.)

_____ No writing

_____ Average less than 1 page per week (per course or subject)

_____ Average between 1 and 3 pages per week

_____ Average between 3 and 5 pages per week

_____ Average over 5 pages per week

Instructional Practice (Check all that apply to your teaching.)

_____ 1. I judge whether students' background is adequate before they read.

_____ 2. I try to refresh or add to students' knowledge before they read.

_____ 3. I introduce new technical terms before students read about them.

_____ 4. I stress the relationships among technical vocabulary terms.

_____ 5. I ensure that students have specific purposes for reading before they begin.

_____ 6. I relate postreading discussions to the original purposes students read to achieve.

_____ 7. I involve all students in class discussions.

_____ 8. I sometimes allow students to question and respond to one another during discussions.

_____ 9. I interact with students through journals or other forms of written interchange.

_____ 10. I provide opportunities for students to reinforce and extend their vocabulary knowledge after they read about new terms.

_____ 11. I provide opportunities for extended writing after some reading assignments.

_____ 12. I constantly look for ways to relate new material to previous material.

_____ 13. I occasionally assist students in developing good study habits and note-taking skills.

_____ 14. I occasionally discuss test-taking strategies with my students.

_____ 15. I talk with special educators in my school about students with special needs.

_____ 16. I modify reading assignments and other tasks, where appropriate, for special students.

_____ 17. I attempt to modify my teaching where possible to accommodate students with special needs.

_____ 18. I use alternative means of testing for special students when appropriate.

_____ 19. I attempt to discover which aspects of my subject specialty students would like to read more about.

_____ 20. My classroom is filled with examples of print materials related to my subject.

_____ 21. I occasionally apportion some time for free reading by students.

_____ 22. Whenever possible I point out links between course material and students' everyday lives.

_____ 23. I vary my teaching methods occasionally to avoid boredom.

_____ 24. I occasionally read aloud to my students.

_____ 25. When I can, I point out to students how course material is connected to other subject areas.

_____ 26. I try to provide students with choices as often as possible.

_____ 27. I find ways to integrate computers into my teaching.

than thirty pages. Moreover, Mr. Ross does not introduce technical vocabulary, nor does he ensure that students have specific purposes for which to read. From these responses alone, Mr. Ross might begin to think about some possibilities for improving his students' reading performance (and consequently the amount of biology they learn). He might, for example, become more selective in his assignments, using other means (such as lecture, discussion, and demonstration) to introduce some of the material. He might also try some of the techniques outlined in Chapters 5 through 8 in preparing his students for the assignments he does make. But Mr. Ross may never reach these conclusions unless his idea of assessment includes his own instructional practice and unless he occasionally reflects on that practice in a more or less structured way. The inventory presented in Figure 3.9 may help you achieve this kind of reflective practice.

Three Struggling Readers

In Chapter 2, we described the stages through which children pass as they become proficient readers (review Figure 2.2). Perhaps the best way to think of struggling readers—those having difficulty becoming proficient—was offered by Spear-Swerling and Sternberg (1996). They suggested that the vast majority of these students have gotten "off track" at a particular stage. Consider three such students.

Josh

Josh struggles to pronounce unfamiliar words. He sometimes guesses at them and sometimes attempts to sound them out from left to right. His pace is plodding and uncertain. He does, however, know a fair number of words by sight, and whenever he encounters one of them he can pronounce it immediately. Josh has gone off track at the decoding stage. Unless he receives appropriate instruction in phonics and other word recognition skills, he will not progress.

Latrelle

Latrelle has a good store of words she recognizes at sight, and she can successfully pronounce almost any unfamiliar word she encounters while reading. Her pace is slow, however, and her oral reading is expressionless. She does not group words into meaningful phrases as she reads, and she tends to ignore punctuation. She needs plenty of practice in real reading, both oral and silent, if she is to become fluent.

Pablo

Pablo is a proficient oral reader, but when faced with new material he often has problems comprehending. This difficulty is especially evident when he is asked to read nonfiction and when he is expected to draw logical conclusions about what he reads. He is a fair student when new content is thoroughly explained by his teacher, but he has problems whenever he must learn it on his own from print. Pablo represents the most common type of struggling reader at the

---

NET Worth

IRA's Adolescent Literacy Site. This site combines IRA's board position regarding adolescent literacy with useful links.

www.reading.org/resources/issues/focus_adolescent.html

AdLit houses many resources for fostering adolescent literacy.

www.adlit.org

---

middle and high school levels. He requires instruction in comprehension strategies as well as careful preparation and guidance when he needs to read new selections.

Teachers in content classrooms need to become aware of the Joshes, the Latrelles, and the Pablos they encounter in their classes. Day-to-day classroom interaction will soon provide all the evidence required to identify them. The hard part is then attempting to accommodate their problems while ensuring that content instruction takes place. While there is no "magic bullet" for meeting their needs, we will suggest steps you can take to do so throughout the remaining chapters of this book.

SUMMARY

In order to make instructional decisions that turn content literacy into an asset, a teacher must have three types of information. These involve (1) the proficiency of the students, (2) the nature of the written materials, and (3) the literacy-related demands made by the teacher. A balance of the three should be an important goal.

Reading ability is a concept that has proved very difficult to measure. Many formats have been used in testing it, and many scales have been devised for describing the extent of an individual's proficiency at reading. One of the most common is the use of grade levels. All attempts to measure or describe reading ability are imprecise.

A useful idea in conceptualizing an individual's reading ability is to speak of three distinct levels based on a grade-level frame of reference. The independent level is the highest at which comprehension is good and no assistance is necessary. In contrast, the frustration level is the lowest at which comprehension is poor even when help is available. The instructional level lies between these two and represents materials that are challenging but not frustrating—materials that are neither too easy nor too difficult and that are therefore appropriate for instructional purposes. Like reading ability in general, these three levels are never precisely measurable, but they can be estimated.

The word *readability* refers to the overall difficulty of text and is often estimated in grade-level terms. A useful method is to think of a student's reading ability and an assignment's readability on the same scale so that the two can be compared and a judgment reached as to whether the match is a good one.

NET Worth

Federal Resources for Educational Excellence (FREE!). This site offers hundreds of educational resources supported by federal government agencies in various subjects including the arts, educational technology, foreign languages, health and safety, language arts, mathematics, science, social studies, and so on.

www.ed.gov/free

There are two approaches to making such a judgment. The first is to judge students and materials separately. The advantage of such an approach is that these assessments can be made without the use of regular class time. Students' reading levels can be estimated from standardized test results, which are typically available at the beginning of the school year. The readability of materials can be estimated through the use of formulas designed for this purpose. The difficulties with this approach are numerous, however. One problem is that because standardized test results are not designed for use with readability formulas, they yield crude and misleading estimates. Another is that readability formulas tend to ignore a host of factors that influence the difficulty of text.

The second approach solves these problems by assessing students and materials together. A brief test is made from the actual materials students will be using, and the results can provide an instructor with useful information about whether the match between students and text will be a good one. A cloze test is one exercise of this sort. It involves systematically deleting words from a representative passage and then asking students to guess the missing words based on context. A more traditional approach is to ask the students to complete a reading guide as they read a short passage assigned by the teacher. The accuracy and quality of their responses to questions and other tasks will reveal much about their ability to read assigned material.

In addition to assessing students' abilities and the difficulty of assigned readings, it is also important for teachers to assess their instructional practices. An individual profile of such practices may assist teachers in recognizing which teaching behaviors may help and which may hinder students as they attempt to use literacy to learn content. Self-assessment can be organized through the Content Literacy Instructional Practice Survey presented in Figure 3.9.

Most of the struggling readers found in content classes from the upper elementary grades through high school can be described as having gone off track at a crucial developmental stage. Some may never have acquired sufficient skill at decoding; others may not be able to read fluently; and still others may be unable to read with good comprehension. Teachers must be aware of these types of students and attempt to accommodate their needs.

NET Worth

The Lexile Framework

The Lexile Framework provides a quick way to learn the approximate difficulty level of any book. Lexiles are difficulty estimates that range from 200 to 1700 (from Amelia Bedelia to Darwin). Corresponding grade-level ranges and familiar titles are provided to give you a frame of reference.

There are several ways to use the Framework. First, you can look up a title in the extensive online database. Most textbooks are included. Second, you can upload a file from your computer. Such a file could contain a text sample that you have scanned or keyboarded, a sample of student work, or any other text. It must be saved as plain text, however.

You can also use the Lexile Framework to judge the match between a book and a student's reading level. Most tests of reading comprehension, including group achievement measures, now report student scores as lexiles. By comparing the student's lexile score with that of the materials that the student is asked to read, a teacher can quickly judge the potential difficulty the student is likely to experience.

The Lexile Framework was developed by MetaMetrics, Inc., through grants from the National Institute of Child Health and Human Development, the National Institute of Health, and the U.S. Public Health Service. Its use is free, although you must register.

www.lexile.com

FIGURE 3.10

Answers to cloze test

The term *hurricane* has its origin in the indigenous religions of old civilizations. The Mayan storm god was named *Hunraken*. A _____god_____ considered evil by the _____Taino_____ people of the Caribbean _____was_____ called *Huracan*. Hurricanes may _____not_____ be considered evil but _____they_____ are one of nature's _____most_____ powerful storms. Their potential _____for_____ loss of life and _____destruction_____ of property is tremendous. _____Those_____ in hurricane-prone areas _____need_____ to be prepared for _____hurricanes_____ and tropical storms. Even _____inland_____ areas, well away from _____the_____ coastline, can experience destructive _____winds_____, tornadoes, and floods from _____tropical_____ storms and hurricanes. Tropical _____depressions_____ and tropical storms, while _____generally_____ less dangerous than hurricanes, _____still_____ can be deadly. The _____winds_____ of tropical depressions and _____tropical_____ storms are usually not _____the_____ greatest threat. Heavy rains, _____flooding_____, and severe weather, such _____as_____ tornadoes, create the greatest _____threats_____ from tropical storms and _____depressions_____.

On average, each year, _____ten_____ tropical storms, six of _____which_____ become hurricanes, develop in _____the_____ Atlantic Ocean, Caribbean Sea, _____or_____ Gulf of Mexico. In _____a_____ typical three-year span, _____the_____ U.S. coastline is struck _____on_____ average five times by _____hurricanes_____, two of which will _____be_____ designated as major hurricanes. _____Tropical_____ cyclones are sometimes steered _____by_____ weak and erratic winds, _____making_____ forecasting a challenge. Warnings _____issued_____ from the National Oceanic _____and_____ Atmospheric Administration's (NOAA) National _____Hurricane_____ Center continue to improve _____and_____ have greatly diminished hurricane _____fatalities_____ in the United States. _____Despite_____ improved warnings, property damage _____continues_____ to increase due to _____growing_____ population on our coastlines. _____Federal_____ agencies, such as the _____Federal_____ Emergency Management Agency (FEMA), _____and_____ organizations such as the _____American_____ Red Cross, have combined _____with_____ state and local agencies, rescue and relief organizations, the private sector, and the news media to improve preparedness efforts.

The *Saffir-Simpson Hurricane Scale* is a 1 to 5 rating based on the hurricane's intensity. This scale estimates potential property damage.

Getting Involved

1. Apply the Raygor formula to samples you choose from this text. Do the results reinforce your own insights about its difficulty level? Do different portions of the text vary markedly in estimated readability, or are they relatively similar?

2. Figure 3.11 contains the information Mr. Ross might have collected about his tenth-grade biology students. Based on these data, which students, in your opinion, are most at risk of doing poorly on the literacy activities Mr. Ross may plan? For which students is the profile

information unclear or contradictory? How might you explain these ambiguities? How might you deal with the contradictions? Would it help to give only one of the tests?

3. Remember that Figure 3.10 presents the answers to the cloze test in Figure 3.8. Use these answers to check your own answers to the cloze test.

FIGURE 3.11

Information for Mr. Ross's biology class

Student	Cloze Percentage	Reading Guide*
Maria	30	A
Tom	32	M
Kanesha	40	A
Rick	64	S
Sam	70	M
Sarah	20	S
Ming Fang	50	A
Tran	52	W
Bill	10	A
Lynn	18	W
Mike	40	M

*S = Strong, A = Adequate, M = Marginal, W = Weak

CHAPTER 4

Teaching for Diversity

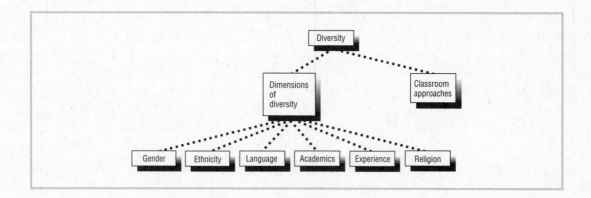

Differences challenge assumptions.

—Anne Wilson Schaef

American classrooms continue to reflect the increasing diversity of a rapidly changing population. The most recent census, for example, found that more than 17 percent of school children live in households where a language other than English is spoken (U.S. Census Bureau, 2002). Many of these children and their families immigrated to the United States overwhelmed by forces of war, political oppression, economic struggles, and language barriers (He, 2003). They bring with them complex differences in culture, ethnicity, race, and language into inner-city, suburban, and even rural classrooms. These children's reading and communicative styles can differ considerably from those of their teachers and peers who speak English as their native language (He & McKenna, 2005).

Ignoring differences among students leads not only to ineffective instruction, but also risks excluding and devaluing some students. Consider Ms. Stevens's ninth-grade general science class. Of her twenty students, nine are girls and eleven are boys. Five are black, three are Hispanic, one is Native American, two are of mixed race, eight are white, and one is Asian. Two of the students have been categorized as learning disabled, but because of a policy of inclusion they are members of Ms. Stevens's class. Yet another of the students has been labeled as having ADHD (attention deficit hyperactivity disorder) and another has been labeled gifted. Language differences also characterize some of the students. The Asian student, for example, has only limited proficiency in spoken English, as does one of the Hispanic students. Five of the black students speak a dialect of American English known as Black English. Seven of Ms. Stevens's twenty students qualify for free or reduced-priced lunches. A total of eight are bused to the school from affluent suburban neighborhoods because of the school's magnet pro-

FIGURE 4.1

Demographic breakdown of Ms. Stevens's ninth-grade science class

Student	Gender	Ethnicity	Exceptionality	First Language	Lunches	Religion
Amber	girl	white	none	English		Mormon
Ann	girl	white	none	English		Presbyterian
Arliss	boy	black	none	English	Free/R	Baptist
Bess	girl	white	LD	English		Catholic
Bryan	boy	mixed	none	English		unknown
Chuck	boy	white	none	English	Free/R	Protestant
Eli	boy	mixed	none	English		Muslim
Jorge	boy	Hispanic	none	Spanish		Catholic
Karl	boy	white	none	English		unknown
Latrelle	girl	black	none	English	Free/R	Baptist
LiQuiang	boy	Asian	none	Chinese		Taoist
Leroy	boy	black	LD	English	Free/R	Catholic
Maria	girl	Hispanic	none	Spanish	Free/R	Catholic
Mike	boy	white	ADHD	English		Jehovah's W
Nora	girl	white	none	English		Methodist
Paula	girl	Native Amer.	none	English	Free/R	Methodist
Ricardo	boy	Hispanic	none	Spanish		Catholic
Ruthie	girl	black	none	English	Free/R	Catholic
Steven	boy	white	gifted	English		Baptist
Tanya	girl	black	physical	English		Pentacostal

gram in computer science. Also, a significant variety of religious preferences are represented in Ms. Stevens's class. Ten of the students are Protestant (loosely defined), six are Catholic, one is Muslim, and one is Taoist, while two are not associated with an organized religion.

Figure 4.1 presents the class roster for Ms. Stevens's class, with each student characterized along all of these lines. As you can easily see, she faces a tremendously varied group of students, especially when so many different factors are taken into account. These differences represent a

Objectives

In this chapter, we describe the major dimensions of diversity present in American classrooms today. We will use Ms. Stevens's class as a way of anchoring our discussion in a real-life context. We will also indicate how various dimensions of diversity pose challenges to teachers. We offer suggestions that may help you to contend with the instructional issues related to diverse classrooms and to become a culturally responsive teacher.

When you finish this chapter, your knowledge of diversity and the steps you can take to affirm it in your classroom should be increased. You should by then:

1. be aware of the major dimensions of diversity within American classrooms;

2. be cognizant of the instructional challenges posed by diverse classrooms; and

3. be able to develop culturally responsive strategies for better addressing the needs of a diverse classroom.

circumstance that Ms. Stevens must acknowledge if her instruction is to be effective. The variation suggests that her students will tend to learn in different ways and filter content according to their culture and background. If Ms. Stevens chooses to ignore these differences and teach instead to a mythical "mainstream," she will risk limiting the degree to which some of her students will learn.

Dimensions of Diversity

The students in Ms. Stevens's class are members of different groups. They can be grouped by gender, ethnicity, academic characteristics, language attainment, religion, and social class. We might have grouped them according to other characteristics as well, such as their leadership capacity or their personal fitness, but the six groupings listed above represent important features useful in planning and delivering instruction. Let's examine each.

Gender Diversity

On the first day of class, Ms. Stevens described the work scientists do. She then made an unusual request—at least for ninth graders. She asked them to draw a picture of a scientist at work. Her class busily created renditions of figures clothed in white lab coats and surrounded by beakers and test tubes, but there was something much more striking about nearly all of the depictions—they were men! These students, even the girls, were relying on a gender stereotype, one that might very well affect their attitude toward science and their success in learning. If science is viewed by girls as a masculine pursuit, then the extent to which they are engaged in learning may be limited. Ms. Stevens would do well to reflect on how the gender of her students might affect just how seriously they take science. She might also consider ways of popularizing science among girls.

Some have argued, however, that it may be possible to "overcorrect" in confronting gender stereotypes and to actually do a disservice to boys by favoring girls. In her book, *The War against Boys,* Christina Hoff Sommers (2000) warns that boys may be systematically shortchanged by teachers striving to correct the inequities of the past. Obviously, what matters most is that teachers like Ms. Stevens attempt to dispel gender stereotypes that could influence the learning of girls. We believe that this can be done without disadvantaging boys in any significant way.

Ethnic Diversity

Ethnic groups, which reflect racial and cultural associations, constitute a critical consideration in instructional planning. A teacher from South Dakota recently described an "Ethnic Fair" planned to make both teachers and students more aware of cultural differences. She spoke of walking from booth to booth and learning about the cultural heritage of Denmark, Norway, Sweden, and Finland. "It was like visiting an ice-cream store," she joked, "where all the flavors were vanilla." The ethnic diversity present in Ms. Stevens's class, however, is a very different matter. It is important for her to recognize that membership in an ethnic group will influence her students' attitudes toward schooling, their expectations, the kinds of questions they ask and respond to, and what they accept as evidence within content subjects.

Shirley Brice Heath (1983) stressed how important it is for teachers to become aware of the "ways of knowing" associated with various ethnic groups they serve. For example, ethnic peers may exert either a positive or negative influence on the effort an individual student expends. A striking example occurs in the movie *Stand and Deliver,* the true story of high school math teacher Jaime Escalante. He was able to create an interest in learning mathematics by appealing to the cultural background of the disadvantaged Hispanic students he taught in California. By pointing out how the Mayans (their ancestors) had built observatories long before the Europeans, he was able to make an important connection, one that dispelled ethnic stereotypes. You can do mathematics, he admonished them. "It's in your blood." In one notable scene, Mr. Escalante confronted a gang leader who finally consented to make the effort to learn math. Surprisingly, however, he demanded a second set of textbooks. Puzzled, Mr. Escalante asked him why he wanted a second set since he had a perfectly good set as it was. Because, the gang leader responded, "I can't be seen carrying these books on the street." This episode illustrates how deeply influential ethnic identity can be in shaping expectations.

Guadalupe Valdés, in her book *Learning and Not Learning English* (2001), describes the experiences of four Mexican-American middle schoolers. These immigrant children find themselves suddenly immersed in the linguistically and culturally alien world of an American middle school. Her account makes clear that learning English is not simply an academic objective, it has cultural and political overtones as well. The children feel pressure from some of their peers *not* to learn English. Doing so is seen by some as compromising their cultural identity. For their part, the non-Hispanic white students in the school tended to view the newcomers stereotypically and, perhaps surprisingly, so did many of the teachers. Challenging one's own stereotypes is the first step toward culturally responsive teaching (Conway, Browning, & Purdum-Cassidy, 2007; Ferguson, 2007; Nieto, 2000; Villegas & Lucas, 2007).

If Ms. Stevens were to conclude that her five black students shared mutual cultural beliefs and values, she might be greatly mistaken. If Ms. Stevens were black, she would undoubtedly be more cognizant of the cultural differences among blacks, but she might be likely in turn to think stereotypically in terms of her white students. Teachers must try hard to get beyond the ethnic stereotyping that can lead to quick and frequently erroneous conclusions about their students.

Linguistic Diversity

Language differences among students in American classrooms present one of the most urgent challenges facing teachers. UNESCO reported that 6,809 different languages were in use (including 114 sign languages) in 228 countries as of the year 2000 (UNESCO, 2003). Although all of these languages are not encountered in American classrooms, the language diversity in the United States is increasing. By 2000, the foreign-born population of the United States was 31.1 million, which represented 11.1 percent of the total population (218.4 million) (U.S. Census Bureau, 2000).

Language Differences.   Linguistic diversity presents itself in two principal ways. The first of these is the acquisition of English as a second language. The majority of such children are not perfectly bilingual, and their skills in English are nearly always inferior to their native (home) language. This discrepancy can cause learning difficulties, of course, and a number of approaches have been developed in the past for contending with the problem. Students of limited English proficiency (LEP) may be taught in a context of bilingual education, in which instruction in both English and the native language occurs in the same classrooms. During one period, instruction might be conducted in the native language whereas during another it might be conducted in English. In contrast, the ESL approach (English as a Second Language) is one in which intense instruction in basic English is conducted in separate classrooms so that students can become proficient as quickly as possible.

The relative merits of these approaches have been hotly debated. Some research indicates that bilingual education can be effective in helping students evolve in their personal language acquisition to the point that they are capable of learning from written materials and oral presentations in English. However, many Hispanic parents object to instruction in Spanish because they believe that their children may be disadvantaged. In 1998, this sentiment led to passage of Proposition 227, the English for the Children Initiative, in California. This proposition called for an end to bilingual education and reliance instead on total immersion of California schoolchildren in English-speaking classrooms. Proponents of the proposition pointed to increases in the test scores of immigrant children as evidence that immersion works better than bilingual education. The debate continues.

Dialect.   The second facet of our linguistic diversity involves dialect. Dialects are variations within the same language. Dialect differences are marked by vocabulary, pronunciation, and syntax (grammar). Dialecticians make a distinction between regional dialects, those spoken by individuals living in the same area, and social dialects, those spoken by members of a particular social or cultural group. Historically, the United States has three regional dialects: Northern, Midland, and Southern. Speakers of these dialects tend to be divided on matters of vocabulary and pronunciation but not on issues of syntax (that is, the way words are ordered in sentences). Think about how you pronounce the word *greasy*. If you give the letter *s* a *z* sound (so that the word rhymes with *easy*), your pronunciation is historically Southern. If you give it an *s* sound, your pronunciation is traditionally Northern. By the same token, ask yourself what word you might use to describe a vessel used to carry water from a well. The word *pail* is historically Northern, whereas the word *bucket* is historically Southern. Because of mass media and population movement, differences among the regional dialects are slowly fading.

Social dialects, however, are still very apparent among the U.S. population, and the most important minority social dialect is Black English. William Labov (1971), who was one of the first to study Black English, identified such features as dropped *l*'s (*hep* for *help*), dropped *r*'s (*fust* for *first*), and the use of the infinitive *be* instead of its conjugated forms ("He be sick" instead of "He is sick"). Like the issue of second-language learning, the challenge presented by social dialects has been vigorously contested. It was once thought that speakers of black dialect, for instance, were disadvantaged in learning from materials printed in Standard English. We know of no evidence to support this claim. In fact, Labov pointed out that most of the speakers of minority dialects develop the capacity to shift their "styles" depending on whom they are addressing. He found that the ability to make these dialect shifts was facilitated by the exposure of students to those who speak other dialects.

Social dialects simply do not seem to be a great cause for concern. Past attempts to accommodate them by using materials written in a minority dialect have been disastrous. Such approaches are based on the fallacy that all blacks speak black dialect. Moreover, past attempts at dialect accommodation have provoked a justifiable objection on the part of black parents, who believe that such approaches risk sidetracking their children from becoming proficient in Standard English. They view such proficiency as the key to success in American society. Indeed, Lisa Delpit, a prominent African American literacy scholar, has described Standard English as the "power code," the one required in order to prosper financially (Delpit, 1988, 1995). The lesson for teachers is reasonably clear: Social dialect differences are not likely to pose serious challenges to students as they learn through text; Standard English, however, should be the expectation in student writing.

Academic Diversity and Exceptionalities

Children vary immensely in their academic ability. Some children have been formally categorized into established exceptionalities. In Ms. Stevens's class, for example, two of the students have been identified as learning disabled, another as gifted, and still another as having ADHD. This does not mean, of course, that the *other* children are extremely similar or, for that matter, that the special students conform to standard expectations associated with each category. The picture is clearly complex, and an overview of major exceptionalities may help.

As we entered the twenty-first century, more than 4.5 million American students had physical, mental, or behavioral handicaps. Federal funding has been appropriated to help ensure that these students receive education that is best suited to their needs. The Education for All Handicapped Children Act of 1975 guarantees a free and appropriate public education to all children in the United States between the ages of three and twenty-one. The law provides funds for special education programs to states and local districts that comply with a set of regulations. It is important to remember that students classified as gifted are also recognized as requiring special services if their potential is to be recognized, and these students are also covered under the 1975 law. Let's briefly examine the major exceptionalities teachers may be faced with in diverse classrooms.

Learning Disabilities. The largest group of exceptional children, slightly less than 5 percent of the American population, have learning disabilities. There is a discrepancy between their measured ability to learn and their actual achievement—a discrepancy that is not the result of intellectual retardation, emotional disorder, or sensory impairment. Intelligence scores for children with learning disabilities range from average to gifted levels. These children may be educated in self-contained classes if their problems are severe, but more often they remain in regular classes with the support of special educators.

Giftedness. Giftedness is broadly defined and may involve academic, intellectual, creative, artistic, or leadership abilities. Nevertheless, the education of students with special gifts and talents is still largely ignored. Approximately half the states now mandate some form of special services for these students, including allowing students to skip grades, providing enrichment experiences, grouping students by intellectual ability rather than by chronological age, and offering counseling to support the development of personal and social skills.

Physical Handicaps. Children with physical handicaps make up about 1 percent of the school population. These handicaps include blindness and visual impairments, deafness and hearing impairments, and orthopedic disabilities. Depending on the degree of the disability and on individual characteristics, these children may be educated in residential schools, separate classes, or regular classes with support services provided by special teachers.

For children who are blind, instruction in braille and mobility is required. Children with visual impairments need materials such as large-type books, special typewriters, and proper lighting. Children who are deaf require language instruction that often combines signing, lip-reading, intensive work in speech production, and amplified aural training. Children with orthopedic handicaps may need the services of a speech pathologist, physical or occupational therapist, psychologist, or social worker. They may also require modifications in their surroundings such as wide doorways to accommodate wheelchairs, toilets at appropriate heights, and ramps or elevators.

Mental Handicaps. Fortunately, less than 2 percent of all children in the United States are classified as mentally handicapped. Children with severe mental handicaps often have multiple disabilities. A variety of educational options are available for these children, including residential schools, special day schools, separate classes, and regular classes with special education support services. The appropriate option for each child depends on the child's characteristics and individual abilities. A variety of terms have been used over the years to describe mental handicaps in an effort to speak and write tactfully about this sensitive topic. Typically, three levels of severity are recognized, and in the most conventional terms these are mild, moderate, and profound.

Behavior Disorders. Children with recognized emotional disorders constitute about 1 percent of the population. These children constitute one of the greatest challenges to educators. Such children may be withdrawn or overly aggressive. Their education is usually provided in regular or special classes with support services provided by psychiatrists, psychologists, social workers, and speech and language pathologists.

Speech and Language Disabilities. Speech or language impairments include problems in articulation, language, fluency, or voice that affect a student's ability to learn or communicate effectively with others. Approximately 3 percent of all U.S. students must contend with such disabilities. The educational treatment provided to these children depends on the severity of the impairment and may include the services of special education teachers and speech and language pathologists.

Specialized Health Care Needs. This is a relatively new term applied to a group of students who previously were unserved in educational settings. Although these students are often considered similar to students with other health impairments, their educational needs are complicated by extreme medical needs. Other terms sometimes used are medically fragile and technologically dependent. Many of these students have survived catastrophic medical events that require intensive and prolonged health care.

Experiential Diversity

Students vary considerably in the range of their personal experiences, and as a result their world knowledge ranges from very limited to broadly developed. Students who are economically disadvantaged tend to have a narrower range of experiences, which may put them at a disadvantage when it comes to comprehending informational text. In other words, as we will see in Chapter 5, their prior knowledge is likely to be limited and their teachers are challenged to find ways of making new material comprehensible.

Experiential diversity is a complex concept. For example, the fact that students live in poverty does not mean that they are deprived of meaningful experiences, but it could well mean that the range of their experiences is so limited as to threaten their comprehension as they read about certain topics. Moreover, many children who are economically disadvantaged are still able to acquire a broad world knowledge by means of television, movies, reading, and personal interaction. It is important for teachers to ascertain quickly which children are most at risk of comprehending poorly because of limited experiential background.

Religious Diversity

The religious background of students adds yet another layer to the present-day diverse classroom. Outside of parochial schools, it is unlikely that any group of students will share uniform beliefs, and the differences may well affect content learning. For example, religious convictions have implications for social issues (e.g., abortion, school prayer, capital punishment) as well as for science (evolution, cloning, transfusions, etc.). Such convictions will surely influence discussions about what students read and will contribute to the nature of their critical thinking. The more religiously diverse a classroom, the more likely it is that opposing views will be voiced. It is the teacher's role to honor differences when they emerge and to strive to develop understanding of divergent views, especially those of the minority.

Meeting the Challenge of Diversity

Understanding how a diverse classroom can influence the nature of student learning and developing culturally responsive strategies for promoting learning are important first steps in contending with the challenges such classrooms pose. In this section, we suggest steps teachers can take based on this understanding.

Assess Your Students

Make it the first order of business to learn all you can about your students. Use not only the records that are formally accumulated (test scores, etc.) but information supplied by the students as well. Consider having them construct a "Map of Me" (see Figure 4.2). Such a diagram is in reality a semantic map with the student at the center. Use yourself to model your expectations.

Once you've gathered the results, construct a profile such as the one for Ms. Stevens's class (Figure 4.1). Doing so will lead you to greater cognizance of the elements of diversity present in your class and will provide a solid basis for instructional planning.

Assess Yourself

If you use yourself to model the process of how to construct a personal map, you may in fact take a first step toward seeing yourself as a member of various groups. If you are white, this kind of thinking may take some getting used to. Sarah McCarthey and her colleagues (2000) have pointed out that many whites think of themselves as not having a culture because "it is almost invisible" to them (p. 550). One of the more productive actions white teachers can take is to consider their own cultural identity and to begin to view their culture for what it is—one among many.

FIGURE 4.2

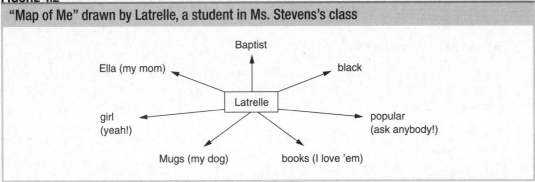

"Map of Me" drawn by Latrelle, a student in Ms. Stevens's class

Share the Results

It is vital that class members realize how diverse they truly are. Some differences are obvious, others are more subtle. Strive to create a more inclusive classroom environment within which all students realize that the world (and content, for that matter) are seen differently by individuals because of their group membership. Encourage your students to celebrate these differences.

McCarthey and her colleagues (2000) offered two metaphors to describe how society (and teachers!) may come to view the presence of multiple cultures. They may be seen as a quilt in which cultural differences fit together in complex ways to make up a colorful whole, or they may be viewed as a pyramid, with a dominant white culture looking down on the others. There can be little debate about which view leads to the most desirable kinds of learning for all students.

Be Culturally Responsive

Au and Jordan (1981; also see Au, 1993; Trueba, Guthrie, & Au, 1981; Williams & Callins, 2007) suggested that one way for teachers to become more responsive to the cultural differences among their students is to develop learning situations that are more "congruent" (p. 151) with what these children have experienced in their homes and communities. In order to do so, a teacher must make a commitment to learn about these cultures by investigating, reading, asking, and listening. Teachers who decline to do so risk isolating minority-culture students and teaching in a vacuum.

Radencich (1998) spoke of "culturally responsive instruction" (p. 186). She stressed the need for teachers to find ways to use students' cultural knowledge in positive ways. Learn about the cultures that are represented in your class so that you have a working knowledge about how their members think, what their traditions are, and what they believe. Consider carefully how cultural norms may influence learning in your content area.

Gay (2000) illustrates some key components of culturally responsive teaching, such as teacher caring, teacher attitudes and expectations, a formal and informal culturally relevant curriculum, culturally informed classroom discourse, and cultural congruity in teaching and learning strategies. Ladson-Billings (1992, 1994, 1995, 2001) advocates a "culturally relevant pedagogy" for culturally and linguistically diverse classrooms that

> . . . prepares students to effect change in society, not merely fit into it. These teachers support this attitude of change by capitalizing on their students' home and community culture. These teachers . . . empower students intellectually, socially, emotionally, and politically by using cultural referents to impart knowledge, skills, and attitudes. (1992, pp. 382–383)

Acknowledging students' cultural and linguistic heritages is the starting point for developing culturally responsive instruction for your students.

Consider also the best methods of instruction for your students. We note in particular a disturbing trend toward "accommodating" cultural differences by abandoning direct instruction. Delpit (1988) observed that some teachers may tend to avoid direct instruction with black students because they believe it may seem too authoritative. They wish instead to engage such students in discovery learning and a negotiated curriculum. She warned that black students may be ill-prepared for such an approach and that direct instruction may be better aligned with their needs.

Delpit (1995) challenged mainstream teachers to look closely at how they meet the needs of "other people's children"—those from diverse cultures and backgrounds. She demands that children of color be challenged and held to high standards, but she stresses that they must have the tools to do so. Delpit emphasizes that teachers should challenge their stereotypes and assumptions; teach to student strengths, not deficits; and respect the value of community and family.

It is important for teachers to connect students' prior knowledge and cultural and linguistic experiences with the texts they are asked to read; to instill decoding proficiency; to create an inclusive and accepting classroom environment; to develop positive relationships with students; to gain an understanding of students' cultural and linguistic knowledge and experience outside of the classroom and select culturally appropriate reading material; and to develop engaging and culturally sensitive teaching strategies, assessments, and evaluations. We also encourage teachers to use life-based, culturally relevant literary texts (He & McKenna, 2005), particularly those written in students' voices, as a means of making sense of a complex world, of creating bridges to worlds other than their own, and of seeing themselves in the stories of others.

There are many other culturally responsive approaches to teaching through text—approaches designed to foster cultural awareness and thereby enhance children's comprehension of text in diverse classrooms. Teachers could invite students to bring their personal experiences to the context of reading through discussions, reflective reading journals, autobiographical sketches, narrative imagination drawing, music circles, show-and-tell, parent or guardian interviews, and collaborative group work. Teachers could search for ways to allow students to reflect on their backgrounds, experiences, values, and ways in which their personal histories, cultures, and experiences affect who they are, how they interact with others, and how they perceive the world. The power of such culturally responsive approaches

FIGURE 4.3

Suggestions for the culturally responsive teacher

- Create and nurture a classroom climate that honors and appreciates the diverse origins of students.
- Begin by making mainstream students aware (and by becoming more fully aware yourself) of the multiple cultures present in the class. Make an effort to learn more about these cultures and their languages as a matter of professional development.
- Employ a variety of instructional techniques to raise awareness, including discussions, reflective reading journals, autobiographical sketches, narrative imagination drawing, music circles, and show-and-tell.
- Select literature, both for students to read and for teacher read-alouds, that embodies relevant cultural experiences.
- Focus discussions of this literature on cultural differences and on the universals that underlie them.
- Forge links with parents, whose notions of literacy education and its importance may differ from your own.
- Be cognizant of how cultural differences can affect comprehension and be creative in attempting to address discrepancies in prior knowledge (He & McKenna, 2005).

lies in their ability to assist students in developing empathy and respect for cultural heritages different from their own (See Figure 4.3).

Affirm Linguistic Differences

Students whose home language is not English may require special attention. ESL teachers may be able to offer suggestions for specific students. You may also be able to pair students with others whose English proficiency is stronger. Volunteer tutors proficient in the home language may be available, and after-school tutoring programs targeting LEP students might be offered. Look into these possibilities at once. Cooperative learning groups can also afford a useful means of getting LEP students the help they need in understanding content. You might also modify discussions to assist LEP learners. Here are some suggestions for doing so:

1. Incorporate frequent rewordings.
2. Supply written notes prior to lecturing.
3. Put key terms on the board as you speak.
4. Supply equivalent terms in the home language when you know them.
5. Reduce the total amount of time spent lecturing.
6. Reduce the duration of any single lecture.
7. Speak at a moderate pace and enunciate clearly.
8. Incorporate frequent review and summaries.
9. Refer to pictures and diagrams where possible to reinforce word meanings.
10. Incorporate language objectives into content lessons (Hernandez, 2003).
11. Be precise in the use and pronunciation of technical terminology.

If one student is highly proficient in both English and the home language, he or she might be asked to translate quietly as you speak, moving near the desks of LEP students before you begin. This remedy has drawbacks, however. It may disadvantage the translator, who might become more concerned with communicating than with thinking about the content. It may also prove distracting to other students. On balance, however, it is an approach well worth considering if

NET Worth

Language Differences

iT's Magazine. This publication is for teachers and students of English (ESL) around the world and provides materials for both. It offers pen pal/keypal opportunities for the exchange of ideas. There is an archive of teacher materials from back issues with notes for the teacher and steps in using the materials.

www.its-online.com

Internet TESL Journal. This well-designed forum offers materials that one can download as well as articles, teaching techniques, and links to issues of interest to ESL teachers. It includes electronic discussion lists and news groups.

http://iteslj.org

English-to-Go. Classroom-ready ESL activities, based on articles that have appeared in Reuters; new lessons posted weekly, with complete lesson plans.

www.english-to-go.com

Foreign Language Translation Services. This site is a good starting point for free on-line translation services.

http://translatefree.com

Barahona Center for the Study of Books in Spanish for Children and Adolescents. Contains a searchable database of "more than 6,000 in print books that deserve to be read by Spanish-speaking children and adolescents (or those who wish to learn Spanish)." Headings and descriptions are bilingual. Updated weekly. Sponsored by California State University, San Marcos.

www.csusm.edu/csb/intro_eng.html

NET Worth

Exceptionalities

Council for Exceptional Children. Home page for the CEC, this Internet site provides teachers with valuable resources for their exceptional students.

www.cec.sped.org

LD OnLine. Provides information and suggestions for parents, teachers, and students. Useful links and activity section.

www.ldonline.org

you are blessed with a student who is fluent in two languages and who is willing to undertake the challenge.

Translations of print material can be helpful, provided the LEP student reads the home language. Finding translations of the materials you expect students to read will be difficult, however. Check first to see if such translations are available from the publisher. On-line translations of classics are sometimes available, and free translation programs are available on the Internet. These programs are far from perfect and require you to keyboard or scan the selection you wish to translate. You may be pleasantly surprised with the results, however, and it is now clear that such software is rapidly improving.

Promote Academic Differences

School records can be useful in understanding the needs of special learners who have been formally categorized. Check to see who these students are and whether an individual educational plan (IEP) has been developed. If available, an IEP can be consulted for background about the nature of the problem and suggestions about teaching methods. Special educators and reading specialists can also be called on for advice and support concerning struggling readers, regardless of whether they fit neatly into an existing category.

Throughout this text we have made a point of indicating ways of assisting special learners. As you know, we have placed suggestions in boxes located adjacent to discussions of various topics. An exploration of diversity is a good point to recap, in list form, some key ideas for meeting the needs of these learners.

- Use Listen-Read-Discuss to ensure adequate prior knowledge (see Chapter 9).
- Consider computerized versions of texts, textbook modifications, and tape-recorded text to ease decoding difficulties.
- Use feature analysis, graphic organizers, and other forms of charts and diagrams to reduce reading demands and to stress thinking.
- Provide guided notes as a way of focusing attention and making reading more purposeful.
- Allow students opportunities to generate comprehension questions.
- Use bottom-up question clusters to model how inferences and critical judgments should be based on facts.
- Use top-down question clusters to troubleshoot whenever inaccurate inferences or inappropriate judgments are offered in response to higher-level questions.
- Accommodate special learners, whenever appropriate, by modifying the types of classroom tests you give and the conditions under which they are given. (See Chapter 12 for specific suggestions.)

SUMMARY

Demographic shifts in the twentieth century now challenge teachers of the twenty-first to become sensitive to the diversity that exists among their students and to provide instruction that accounts for it appropriately. Diversity exists along many dimensions. Among the most important are gender, ethnicity, language, exceptionalities, experience, and religion. Differences in these dimensions can influence how students learn and how they interpret content.

Teachers can begin to contend with these dimensions by first taking stock of them and by then adjusting their instruction to meet the needs of students who may not be able to learn well through conventional teaching. This book has offered many suggestions for assisting students with special needs, and these suggestions have been briefly revisited in this chapter.

The Internet now offers teachers exciting resources and contacts for dealing effectively with diversity. Web sites devoted to multicultural awareness abound, as do sites affording help with students of limited English proficiency and various exceptionalities.

Getting Involved

1. Study the profile of Ms. Stevens's class presented in Figure 4.1. Identify what in your opinion seem to be the most important issues of diversity in terms of instruction in a content subject. Formulate a plan for contending with these issues.

2. Interview a teacher faced with a highly diverse class. Ask what strategies he or she employs in response to diversity. Judge whether these strategies are designed to minimize the effects of diversity or to celebrate them. How might you have approached the teacher's class differently?

3. Explore the Web sites presented in this chapter. Discuss which of them seem to hold the most promise for contending with diverse classrooms.

Prereading Strategies

Whenever a teacher requires students to read, it is vital to prepare them for the task. This is true regardless of how extensive their background may be or whether the selection to be read is a textbook chapter or outside reading. Simply assigning the material, whether by identifying the pages to be read or by distributing an extra selection with the warning to "read with care," is totally inadequate. In this section, we examine methods by which teachers can facilitate students' reading by ensuring that their background is adequate for the task. We might have approached this topic in one lengthy chapter but chose instead to separate into two chapters our discussion of activities for building background: those that are directly concerned with introducing new vocabulary and those that are more general in nature.

Chapter 5 examines why it is vital first to take stock of prior knowledge by comparing what an author assumes students already know with what they actually do know. We then present numerous activities designed either to "activate" (that is, "switch on") relevant background knowledge or to add to students' background specific information needed for comprehension.

Chapter 6 continues the topic of prereading activities by presenting those useful in introducing new vocabulary. We describe a great variety of techniques that have proved effective for presenting terminology and other vocabulary. An important distinction is that most of the methods described in this chapter are especially designed for content area teachers because they rely on the knowledge that new words are neither taught nor learned one at a time in isolation but are often closely interrelated, making them best approached in clusters.

Building Prior Knowledge

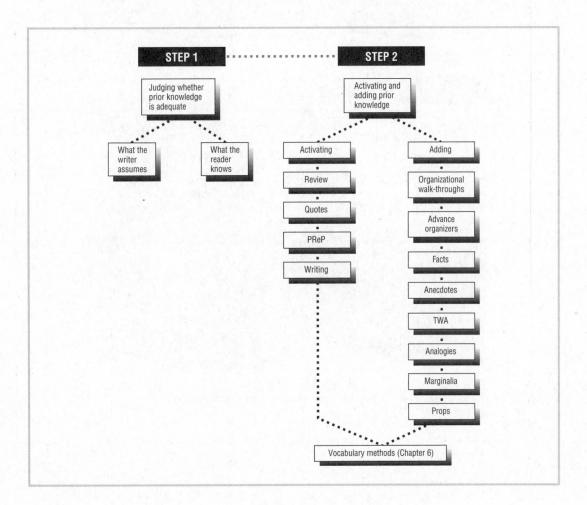

*I suggest that the only books that influence us are those for which
we are ready, and which have gone a little further down our particular
path than we have yet got ourselves.*

—E. M. Forster

Before we begin, take a moment to examine the political cartoon in Figure 5.1. This nineteenth-century cartoon by Thomas Nast requires a great deal of prior knowledge before a present-day reader is likely to "get it." Recognition of the Trojan horse is required, of course, but so is familiarity with Horace Greeley, what he looked like, and what he stood for.

FIGURE 5.1

An example of the need for prior knowledge

ANY THING TO GET IN

YOU CAN'T PLAY THE OLD TROJAN HORSE GAME ON UNCLE SAM

It would certainly help to know that Nast viewed him as a champion of democracy who was kept out of the federal government by self-serving interests in the Washington establishment. Even a familiarity with the shape of the Capitol building is needed.

Once this information is acquired, the point of the cartoon is clear (or at least clearer). Without it, the point is hopelessly lost, and any social studies teacher who expected students to appreciate its message without thoroughly introducing it beforehand would be disappointed. Nast could safely assume that the vast majority of his readers possessed the prior knowledge they needed to interpret his meaning, but he did not have twenty-first-century students in mind.

In much the same way that the artist conceived his cartoon, an author writing for students makes assumptions about their previous familiarity with certain topics, concepts, and ideas. In making these assumptions, the author is handicapped by two limitations. First, the author's knowledge considerably exceeds that of students, making it difficult to identify with student readers and to predict what they might or might not be likely to know already. Second, the background knowledge of individual students tends to vary widely so that generalizations about what the "typical" student may know are impossible. Writing that is appropriate for the background of some students is sure to be inappropriate for others.

Additional factors can make the issue of background even worse. Some writers, for example, are less sensitive than others to the limits of their readers' prior knowledge. In addition, teachers sometimes find it useful to assign reading selections not expressly written for students—articles, essays, short stories, and so on. In these cases, the authors were obviously in no position to consider the needs of students.

Objectives

In Chapter 2, we examined the role of prior knowledge in assisting readers as they attempt to make written materials meaningful. In this chapter, we look at methods of determining differences in what students need to know before they read a given selection and what they actually do know. We suggest techniques useful in filling gaps in prior knowledge and present ways of "activating" relevant knowledge that already exists. When you have completed this chapter, you should be able to

1. know what is meant by considerate and inconsiderate text;
2. assess the prior knowledge demands of reading assignments;
3. assess the adequacy of students' prior knowledge;
4. select and use appropriate techniques of building background; and
5. select and use appropriate techniques of activating existing prior knowledge.

Judging Whether Prior Knowledge Is Adequate

All authors make assumptions about what their readers are likely to know before they read. This is true regardless of the type of writing, as the following two examples plainly show. First, when writing the second chapter of a textbook, the author may well assume that the student has understood the content of the first chapter. Because of this assumption, knowledge of the initial chapter's content may be necessary for the reader to grasp the facts and concepts introduced in the second chapter. Likewise, an eighteenth-century English novelist might expect a reader to be rather familiar with life and customs in England during the 1700s. The novelist would therefore not bother to provide detailed accounts of these subjects, and consequently, a modern reader unfamiliar with them will have difficulties whenever such knowledge is assumed.

Information's pretty thin stuff, unless mixed with experience.
CLARENCE DAY

Considerate and Inconsiderate Text

We have suggested that some writers are more sensitive than others to the prior knowledge of students. Such writers make an effort to review or reference earlier material whenever its content is needed to comprehend new information. They are careful to define new concepts clearly and, where possible, to relate abstract ideas to the everyday experiences of students. These writers have a well-developed *sense of readership,* an idea of what sorts of readers are likely to read what they've written. Armbruster (1984) has called writing of this kind "considerate" (see also Lipson & Wixson, 2003), in that the author carefully considers the limitations of what students are likely to know and writes with these limitations in mind.

Inconsiderate writing, on the other hand, is the result of a poor sense of readership so that too much reliance is placed on the reader's background. This can and does happen in content area texts, but the issue is rather complicated. First, a given selection may be considerate of some readers and inconsiderate of others. This is because of differences in their prior knowledge. Moreover, some portions of the same textbook may be considerate, others inconsiderate. This may be the result of multiple authors' having contributed different

Remember the cricket example in Chapter 2? That was surely an example of inconsiderate text—for any reader!

portions to the book or of a single author's being less cognizant about student knowledge in some areas than in others.

When reading materials are assigned that were not written with students in mind, the chances of inconsiderate writing are especially high because the author's sense of readership may be off target. As an extreme example, consider a health instructor who asks students to read an article appearing in the *Journal of the American Medical Association*. Because the author anticipated a readership made up of physicians, the writing would not be considerate of the needs of secondary school students. This example is admittedly exaggerated to illustrate our point, but similar results can befall the language arts teacher who assigns a Shakespearean play, the biology teacher who duplicates an article from *Scientific American*, or the government teacher who distributes a column by George Will.

Our point is that teachers must be aware of the assumptions writers make about prior knowledge. Such awareness can occur only if a teacher inspects the material to be assigned.

Judging What the Writer Assumes

Regardless of how considerate a writer attempts to be, there is always some reliance on the reader's background. We know of no precise way to itemize that dependence, but the following guidelines are useful for identifying major instances of reliance.

1. *Look for references to previous material.* Examine the selection for references to earlier chapters. If the selection is a stand-alone (that is, an article, poem, essay, etc.), look for references to other sources with which the author may assume the reader is familiar.

Assisting Students with Special Needs

Electronic Texts

Imagine a computerized textbook, one in which all of the material, complete with graphics, appears on-screen. Readers could scroll through it in a linear way, exactly as they might read a conventional text, but a computer format offers much more. It enables the reader to branch to other text and resources on demand, making one's progress through the material *nonlinear* as alternative pathways are explored. The linear text remains, but a wide variety of branches are available. Such an environment is called *hypertext*. When nonprint options, such as audio clips and QuickTime movies, are available to complement a web of text, the result is called *hypermedia,* possibly one of the most important recent innovations in educational software (McKenna, 2002).

The branching options are of two kinds: (1) those that are meant to support the poor reader and (2) those that are designed to enrich and extend students' thinking. Resources for poor-reader support include the following:

- Stored digital pronunciations, available on demand
- Stored listening versions of sentences, paragraphs, or chapters
- Glossary entries that appear as sidebars on request
- Simplified paraphrases of difficult passages
- Marginal notes created by the author or by the teacher

Enrichment and extension resources include the following:

- Video footage stored as QuickTime movies
- Digitized audio recordings
- Graphics (pictures, diagrams, etc.) related to the content but not likely to be included in a conventional textbook
- Other textual material, such as articles, sidebars, and even other textbooks
- Interactive exercises that involve higher-order thinking

Bad authors are those who write with reference to an inner context which the reader cannot know.
ALBERT CAMUS

Although in their infancy, and though presently faced with the problem of limited hardware, electronic textbooks will offer advantages for good and poor readers alike. They will also raise a host of issues. Consider a few of the questions educators are already beginning to ask: Who should get priority when resources are limited, the poor reader or the good one? Can students "navigate" responsibly through hypertexts without getting endlessly sidetracked? What happens to the notion of readability (as discussed in Chapter 3) when textbooks have the capacity to rewrite themselves on demand? Indeed, must we revise the very concept of literacy to accommodate electronic texts? Further, are we ready for electronic textbooks that permit branching not only to other stored materials but to resources accessible through the Internet, such as library holdings and on-line magazines? In a system such as this, where are the boundaries of the "textbook"? Or do any true boundaries exist?

These are not issues that lurk in the remote future. They will confront the present generation of teachers, yourself included!

2. *Examine the new vocabulary introduced.* We say much more about this subject in Chapter 6, but for now it is important to note that newly introduced terms offer a major hint as to the background a reader will need. This is because words are not learned in isolation but by association with word concepts previously learned. The point of listing new words is to gain a perspective on which words must be known in advance in order to make sense of them. Often teachers' editions of textbooks list new words in advance so that the only real task confronting the teacher is to decide which previously introduced words the new terms build on.

3. *Look for references that are not adequately explained.* An author may refer to facts or ideas that were not previously introduced and that may require additional explanation. This happens frequently in literature but can occur in textbooks as well. The issue is whether the reference is critical to understanding the content. When a biology text mentions that fossils of ancient fish were studied by Agassiz, a famous nineteenth-century naturalist, the teacher must ask whether the time needed to explain who Agassiz was would substantially improve the students' understanding of a chapter on fossils.

Judging What the Reader Knows

The relationship between a reader's prior knowledge of a topic and the prior knowledge actually needed for adequate comprehension is depicted in Figure 5.2. The left-hand circle represents all that a given reader knows about the topic, the right-hand circle all that the author assumes the

FIGURE 5.2

Prior knowledge needs: What the author assumes versus what the reader knows

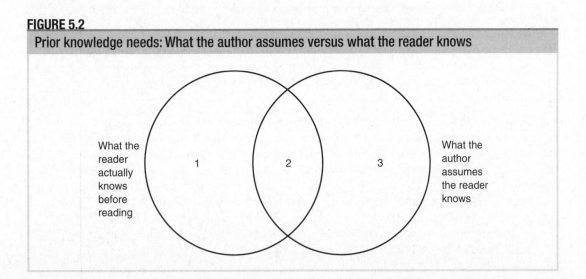

reader knows. Region 1 contains information known to the reader that is not essential to under- standing the selection. Region 2 comprises information known to the reader that is crucial to comprehension. Region 3 represents information that is assumed to be known to the reader but that is in fact not known.

In Section 1, we examined guidelines for determining the demands a reading selection makes on prior knowledge. We now look at methods of determining whether students' prior knowledge is equal to these demands. Answering this question gives a teacher a good notion of what Region 3 contains. Answering it need not be involved, and a variety of quick and simple techniques is pos- sible. Holmes and Roser (1987) offer the following:

1. *Free recall.* The teacher suggests a topic and asks students to brainstorm, saying anything they suspect a treatment of that topic might contain.

2. *Word associations.* Using a list of topics or subtopics, the teacher tells students they are to react with whatever association occurs to them. Then each topic is read aloud.

Assisting Students with Special Needs

Taped Texts

Tape-recorded textbooks are also a popular accommodation offered to special-needs students. However, students need both good listening skills and supplements to the recordings if they are to derive maximum benefit from tape-recorded texts. Essentially, providing students with a tape recorder and a verbatim recording of the reading assignment does little to improve the student's comprehension of content (Schumaker, Deshler, & Denton, 1982). However, (1) listening to taped readings while following along with the textbook and (2) beginning taped readings with a review of previous readings appear to help some students (Rivers, 1980). Although limited research exists regarding the effectiveness of taped text material, Deshler and Graham (1980) maintain that in taping content material, several elements must be considered:

1. Instructional goals and objectives must be identified.
2. Specific aspects of the text relating to the objectives should be considered.
3. When the entire reading is not recorded, a summary or outline of the entire reading should be provided for students to lend a context to the major concepts that are recorded.
4. Important concepts should be differentiated from unimportant and distracting details.
5. Emphasis on maps, tables, charts, chapter titles, and headings should be considered.
6. A marking system that coordinates text with recordings to prevent students from getting confused or lost should accompany each recording.

Schumaker and associates (Schumaker et al., 1982) contend that recordings that are organized to emphasize active student participation and that are followed by direct instruction that reviews important concepts result in significant achievement gains in special-needs students. To relieve the teacher, peer tutors, paraprofessionals, or trained volunteers may provide the direct instruction review.

If you will carefully consider the six recommendations of Deshler and Graham (1980) above, you will see that departures from a word-for-word oral reading of the text are often in order. This is why the content teacher is the best possible person to do the recording. Consider a few possibilities. The teacher can judiciously skip extraneous material. Likewise, the background of the content teacher makes it possible to paraphrase difficult prose, to restate and summarize main ideas, and to inter- ject additional facts and observations that may enhance comprehension. Moreover, the teacher can embed writing tasks, questions to think about, and other directive remarks at key points in the material. In short, the taped version can incorporate most of the advantages of a content literacy guide, marginal notes, and other background-building devices.

The fact that the content teacher is the one individual with adequate expertise to skillfully create taped versions of text assignments may present a depressing prospect. You cannot safely relegate the task to a paraprofessional or a gifted student. There are, however, some compensating advantages. First, taping affords a marvelous opportunity to become acquainted with your own text. Creating a tape is a good way to assess the demands your materials make on students—a necessary and enlightening process we discussed in Chapter 3. Second, once a tape is finished, it becomes a resource for as long as the materials will be assigned, and dubbing multiple copies is easy. Third, if you teach in a setting large enough that other teachers are assigning the same materials, collaboration becomes possible. If, for example, three teachers use the same text, each must record only a third of the material. Even if you teach in a smaller setting, you can readily locate colleagues in other schools who use the same text. The publisher's area sales representative can help, as can state organizations of which you are a member that are associated with your content area.

3. *Structured questions.* The teacher begins by asking a relatively simple question concerning the content of a reading selection. If students successfully answer it, the teacher proceeds to a second question that is an outgrowth of the first and that is slightly more difficult. Sequences of carefully crafted, progressively more difficult questions can tell a teacher a great deal about the limits of prior knowledge.

Diagnostic Assessment ideas

4. *Recognition questions.* The teacher prepares and distributes a number of multiple-choice questions about the topic. The idea is to assess misinformation as well as prior knowledge.

5. *Unstructured discussion.* The teacher attempts to elicit from students their own experiences as they relate to the topic. This technique seems especially well suited to fiction.

To these we can add structured writing assignments as a means of assessment. Any task that calls on students to summarize what they know about a topic, categorize key concepts, and so forth will provide useful information. It may be natural to think of time as a limiting factor in using writing tasks in this way—time to write and time, subsequently, for the teacher to read the written products. There are ways around this limitation, however. First, students could be asked to work on a task collaboratively, thus producing less material for the teacher to scrutinize. Second, the teacher can inspect student work as it is being written by circulating about the room. Third, writing tasks need not produce full-blown compositions but can involve single paragraphs, even sentences, and can include categorization tasks in which only a few words are used. Last, writing often has the effect of clarifying and organizing prior knowledge as well as activating it. The writing task can therefore be designed to do double duty. It is for this reason that we will revisit writing techniques in Section 3.

Approaches such as these serve a variety of functions. Their main role, of course, is to allow the teacher to plan and modify how background is to be built for a reading assignment. They also serve to focus attention on the topics to be covered and are therefore appropriate to the initial steps of the DRA (Directed Reading Activity) and the explicit teaching model. When discussion is involved, they fit quite well within the framework of the DR–TA (Directed Reading–Thinking Activity) and K-W-L*. Finally, they give the teacher a benchmark by which to gauge the extent of student comprehension and learning.

Ways to Add and Activate Background Knowledge

Comprehension can be improved when a reader's relevant prior knowledge is "activated" before reading (Ambe, 2007; Heffernan, 2003; McKenzie & Danielson, 2003; Walsh, 2003). By assisting students to recall knowledge needed for a given reading assignment, teachers help

---

*Full descriptions and discussion of DRA, DR–TA, and K-W-L are provided in Chapter 9.

Assisting Students with Special Needs

Textbook Modifications

In addition to adding marginal notes, two additional textbook modifications are fairly simple and effective for many special students. The first involves highlighting topic sentences, key terms and definitions, and other important information with a pastel-colored felt-tip marker. It is especially helpful to color-code related concepts and include a key explaining the color-coding system. For example, all topic sentences might be highlighted in yellow, terms and definitions in pink, and important information (e.g., people, dates) in green.

The second modification requires a photocopier with an enlarging option. First, photocopy each page of the reading assignment and then enlarge each photocopy as much as possible. A print size that is at least as large as the print used in primary picture books works best, so the original photocopies may need to be cut in half before enlarging. This is a good assignment for an aide or paraprofessional.

them in "building bridges from the new to the known" (Pearson & Johnson, 1978, p. 24). Prince (1987) found that comprehension was even improved by conducting certain enrichment activities before reading rather than afterward (the usual practice). Comprehension can also be enhanced by adding important background knowledge that students lack. When background is *activated*, Region 2 of Figure 5.2 is involved. When background is *added*, Region 3 is involved. We now present a variety of methods useful in adding or in activating background knowledge.

Activating Prior Knowledge

The notion of activating, or "switching on," appropriate background knowledge is important because new knowledge, if it is to be well learned and understood, must be integrated into existing knowledge. Menke and Pressley (1994) put the matter succinctly: "Having prior knowledge is not enough to increase comprehension and learning—it must also be activated" (p. 642). The teacher's job is to help students bring relevant facts, concepts, and experiences to consciousness. While the methods for doing so are probably limitless, we offer three that are broadly useful, and we discuss more in relation to vocabulary in Chapter 6.

Review. Whenever an upcoming reading assignment builds on information previously provided, review can be an effective first step in introducing the new material. This circumstance arises, for example, when a mathematics textbook chapter introduces a more advanced version of a problem type. Review is not as relevant, however, to a chapter (perhaps a chapter in the same textbook) in which a major shift in topics occurs.

Quotes. A brief way to "switch on" appropriate schemata is to write a provocative quotation on the board at the beginning of a lesson. When students arrive after a passing period, displaying the quote in advance can serve as an effective sponge activity that leads directly into a lesson. The quotation must not be too abstract or arcane—it must be comprehensible to the students based on their existing knowledge. Here are some examples:

■ For a history unit:
  War is a biological necessity.

—*Friedrich von Bernhardi*

■ For a unit on the environment:
  Over increasingly large areas of the United States, spring now comes unheralded by the return of the birds, and the early mornings are strangely silent where once they were filled with the beauty of bird song.

—*Rachel Carson (1962)*

The traditional anthologies of quotations can be useful resources, but more current examples come in the daily paper or weekly newsmagazines. Becoming a collector of quotes will allow you to add an element of spice to lessons as prior knowledge is put in gear. We will return to the uses of quotations in the next chapter.

PReP. Langer (1981) has suggested a PreReading Plan (PReP) that can be used to activate prior knowledge and at the same time provide the teacher with an idea of problem areas. PReP has three goals: (1) to determine the extent of students' prior knowledge and how that knowledge is organized, (2) to ascertain how well students can express their understanding of the topics to be studied, and (3) to discover what additional background students might need in order to understand the new material.

PReP has two steps, the first involving a three-phase class discussion, the second involving teacher analysis of the responses given by students.

Step 1: Class discussion
- **a.** *Initial associations with the concept.* Questions such as the following are asked during this first phase of PReP:
  - "What do you first think of when you hear this word [see this picture, and so on]?"
  - "What do you associate with this idea based on your past experiences?"

  The teacher records on the chalkboard the student responses to this initial presentation of the new word.
- **b.** *Reflection on initial associations.* The teacher then asks the students to reflect on why they said what they did in phase 1. Questions might be similar to the following, though phrased more specifically in an actual classroom setting:
  - "What are some reasons for your suggestions in our initial discussion?"
  - "Why do you think others in class made the suggestions they did?"
- **c.** *Reformulation of associations.* The third phase of the PReP reading strategy gives students the opportunity to reflect on the various ideas that have been presented to this point. The teacher could ask the class to discuss the following:
  - "Based on our discussion to this point, do you have any new ideas or feelings on our topic of discussion?"
  - "What do you think of the ideas presented by your classmates?"

  The teacher summarizes the class discussion in this phase as well as the others without commenting or making a critical judgment of what was said.

Step 2: Analysis

Langer suggested that the teacher then evaluate the total responses of the group on the basis of the following guidelines:
- **a.** Students with a high level of prior knowledge about a particular subject will answer using definitions, analogies, linkages, and superordinate concepts.
- **b.** Students with some prior knowledge will most often respond by noting examples, attributes, or defining characteristics of the idea.
- **c.** Students with little prior knowledge show this lack of information by answering with low-level associations, words that sound like the primary word, and not quite relevant experiences.

  Analyzing the discussion provides the teacher with an idea of which students may have inadequate prior knowledge. It also helps in making decisions about how best to add to that knowledge.

Writing. We have stated repeatedly that writing can be used as a means of clarifying one's thoughts about a subject. By confronting students with a brief writing task, a teacher compels prior knowledge to be activated and applied. Moreover, the teacher who circulates among students as they write, or who collects their written products for inspection, has a good means of assessing prior knowledge as well as activating it. Writing tasks can be used for these purposes in virtually all content areas, as the following examples show:

- A math teacher, preparing to introduce a theorem to be used in the upcoming chapter, asks students to write out the proof of the theorem based on previous material.

There are many virtues in books, but the essential value is the adding of knowledge to our stock by the record of new facts and, better, by the record of intuitions which distribute facts.

RALPH WALDO
EMERSON

■ A language arts teacher, before assigning a short story about a wilderness expedition, asks students to write about an experience they may have had while camping.

■ A chemistry teacher, preparing students for a chapter that describes a particular experiment, tells the students to formulate a hypothesis based on what they have already learned.

■ A history teacher invites students to work in groups to write a possible scenario for the Battle of Waterloo. The students do not know the outcome of the battle but have read an account of events up to the point of the conflict. They then read the selection to contrast their scenarios with what actually happened.

Writing, as these examples indicate, not only provokes thinking based on prior knowledge but lends itself to collaborative activities. Such activities can also be linked to setting purposes for reading, a topic we address in Chapter 7.

Adding to Prior Knowledge

Whenever a reader's background is inadequate for the task of reading a particular selection, the teacher can improve comprehension by enhancing background knowledge. There are numerous methods for achieving this goal, and they vary widely depending on what kind of information the teacher wants to supply. Some techniques deal with how the author has organized a selection, others with providing specific knowledge the author may have assumed on the part of students. Still others are concerned primarily with vocabulary. These last are examined in the next chapter.

Organizational Walk-Throughs. It is often helpful (especially with expository writing) for students to know in advance how material is organized (Holbrook, 1984). One way of accomplishing this is to "walk through" the selection in a teacher-led discussion, noting subheads and reasoning aloud about how the subtopics are organized. This technique has acquired a very consistent basis in research (Alvermann & Swafford, 1989) and deserves our close attention.

We begin by considering the various types of organizing patterns used by textbook authors. Fortunately, the number of effective patterns is relatively limited.

1. *Time order*. Topics are arranged chronologically. A chapter on the Civil War in a history text might be organized as follows in terms of *major* headings:
   - I. Precursors of war
   - II. Early phases of conflict
   - III. The tide turns
   - IV. Appomattox and after

2. *Comparison-contrast*. Major viewpoints, theories, concepts, or ideas are contrasted and compared. The same history chapter might have been organized alternatively as follows:
   - I. What the Confederacy believed
   - II. What the Union believed
   - III. Irreconcilable differences

3. *Cause-and-effect*. Writing about an event, phenomenon, or process, an author may focus on causal relationships. Our Civil War chapter might have been handled like this:
   - I. Why the war was fought
     - A. The slavery issue
     - B. States' rights
   - II. Changes brought about by the war
     - A. Emancipation
     - B. Civil rights movement
     - C. Reconstruction

4. *Problem-solution*. The author's principal focus is on a major problem with a view to possible solutions. Our hypothetical chapter would certainly be an appropriate candidate for this pattern. For example:
   - I. The impasse in 1860
   - II. Solutions that failed
     - A. Negotiation and diplomacy
     - B. Missouri compromise continued

    C. Influence of Great Britain

    D. Congressional initiatives

5. *Simple listing*. Subtopics are ordered at random in the absence of any rationale for determining their order. A portion of the Civil War chapter might have been organized this way:

  I. Portraits of generalship

    A. Hood

    B. Grant

    C. Sherman

    D. Lee

6. *Systematic listing*. As in simple listing, the author wishes to enumerate several relatively unconnected subtopics but chooses to arrange them in some systematic way, such as by importance, location, or some other criterion. For example, the generals in the previous illustration might have been listed in terms of how the author viewed their skills or eminence:

  I. Portraits of generalship

    A. Lee

    B. Grant

    C. Sherman

    D. Hood

Discussing the organizational pattern is a good way to ensure that students have in mind the proper skeletal framework into which details will eventually be fitted. The process is usually not lengthy and can easily be combined with other background-building techniques.

We offer some specific observations before considering these additional methods. First, selections are rarely organized around a single pattern. Rather, authors tend to employ nested schemes, in which the overall organizational pattern is of one kind while subsections are organized differently. A good example is the outline just discussed for the problem-solution pattern. The four alternative solutions mentioned follow a simple-listing format.

Walpole (1998–1999) has pointed to a questionable trend away from linear text and toward arrangements that present students with potentially confusing, magazine-type layouts filled with sidebars and other digressions. This trend produces visually appealing material, to be sure, but such material can also require sophisticated reading strategies in order to navigate successfully through a chapter. This is all the more reason to walk students through a chapter carefully before asking them to read it.

Figure 5.3 is an excerpt prepared by the National Oceanic and Atmospheric Administration (NOAA) on the subject of hurricanes. (You may recognize it as the source of the cloze passage presented in Chapter 3.) As you can see, there is much more to the passage than linear text. It also contains maps, photographs (one with vocabulary labeling), a sidebar defining key terms, and a chart of the Saffir-Simpson scale. Students might have difficulty navigating through this material. They must decide what to read first and how the pieces fit together. A teacher can help by previewing these graphic features during the walk-through.

Introducing the organizational patterns can also help students *write* about content. With a clear prompt after having discussed textbook examples of organizational patterns, students might be asked to tackle assignments like these:

■ Write a comparison-contrast description of the three major types of rocks.

■ Use a time-order pattern to describe how to solve a quadratic equation.

■ Using a problem-solution pattern, discuss the problem of global terrorism.

■ Think of three of your favorite books and write a short paragraph about each book. Tell about your most favorite first.

Advance Organizers. Ausubel (1960) introduced an effective technique for preparing readers for a selection likely to prove challenging. An advance organizer is a brief prose introduction to the topic or topics presented in the actual selection. It is similar to the abstract of a journal article or the blurb located on the inside of a book jacket (Kirkman & Shaw, 1997).

We suggest four sources of advance organizers: (1) chapter introductions, (2) chapter summaries, (3) teacher-composed organizers, and (4) student-composed organizers. First, authors and editors of content area textbooks are more likely now than in previous years to provide an

FIGURE 5.3

Example of a nonfiction selection

What is a Hurricane?

The term hurricane has its origin in the indigenous religions of old civilizations. The Mayan storm god was named *Hunraken*. A god considered evil by the Taino people of the Caribbean was called *Huracan*. Hurricanes may not be considered evil but they are one of nature's most powerful storms. Their potential for loss of life and destruction of property is tremendous. Those in hurricane-prone areas

need to be prepared for hurricanes and tropical storms. Even inland areas, well away from the coastline, can experience destructive winds, tornadoes and floods from tropical storms and hurricanes.

Hurricane Iniki/NOAA

A hurricane is a type of tropical cyclone—an organized rotating weather system that develops in the tropics. Hurricanes rotate counterclockwise in the Northern Hemisphere. Tropical cyclones are classified as follows:

■ **Tropical Depression**—An organized system of persistent clouds and thunderstorms with a closed low-level circulation and maximum *sustained* winds of 38 mph (33 knots) or less.

■ **Tropical Storm**—An organized system of strong thunderstorms with a well defined circulation and maximum *sustained* winds of 39 to 73 mph (34-63 knots).

■ **Hurricane**—An intense tropical weather system with a well defined circulation and *sustained* winds of 74 mph (64 knots) or higher. In the western North Pacific, hurricanes are called typhoons, and similar storms in the Indian Ocean are called cyclones.

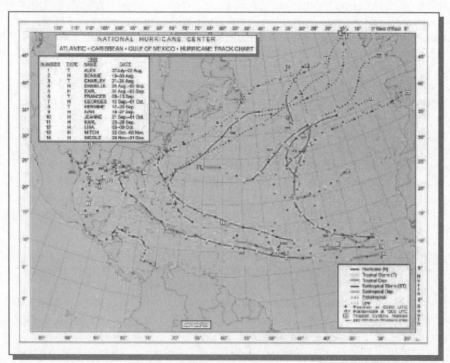

1998 Atlantic Ocean Hurricane Season Summary/NOAA

FIGURE 5.3
Example of a nonfiction selection *(continued)*

Tropical depressions and tropical storms, while generally less dangerous than hurricanes, still can be deadly. The winds of tropical depressions and tropical storms are usually not the greatest threat. Heavy rains, flooding and severe weather, such as tornadoes, create the greatest threats from tropical storms and depressions.

On average each year, 10 tropical storms, 6 of which become hurricanes, develop in the Atlantic Ocean, Caribbean Sea or Gulf of Mexico. In a typical 3-year span, the U.S. coastline is struck on average five times by hurricanes, two of which will be designated as major hurricanes.

Hurricane Camille, Category 5
Hurricane/NOAA

Tropical cyclones are sometimes steered by weak and erratic winds, making forecasting a challenge. Warnings issued from the National Oceanic and Atmospheric Administration's (NOAA) National Hurricane Center and Central Pacific Hurricane Center continue to improve and have greatly diminished hurricane fatalities in the United States. Despite improved warnings, property damage continues to increase due to growing population on our coastlines. Federal agencies, such as the Federal Emergency Management Agency (FEMA), and organizations such as the American Red Cross, have combined with state and local agencies, rescue and relief organizations, the private sector and the news media to improve preparedness efforts.

Saffir-Simpson Hurricane Scale

The *Saffir-Simpson Hurricane Scale* is a 1 to 5 rating based on the hurricane's intensity. This scale estimates potential property damage. Hurricanes or typhoons reaching Category 3 and higher are considered *major* hurricanes because of their potential for loss of life and damage. Category 1 and 2 storms are still very dangerous and warrant preventative measures. In the western North Pacific, the term "Super Typhoon" is used for tropical cyclones with sustained winds exceeding 150 mph. For more information on the Saffir-Simpson Hurricane Scale, go to **www.nhc.noaa.gov/aboutsshs.html**.

Saffir-Simpson Hurricane Scale

Scale Number (Category)	Sustained Winds (MPH)	Types of Damage	Hurricanes
1	74-95	**Minimal:** *Damage primarily to shrubbery, trees, foliage and unanchored mobile homes. No real damage to other structures.*	*Irene, 1999*
2	96-110	**Moderate:** *Some trees blown down. Major damage to exposed mobile homes. Some damage to roofing materials, windows and doors.*	*Georges, 1998 Floyd, 1999*
3	111-130	**Extensive:** *Large trees blown down. Mobile homes destroyed. Some structural damage to roofing materials of buildings. Some structural damage to small buildings.*	*Betsy, 1965 Alicia, 1983*
4	131-155	**Extreme:** *Trees blown down. Complete destruction of mobile homes. Extensive damage to roofing materials, windows and doors. Complete failure of roofs on many small residences.*	*Andrew, 1992*
5	>155	**Catastrophic:** *Complete failure of roofs on many residences and industrial buildings. Extensive damage to windows and doors. Some complete building failure.*	*Camille, 1969*

NOTE: Damage can vary greatly and may not apply to all areas, such as Hawaii.

(Continued)

FIGURE 5.3
Example of a nonfiction selection *(continued)*

How Hurricanes Form

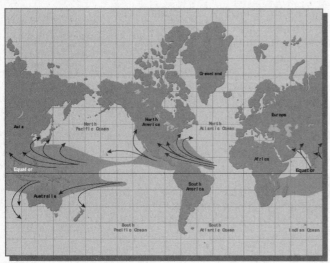

NOAA

Breeding Grounds

Hurricanes are products of a tropical ocean and a warm, moist atmosphere. Powered by heat from the sea, they are typically steered by high-level easterly winds while in the tropics, generally south of 25° north latitude and by high-level westerly winds north of 25° north latitude. When hurricanes become very strong, they can create their own steering winds.

The Atlantic hurricane season starts on June 1. For the United States, the peak hurricane threat exists from mid-August to late October, although the official hurricane season extends through November. Over other parts of the world, such as the western North Pacific, typhoons can occur year-round.

Storm Structure

The process by which a disturbance forms and strengthens into a hurricane depends on at least three conditions. First, a disturbance gathers heat and energy through contact with warm ocean waters. Next, added moisture evaporated from the sea surface powers the infant hurricane like a giant heat engine. Third, the hurricane forms a wind pattern near the ocean surface that spirals air inward. Bands of thunderstorms form, allowing the air to warm further and rise higher into the atmosphere. If the winds at these higher levels are relatively light, this structure can remain intact and further strengthen the hurricane.

The center, or eye, of a hurricane is relatively calm with sinking air, light winds and few clouds. The most violent winds and rain take place in the eyewall, the ring of thunderstorms immediately surrounding the eye. At the top of the eyewall (about 50,000 feet), most of the air is propelled outward, increasing the air's upward motion. Some of the air, however, moves inward and sinks into the eye, creating a cloud-free area.

Eye and Ocean Surface

Eyewall — Eyewall

Hurricane Mitch/NOAA

4

introduction or abstract to each chapter. Check the selection to see whether such a device is already available. Then discuss it with students as you read it together. Second, chapter summaries offer another good source. Although their primary function is to synthesize and review chapter content, they can also serve as a focal point of prereading discussion, provided the teacher elaborates on the extremely condensed and cryptic treatment of the content. (After all, the author assumes the students have completed the chapter when they reach the summary.) Third, you can write your own organizers. While this prospect is a little demanding, it does afford the chance of organizing your own thoughts about a topic and of deciding at the outset what's vitally important to emphasize. Last, you can ask students to compose such an organizer after they read. This is an excellent writing activity in which the students' task is to prepare the next group of students for what lies ahead in the selection. Exemplary organizers can be saved for future use.

Factual Information. For some reading selections, specific facts are needed for adequate comprehension. As we have mentioned, there are two principal reasons that such information was not included in the selection. One is that the author is unable to anticipate the prior knowledge limitations of students. The second is that the selection may have been originally intended for a different readership. It is up to the teacher to determine which information is likely to be needed.

As an example, read the following description of an airplane flight and ask yourself whether there is a factual error:

> The pilot guided his single-engine Cessna over downtown Detroit. Below him he could make out the four towers of the Renaissance Center. His heading was due south. A few moments later, still traveling south, he radioed for permission to enter Canadian airspace.

Everyone knows Canada lies to the north of the United States. So how could a southbound plane enter Canada? Residents of the Detroit area know that a tiny arm of Canada stretches to the south of the city. Had we mentioned this fact in advance, perhaps by displaying a map, your comprehension would not have been threatened. This example presents an obvious need for advance clarification. In typical classroom practice, the facts students may need to make sense of text are often harder to anticipate.

Anecdotes. Occasionally a reading selection can be made more engaging, more personal, and more comprehensible when the teacher offers a brief story in advance (Flood, Lapp, & Wood, 1998; Millstone, 1997; Norton & Anfin, 1997). The story might involve the author, it might represent some historical oddity not very important in itself, or it might concern the teacher's experiences. The benefits of anecdotes in terms of motivation and comprehension easily outweigh the short time needed to tell them. Their use requires teachers to draw on their own knowledge of the content, which is likely to be much more extensive and diverse than what is included in a given reading selection.

Anecdotes can be used with virtually any topic, even one as dry (in our opinion) as the rectangular coordinate system used to plot points on a graph. In the seventeenth century, this system was invented one morning by the French philosopher Descartes, who was lying in bed watching a fly crawl across the ceiling of his room. "No matter where that fly is on the ceiling," Descartes remarked to himself, "I can describe its position with two numbers." He proceeded to develop the Cartesian coordinate system, which forms the basis of analytic geometry and calculus—all because of a fly! Such a story could do much to enliven a topic that students might otherwise find uninspiring.

Analogies. Abstract ideas are often so far removed from the experiences of students that they prove difficult to grasp. This may even be so when the writing itself is competent and considerate. An effective strategy can be the introduction of an analogy to enable students to compare a new abstract idea with one that is familiar and concrete (Hayes & Tierney, 1982). Analogies can make abstract content more interesting as well as understandable (Brown et al., 1996; Glynn, 1996).

Imagine, for example, that a biology teacher is about to begin a unit on the digestive system. A good way of prefacing what the students will read is to compare this system with an automobile. (Gasoline is the equivalent of food, the motor the equivalent of muscles, exhaust the counterpart of body waste, and so forth.) We have made frequent use of this device in writing this text—for instance, by comparing comprehension with "building bridges," earlier in the chapter.

Although authors of content materials often attempt to build analogies into their own writing, it is advisable to be on the lookout for useful comparisons whenever you deal with your discipline. When you come across one, or produce an original, make a note of it for future use with your students. Moreover, encouraging students to create their own analogies can be an effective way to deepen understanding by causing them to connect the new with the known (Kuse & Kuse, 1986).

We offer one caution concerning the possible side effects of analogies. Spiro (1991) warns that analogies can have such a powerful effect on thinking that some students may find it difficult to learn detailed information in cases where it does not conform to the original analogy suggested by the teacher. His solution is not to avoid analogies but rather to use *more than one* wherever appropriate. Suggesting to students the limitations of an analogy may also be helpful.

TWA. Shawn Glynn has suggested a method teachers can use to bring new content to life through analogies. His six-step method, called Teaching with Analogies (TWA), is easy to use and gives structure to the lesson:

Step 1: Introduce the concept to be learned.
Step 2: Review the analogous concept.
Step 3: Identify features that both concepts possess.
Step 4: Explain the similarities.
Step 5: Discuss where the analogy breaks down.
Step 6: Draw conclusions.

Glynn's research confirmed that students' comprehension of new ideas was substantially improved by this process when all six steps were followed (Glynn, 1989, 1995, 1996; Glynn, Aultman, & Owens, 2005). Figure 5.4 describes these steps in the context of an example from science.

TWA can be modified in many ways. Here are just a few:

- At the conclusion of a unit, suggest several analogies and ask students to critique them. (Which analogies work and which don't?)
- When students have worked with analogies for a while, ask them to suggest their own analogies for selected concepts.
- Ask students to engage in reciprocal teaching, explaining a new concept to another group by means of an analogy.

Marginalia. Marginal notes, sometimes called *glosses*, represent a good way of providing additional background information at the precise moment it is needed by students as they read. Marginalia can include definitions, restatements of complex information, additional background notes, synonyms for difficult terms, and so forth. A recent trend has involved the inclusion of such glosses in textbooks as they are written. For other texts, the teacher can supply marginalia. Richardson and Morgan (2003) suggest that glosses are like "having the teacher go home with the students and look over their shoulders as they read" (p. 190).

Because the task must be done by hand, it may seem formidable, but we suggest the following guidelines for making it a realistic way of building background:

Think about the glosses you've read in this book—like this one! They're not meant to clarify, of course, but to extend your thinking. Have they succeeded?

1. Analyze your text for difficult terminology, unclear statements of important ideas, and points at which added background might be helpful to students.
2. Write appropriate marginalia into your own copy of the text as a master.
3. During your planning days just prior to the start of the school year, transcribe your glosses into several (but not all) student copies. An aide or student volunteer could assist.
4. When school begins, identify those students most at risk of failing to comprehend assigned reading, using the techniques described in Chapter 3.
5. Make sure that the glossed copies are distributed to these students.

FIGURE 5.4

Example of TWA: Photosynthesis

1. Introduce the concept to be learned.

   The teacher defines the term *photosynthesis* and provides background information. Graphic organizers might be used, such as time lines and labeled pictures (see Chapter 6).

2. Review the analogous concept.

   The analogy involves a factory. The teacher engages the students in a discussion of how a factory operates, possibly using a local example. (For our example, let's consider a paper factory.) The teacher stresses how energy and raw materials are converted in the factory into some sort of desirable good.

3. Identify features that both concepts possess.

   The teacher lists elements common to both photosynthesis and a factory. They both use energy, start with raw materials, produce a desirable finished product, and create waste products along the way.

4. Explain the similarities.

   The teacher lists these elements in chart form. At this point the specifics of each concept are included. Such a chart might look like this:

	Photosynthesis	Paper Factory
Raw Materials	water	wood pulp
	chlorophyll	acid
	carbon dioxide	
Energy	sunlight	coal
Product	wood, fruit, etc.	paper
Waste	oxygen	sulphur dioxide

5. Discuss where the analogy breaks down.

   The teacher explains that photosynthesis, unlike a factory, does not involve waste products, unless we consider the dead leaves and rotting vegetation that eventually result.

6. Draw conclusions.

   Photosynthesis is similar to a factory, but it is far more efficient and rarely creates environmental problems (except in the case of weeds!).

6. Take the at-risk students aside, privately, and explain that you were the person responsible for the notes. Explain their purpose and convey the expectation that the students will read the notes in the course of reading each assignment.

An alternative to writing directly onto the pages of the book is to prepare gloss sheets (Richgels & Hansen, 1984). The results might be called "portable footnotes." These offer the advantage of easy availability to all students but at the same time their use requires a conscious effort. We suspect notes written on the actual pages of a book are more likely to be read.

Props.   Physical objects can occasionally provide a visual referent that will enhance comprehension enormously. Such props might include the following:

- A three-dimensional model of a DNA molecule
- A terrarium or aquarium
- Conic sections used in geometry
- A miniature representation of a theater stage
- A Native American artifact
- A map, diagram, painting, or photograph not reproduced in the text
- A box of black and white marbles used to teach probability

Think back to the notion of accommodation introduced in Chapter 2. You may have found it necessary to accommodate the concept of electronic hypertexts into your schema for textbooks.

- Audiotapes, videotapes, films, filmstrips, records, or CDs
- Naturally occurring objects (wood, rocks, plants, animals, etc.)
- Scientific equipment (telescope, barometer, etc.)

The list is endless. These examples illustrate the variety of ways in which props can be used to introduce written material. As in the case of anecdotes, their use can be attention getting but requires that teachers draw on personal knowledge of the discipline. The use of props has been shown to be effective in a variety of disciplines, from science (Leach, Konick, & Shapiro, 1992; Sukow, 1990) to language arts (Dalle & Inglis, 1990; Fisher, 1990).

A collection of props and other resources useful for teaching a particular topic is called a *jackdaw*. Over the years, a teacher might build jackdaws as new resources are acquired and "field tested" in class. The Internet has become invaluable in locating resources (Richards & McKenna, 2003; Shiveley & van Fossen, 2000).

SUMMARY

Prior knowledge of a subject is always needed in some degree if we are to comprehend what we read. This is true because new knowledge must be stored in connection with existing memory structures. Authors inevitably make certain assumptions about the prior knowledge of their readers. When too much is assumed, comprehension suffers. Authors who are sensitive to the possible background limitations of their readers produce what has come to be called considerate writing, but even these authors cannot completely anticipate the prior knowledge needs of individual readers.

It is therefore important for teachers to consider the assumptions an author has made in writing a selection—to assess what the author assumes. In particular, references to previous material should be noted, new vocabulary should be inspected in terms of links with previously introduced words, and important references not fully explained should be identified.

It is equally important for teachers to gain a clear idea of how much students actually know about the topics contained in a selection. Many techniques are available for making assessments of this kind, including asking students to use free recall to tell what they know about a topic, providing word associations, asking structured questions that grow successively more specific, posing written multiple-choice questions that may help to identify misconceptions, conducting unstructured discussions whereby students can relate their previous experiences, and presenting writing tasks that require students to recall and apply their prior knowledge.

Because new content is learned in association with existing knowledge, it is important for the teacher to activate, or "switch on," relevant prior knowledge. A traditional way of doing so is to conduct a brief review of material if the selection to be read is a continuation of a topic already being studied. A second method is Langer's (1981) PreReading Plan (PReP). Step 1 of PReP involves conducting a brief discussion, in which students begin to organize their prior knowledge, associations with key concepts are generated, and the associations are carefully inspected and reformulated if need be. In Step 2 the teacher analyzes what students have contributed to the discussion and judges just how thorough their knowledge is. A third technique is to present students with structured writing tasks that call on them to recall and apply their prior knowledge. Writing can serve both to assess and to activate prior knowledge.

It is also important for teachers to add knowledge assumed by the writer but not available to the reader. Numerous effective methods of enchancing prior knowledge have been developed. In organizational walk-throughs, the teacher may discuss the formats an author has used to structure the writing. Other methods of building background prior to reading include using advance organizers; introducing facts assumed but not provided by the author; telling anecdotes that may personalize, clarify, and enliven the topic; offering analogies by which abstract new concepts can be related to concrete familiar concepts; using marginalia to fortify a textbook for those students whose prior knowledge is apt to be weak; and presenting props, including physical models, artifacts, audiovisual materials, and so forth.

Getting Involved

1. Choose a reading selection you plan to use with your students at some point in the future. If you are not now teaching, select an article or work of literature you might be likely to assign. Analyze the selection in terms of (1) references to other materials, (2) new terms introduced, and (3) references not fully explained. Develop methods of preparing your students for these potential problem areas by using the suggestions made in this chapter.

2. Using the same selection, develop a set of structured questions designed to assess students' prior knowledge of the content. Remember that the first question is quite general and that each succeeding question is more specific and requires more extensive background. The questions should be logically linked so that each is related in some way to the one before.

CHAPTER 6

Introducing Technical Vocabulary

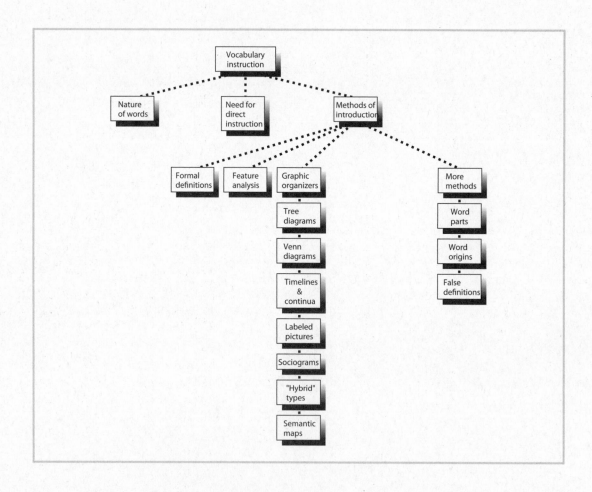

The investigation of the meaning of words is the beginning of wisdom.

—Antisthenes

One of the more painful memories many people have of their early school experiences is the vocabulary lesson. You may recall being faced with a list of words and their definitions and being asked by your teacher to associate one with the other. The words may have had little relationship to one another or, if they did, such relationships were lost because the words were presented randomly, in list form. We suggest that the memories of such experiences may be painful because this approach to vocabulary instruction tends to be inefficient and tedious. Research indicates that the most effective methods of introducing new words involve introducing them in groups that share some characteristic or relationship (Blachowicz & Fisher, 2004; McKenna, 2004).

Research has also confirmed the need to introduce terminology before students read, as a means of removing roadblocks to comprehension. No matter which of the global lesson designs you select, there is a place for the introduction of new key words prior to reading. Bromley (2007) underscores the importance of preteaching key words to improve comprehension. However, choosing which words to preteach and how much time to devote to them can be perplexing. Flanigan and Greenwood (2007) suggest that there are four types of vocabulary contained in a reading selection. Some words are essential in order to grasp the meaning of the selection and must be carefully taught before students read. Others are important for comprehension but teachers can get by with introducing them quickly. Still other words will be useful for students to learn eventually, but are not immediately necessary to understand the selection; these can be visited during a postreading discussion. Finally, some words, although rare and unknown to students, are not closely connected to the content of the selection and should not be taught at all. Once a teacher has identified which words to introduce, the key is to employ effective instructional strategies. That is the focus of this chapter.

Let us consider two teachers who are preparing to introduce such terms. One is a language arts teacher who will ask the students to read "The Gold Bug," a short story by Edgar Allan Poe. The teacher carefully lists all the words likely to be unfamiliar to the students—words like *mortification, consequent, palmetto,* and *horticulturists* (all from the first page!). The teacher writes out a brief definition or common synonym for each of these terms and makes a transparency to introduce them to the students. The second teacher is a biology instructor about to assign a chapter devoted to insects. This teacher also looks through the material and lists terms that might be troublesome: *thorax, pupa, antennae,* and so forth.

Although their actions were similar, there is a crucial difference in the lists of words produced by these two teachers. The biology teacher has concentrated on *key* terms, that is, the important new concepts introduced in the chapter. Many of the terms have natural relationships to one another, a feature that makes them easier to introduce, as we will see. The language arts teacher has listed words that, while useful to know, are not central to understanding the story. Moreover, they will prove very difficult to introduce (many transparencies will be needed!) because they lack logical relationships that link them together.

Of course, there is another difference in the assignments about to be made by these two teachers. One assignment is nonfiction, a textbook chapter designed for the specific purpose of introducing important new terms that are linked in meaningful ways. The other is fiction, and its primary purpose is not to instruct. Even in the example of the short story, however, we suggest that there are key terms, concepts so central to understanding the story that they warrant brief discussion by the teacher prior to reading. Such terms would include the names of characters and places as well as any critical words not adequately defined in context.

Our point in contrasting these two teachers is that introducing key terminology during the prereading phase is important for any reading assignment. It is up to the teacher to decide *which* words to present and *how* to present them.

It is impossible to dissociate language from science or science from language. To call forth a concept, a word is needed; to portray a phenomenon, a concept is needed. All three mirror one and the same reality.

ANTOINE LAVOISIER

Objectives

Your reading of this chapter should improve your ability to make these kinds of decisions. Specifically, when you have finished, you should be able to

1. describe the nature and function of words and their relationship to human experience;
2. identify the two elements of a classical definition;
3. incorporate feature analysis into prereading discussions;
4. construct and use graphic organizers of various kinds; and
5. describe the Guided Writing Procedure, List-Group-Label, and other techniques.

The Nature of Words

Words are symbols for concepts. As we noted in Chapter 2, a schema is all the information and experiences that an individual has learned in association with a given concept. Your schema for books includes all your many experiences with having read and used books. It may include a formal definition, and it probably involves emotional associations you tend to make with the notion of books. Such a process, which depends heavily on personal experiences, obviously leads to differing conceptualizations of just what is meant by the word *book*. The written symbol itself does not "carry" meaning; rather, the reader *brings* meaning to the symbol (Smith, 2004).

"When I use a word," Humpty Dumpty said in a rather scornful tone, "it means just what I choose it to mean— neither more nor less."

LEWIS CARROLL,
Through the Looking Glass

Words therefore come to have many associations for us. Those associations concerned with the word's general meaning and which are likely to be shared by most users of the word are said to be *denotative*. The word's dictionary definition is sometimes called its denotation. Associations that are not directly connected to a word's denotative meaning are described as *connotative*. Such associations vary with individuals because their experiences vary. To some, the word *golf* might connote doctors, presidents, and country clubs. To others it might connote frustration, fatigue, and wasted hours. These diverse sets of connotations are not directly connected with what the word *golf* denotes. Both denotations and connotations are very much a part of a student's schema for a given word.

As students mature, their schemata for various concepts develop more fully and new concepts are continually added, each represented by a word. Research into vocabulary knowledge has suggested these rather startling facts:

> There is good reason to believe that the average high school senior's vocabulary is in the neighborhood of 40,000 words. Such vocabulary size estimates imply a tremendous volume of word learning, around 3,000 words per year during the school years. This astounding rate of vocabulary growth by average children sets a mark against which the contribution of any program of vocabulary instruction must be measured. (Nagy & Herman, 1984, p. 6)

If each of these newly acquired concepts were associated with only one visual symbol (word), vocabulary learning would be difficult enough. It is complicated, however, by the fact that many concepts may share the same word. Vocabulary users must be able to distinguish which of several meanings is the intended one, and problems can result when a reader's knowledge and experiences are limited to definitions not intended by a writer. As an extreme case, consider the following:

> When they took their sixth wicket in the 30th over, there appeared to be some hope for Surrey. But when the fly slip couldn't stop Allan Warner's drive from becoming a four, Derbyshire looked in good nick, and Geoffrey Miller's 4-bye in 38 was sufficient to make sure Surrey was pipped at the post. (Margolis, 1990, p. 3)

Unless you happen to be familiar with the game of cricket, this paragraph has little, if any, meaning for you. The reason for the difficulty in understanding the example is not entirely that the vocabulary is unusual; for most readers the example does not bring to mind any previous experiences with the topic being discussed.

Many of the technical terms likely to be introduced in content areas have everyday meanings that can distract and confuse students. Such words as *set, field,* and *ring,* for example, have highly specific applications in mathematics—meanings that have little or no relationship to their more common ones.

Introducing vocabulary must therefore account for, and build on, the past experiences of students (Stahl, 2004). Techniques must be sought that relate new vocabulary to old and that stress the interrelationships among words. We shall discuss several major techniques for accomplishing this aim, but first it is necessary to dispel a myth that frequently surrounds vocabulary acquisition.

The Myth That Words Teach Themselves

Many adults, including a great many teachers, are convinced that deliberate teaching of new terms is largely unnecessary. This belief may in part be the result of ineffective teaching episodes recalled from past experiences, episodes based on the teaching of words one by one, in relative isolation. They account for knowing so many words by having met each word in their vocabulary countless times in a variety of contexts. They believe that, over a long period, these repeated exposures allow an individual to internalize word meanings.

The difficulty with this notion is that it is partly true. We suggest, for example, that no one directly taught you the word *book*, certainly not by stating its formal definition for you to remember. Instead, you learned what a book is by encountering numerous examples, both physical (that is, books you came across in the real world and that others referred to as books) and linguistic (uses of the word *book* to describe books that were not actually present). By exposure to so many examples of books, you were able to arrive at certain generalizations about what makes a book a book. Your conceptualization became more fully developed with each new example you encountered. This is an *inductive*, or incidental, approach to vocabulary acquisition, in which general rules or characteristics are inferred from numerous examples.

The meanings of many common words are acquired inductively. It may therefore be natural to suppose that such a method is adequate for introducing virtually all new words. That is, it is easy to assume that by providing students with enough contexts (both physical and linguistic) in which a word is encountered, a teacher can assure conceptualization. This assumption has three major difficulties.

First, research has revealed that context is often not very useful in helping students infer new word meanings (Beck, McKeown, & Kucan, 2002). Context is always helpful for narrowing the range of possible meanings a word might have, but it is seldom sufficient to allow a reader (or listener) to conceptualize the meaning of a word not previously encountered.

But in an inductive approach, one can argue, the student is confronted by so many instances that the deficiencies of any particular occasion will be offset by others. The result would be adequate conceptualization. This reasoning leads to the second difficulty: Such conceptualizations are often inadequate, even after innumerable encounters with a word in context. The notion of a book, which we have used as a familiar, thoroughly internalized concept, is probably not rigorously conceptualized at all. You would have no difficulty classifying a hardbound volume like this one as a book, but there are less clear examples that would challenge how precise your idea is. If the cover were removed, would it still be a book? What if the spine were severed so that it became a stack of unattached pages? What about its word-processed form? The content is, after all, the same, but is it a book in that form? Despite your many encounters with the word, the notion of a book remains a bit murky. This circumstance may be acceptable in a case like the word *book*, but with technical terms possessing precise definitions and important features that distinguish them from related terms, this lack of precision is unacceptable.

The last difficulty with the inductive approach is that many technical terms are not encountered frequently enough to expose students to an adequate number of examples. For instance, the following terms, associated with the content of science and art, were estimated by Nagy and Anderson (1984) to occur less than three times in a billion words of text:

ammeter
cyanide
anneal
template
fresco
ventilate

To argue that the student will encounter such words with far greater frequency while studying them in a given course is true, but the number of repetitions needed for induction to occur may still not be reached. (Nagy and Herman, 1985, suggest that twenty contextual encounters with a new word are required for adequate learning to occur.) Moreover, the authors of textbooks used in these courses do not rely on the inductive approach. Rather, they tend to introduce new terms along with formal definitions, an approach we consider in the following section.

Formal Definitions

When a teacher (or text) introduces a new word by stating its definition and then offering examples that may or may not conform to the definition, the approach is *deductive*. In deductive instruction, learners progress from a general rule (in this case, a definition) to the consideration of individual examples (here, encounters with the word in contextual settings).

Aristotle suggested that the formal definition of a noun should contain two elements: (1) the class, or category, to which the concept belongs and (2) specific features that allow us to distinguish examples of the concept from any other member of the category. Consider the following definition of the word *hammer*:

a tool for driving nails

We see that any hammer is a member of the larger category, tools, and that we can distinguish a hammer from other tools by its primary function, driving nails. If other tools were used to drive nails, it would be necessary to add more specific features. Plato, half in jest, once defined a man as simply "a two-legged animal." When a friend good-naturedly pointed out that this definition would not enable him to distinguish a man from a chicken, Plato modified his definition: "a two-legged animal without feathers."

Knowing the nature of formal, or classical, definitions can assist teachers in a number of ways. First, the class and distinguishing features can be identified for the students as the definition is presented. Schwartz (1988) has suggested that content teachers take the few moments required to acquaint students with the two elements of classical definitions (see also Schwartz & Raphael, 1985). Second, students can be asked to *construct* formal definitions once they know the two required components. They begin by selecting the category to which a concept belongs and then proceed to add features that would allow it to be distinguished from other category members. They can then compare their definitions with those of a dictionary or glossary. Finally, knowledge of the classical components of a definition makes possible a number of recent techniques that have proved to be highly effective in the introduction and reinforcement of vocabulary. We now examine these approaches.

Feature Analysis

When introducing a group of concepts, all of which are members of the same category, a teacher can employ an efficient approach called feature analysis (Johnson & Pearson, 1984). This technique makes use of a simple chart, like that in Figure 6.1. In the upper left-hand corner of the chart, the name of the category is written. The category members are written in the first column. Across the top of the chart, the column headings identify various features that each concept might or might not possess. The chart is completed by placing a plus sign (+) in a particular position if the concept in that row has the feature for that column. If not, a zero (0) is indicated. Some teachers find the letter *s* helpful if the concept *sometimes* has that feature.

The feature analysis chart permits comparisons of any pair of concepts by noting features shared, features possessed by only one of the concepts, and features possessed by neither concept. The chart also facilitates the analysis of each feature by considering which concepts possess it (Blachowicz & Fisher, 2004).

The relationship of feature analysis to formal definitions is obvious. Both are ways of considering a concept in relation to its category membership and its key features. From a completed

FIGURE 6.1

Feature analysis chart based on tools

Class: Tools	For driving nails	For inserting screws into wood	For gripping with leverage	For cutting metal	Has c-shaped frame	No movable parts
Hammer	+	0	s	0	0	+
Phillips-head screwdriver	0	+	0	0	0	+
Flathead screwdriver	0	+	0	0	0	+
Hacksaw	0	0	0	+	+	+
Pliers	0	0	+	0	0	0
...						

Note: A plus indicates the tool has the feature; a zero indicates it does not; *s* indicates it sometimes has the feature.

feature analysis chart, definitions of the concepts could actually be written. From Figure 6.1, the following definition of the word *hacksaw* can be composed:

a tool used for cutting metal and consisting of a thin blade attached to a c-shaped frame

This is close to the dictionary definition, though some of the definitions composed from a feature analysis chart tend to be longer and more awkward. Nevertheless, the two required elements are present: the category and the distinguishing features. Definition construction is an excellent writing activity that can be used to follow up a reading assignment that has been introduced by means of feature analysis.

The link between feature analysis and formal definitions has an important implication for determining which features to include in a chart. If any two concepts have the same set of codings (+, 0, and *s*), the chart is incomplete. Note that in Figure 6.1 there is no way to distinguish a Phillips-head screwdriver from a traditional flathead screwdriver. The codings are identical. The chart must be expanded by adding one more feature concerned with the tips of these tools—for example, "has a flat, bladelike end." The coding would then differ for the two concepts.

Feature analysis is not limited to a particular subject or even to technical terminology in the usual sense. For example, a useful chart involving characters from a short story or novel, analyzed by character traits, is quite possible. Such charts are so useful and versatile that we offer a blackline master in Figure 6.2 that can be duplicated as needed.

Graphic Organizers

The term *graphic organizer* has been defined in a perplexing variety of ways (Rice, 1994). We adopt here a rather narrow definition and suggest that a graphic organizer is *a diagram showing how key concepts are related*. While diagrams of this sort have existed for years, Barron (1969) first suggested their use for introducing related clusters of new terms. He viewed the graphic organizer as a streamlined version of the advance organizer, a technique pioneered by Ausubel (1960) and consisting of a prose introduction to a reading assignment. Research has demonstrated that graphic organizers are highly effective devices for helping students understand the relationships among concepts (Baxendell, 2003; Brunn, 2002; Merkley & Jefferies, 2001). In addition, graphic organizers have been used successfully with a wide variety of populations, such as students with various types of language disorders (Ives & Hoy, 2003), physical disabilities (Luckner, Bowen, & Carter, 2001), learning problems (DiCecco & Gleason, 2002), and LEP children (Johnson & Steele, 1996; Webster, 1998). Other beneficial applications

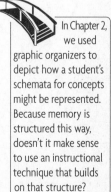

In Chapter 2, we used graphic organizers to depict how a student's schemata for concepts might be represented. Because memory is structured this way, doesn't it make sense to use an instructional technique that builds on that structure?

FIGURE 6.2

Master feature analysis chart for duplication

Feature Analysis Chart

Class:

include improving media literacy (Hobbs, 2001), promoting general vocabulary development (Ainslie, 2001; Allen, 2002), and enhancing comprehension ability (Vasilyev, 2003). It is hardly surprising that the National Reading Panel (2000), in its comprehensive review of research, concluded that using graphic representations of a text's content is a highly effective instructional technique.

NET Worth

Graphic Organizers

The Graphic Organizer. Lots of resources for teachers. Allows you to create your own organizers online, and more.

www.graphic.org

FIGURE 6.3

Graphic organizer: Tree diagram for musical instruments

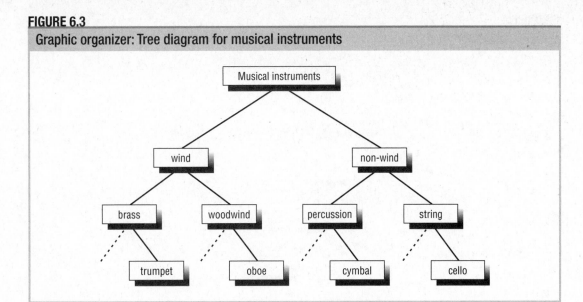

Types of Graphic Organizers

Barron's (1969) original notion of graphic organizers entailed only one type, the tree diagram. Fry (1981), however, has demonstrated the great variety of diagrammatic forms available. We will consider a few of the most broadly useful types.

Tree Diagrams. When some of the concepts to be taught represent subdivisions of other, broader concepts, the relationship can be depicted by means of a branching arrangement known as a *tree diagram.* The branching usually runs downward so that one encounters smaller and smaller subdivisions as one moves down the page. (These "trees" grow upside down!) Figure 6.3 depicts how a large concept, musical instruments, could be delineated into subconcepts. (Broken lines indicate undeveloped portions of the diagram.)

Because so many concepts bear this sort of relationship, it was perhaps natural for tree diagrams to be developed first, as a principal type of organizer. Some have argued that much of human knowledge is organized in this hierarchical fashion. Figure 6.4 illustrates how biologists systematize the classification of organisms. It is reasonably clear that semantic memory (our personal store of concepts) is organized as a network of associations that can be diagrammed in this way. The biology teacher who constructs a portion of Figure 6.4 on the chalkboard to introduce a new plant or animal is actually providing instruction that is consistent with the nature of memory. Imagine how useful such a framework might be to the student struggling to relate species after species encountered in class.

Venn Diagrams. When concepts cannot be broken down cleanly into narrower concepts—that is, when overlapping is possible—a Venn diagram may be helpful in depicting the relationships (Moyer & Bolyard, 2003; Padak, 1997; Tompkins, 1998; Yopp & Yopp, 1996). This device is borrowed from mathematical set theory and employs overlapping circles to represent related concepts. Figure 6.5 illustrates the relationship between liberals and Republicans. An individual can be classified in one of three ways: (1) as a non-Republican liberal (the left-hand crescent), (2) as a nonliberal Republican (the right-hand crescent), or (3) as a liberal Republican (the overlapping, football-shaped intersection). If it were not possible to be both a liberal and a Republican, a tree diagram would be more appropriate because the two Venn circles would not overlap.

To illustrate this difference, consider a science textbook chapter on birds. Assume that the author has employed a very simple organizational pattern in which each species is discussed in succession. If we choose two of the concepts (say, turkeys and robins), we might depict the relationship by means of the simple tree diagram in Figure 6.6. The division is clear-cut in that it is

FIGURE 6.4

Graphic organizer: Tree diagram for biological classification system

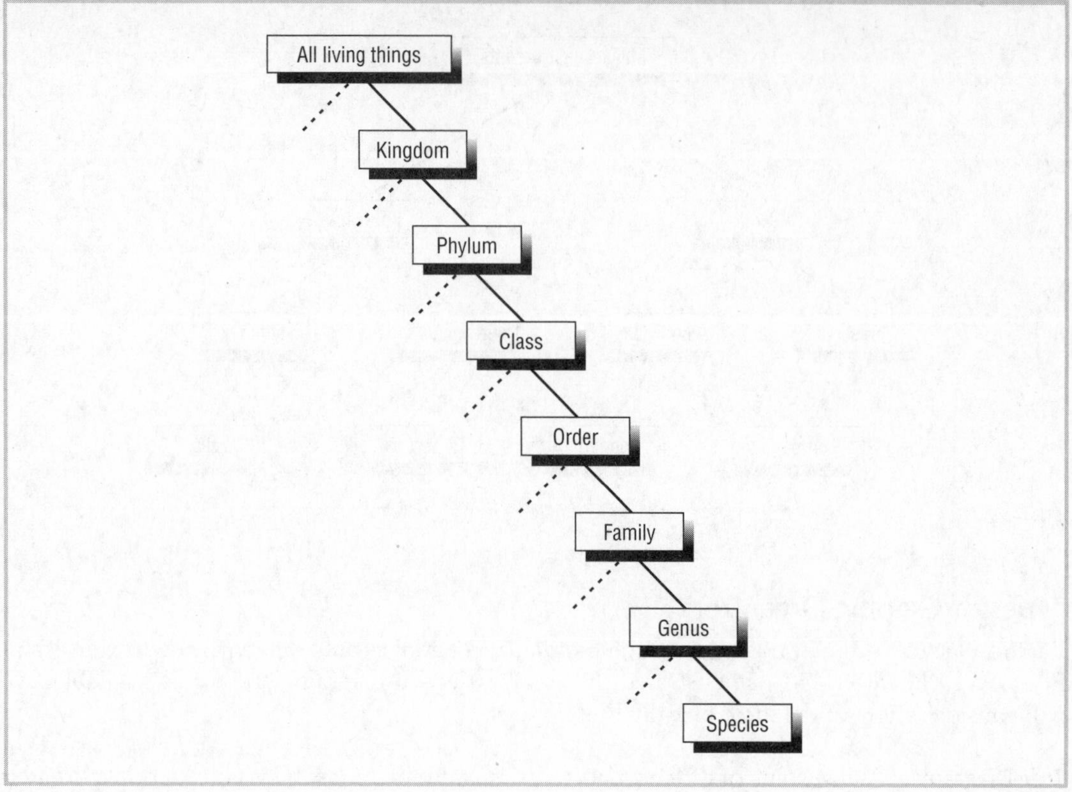

```
                    All living things
                         Kingdom
                          Phylum
                           Class
                            Order
                             Family
                              Genus
                               Species
```

impossible for a bird to be both a turkey and a robin. If we used a Venn diagram, the result would be Figure 6.7, showing lack of overlap.

A special kind of Venn diagram is useful in depicting concepts that are contained (or "nested") within other concepts. Figure 6.8 illustrates the nested nature of number systems, for example. It is true that we could have used this arrangement in our bird example, as in Figure 6.9, but the nested Venn diagram is useful primarily in cases of *successively* nested concepts, as in the case of number systems.

FIGURE 6.5

Graphic organizer: Venn diagram for liberals and Republicans

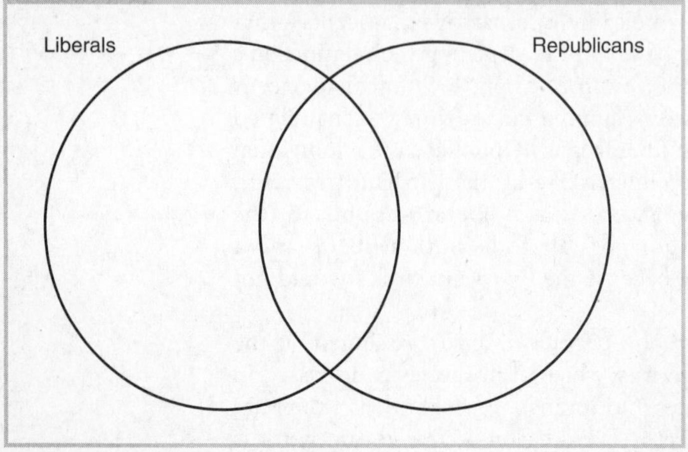

Liberals   Republicans

FIGURE 6.6

Graphic organizer: Tree diagram for birds

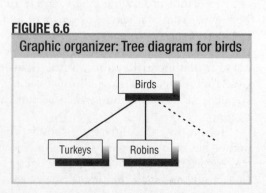

FIGURE 6.7

Graphic organizer: Venn diagram for birds

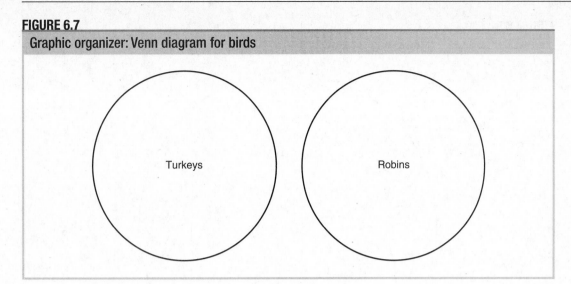

Turkeys

Robins

Timelines and Other Continua.   When concepts are related along some linear dimension, they can be effectively presented by means of a very simple organizer. Timelines (Parker & Jarolimek, 1997), such as the one depicted in Figure 6.10, are appropriate whenever the terms are related by chronology. When specific dates are known, the timeline can be marked off accordingly. When they are not known, as in a novel, a timeline can still be used to sequence the key events (see Figure 6.11).

FIGURE 6.8

Graphic organizer: Nested Venn diagram for number systems

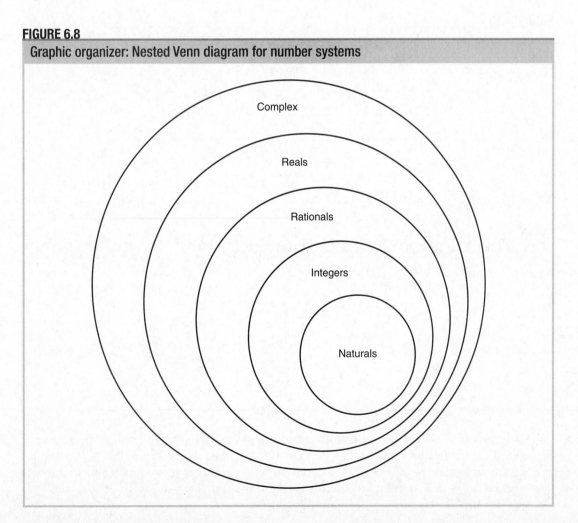

Complex

Reals

Rationals

Integers

Naturals

FIGURE 6.9

Graphic organizer: Nested Venn diagram for birds

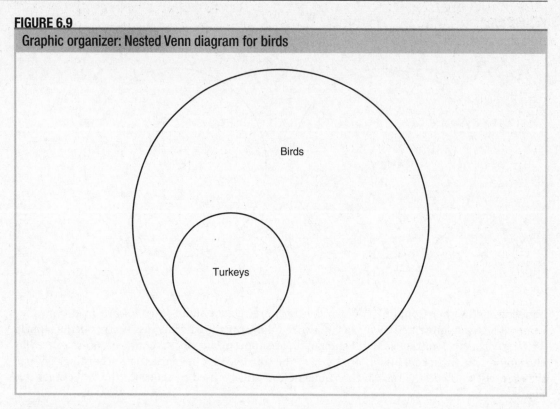

FIGURE 6.10

Graphic organizer: Timeline for World War II

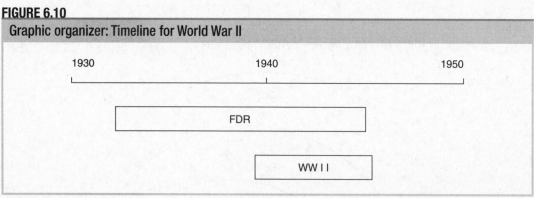

FIGURE 6.11

Graphic organizer: Timeline without specific dates

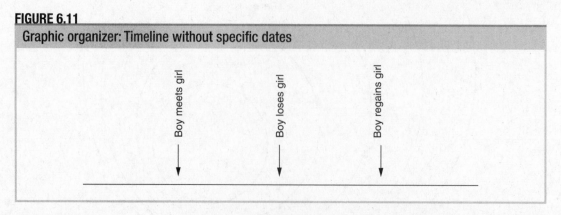

Variations of timelines depart from the traditional left-to-right straight-line arrangement. Figure 6.12 illustrates how the biology teacher we described at the beginning of the chapter might have presented one cluster of closely related terms. Figure 6.13 exemplifies a variation of the timeline developed by computer scientists: the flowchart. Flowcharts are useful whenever decision points are encountered in a repeatable process.

FIGURE 6.12

Graphic organizer: Variation of a timeline

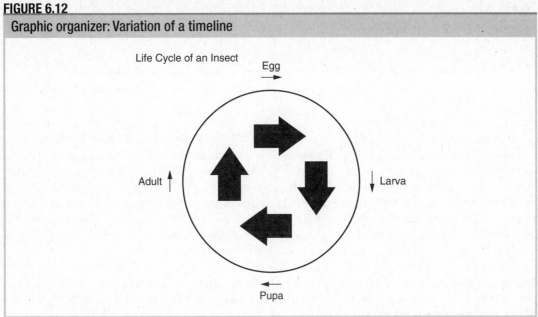

Life Cycle of an Insect

FIGURE 6.13

Graphic organizer: Flowchart for a mathematical process

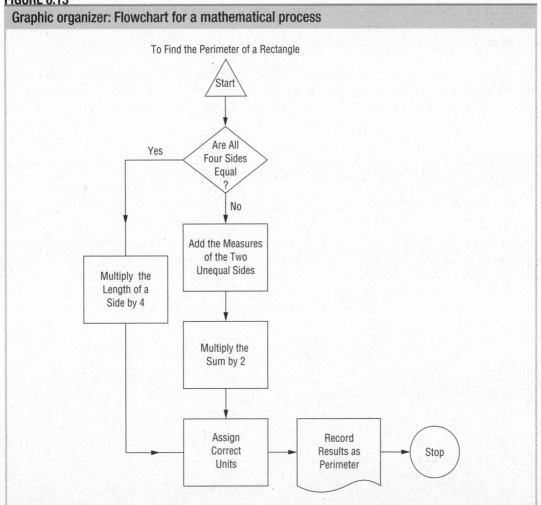

To Find the Perimeter of a Rectangle

FIGURE 6.14

Graphic organizer: Continuum showing political orientations

Liberal	Moderate	Conservative

Turn back to the Saffir-Simpson hurricane chart in Chapter 5. Would the information have been presented more effectively in a straight-line scale?

Straight lines (surely the simplest type of diagram!) can be used to represent nearly any continuum and are not limited to time. Figure 6.14 is sometimes used by social studies teachers to introduce the concepts associated with political philosophies. Well-known politicians might be added to the scale at points determined by the students to be appropriate. A music teacher developed the "speedometer" depicted in Figure 6.15 to demonstrate the distinctions among the Italian terms used by composers to indicate the pace at which a piece is to be played. The diagram was posted as a reference chart on the band-room wall behind the podium. Finally, Figure 6.16 is a straight-line scale used in classifying minerals by their hardness.

Labeled Pictures. When a cluster of terms is related chiefly by the *location* of the things to which they refer, a picture with the terms as labels can be highly effective. Consider again the biology teacher preparing to assign a chapter on insects. Some of the terms to be introduced may represent the main body parts of any insect. The labeled picture in Figure 6.17 presents these terms in an extremely efficient way.

We suspect that the oldest form of graphic organizer is a map. Note that maps serve the function of graphic organizers perfectly: They present key terms (the names of places) in a diagram depicting their most important interrelationships (location). Imagine the task of converting all the information contained on an ordinary highway map into the form of prose. Volumes would be required!

Sociograms. When the terms to be introduced represent people or groups of people linked by social relationships, a sociogram can be used to depict these relationships diagrammatically. Figure 6.18 contains an organizer often used by social studies teachers to convey how the system

FIGURE 6.15

Graphic organizer: A musical "speedometer" (some elements omitted)

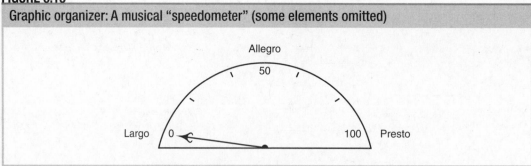

FIGURE 6.16

Mineral hardness scale used by geologists

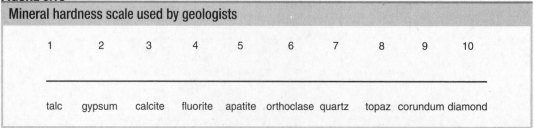

1	2	3	4	5	6	7	8	9	10

talc   gypsum   calcite   fluorite   apatite   orthoclase   quartz   topaz   corundum   diamond

FIGURE 6.17

Graphic organizer: Labeled picture for parts of an insect

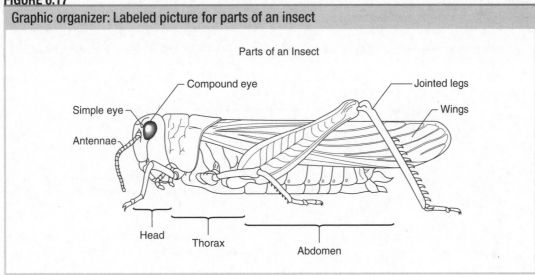

of checks and balances operates among the three branches of government. The arrows represent methods of exercising power or influence. Sociograms vary widely in nature but are always designed to depict some form of social relationship. The organizer used in Figure 2.1 (page 16) depicts a very specific relationship linking a reader and a writer in the social process of written communication.

"Hybrid" Types.   Some graphic organizers combine the characteristics of more than one basic type. The family tree in Figure 6.19, for example, is an effective combination of basic types of organizers. The organizer has the appearance of a tree diagram (it is a *family* tree, after all), but it differs from most tree diagrams in that large concepts are not delineated into narrower components. It is, in some respects, a timeline since the generations progress in time from top to bottom, but it is also a sociogram in that it portrays familial relationships. In constructing a graphic organizer, it is less important to stick with one of the conventional types described here than to produce a diagram that effectively communicates the relationships that link concepts.

Semantic Maps.   A more open-ended approach to graphic organizers is the semantic map (e.g., see Johnson & Pearson, 1984; Stahl & Nagy, 2006). Open-endedness means that students contribute to the map as it is being constructed by the teacher on a chalkboard, overhead, or wall chart. Stahl and Vancil (1986) offer a description of how semantic maps are used (see Figure 6.20).

FIGURE 6.18

Graphic organizer: Sociogram for checks and balances among the three branches of government

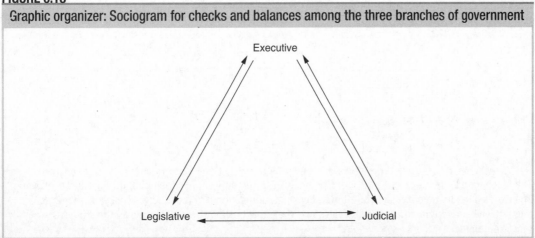

FIGURE 6.19

An American family tree: Part timeline, part sociogram, part tree diagram!

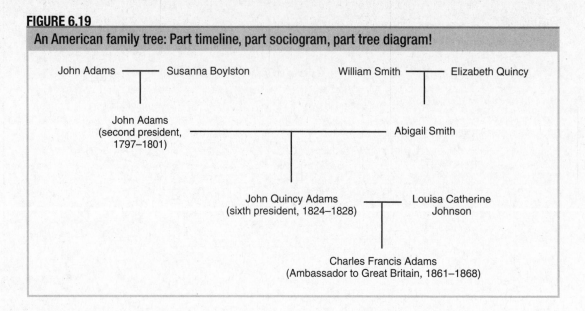

FIGURE 6.20

Semantic map for polygons

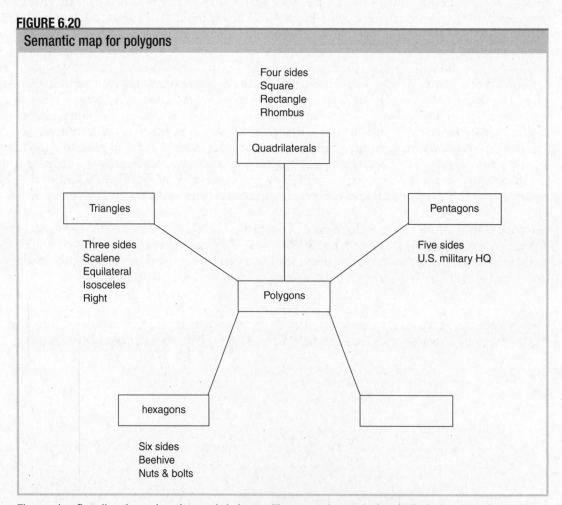

The teacher first directly teaches the words in boxes. The semantic map is then built during class discussion. The words outside the boxes are contributed by the students. Some of these (e.g., isosceles, rhombus) might have been taught during previous lessons. The blank box may be contributed by the students as well (e.g., heptagons).

In semantic mapping, a teacher chooses a key word and other target words from material that the students will read. The key word is listed on the board and students are asked to suggest terms associated with the key word. The teacher writes the suggested words in a list on the board as the students suggest them.

From this list, a map is constructed. The relationships between the key word and the target words are discussed thoroughly. Students are then asked to try to categorize each section of the map.

A copy of an incomplete semantic map is next handed out to the students. They are asked to fill in the words from the map on the board and any other additional categories or words they can add. . . .

The reading is assigned, with instructions for students to work on their maps during reading. After reading, the maps are discussed once more and new terms and categories are added.

In the map shown, the categories and boldfaced words were provided.

The other words listed were student contributions and their relation to the categories and the boldfaced words were discussed in class. The blank category was filled in by a number of students after reading.

Semantic mapping offers an interesting alternative to the use of preplanned, conventional graphic organizers. It has the advantages of encouraging student involvement during the introduction of words and of helping students discern relationships between new terms and those previously encountered (Avery et al., 1997; Lipson, 1995; Parker et al., 1996; Stahl, 1999; Zapprich, 1997). Not surprisingly, the research base underlying semantic mapping supports its effectiveness (Avery et al., 1996; Johnson & Steele, 1996; Lipson, 1995; Rosenbaum, 2001; Webster, 1998).

Recall that in Chapter 5 we stressed the usefulness of analogies in linking the new with the known. We hope our own analogy comparing semantic maps with spiderwebs illustrates their power.

The freewheeling nature of semantic maps offers a unique advantage as well. In addition to the vital links between the target word and its category membership, other associations can be attached as offshoots of the diagram. A word's connotations, for example, as supplied by students, can be added. The result, admittedly, can be a cluttered, weblike maze (semantic maps are often called webs), but they act in much the same way that a spiderweb traps insects: The more strands the insect touches, the less likely it is to escape. Similarly, the more associations a teacher can provide for a new word, the more likely it is to remain in the student's memory.

Constructing Graphic Organizers

Many textbook authors have begun incorporating graphic organizers and other aids into prose material. In these cases it is merely a matter of discussing the diagram with students before they read (Fiderer, 1998; Readence, Moore, & Rickleman, 2000). Where no organizer exists, one or more can be developed easily, and we offer the following steps.

1. *Make a list of key terms.* Such a list may have been produced by the textbook authors, but it may be necessary to construct one. Do not be concerned with how long the list becomes. In fact, it is a good idea to include terms introduced in previous lessons that bear directly on the new content. The biology teacher discussed earlier might have produced the following rough list:

pupa
thorax
abdomen
larva
egg
wings
head
adult
compound eye
simple eye
jointed legs

2. *Identify clusters of highly related terms.* Go through the list and mark terms that are highly related to one another. You may have several clusters in the overall list constructed in Step 1. The idea is to construct a graphic organizer for each cluster (or for those clusters that organizers might in your judgment help to teach). Attempting to construct a single organizer that incorporates all of the terms from the master list is nearly always a mistake, because the interrelationships are too varied and complex. Simple diagrams are almost always more effective than complicated diagrams. The biology list would have been earmarked into clusters as shown:

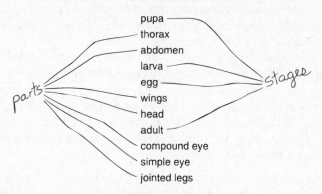

3. *Choose a diagram type that reflects how the clustered terms are related.* Study each word cluster. Ask yourself what the chief relationship is that links the terms together. The answer to this question will suggest the type of diagram that will be most useful in communicating this relationship. If the terms are related chronologically (steps in a process, phases, events), a timeline is called for. This is true for one of our biology clusters; the result was Figure 6.12. If the terms represent people, groups, or institutions, a sociogram may be best. If the terms are hierarchically related, so that some are components, aspects, or examples of others, a tree diagram is suggested. When the terms are spatially related, a labeled picture (such as the one in Figure 6.17) is called for. This brief analysis is essential to the construction of a straightforward organizer that efficiently conveys the most important relationships.

Presenting Graphic Organizers

A sizable body of research has determined that graphic organizers are highly effective tools for helping students understand the important relationships that exist among technical concepts (Dunston, 1992). Researchers have therefore often looked at how best to use organizers. (The question of *whether* to use them has been answered affirmatively!)

Moore and Readence (1980) observed that while graphic organizers are effective devices for introducing vocabulary prior to reading, they may be even more effective when used *after* reading; accordingly, we reconsider their use in Chapter 11. Of course, these uses do not preclude one another: An organizer used to introduce terminology could be revisited following reading.

Darch, Carnine, and Kameenui (1986) contrasted the use of graphic organizers with groups of students and with individuals. They observed that group settings produce the best results, perhaps because of the contributions students might make to the *discussion*. Stahl and Vancil (1986) found indeed that discussion is a critical component during the introductory process. Students must become involved with the organizer—cognitively engaged in considering what it conveys—in order for learning to be maximized (Dinnel & Glover, 1985).

Reinking (1986) has indicated the need of some students to learn exactly what graphic aids are for. Teachers should not take for granted that an organizer, perfectly comprehensible to them, will be equally meaningful to their students. A few moments spent explaining how an organizer "works" and what its purpose is will be time well spent.

In summary, we offer the following tips regarding the most effective uses of graphic organizers:

1. Keep them simple.
2. Discuss them thoroughly while you present them.
3. Include previously encountered terms where appropriate.
4. Be flexible in using them before or after reading—or both.
5. Make use of organizers developed by others.

Writing with Graphic Organizers

Constructing a graphic organizer is an excellent means of preparing to write. Because the diagram depicts important relationships among concepts, the student's task is to note those relationships and turn them into prose. There often is a close connection between a graphic organizer and one of the organizational patterns presented in Chapter 5. For example, Figures 6.10, 6.11, and 6.12 consist of timelines, and the Time Order pattern would be useful for writing a summary of the diagram's content. A student might organize a summary of Figure 6.12 like this:

Stage 1	Egg
Stage 2	Larva
Stage 3	Pupa
Stage 4	Adult

A few sentences would then be devoted to each stage. Another good example is the semantic map represented in Figure 6.20. This diagram suggests a Systematic Listing pattern. The student might write about each type of polygon, but not at random. It would be better to start with triangles and then add to the number of sides (quadrilaterals, pentagons, and so forth).

Centering a short writing activity around a graphic organizer presented in class is a good first step toward content area writing. The next step is to encourage students to rough out their own graphic organizers in a situation in which they are asked to write but do not have an organizer already in hand. A teacher must first model how to construct graphic organizers and then how to convert them into prose.

Additional Methods

The techniques we have presented thus far are nearly always useful, regardless of the nature of the material to be read. We now offer some approaches that will occasionally be appropriate, depending on the specific vocabulary to be introduced.

Word Parts

Many words, especially technical terms, were originally coined by combining familiar word elements from Greek and Latin. In mathematics, for example, the family of polygons is made up of words containing clues to the number of sides: *triangle, quadrilateral, pentagon, hexagon,* and so on. The terminology of the entire metric system was similarly constructed from these and other word elements.

When a teacher takes a few seconds to discuss a word's structure, the connection between the word and its meaning is strengthened. The language arts teacher who writes the word *autobiography* in parts on the chalkboard, and then discusses its meaning in terms of these parts, has given students an added tool for remembering and understanding. Of course, not all words lend themselves to this sort of structural analysis; stay alert for those that do.

Word Origins

Most words have historical sources in languages no longer spoken. Tracing their origins through linguistic antiquity has little to recommend it as a means of sparking the interest of students, but some words are different. These words have engrossing, sometimes fascinating, stories that can assist students in learning their meanings.

Some words are based on the names of people (e.g., *chauvinist, einsteinium, pasteurize, decibel, hertz, diesel,* and *sideburns*), whereas others are based on the names of places (*francium, tuxedo, bayonet, hamburger, limerick*).

Some words—called *portmanteaus,* or blends—are combinations of other words:

smog	=	smoke + fog
lox	=	liquid oxygen
bit	=	binary unit
brunch	=	breakfast + lunch
motel	=	motor hotel

Assisting Students with Special Needs

Which Vocabulary Techniques Work Best?

Introducing key terms prior to reading assignments can effectively enhance the comprehension of *all* students. However, some of the techniques presented in this chapter have been shown to be especially useful with poor readers. Outstanding examples are feature analysis (Bos & Anders, 1990) and graphic organizers (Horton & Lovitt, 1989; Langer, Bartolome, & Vasqueze, 1988; Torgesen & Kail, 1985).

Several possible factors may explain the effectiveness of these techniques. Poor readers tend to decode slowly and to direct their attention and effort toward word recognition rather than meaning construction. Diagrams and charts, although rich in meaning, require little effort to "read." In addition, the content presented in many assignments tends to be abstract and difficult to visualize. Charts and diagrams provide a means of envisioning concepts and their interrelationships. Finally, poor readers often do not recognize the need to organize concepts. To combat this tendency, Tobias (1982) recommended techniques that make concept organization clear and salient. Feature analysis and graphic organizers do exactly that.

Portmanteaus have an important significance for teachers in content areas because a surprisingly large number of new technical terms are deliberately coined in this manner (Simonini, 1966). For a discussion of these interesting words, see McKenna (1978).

A few words have unusual stories associated with their origins. When a new type of heavily armored vehicle was shipped from England to the Continent in World War I, these vehicles were packed in huge wooden crates commonly used for shipping benzene tanks. For security reasons, the word *tank* was painted on the side of each crate. The name stuck.

Discussing word origins does more than increase student interest and engagement. It adds connotative associations to the denotative values of words. The web of meanings for the new word becomes stickier! Locating words with unusual origins is easy. While books on word origins are available, there is a simpler way. All standard dictionaries include an etymology for each word as part of the entry. The *etymology*, or history of the word, is usually in brackets. While most etymologies recount the evolution of words from dead languages, brief anecdotes are also included when the origin is more colorful.

 In Chapter 5, we discussed anecdotes as a stimulating way of building prior knowledge. Stories about words like *tank* represent a specific kind of anecdote.

False Definitions

Common words are occasionally "redefined" by skillful writers in ways that are thought-provoking and often humorous. Consider a few of these false definitions drawn from a variety of content areas. (In the case of *hammer*, contrast Bierce's definition with its real definition, given on p. 82!)

hammer	an instrument for smashing the human thumb (Ambrose Bierce)
government	the worst thing in this world, next to anarchy (Henry Ward Beecher)
football	committee meetings, called huddles, separated by outbursts of violence (George Will)
esophagus	that portion of the alimentary canal that lies between pleasure and business (Ambrose Bierce)
engineering	the art of doing that well with one dollar which any bungler can do with two after a fashion (Arthur M. Wellington)
literature	news that *stays* news (Ezra Pound)
mathematics	the science that draws necessary conclusions (Benjamin Pierce)
science	an exchange of ignorance for that/which is another kind of ignorance (Lord Byron)

circle	the highest emblem in the cipher of the world (Ralph Waldo Emerson)
GOP	Grand Old Platitudes (Harry Truman)
grammar	that which knows how to lord it over kings and with high hands makes them obey its laws (Molière)
education	what survives when what has been learnt has been forgotten (B. F. Skinner)

False definitions have the form of real definitions and are therefore useful in making contrasts with their dictionary counterparts. As in the case of word origins, they are peripheral to teaching denotative meanings but add additional associations that may help students retain the actual meanings. Any book of quotations can be scoured for quips that have the form of classical definitions; also, McKenna (1983) has compiled an entire volume devoted exclusively to false definitions.

SUMMARY

An important part of teaching in content areas is the introduction of new concepts, represented by words. Vocabulary instruction is complicated by the fact that the same visual symbol (word) can represent numerous concepts and that what a word formally signifies (what it denotes) is only one of many associations a reader may have for the same word, including what the reader may have experienced in regard to that concept (what the word connotes). Many teachers assume that as students are exposed again and again to a given word, the word's meaning will be acquired inductively. However, while this process may occur to a degree, the precise meanings of key terminology often need to be explicitly taught through a more deductive approach.

Numerous methods have been developed for introducing new words. One of the most effective is feature analysis, which involves construction of a chart in which the left-hand column lists category members and additional columns represent various features either possessed or lacked by the members.

One of the most important advances in our ability to introduce new words is the graphic organizer, a diagram that depicts relationships among key terms. Major types of organizers include tree diagrams, Venn diagrams, timelines, labeled pictures, and sociograms, although many others are possible, including combination (hybrid) types. Semantic maps are a modified form of graphic organizer with a more freewheeling structure conducive to student input. To construct a graphic organizer, students first list all key terms in a selection, then identify clusters of closely related terms, and finally construct a diagram for each cluster that best represents the relationship among the terms.

Numerous other techniques have been used successfully to introduce new terminology, either alone or in association with the techniques previously mentioned. One approach is to analyze words on the basis of meaningful word elements (prefixes, suffixes, root words, etc.). Another approach is to explore the historical origins of words whenever the origin offers insights into a word's meaning or provides an additional colorful association that may create an interest in the word *and* improve the chances that students will retain it. False definitions are quotations from writers who have offered their own renditions of what certain widely used words mean. These "definitions" can provide the basis of useful contrasts with the word's denotation.

Getting Involved

1. For each of the following sets of terms, select the most appropriate type of graphic organizer. Choose from among the following types:
   a. timelines and other continua
   b. tree diagrams
   c. Venn diagrams
   d. labeled pictures
   e. sociograms

1. cats, tiger, leopard, jaguar
2. adulthood, infancy, adolescence, childhood
3. cerebrum, cerebellum, cranium, brain stem
4. fuselage, wing, rudder, tail
5. generals, presidents, Grant, Lincoln, Lee
6. student, teacher, principal, superintendent
7. cars, U.S. cars, foreign cars, Japanese cars, Saab, Honda, Ford
8. Republicans, Democrats, conservatives
9. general practitioner, specialist, referrals, consultations
10. red, blue, yellow, orange, purple, green, brown

There is often more than one way to depict a cluster of terms using a graphic organizer. The following answers are *suggested* for the sets of terms presented above:

1. b, 2. a, 3. d, 4. d, 5. c, 6. e, 7. b, 8. c, 9. e, 10. c

For additional practice, try actually constructing the diagrams for these clusters.

2. Figure 6.21 provides an incomplete feature analysis chart based on the instructional techniques described in this chapter. Use the codings +, 0, and *s* to complete the chart, based on your knowledge of the techniques.

3. The following words are drawn from a variety of subject areas. Each has an interesting origin that is provided in the etymology section of a standard dictionary entry. Choose the words associated with your own area and look up their histories in a dictionary. Don't be surprised if you find yourself looking up *all* the words!

sandwich	gorilla	transistor	saxophone
Teflon	quark	boycott	crowbar
nylon	googol	agnostic	Dixie
scuba	Pacific	bazooka	forsythia
quasar	magenta	braille	poinsettia
shrapnel	silhouette	radar	laser
bikini	badminton	calico	damask
marathon	plutonium	uranium	bloomer
derringer	gardenia	sousaphone	bolt
watt	zinnia	good-bye	gas
blurb	bleacher	boondocks	cowlick
dynamite	goatee	hydrogen	iron curtain
jackrabbit	jeep	serendipity	spoof
teetotaler	zilch	yippie	jumbo

For additional reading on the educational uses of word origins, see McKenna (1977a).

FIGURE 6.21

Feature analysis chart for selected chapter terms

Class: Vocabulary introduction devices	Type of graphic organizer	Used only with highly related terms	Developed by Aristotle	Most open-ended of organizers	Helps categorize terms by class and characteristics
Timeline					
Word parts					
Formal definition					
Semantic map					
Venn diagram					
Tree diagram					

Strategies for Guided Reading

In Chapter 2, we examined the roles played by prior knowledge of content and purpose for reading in the process of learning through text. We suggested that content area teachers are perfectly positioned to influence these factors as students undertake assigned reading. We now turn to the second factor: the purposes for which students read.

Chapter 7 presents a variety of techniques for making reading purposeful in a specific sense. The use of questions as a purpose-setting device is discussed in detail. While questions are a mainstay, other methods are also examined. These include reading to confirm a hypothesis or prediction, reading to satisfy a stated objective or outcome, reading to construct (or complete) a graphic organizer or chart, reading to solve a specific problem, reading for the purpose of writing a summary, and reading in order to prepare an outline of the written material.

Chapter 8 presents a method of incorporating the basic purpose-setting devices described in Chapter 7 into a content literacy guide. These guides are designed to be completed by students as they read. The chapter begins with a discussion of the advantages of written guides and when to use them. Numerous guide formats are introduced. This chapter also offers advice on how to construct and use such guides.

Chapter 9 explores the practical issues and decisions involved in actual reading. Should material be assigned for reading at home? Should class time be allotted for silent reading? Should students cover assigned material in pairs or in groups? Workable options are examined in this chapter.

CHAPTER 7

Making Reading Purposeful

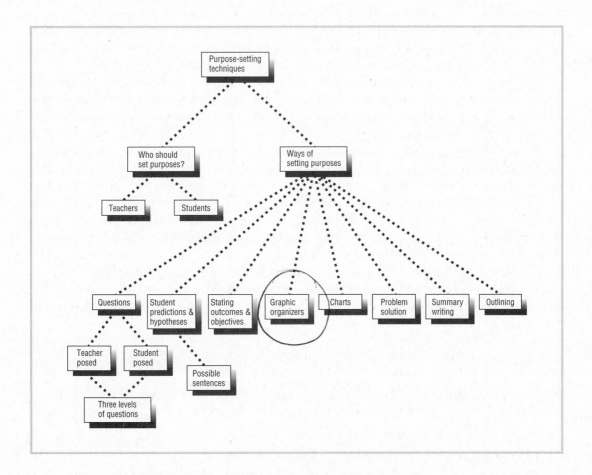

The secret of success is constancy to purpose.

—Benjamin Disraeli

Dr. Samuel Johnson, whose comments about reading and writing we have quoted liberally in this text, enjoyed a reputation as one of the world's foremost authorities on these subjects during the eighteenth century. The Scottish economist Adam Smith once remarked that Johnson "knew more books" than anyone in the world. The question of how Johnson was able to read so extensively on such a wide variety of subjects was a frequent topic of discussion. An acquaintance once asked him if, when he read a book, he proceeded through it line by line from cover to cover, reading every word as he went. Johnson's reply astonished his friend.

He said that he rarely if ever read a book in that manner, for few books were worthy of that sort of reading. Instead, he read selectively to accomplish his own purposes for reading. Johnson's interviewer was surprised because he, like many of us, believed that to do anything less than read every word is not reading at all. In our print-oriented society, however, in which the demands of reading are apt to be extensive, skillful readers tend to adopt strategies like Johnson's and read to accomplish their own purposes. The need to *have* clear purposes is obviously great, especially when materials are challenging and prior knowledge is limited.

Reading without a clear idea of purpose can lead to frustration for students, who may not achieve the results their teachers expect, and to exasperation for teachers, who often fail to understand how their students' comprehension can be so inadequate. For many students, however, it is not enough to read a textbook for the broad purpose of "getting all the facts" or a narrative with the aim of "finding out what happens." They often need specific direction in determining what is important in the midst of what may seem an avalanche of print.

Consider your own experience with this text. Have you caught yourself wondering, or perhaps even inquiring, about what you will need to know for testing purposes? There is nothing wrong with such a question, for it reflects the thinking of a strategic reader—one who reads purposefully, using whatever strategies may help to achieve specific goals. When, as in many classroom situations, the purposes are determined by the teacher, it makes sense to discover them by asking.

Teachers who are not forthcoming about what they expect their students to derive from reading are inviting poor comprehension. Some teachers defend this policy, however, by suggesting that any effort on their part to limit the scope of reading assignments will result in their students' reading only for the prestated purposes. This response acknowledges how powerful purpose setting can be! The object is to set the *right* purposes: those that go beyond literally stated facts and get at their significance. Teachers who establish purposes in this manner can have the confidence to permit, and even encourage, students to read strategically. Whenever purposes for reading encompass the curricular goals envisioned by a teacher, the goal of reading should be to achieve those purposes and not simply to reach the last page of an assignment. Students are then free to model themselves after Dr. Johnson and read for what they need.

> *He has only half learned the art of reading who has not added to it the even more refined accomplishments of skipping and skimming.*
>
> ARTHUR, LORD BALFOUR

Objectives

This chapter will acquaint you with ways of making your students' reading more purposeful. When you have completed it, you should be able to

1. describe the reasons for setting purposes prior to reading;
2. pose questions at the literal, inferential, and critical levels;
3. explain how student-posed questions might best serve certain reading assignments;
4. describe and use alternative methods of purpose setting, including hypothesizing, stating objectives, completing graphic organizers and charts, solving problems, writing summaries, and outlining;
5. identify the strengths and limitations of these techniques that may make them more suitable to some global plans than to others; and
6. vary and combine purpose-setting techniques.

Who Should Set Purposes for Reading?

Few would dispute that an important goal of schooling is to produce strategic readers capable of setting their own purposes and of reading flexibly to achieve those purposes (Damico & Baildon, 2007; Janzen, 2003; Petersen & VanDerWege, 2002). Our recommendation, however, is that content teachers be somewhat directive in the process of setting purposes. There are three good reasons behind this suggestion. To begin with, the teacher's prior knowledge of the subject is apt to exceed that of students to such an extent that the teacher is better able to establish reasonable goals for reading. In addition, many students have limited experience in setting purposes, regardless of their knowledge of content. Finally, we would argue that the ability to read strategically in order to achieve purposes set by others will eventually be at least as important to students (when they reach the workplace) as reading to satisfy their own purposes.

We are not suggesting that teachers give their students no choices as to what to read or what to read for. We do recommend that, while guiding the process of purpose setting in these techniques, they continue to realize that student-generated purposes may be unsophisticated, vague, and incomplete. In these cases, teachers may be wise to encourage students to modify their purposes in accordance with teacher suggestions. Tact is important in order not to dampen student initiative and thought.

Ways of Setting Purposes

The goal of purpose setting is to "direct student attention to the most important information" (Marshall, 1989, p. 64). There are several methods for accomplishing this goal. No one method is best for all reading assignments, and familiarity with several techniques will give you the power to select one that is well suited to a given occasion. In the next chapter, we take the additional step of incorporating these methods, often in combination, into reading guides used to focus the efforts of students as they read.

Questions Posed by the Teacher

A traditional means of focusing students' attention is by posing prereading questions. This practice, more than most, is likely to occasion the complaint we mentioned earlier: that if students are told what to read for, told in advance which questions they'll be called on to answer, they will read for this purpose alone. Indeed, there is research evidence indicating that prereading questions tend to focus attention so distinctly that content not associated with the questions can be missed. Such findings merely indicate the power of prereading questions. It is up to teachers to ensure that questions cover the desired range of content and that they do more than call for a litany of factual details.

Moreover, questions can have an important dual effect. Not only do they focus thought on the important dimensions of content, but they also activate some of the relevant schemata readers will need to process the material (LeNoir, 1993).

Types of Questions.   Knowing the right questions requires knowing something about the types of questions one might ask. In the past, reading researchers have examined detailed lists, or taxonomies, of comprehension skills (e.g., Barrett, 1972; Pearson & Johnson, 1978). The skills contained in these taxonomies, such as inferring cause-and-effect relationships or predicting outcomes, can be used to define types of comprehension questions. This highly detailed approach to question formulation is not really necessary for most purposes, however. Instead, we recommend a simpler approach based on three widely acknowledged *levels* of comprehension. These levels, along with the kinds of questions they suggest, are depicted in Figure 7.1.

At the lowest level, the literal, questions call for students to recognize explicitly stated information. Some years ago, an eighth-grade student of the first author described them as "Christopher Columbus" questions because "you search for the answer until you land on it." It is no doubt that literal questions cause some teachers to have reservations about the notion of posing prereading questions at all.

Students can look up answers to literal questions without giving much thoughtful attention to an answer's context and implications. It is for this reason that such questions should seldom form the sole basis of a reader's purpose. There are exceptions to this rule, as when we look up a population figure in an almanac or a pronunciation in a dictionary. But the reading of longer selections with the goal of fully comprehending their content requires more than the acquisition

FIGURE 7.1

Three levels of questions

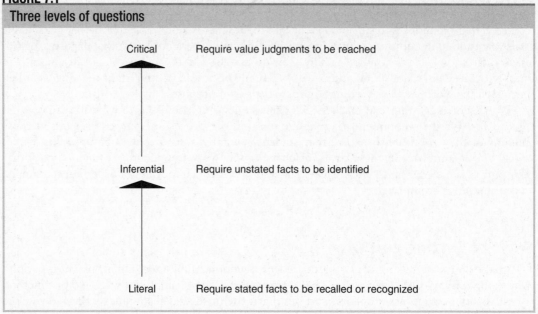

Critical   Require value judgments to be reached

Inferential   Require unstated facts to be identified

Literal   Require stated facts to be recalled or recognized

of individual facts. The student must integrate facts, both with one another and with prior knowledge, in order to make sense of them, to apply them, and, in Aquinas's words, to realize their significance. Purposes of this sort call for questions of a different kind. Although literal questions have their uses in helping students acquire the facts they need, they should not be an end in themselves.

Truth is not facts. Truth is the significance of facts.

THOMAS AQUINAS

Inferential questions require students to use explicit facts in order to reach unstated, or implicit, conclusions. Teachers should encourage students to draw on prior knowledge in this process as well. The result is the identification of new (that is, unstated) facts or *suspected* facts (Basche et al., 2001). Some inferences are clearly and indisputably correct. When we read that a painter mixes equal portions of blue and yellow paint, we can safely infer that the result is green even though this fact may not be stated. (Note that we used prior knowledge along with information provided through reading in order to reach this particular conclusion.) On the other hand, some inferences are less than certain. Consider the social studies teacher who assigns a series of newspaper and magazine articles about a coming election and then asks students who they think will win. Even though the students cannot be sure of their answers, the reasoning process is nevertheless inferential. This is because known facts are being used to determine unstated ones. Noted linguist S. I. Hayakawa (1939) once defined an inference as "a statement about the unknown made on the basis of the known" (p. 41). It is less important that a student's "statement" about the election's outcome eventually be proved correct than that it be based on presently known facts.

At the critical level, questions call on students to judge what they read. These judgments can serve a variety of purposes.

■ Synthesizing information from a variety of sources
■ Selecting facts that support a particular viewpoint
■ Identifying biased writing
■ Recognizing inadequacies in an author's treatment of a topic
■ Evaluating the literary merits of writing
■ Interpreting information in order to apply it to a new situation
■ Deciding how to read a given assignment selectively in order to accomplish one's purposes
■ Comparing one reading selection with others
■ Choosing the most efficient method of solving a problem in mathematics or science

Critical questions do not have factual answers. Reasonable, comprehending readers may differ in their responses to such questions because the answers depend on personal values, experiences,

FIGURE 7.2

Description of Pluto at the NASA Web site

Once known as the smallest, coldest, and most distant planet from the Sun, Pluto has a dual identity, not to mention being enshrouded in controversy since its discovery in 1930. On August 24, 2006, the International Astronomical Union (IAU) formally downgraded Pluto from an official planet to a dwarf planet. According to the new rules a planet meets three criteria: it must orbit the Sun, it must be big enough for gravity to squash it into a round ball, and it must have cleared other things out of the way in its orbital neighborhood. The latter measure knocks out Pluto and 2003UB313 (Eris), which orbit among the icy wrecks of the Kuiper Belt, and Ceres, which is in the asteroid belt.

Discovered by American astronomer Clyde Tombaugh in 1930, Pluto takes 248 years to orbit the Sun. Pluto's most recent close approach to the Sun was in 1989. Between 1979 and 1999, Pluto's highly elliptical orbit brought it closer to the Sun than Neptune, providing rare opportunities to study this small, cold, distant world and its companion moon, Charon.

Source: www.nasa.gov

desires, and tastes. As in the case of inferential questions, the important aspect of a critical response is not the response itself but the reasoning behind it. Answers to critical questions are not correct or incorrect; they are more or less *defensible* depending on their basis in fact.

To illustrate the difference between literal, inferential, and critical questions, consider the passage presented in Figure 7.2 about the planet Pluto. This objectively written, highly factual, expository selection invites many sorts of questions, and we offer one at each level of comprehension.

1. How long does it take Pluto to orbit the sun?

This question has a factual answer that is clearly stated in the selection. It is a clear-cut, "Christopher Columbus" example. Contrast it with this one:

2. Is there life on Pluto?

This question has a factual answer (there either is or is not life on Pluto), but you will find no mention of life in the selection. The question is therefore not literal but inferential. Because it is not a certain inference, some teachers might categorize it as critical, but the answer is factual, like our earlier example of predicting the results of an election. The third question is undeniably critical. Contrast it with the second in terms of the sort of answer it calls for.

3. Should the United States send a space probe to explore Pluto?

Here, the answer is not a fact but a judgment—an answer that may well vary from one reader to the next despite how well those readers have understood the selection. The usual confusion between critical questions and questions that call for probable (less than certain) inferences is that each asks the reader for an *opinion*. However, the inferential question asks for an opinion based on facts while the critical question calls on the reader to examine values and desires.

We emphasize that these three levels are not entirely distinct. There is a "gray" area between the literal and inferential levels, where some questions appear to fall, and another between the inferential and critical levels. This is of little concern to us, however, because the three-level system is designed as a tool for formulating new questions, not classifying existing ones. In Figure 7.3, we offer a few tips for using the three-level approach more effectively in setting purposes.

Teacher-posed questions have an obvious influence on any postreading discussion, because the teacher's blueprint for discussing the material is in fact the questions posed in advance. Other questions are asked as well, as we describe in Chapter 10, but the framework of the discussion is planned before the reading assignment is ever made.

The value of suggesting questions during reading has not been lost on nonfiction writers for youngsters. Figure 7.4 illustrates how using questions as subheadings can focus attention. Each subsection is devoted immediately to answering the question posed at the outset. The text then goes on to elaborate. Do you think students would find the material just as engaging with different headings?

FIGURE 7.3

Characteristics of questions

Critical questions
- Always open-ended; never have a single answer
- Have answers that are not facts but that reflect values
- Often contain the word *should*

Inferential questions
- Have factual answers even though the answer may not be certain
- Require that two or more facts be considered together in order to produce an unstated (or suspected) fact
- May rely on facts in the reader's prior knowledge as well as facts stated in the reading selection

Literal questions
- Have answers that can be located in the reading selection
- Require minimal use of prior knowledge

Questions Posed by Students

The National Reading Panel (2000) concluded that activities in which students generate questions themselves tend to improve comprehension. One reason for this is that in order to ask a good question we must understand the material ourselves—at least to a degree. But can students ask reasonable questions? Our classroom experience says that they can. We have observed children as young as third grade generate productive questions about fiction and nonfiction alike. Many teachers, however, hesitate to relinquish the traditional role of questioner. In our experience, they have little to fear, and they can always complement student questions to fill gaps.

As an experiment, we described the Pluto selection (Figure 7.2) to a group of eighth graders without allowing them to see the selection. We told them the source was a NASA article and asked them what they would expect to be able to learn from reading the selection. Here is a sample of what they suggested:

- How cold it is on Pluto
- How far Pluto is from Earth
- What Pluto looks like
- What life-forms might exist on Pluto
- What kinds of rock might be on Pluto
- How big Pluto is
- Whether Pluto has any moons
- Where you might look for Pluto in the sky

Examining the list might give confidence to teachers who are skeptical that students are capable of setting prudent, defensible purposes for reading when encouraged to do so. Note that the items in our list are in the form of indirect questions because of how we had asked our question. Note, too, that these questions are either literal or inferential, depending on how the encyclopedia author treated the topic. The students had no way of knowing whether they might actually find the information literally stated in the selection. In cases where the information was not explicit (such as "what life-forms might exist on Pluto"), the students' purpose would be to identify facts that support an eventual inference (such as the extremely low temperatures, the near-absence of life, and the hostile atmosphere). Finally, note that critical questions are not present. This may well have been because the students did not expect such issues to be addressed in an encyclopedia. It may also have been the result of their limited experiences with critical thinking and reading. Teachers interested in encouraging these processes may find it necessary to nudge students in this direction during the prereading discussion.

FIGURE 7.4

Example of embedded questions, U.S. Geological Survey

The Mountain That Moved

Geologic Wonders of the George Washington and Jefferson National Forests

No. 2 in a Series
Blacksburg/Wythe Ranger Districts

USGS U.S. Department of Interior
U.S. Geological Survey

in cooperation with

U.S. Department of Agriculture
Forest Service, Southern Region

2000

Prehistoric, giant landslides in Montgomery and Craig Counties, Va., in the Blacksburg/Wythe Ranger Districts of the Jefferson National Forest, are the largest known landslides in eastern North America and are among the largest in the world. One of the landslides is more than 3 miles long! The ancient, giant landslides extend for more than 20 miles along the eastern slope of Sinking Creek Mountain. Enormous slabs of rock ranging from about 0.2 to more than 1.5 square miles in size broke loose and slid downslope under the influence of gravity. The movement of some slides may have been slow, but the movement of others was probably sudden and catastrophic.

These landslides are called rock-block slides and rockslides. In rock-block slides, a slab or block of bedrock moves down a slope intact. If the slab or block breaks up as it slides, it is called a rockslide.

How were the landslides discovered?

The landslides were discovered in the 1980's during geological mapping, which showed that rock layers were displaced (fig. 1). The landslides had not been recognized before because they are so large they are not easily seen. The zone of landslides was identified by geologists who noticed a combination of unusual hills and hollows, geologic structures, and unexpected vegetation patterns. These landslide features include cliffs where the rock has broken away, isolated flat areas or benches, and isolated knobs. The benches have springs, small streams, swamps, ponds, and circular to elliptical depressions from 30 to 300 feet across—features that are rare on slopes without landslides. The unusual landforms can be seen on topographic maps and aerial photographs.

Many of the rockslides have evergreen vegetation, while slopes below the slides have deciduous (hardwood) vegetation. Also, swamps and ponds on the slides contain ferns that do not normally grow on the steep eastern slopes, which are usually too dry for these plants. These changes in vegetation reflect the disruption of soils in the landslide zone.

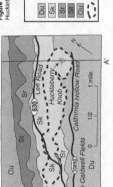

Figure 1. Cross section and geologic map, Huckleberry Knob area.

EXPLANATION

- Du Mostly shale
- Sk Keefer Sandstone
- Sr Rose Hill Formation
- St Tuscarora Sandstone
- Ou Older sedimentary rocks
- --- Boundary of landslide

FIGURE 7.4 (continued)
Example of embedded questions, U.S. Geological Survey

When did the landslides happen?

The exact time of movement is uncertain, but evidence suggests that the landslide movement was between about 10,000 and 25,000 years ago. This would be during the Pleistocene Ice Age, but before the arrival of humans in the area. Pollen and organic matter from a sag pond on one of the landslides show that sediments were deposited in the pond as early as 10,000 years ago. Native American artifacts of the Woodland period (about 1,000 B.C. to A.D. 1,000) were found on landslide slopes at three places. There is no evidence of recent movement of the landslides.

Where can you see them?

The large size of the landslides, dense vegetation, and deep erosion make them difficult to see. But, if you look carefully from certain locations, you can see the unusual landforms that are a result of these ancient landslides. They are seen best when the leaves are off the trees.

From Caldwell Fields and Lee Road. From the Caldwell Fields (fig. 2) parking area, look north along Lee Road (Rt. 630) (fig. 1). You will see the steep, straight "flat-irons" of

Figure 2. Map showing location of ancient giant landslides.

sandstone that are characteristic of the undisturbed parts of the east slope of Sinking Creek Mountain. Then look to your left, where the slope is broken by "lumpy" topography, and the lower bench of a large landslide can be seen below the crest of the mountain. If you look closely at the powerline at the top of the mountain, you can see a cliff where bedrock is exposed. This is the scarp from which the slab of rock in the slide broke away. If you drive up Lee Road from Caldwell Fields, you will cross one of the ancient landslides, but the changes in topography, geology, and vegetation are subtle and not readily recognized.

Huckleberry Knob. Huckleberry Knob (fig. 3) can be seen best when the leaves are off the trees from near the end of the Lee Road or by hiking on California Hollow Road (fig. 1). Huckleberry Knob is one of the best examples of an isolated landslide block sitting out in the valley. Notice the evergreens on the knob and the reversal in slope of the bench northwest of Huckleberry Knob. This is typical of the unusual landslide topography.

From Rt. 621 and Hall Road. Landslide benches can also be seen at some places from Rt. 621 on the slopes of Sinking Creek Mountain between Caldwell Fields and Rt. 209 (Hall Road). If you drive up Rt. 209, you get a good view of "lumpy" landslide ridges below the straight ridge at the skyline (fig. 4). As you continue on Hall Road to the top of Sinking Creek Mountain, you drive across an ancient giant landslide.

From Brush Mountain. Another viewpoint from which the landslide benches can be seen is the crest of Brush Mountain, looking north

Figure 3. View of Huckleberry Knob, which is an escarpment on the front of a landslide. Crest of the mountain and source of the slide are to the left.

to Sinking Creek Mountain (cover photograph). You can drive to the crest of Brush Mountain on the gravel road (P188-1) off State Route 624.

From the Appalachian Trail. Hikers on the Appalachian Trail ascending Rt. 621 to the top of Sinking Creek Mountain will walk across the benches of one of the ancient giant landslides. Along the crest of Sinking Creek Mountain, hikers can look down the eastern slope toward Huckleberry Knob and see benches on the ancient giant landslides.

Why did the mountains move?

Erosion that undercut the base of the slope or erosion related to heavy rainfall might have produced unstable slopes that resulted in landslides. Another possibility is that the landslides were triggered by earthquakes because the landslides border on the presently active Giles County earthquake zone.

Will there be more landslides?

Even though there is no evidence of recent movement of the ancient, giant landslides on the slope of Sinking Creek Mountain, other types of landslides (rockslides and debris flows) do occur during rainstorms on slopes in

the Appalachian Mountains. In the past, most landslides occurred in uninhabited areas. Today, knowledge of the geologic setting of existing and planned development can help identify the potential for landslides. Research on how and where slope failures occur can help reduce the risk to human lives and property from landslides.

Have the rocks been useful?

Yes. The rocks that form the high ridge of Sinking Creek Mountain are composed of sandstone (Keefer Sandstone), sandstone and quartzite (Tuscarora Sandstone), and interbedded sandstone and shale (Rose Hill Formation). Rocks from these units, both in the landslides and in the intact parts of the ridges, have long been used for building stone. Sandstone of the Rose Hill Formation commonly forms one- to two-inch thick, grayish-red to reddish-black layers that make good flagstone. The layers of the Rose Hill Formation may have provided surfaces along which overlying blocks of rock slid. (Note: If you wish to remove stone from the national forest, first stop at the Blacksburg Ranger Station and get a permit.)

Figure 4. "Lumpy" ridge line (accentuated by the dashed line) formed on a landslide. View from Hall Road near Craig Creek.

Question–Answer Relationships (QARs).   Raphael (1984) has suggested a straightforward method of teaching students about the levels of questions. Rather than use technical terms like *literal, inferential,* and *critical,* Raphael and her colleagues recommend the following easy-to-understand category labels:

1. *Right There.* The answer is in one place in the text. Words from the question and words that answer the question are often "right there" in the same sentence.

2. *Think and Search.* The answer is in the text. Readers need to "think and search," or put together different parts of the text, to find the answer. The answer can be within a paragraph, across paragraphs, or even across chapters and books.

3. *On My Own.* The answer is not in the text. Readers need to use their own ideas and experiences to answer the question.

4. *Author and Me.* The answer is not in the text. To answer the question, readers need to think about how the text and what they already know fit together. (Raphael, Highfield, & Au, 2006, pp. 23, 26)

Raphael and her colleagues describe the first two types as "In the Book" QARs. The second two are "In My Head" QARs.

Other researchers have validated Raphael's notion of QARs. Taking the time to acquaint students with question–answer relationships has been shown to help them answer a significantly larger percentage of comprehension questions (Benito, Foley, Lewis, & Prescott, 1993; Ezell, 1992; Tierney & Readence, 2005).

Student Predictions and Hypotheses

Posing questions prior to reading has the advantage of focusing students on specific aspects of content. Of course, this result can happen only if the students tacitly consent to use such questions to guide their comprehension. There is a danger that teacher-supplied questions may be ignored. In the next chapter, we will examine how reading guides can help ensure that prereading questions are taken seriously by requiring students to jot down answers as they read. For now, let's consider a more open-ended approach, one calculated to increase students' level of mental engagement. What if the teacher asks them to form predictions about what a reading selection will contain? Their focus, once they begin to read, will then be to test their predictions and learn why they were right or wrong.

Possible Sentences.   There are many ways of evoking predictions, and one of the cleverest is an approach called Possible Sentences (Moore & Moore, 1986). This technique blends technical vocabulary introduction with purpose setting and is excellent for content units (Stahl, 1999). It stresses clusters of related terms and the relationships among terms. The procedure is quite simple:

- Choose six to eight unfamiliar words from the new unit.
- Choose an additional four to six words likely to be familiar.
- Put these ten to twelve words on the board.
- Provide short definitions, drawing on student knowledge wherever possible.
- Ask students to think of sentences that use at least two of the words and that express ideas they think they may discover when they read.
- Write these sentences on the board as the students dictate them.
- Include both right and wrong guesses.
- Make sure every word is used in at least one sentence.
- When the students are finished providing sentences, ask them to read the material.
- Afterward, discuss the sentences on the board, noting whether each could be true, based now on the reading.
- If a sentence is true, leave it alone. If it is not, discuss how to modify it to make it true.

Stahl and Kapinus (1991) found that possible sentences improved both vocabulary knowledge and comprehension of material containing targeted words. In fact, it proved more effective than another very useful approach, semantic mapping.

Stating Objectives and Outcomes

One of the most direct ways to set purposes is to make clear to students precisely what they should know or be able to do once they have completed a selection. Consider the teacher about to assign the Pluto article, who says to students:

> After you've read, you should be able to describe the conditions on Pluto.

Naturally, the outcomes or objectives of reading can always be cast in question form and vice versa. Questions have the advantage of merging rather naturally into a postreading discussion. Instead of stating the outcome, the teacher might have asked students to read in order to answer this question:

> What are conditions like on Pluto?

Compare the two approaches. Do see any advantage of objectives over questions, or vice versa?

You've undoubtedly noticed our use of objectives as embedded purpose-setting devices in all the chapters you've read. How effective have they been for you? (Have you taken the time to read them?) Would secondary or middle-grade students be likely to read them? What if a teacher deliberately discussed such objectives before the students read? Would you predict that their comprehension would improve?

Graphic Organizers

In Chapter 6, we discussed how presenting new technical terms by means of graphic organizers can be an effective method of building prior knowledge. Graphic organizers also provide a means of setting purposes for reading. Students who are familiar with the nature of organizers from exposure to them in textbooks and discussions are in a position to produce organizers of their own. A purpose for reading can be to complete, or in some cases to construct, a graphic organizer. This approach can be very effective when several guidelines are observed:

1. Familiarize students with the nature of graphic organizers by introducing organizers frequently in your discussion of course material and by calling attention to the different types of organizers and their characteristics.

2. Suggest the three-step process for construction of a graphic organizer presented in Chapter 6. You will recall that these steps include (a) listing key terms, (b) identifying within the list clusters of closely related terms, and (c) designing a diagram that best predicts the relationship among the terms in a given cluster.

3. Do not begin by requiring students to follow this three-step process in its entirety. Instead provide them with the opportunity to complete graphic organizers by inserting terms at appropriate positions. As students acquire experience in completing the diagrams, present them with progressively more demanding tasks. Such a progression might proceed as follows:

   a. From a list, students select terms and write them into the appropriate positions within a partially drawn organizer.
   b. Without a list, students write terms into a partially drawn organizer, selecting them from the reading material in general.
   c. Students construct an organizer, given only a cluster of terms but no diagram.
   d. Students produce a viable organizer without the teacher's having specified which terms or the type of organizer.

The first three steps in this progression are illustrated in Figure 7.5, which is again based on our reading selection about the planet Pluto.

ConStruct. Vaughan (1982) has suggested a technique in which students with some familiarity with organizers read for the purpose of constructing a single, comprehensive organizer. In this process of *concept struct*uring (ConStruct), the students initially read rapidly, striving only to produce a sketchy, skeletal diagram that involves the main topic and major subtopics. The students read a second time (more carefully) with the goal of elaborating on this scant beginning. A much more detailed organizer results. After studying this diagram, the students read for a third time to clear up any remaining points of confusion. The ConStruct approach clearly requires that students be familiar with graphic organizers in advance, and Vaughan suggests modeling them before using ConStruct itself.

FIGURE 7.5

Three ways of implementing a timeline based on the Pluto passage

(a) The teacher instructs students to place the phrases below on the timeline.

Discovery of Pluto
Pluto's passage inside Neptune's orbit
Pluto's passage outside Neptune's orbit
Pluto's most recent close approach to the sun

| 1900 | '10 | '20 | '30 | '40 | '50 | '60 | '70 | '80 | '90 | 2000 | 2010 |

(b) The teacher lists the four events and instructs the students to create a timeline.

(c) The teacher instructs the students to create a timeline in which key events in Pluto's history are represented, but the teacher does not list these events.

Charts

A good approach to many factually rich reading selections is to provide students with a chart that requires them to categorize information they encounter while reading (McKenna, 2002). The teacher provides students with the structure of the chart, including column headings and, in some cases, the entire *first* column. The feature analysis chart can serve as a purpose-setting device as well as a means, discussed in Chapter 6, of presenting the terms in a prereading discussion. Figure 7.6 depicts how such a chart might be used to guide students through the Pluto selection. Note that the column headings are completely provided, and, in addition, the first column has been completed to further limit the students' focus as they read. Completing an example or two while explaining the chart to students can be helpful.

As in the case of graphic organizers, students will become accustomed to the nature of feature analysis charts when teachers make frequent use of them during the introduction of technical vocabulary. They should come to consider completing such charts while they read as a natural application of charting activities.

FIGURE 7.6

A feature analysis chart for a reading selection on Pluto

The following chart allows students to integrate information about Pluto with information previously learned about other planets.

Planets	Mainly gaseous	Larger than Earth	Has at least one moon	Has an atmosphere	Has rings	Nearer sun than Earth
Mercury						
Venus						
Earth						
Mars						
Jupiter						
Saturn						
Uranus						
Neptune						
Pluto						

A wide variety of charts is available, and feature analysis is only one of many possibilities. To illustrate the range of types, we have included a very simple T-chart in Figure 7.7, also based on the Pluto passage. Like the feature analysis chart, it requires higher-level thinking (inferential and critical). As with the construction of graphic organizers, the completion of charts helps to make reading an active process, one that engages students as they read.

Problem Solution

Providing students with the opportunity to apply what has been learned to the solution of a problem is a good way to direct comprehension toward a higher-level purpose. Dahlberg (1990) argues that students are already experienced problem solvers in out-of-school contexts and that teachers can and should tap their ability. Let's begin by differentiating between two types of problems useful for setting purposes.

One involves mathematics and science content designed to develop students' abilities to solve a particular kind of problem (e.g., solving a second-degree equation using the quadratic

FIGURE 7.7

A T-chart for a reading selection on Pluto

The teacher instructs students to read in order to complete the chart below.

Evidence that argues *against* the existence of life on Pluto	Evidence that argues *for* the existence of life on Pluto

formula or computing force vectors in beginning physics). This type of problem solving differs very little from the technique of merely making the objectives of a reading assignment clear in advance. That is, learning to solve problems of a particular kind is one type of objective that a teacher might specify prior to reading. Naturally, the material to be read focuses on problems of precisely this sort.

The second kind of problem-solving purpose is considerably different. It involves presenting students with a single, overarching problem that can be approached using the information acquired through reading. The selection to be read, however, may not directly focus on such problems. For example, the social studies teacher might assign students the task of creating a plan to contend with their community's air pollution problem. This teacher instructs the students to consider carefully the information acquired by reading a specific selection on air pollution together with information presented through class discussion and lecture. A math teacher might begin a trigonometry unit by providing students with a diagram of their school grounds complete with precise measurements and angles, suggesting to them the need for determining specific missing measurements. Their study of the trigonometry materials should eventually permit them to solve the myriad problems such a framework might provide. These are examples of what Dahlberg (1990) calls "real life problems" (p. 14), the sort most likely to motivate students by demonstrating how content relates to their lives. As a third example, consider again our Pluto selection. A science teacher might provide the following task to students prior to reading:

> Imagine that you are assigned the task of designing a space suit for use on a mission to Pluto. Begin your assignment by reading the selection to discover what conditions are like there. Then describe the special characteristics your suit might need to possess.

Summary Writing

Reading for the purpose of later composing a summary of what is read has a number of distinct advantages. It stresses the interconnectedness of reading and writing. It gives students the opportunity to reconsider content and to reorder it within their own thinking. It also compels students to identify the most important ideas contained in a reading selection. In fact, the most important comprehension skill underlying the ability to summarize is the capacity to distinguish more important from less important information. Finally, summarization is suitable for use with any kind of prose material, expository or narrative. It is perhaps an especially useful device with (1) selections containing a large amount of detailed, though not always highly pertinent, information and (2) narrative selections that involve extremely complex sequences of events (see Coffman, 1994).

It is my ambition to say in ten sentences what everyone else says in a whole book.
FRIEDRICH NIETZSCHE

Hill (1991) has suggested that students often find it more difficult to write summaries of expository material (such as textbook chapters) than of narrative selections. Teachers might be wise to begin summary writing with material organized chronologically (e.g., historical accounts and descriptions of processes). In Chapter 11, we specifically describe a writing activity aimed at summarizing the steps of a process.

Writing good summaries is usually an acquired skill, however, and some direct instruction may be needed. Two recommendations for guiding students in writing summaries have been examined in recent years: (1) a "chaining" approach and (2) a guided approach. Both have proved effective.

In the first approach to expository summaries, the teacher suggests that students write a single summarizing sentence for each section of the assigned reading selection. For example, for a textbook chapter that is divided by a number of subheads, the students might compose one sentence per subsection. The resulting summary is the "chaining" together of these summarizing sentences. Miller and McKenna (1989) have suggested the additional step of segmenting the resulting summary into paragraphs based on major chapter sections. Students also write a topic sentence for each of these paragraphs. Cunningham (1982) conducted a study in which he found that this technique significantly enchanced the comprehension of fourth graders.

The second approach to teaching students how to summarize involves providing them with general guidelines. Bean and Steenwyk (1984) found that instruction based on the following six rules (originally suggested by Kintsch and van Dijk, 1978) resulted in significantly better products than those produced by students who had not been taught the rules:

1. Delete unnecessary and trivial material.
2. Delete material that is important but redundant.
3. Substitute a higher-order term for a list of terms.
4. Substitute a higher-order term for components of an action or process.
5. Select and incorporate topic sentences.
6. Where there are no topic sentences, write them.

One caution about the use of summary writing as a purpose-setting technique is that it tends to focus the attention of students on the most important information they encounter. Not surprisingly, Rinehart, Stahl, and Erickson (1986) found that comprehension of details was not enhanced through summary writing. Whenever a selection presents a large amount of factual information, teachers might consider using summarization as a postreading activity and relying on other techniques to ensure that comprehension is adequately detailed. For this reason, we return to the subject of summary writing in Chapter 11. A further limitation is that summary writing is teacher directed despite its apparent open-endedness.

Outlining

When students read for the purpose of outlining a selection, two important benefits can result (Fernandez, 1998; Kneale, 1998). One is that the *product* they produce—the outline itself—can have later usefulness as a review guide. The other is that the *process* of outlining as they read encourages them to see important relationships that exist among ideas. Disadvantages of outlining are that it can be highly tedious and that many materials are not amenable to outlining (such as narratives and loosely structured nonfiction).

Like summarizing, outlining may require some direct attention from teachers if students are to engage in it successfully. Because one of the most important skills underlying successful outlining is the classification of concepts into categories and subcategories, it is advisable to precede any use of outlining with practice in such vocabulary techniques as List-Group-Label and nested categorizing (presented in Chapter 11). These techniques should adequately familiarize students with the logic skills needed in outlining. Once students are familiar with the notion of subcategorizing ideas, the teacher can provide sample outlines. These are complete, model outlines that represent the content of a given selection. For example, after students have completed a textbook chapter, the teacher might distribute an outline of its content, pointing out key characteristics of the outline and advising students to keep it as a review aid. The teacher should then progress toward providing students with incomplete outlines prior to reading—outlines in which the innermost entries are deleted and marked only with appropriate letters or numbers. These "shells" have most of the entries intact but omit certain details that the students must identify and insert. Figure 7.8 provides an example based on the Pluto selection in Figure 7.2.

FIGURE 7.8

Portion of a shell outline for the Pluto passage

   I. **Background**
       A. Location:
       B. Features:
  II. **History**
       A. Discovery:
       B. Key Events:
 III. **Sources of Information**
       A. Earth-based:
       B. Next step:

In this example, colons indicate points at which students should enter information. The space provided by the teacher should correspond to what the students are expected to record.

Some authorities argue that the final goal of using outlining as a purpose-setting technique is to enable the student to outline a selection without the assistance of a shell. Our opinion is that this goal may be unrealistic for many students, and it is certainly problematic with respect to many of the reading materials they are apt to encounter. We believe it is nearly always better to provide a partially completed shell outline. This practice affords students a degree of structure, content, and focus as they read. Such a technique is similar to providing students with a chart or incomplete graphic organizer for purpose setting. It is also similar to Lazarus's idea of *guided notes* (Lazarus, 1988, 1989, 1991, 1993, 1996; Lazarus & McKenna, 1991) and to the notion of reading guides, techniques we will explore in Chapter 8.

Varying and Combining Techniques

Being able to use a variety of purpose-setting techniques provides four powerful advantages. First, it allows teachers to introduce elements of novelty and variety that are now well recognized as ingredients of effective instruction. Second, teachers can match the type of technique to the nature of the material to be read. Third, they can combine two or more techniques for use with the same reading assignment. Finally, from exposure to a variety of techniques, students not only learn that reading should be purposeful but they also acquire an array of methods for making it so. Eventually, they can use these methods independently.

In the next chapter, we examine ways in which purpose-setting techniques can be varied and combined to produce content literacy guides. These devices focus students' attention on the most important aspects of content, make reading an active rather than a passive process, integrate writing and reading, lead to the production of a useful review guide, and provide students with a resource to assist them in responding during class discussions. Such guides are based entirely on the various approaches to purpose setting described in this chapter.

SUMMARY

The most effective reading is purposeful. Good readers have relatively clear notions of what they hope to accomplish through reading. Good teachers therefore either provide students with specific purposes prior to an assignment or help them establish their own purposes. A variety of techniques is available for purpose setting, and in some the teacher plays a more direct role than in others. The degree to which the teacher directs student purposes depends both on the nature of the material and on the philosophy of the teacher.

Prereading questions are among the most versatile devices for setting purposes. They are well suited to developing multiple levels of comprehension (literal, inferential, and critical); they are useful with virtually any reading selection; they are often embedded by textbook authors; and they can be posed by students as well as teachers.

Numerous alternatives to prereading questions are available. Teachers can lead students to form predictions, or hypotheses, that they will then "test" by reading. This approach is less teacher centered than many but is not equally useful with all assignments. In contrast, teachers can simply specify in advance the objectives, or outcomes, of reading. This approach is highly teacher directed and obviously well geared to explicit teaching.

Graphic organizers and charts provide students with the task of interpreting, classifying, and recording information as they read. In the former, they complete or construct a diagram; in the latter, they organize information in tabular form, given the headings of columns and the nature of rows. These techniques can be more or less teacher directed as desired.

Three relatively teacher-centered approaches have been used successfully in recent years. Providing students with problems to be solved is a traditional mainstay of math and science instruction but can be extended to many disciplines with a little creativity. Summary writing encourages students to integrate content and identify its most important components. Outlining has the advantage of giving students a useful review guide. It works best when the teacher provides an unfinished, or "shell," outline to be completed by students during reading.

This wide variety of techniques allows teachers to match method with materials and to combine approaches for use with the same reading selection. Exposure to a range of purpose-setting techniques also serves to model for students how they can make reading more deliberately purposeful as they work independently.

Getting Involved

1. Group achievement tests of reading comprehension usually present students with short passages followed by questions. Nearly all of these questions are either literal or inferential. Speculate about why this policy is so common.

2. Which method of setting purposes seems best matched to your teaching style and content? Would you consider adopting a variety of approaches?

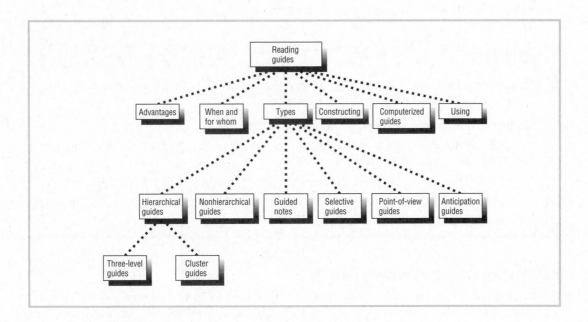

CHAPTER 8

Reading Guides

*The whole art of teaching is only the art of awakening the natural curiosity
of young minds for the purpose of satisfying it afterwards.*

—Anatole France

Imagine that you have arranged a field trip to a large national museum associated with your
content area. Because the trip will afford your students a special opportunity to enhance
their understanding of the subject, you want to do everything possible to ensure that their
time will be well spent. You might begin by contacting the museum far in advance to acquire
information about exhibits, the building's floor plan, and so on. You may then share this
information with your students to acquaint them with what they can expect to find once
they enter the facility. When the day of the trip arrives and you enter the museum with your
class, you discover that for a small fee, tour guides are available to assist with your visit.
While you personally prefer to explore museums on your own, you decide that a certain
amount of guidance may be in the best interests of your students.

Once the tour begins, you become convinced that you made the correct decision. The
guide leads your students along a preplanned route and stops at key points of interest.
During each stop, the guide offers additional information about the exhibits and calls the

students' attention to interesting and important features. Sometimes the guide raises questions or elicits student reactions in other ways.

Now consider the effect of not hiring a tour guide. Do you think that simply "turning the students loose" in the museum would produce results comparable to a guided situation? It is true that some of your more capable students would, like yourself, fare well in such circumstances. For most, however, the museum experience would likely be a random, structureless walk during which much is missed and much more is misunderstood. We suspect that even your more capable students would not benefit to the same degree without a guide.

Our museum analogy closely parallels the situation in which a content area reading selection is assigned. Without guidance, students may wander rudderless through a sea of print, unable to distinguish what is important from what is not and inadequately comprehending its meaning.

Objectives

This chapter introduces methods of guiding your students through assigned reading. When you have completed it, you should be able to

1. list the key advantages of using guides in written form;
2. defend the use of guides for a wide range of reading selections and for students of high reading ability as well as weaker readers;
3. describe the major types of guides and identify their advantages and potential drawbacks;
4. outline the steps of constructing a guide;
5. indicate how such guides are best employed in the classroom.

Advantages of a Written Guide

We concluded the last chapter by suggesting several benefits of providing students with a reading guide. It's true that some purpose-setting techniques can be used orally, such as posing key questions prior to reading. We argue, however, that the advantages of a written format are so persuasive that written guides should easily be the method of first choice. Let's reexamine the benefits in more detail.

First, guides help students focus their attention on important aspects of content. A written format ensures that this focusing occurs at the appropriate time in their reading. The teacher who orally poses a number of questions before students read risks their forgetting one or more of these questions when they reach the appropriate portions of the assigned reading selection. If, on the other hand, the teacher provides these same questions in written form, along with page numbers of the material to which they relate, the student is in a position to reference each question at precisely the moment it will do the most good as a purpose-setting device.

Second, guides make the reading process active rather than passive (Herber, 1978). Suddenly, reading is more than turning pages until the last is reached. The immediate goal is to consult the guide and respond to it—in writing. When reading is made *physically* active, chances are good that it will become *mentally* active as well. No longer can students engage in silent decoding without giving adequate thought to the ideas they encounter, for this is merely the illusion of reading. The guide prompts such thinking at the moment it is most opportune.

Third, responding to guides causes students to *translate* the material into their own words, phrases, and sentences. The process of translation is important in allowing the ideas to become those of the student rather than the author's alone (Pearson & Fielding, 1991). The more that guides can cause this translation to occur, the more successful they will be.

Fourth, guides help integrate reading and writing. We have already described how the use of literacy processes complement one another as the student learns from written materials. Reading provides new information; writing enables students to organize, refine, and extend their understanding of what they have read. Guides permit these processes to work simultaneously, establishing a synthesis that tends to be more productive than postponing all writing activities until after the students finish reading.

Fifth, written guides and students' responses to them produce a useful tool for review. In studying for tests, students with guides will have far more tangible assistance than the help available from the text itself, which they may have comprehended poorly to begin with. Moreover, well-constructed literacy guides serve as note-taking models that students may come to emulate when reading on their own.

Sixth, the completed guide provides students with a valuable discussion aid. Few experiences are as disconcerting for teachers as asking questions that students cannot answer. We are not suggesting that reading guides will completely remedy this problem, but there is no doubt that post-reading discussions will generally be smoother, quicker, and far less frustrating for students and teachers alike when students have completed reading guides. The guide amounts to a blueprint of the ensuing discussion. While postreading talk may occasionally digress, the guide itself serves as the primary source of questions. Regular use of guides will rapidly instill in students an expectation that both discussion and examinations will follow the guides and that they are therefore well worth attending to while reading.

Seventh, a compelling body of research evidence now documents the effectiveness of guides in improving students' comprehension of assigned reading (McKenna, Davis, & Franks, 2003; Tierney & Readence, 2005; Wood, Lapp, & Flood, 1992). In short, guides work!

When Should Reading Guides Be Used?

Vacca & Vacca (2004) have suggested that reading guides be used only with unusually difficult reading selections. They have argued that adequate comprehension will in most cases result when teachers take the trouble to prepare students orally for a reading selection. We strenuously disagree with this reasoning. It may be true that comprehension will be reasonably good without guides for most students and most selections. However, there is now ample evidence that comprehension is better for students who make use of guides. Armstrong, Patberg, and Dewitz (1988, 1989) observed not only superior comprehension, but also better transfer of learned strategies to new material among students who had used literacy guides. These results are hardly surprising, since the advantages we have just discussed will always be present regardless of a selection's difficulty.

Another limitation often ascribed to reading guides is that they are useful primarily for poor readers. It is probably natural for teachers (who tend to be good readers) to infer that because they can comprehend well without guides their better students also don't need them. These teachers tend to forget, however, that even their best students are not likely to be as sophisticated as they are in reading, especially when selections are drawn from the area of the teacher's greatest expertise.

There is now evidence that better students may actually benefit the most from reading guides. Armstrong et al. (1988) found greater comprehension gains for good readers using guides than for poor readers also using guides. This research finding tends to confirm Savage's (1983) recommendation that guides be used with gifted students.

Finally, a long-standing assumption concerning guides is that they are unsuitable for children prior to middle school. A recent Eisenhower research project, however, revealed that even third graders could respond well to guides and that their overall ability to read nonfiction improved compared with children who did not use guides (McKenna, Davis, & Franks, 2003). These results are very much in line with Chall's stages of reading development (1983/1996), discussed in Chapter 2. Third grade is a pivotal year, when most children are developmentally ready to learn through text. Providing support through reading guides is an effective way to help them along this path.

In summary, the three long-prevailing reservations about using reading guides appear to be myths. One is that they are useful only with difficult selections. Another is that they are helpful only to poorer readers. A third limits their use to the middle and secondary grades. The evidence suggests that guides are a powerful tool for a wide range of readers and a wide variety of selections. We now look at various types of guides in common use. As you read about them, it is important for you to consider each type in relation to your own content area. Consciously look for those you feel are most suitable to the sorts of material you intend to assign.

Types of Guides

Reading guides come in an assortment of shapes and sizes. This diversity is natural since written materials vary considerably and the type of assistance students may need will vary also. Some formats are better researched than others and some have a better track record in content classrooms. Below, we examine the most common types together with one or two promising innovations.

Hierarchical Guides

In 1969, Earle suggested a format designed to lead students through three levels of mental processing as they read. His three-level guides consisted first of questions of a literal nature, having factual, explicitly stated answers. Next came a series of inferential questions that required students to arrive at logical conclusions based on stated facts. The final set of questions required students to apply and interpret what they had read. Herber (1978) and later Vacca and Vacca (2004) have subsequently urged content teachers to make use of three-level guides. An example of such a guide, which Armstrong et al. (1988) call a hierarchical guide, appears in Figure 8.1, for use with the hurricane passage (see Figure 5.3, page 70).

The rationale of the three-level guide is appealing. Presumably, it takes students through the proper process of critical reading, namely, by starting with stated facts, inferring other facts, and arriving at judgments and applications. The main difficulty with such guides is that efforts to validate them through research have as yet been disappointing. While the reasons for their failure are not entirely understood, one problem may be that students must answer every literal-level question first before answering a single higher-order question. Consequently, to make an inference based on the first subsection of a textbook chapter, students must wait until they have completed the entire chapter. In our view, timing is a crucial difficulty with the traditional three-level guide and may in some cases actually hinder higher-level thinking.

Nonhierarchical Guides

Armstrong et al. (1988) tested an alternative to the three-level guide, one in which questions at various levels were intermingled. This nonhierarchical guide follows the reading selection from

FIGURE 8.1

A hierarchical guide for the hurricane selection in Figure 5.3

Part 1. *As you read the selection on hurricanes, answer these questions.*

True or False?

A hurricane can cause a tornado._____

People who live away from the coast are safe from hurricanes._____

Average number of hurricanes per year in the Atlantic, Caribbean, and Gulf:_____

What makes hurricanes hard to predict?_____

Where do hurricanes get their power?_____

When they are in the tropics, hurricanes are steered by winds from what direction?

_____

Hurricane season   Starts:_____

                          Ends: _____

In your own words, tell the three conditions needed for a hurricane to form:

1.

2.

3.

The strongest winds are in the

_____ eye

_____ eyewall

_____ bands of thunderstorms

How high is the top of the eyewall?_____

FIGURE 8.1 (*continued*)

A hierarchical guide for the hurricane selection in Figure 5.3

Part 2. *Now that you know some of the facts about hurricanes, answer these questions.*
Look back at the passage as you work.
Use the sidebar to complete this chart:

	Maximum Sustained Winds	
Type of Storm	**Lowest mph**	**Highest mph**
Tropical Depression	0	
Tropical Storm		73
Hurricane		

Check the agency that is most important *before* a hurricane strikes.

_____ American Red Cross

_____ NOAA

_____ FEMA

A hurricane that forms in the Pacific is called a(n)_____.

How would tropical storms be rated on the Saffir-Simpson Scale?

(Warning! Trick question!)

A hurricane with maximum sustained winds of 120 mph would be what category?

Why do hurricanes not form in winter?_____

How many months does the hurricane season last?_____

Which month is probably the worst for hurricanes?_____

Look at the satellite photo. If you were directly above the eye of a hurricane, could you see the ocean?_____

Part 3. *Now you're ready to form some opinions about hurricanes.*
In your opinion, why aren't homes along the coast simply built to be hurricane proof?

In your opinion, why do think there is no Category 6?

In your opinion, how could a building be designed to withstand a Category 5 hurricane? Offer a few ideas.

If you were in a boat, do you think you could stay safe by remaining in the eye? Why or why not?

start to finish. The teacher writes questions without concern for their level and arranges them in the order in which students will encounter the appropriate portions of the selection. Contrast the nonhierarchical guide depicted in Figure 8.2, also for the hurricane passage, with the hierarchical approach represented in Figure 8.1.

Nonhierarchical guides have the advantage of positioning questions at the points where they are most answerable. Teachers merely concern themselves with what is important and leave the issue of levels to take care of itself. Note how the teacher is able to add subheadings and page numbers so that the students can keep their place as they read the passage. It would be awkward to supply these road signs in a hierarchical guide.

FIGURE 8.2

A nonhierarchical guide for the hurricane selection in Figure 5.3

WHAT IS A HURRICANE?

True or False?

A hurricane can cause a tornado._____

People who live away from the coast are safe from hurricanes._____

Use the sidebar to complete this chart:

| Type of Storm | Maximum Sustained Winds | |
	Lowest mph	Highest mph
Tropical Depression	0	
Tropical Storm		73
Hurricane		

Average number of hurricanes per year in the Atlantic, Caribbean, and Gulf: _____

What makes hurricanes hard to predict?_____

Check the agency that is most important *before* a hurricane strikes.

_____ American Red Cross

_____ NOAA

_____ FEMA

In your opinion, why aren't homes along the coast simply built to be hurricane proof?

SAFFIR-SIMPSON HURRICANE SCALE

A hurricane that forms in the Pacific is called a(n)_____.

How would tropical storms be rated on the Saffir-Simpson Scale?

(Warning! Trick question!)

A hurricane with maximum sustained winds of 120 mph would be what category?_____

In your opinion, why do think there is no Category 6?

In your opinion, how could a building be designed to withstand a Category 5 hurricane? Offer a few ideas.

FIGURE 8.2 (*continued*)

A nonhierarchical guide for the hurricane selection in Figure 5.3

HOW HURRICANES FORM BREEDING GROUNDS

Where do hurricanes get their power?_____

Why do hurricanes not form in winter?_____

When they are in the tropics, hurricanes are steered by winds from what direction?_____

Hurricane season   Starts: _____

                                   Ends: _____

How many months does the hurricane season last?_____

Which month is probably the worst for hurricanes?_____

Look at the satellite photo. If you were directly above the eye of a hurricane, could you see the ocean?_____

Storm Structure

In your own words, tell the three conditions needed for a hurricane to form:

1. _____

2. _____

3. _____

The strongest winds are in the

_____ eye

_____ eyewall

_____ bands of thunderstorms

How high is the top of the eyewall?_____

If you were in a boat, do you think you could stay safe by remaining in the eye? Why or why not?

Selective Guides

Cunningham and Shablak (1975) developed a guide that not only focuses attention on elements a teacher feels are important but actually encourages students to skim or skip other portions of a selection. This approach may remind you of Samuel Johnson's remark, quoted in Chapter 7, that he seldom read every word contained in a book. The rationale behind selective guides is the same as Johnson's: All parts of a reading assignment may not deserve equal attention and concentration. By means of a selective guide, the teacher makes these decisions for students in advance, and Cunningham and Shablak reasoned that repeated use of such guides would encourage students to become more flexible and selective readers by themselves.

Selective guides address two of the recurrent problems of textbook reading assignments. One is that readability tends to fluctuate among chapters and even among sections of the same chapter. The other is that the writing is often dense with facts, not all of which are vital to an understanding of the content. Selective guides aid students in selecting the wheat and ignoring the chaff. Teachers must begin by closely examining the selection to be assigned. They must first decide what students should *know* after completing the assignment by identifying important ideas, concepts, and supporting details. They must then decide what students can be expected to *do* as well as identify the information needed to do it. The result is a blend of questions, comments, and suggestions. Tierney and Readence (2005, p. 422) offered these examples of the kinds of remarks a teacher might include in a selective guide. Some focus thinking on key ideas.

■ P. 93, paragraphs 3–6. Pay special attention to this section. Why do you think Hunter acted in this manner? We will discuss your ideas later in class.

> We are too civil to books. For a few golden sentences we will turn over and actually read a volume of four or five hundred pages.
>
> RALPH WALDO EMERSON

- P. 94, subtopic in boldface print at top of page. See if you can rewrite the topic to form a question. Now read the information under the subtopic just to answer the question. You should pick up the five ideas very quickly. Jot down your answers in the space provided below.
- P. 94, picture. What appears to be the reaction of the crowd? Now read the fifth paragraph on this page to find out why they are reacting as they are.
- P. 95, paragraphs 5–8. Read this section very carefully. The order of the events is very important and you will want to remember this information for our quiz.

Other remarks actually guide the student in deemphasizing or ignoring material:

- P. 179, all of column 1. The author has provided us with some interesting information here, but it is not important for us to remember. You may want to skim over it and move on to the second column.
- Pp. 180–181. These pages describe a fictitious family who lived during the Civil War. You may skip this section because we will learn about the lifestyles of the time through films, other readings, and class discussions.
- Pp. 221–222. Recent discoveries in science have improved the information contained on these pages. I will discuss this information with you in class. Now move on to page 223.

Note how the last three examples encourage students to skip and skim particular sections of the assignment.

Vacca and Vacca (2004) have suggested that content teachers gradually wean students away from selective guides. Our belief is that there is little reason to do so. Molding students into independent readers is not likely to result from gradually reducing the support that guides offer for a single textbook. A sizable advantage in prior knowledge of content will always place the teacher in the better position to judge what should be skimmed and what should be read with deliberate care.

In Chapter 5, we discussed how tape-recording textbook material can involve informing the student to skip over less important portions of an assignment. A selective guide accomplishes the same result.

Point-of-View Guides

Wood (1988) introduced a new type of guide designed to assist middle-level students with textbook assignments. Her point-of-view guide uses questions in an interview format "to allow students to experience events from alternative perspectives" (p. 913). A variety of interview questions pushes the student to comprehend at more than one level of thought. The teacher begins

Assisting Students with Special Needs

Guided Notes

Questions provide an effective format for reading guides, but they are not the only format. Lazarus (1988, 1993) developed an approach called guided notes, which consists of an incomplete outline of the material. Originally designed for use with lectures, this technique required teachers to prepare a skeleton outline of the material they wished to present. Enough space was available for students to fill in the outline as the teacher spoke. Lazarus (1993) observed remarkable successes using guided notes with mildly learning-disabled students.

While guided notes can be an effective device for use during lectures, modifying the technique for reading selections is a simple matter. Subheads provide a natural basis for the skeletal framework, but it is probably a good idea to go one step further and indicate the sorts of information and conclusions students should derive from within each subsection. Even though guided notes are not based on questions, the resulting product is nevertheless a useful tool during postreading discussions. In fact, Lazarus and McKenna (1991) found that a combination of guided notes and subsequent review produced the best results. Figure 8.3 provides an example of guided notes applied to the selection on the hurricane presented in Chapter 5 (Figure 5.3). Note how this example differs slightly from the simpler outlining approach (Figure 7.8) by providing additional suggestions about what the student should write. Take a moment to contrast the two examples.

FIGURE 8.3

Portion of a guided notes guide for the hurricane selection in Figure 5.3

History
> *Hunraken:*
> *Huracan:*

Storms
> Tropical Depression:
> Tropical Storm:
> Hurricane:

Threats from tropical depressions and storms:
1.
2.
3.

by choosing an appropriate perspective on the material the students will read. In the example presented in Figure 8.4, we chose the perspective of a hurricane forecaster. The viewpoint a teacher selects, however, might be a real person. We might have chosen the governor of a threatened state, for instance.

The point-of-view guide offers several advantages that we feel make it useful, even with students above the middle grades. First, it encourages writing about what is read, sometimes at length. Second, Wood's experiences reveal that students feel less pressure to use "textbook language." They feel freer to reexpress content in their own words. Third, the point-of-view guide seems applicable to a variety of content subjects. As Wood observes, "In literature students

FIGURE 8.4

Portion of a point-of-view guide for the hurricane selection in Figure 5.3

Imagine that you are a hurricane forecaster. As you read, answer these questions the way you think he or she might have answered them.

WHAT IS A HURRICANE?

Two storms are developing at about the same distance from the United States. One is Tropical Depression Abe and the other is Tropical Storm Bess. Which one will you monitor more closely and why?

As a hurricane approaches, would you issue a warning to people who live inland, away from the coast? Why or why not?

In May, the head of the Red Cross calls you. She asks you how many hurricanes her volunteers should prepare for in the coming season. What do you tell her?

can assume the role of various characters as they react to events in a story. In science, they can describe the process of photosynthesis from the perspective of a plant or the act of locomotion from the perspective of an amoeba" (p. 915). Fourth, such guides encourage perspective taking— seeing issues from another's viewpoint. Gardner and Smith (1987) observed that this ability is related to inferential comprehension. Point-of-view guides may therefore offer the bonus of enhancing student inferences.

Anticipation Guides

Readence, Bean, and Baldwin (1981) developed a very different kind of guide especially for use with materials that involve controversy or factual misunderstanding. Their anticipation guide consists of a series of statements about the material covered by the selection. Students read the statements prior to the selection and indicate whether they agree or disagree with each. The teacher and the class openly discuss the statements, but the teacher refrains from suggesting responses. The rationale of the anticipation guide is simple: The statements serve to activate appropriate prior knowledge, while a student's responses provide hypotheses to be tested through reading.

Figure 8.5 shows an example of an anticipation guide based on the hurricane passage from Chapter 5. This particular illustration is a modification of the basic idea and is sometimes called an anticipation-reaction guide. Students place a check mark in the first column when they agree with the statement prior to reading. They place a check mark in the second column if they *still* agree with the statement after they have finished reading.

Duffelmeyer (1994) warns that in order for anticipation guides to be effective, the statements they contain must be carefully worded. Good statements, he stresses, should have three characteristics: (1) they must center on key ideas, not details; (2) they must activate and draw on prior knowledge; and (3) they must *challenge* students' existing beliefs. He offers four steps leading to an effective anticipation guide:

1. Identify the major ideas presented in the material to be read.
2. Consider what beliefs your students are likely to have.
3. Create statements that elicit those beliefs.
4. Arrange the statements in a manner that requires a positive or negative response.

We have tried to follow Duffelmeyer's advice when we wrote the statements in Figure 8.5. We were especially interested in statements that might run contrary to a student's preexisting beliefs or to "common sense."

FIGURE 8.5

Example of an anticipation-reaction guide for the hurricane selection in Figure 5.3

The teacher instructs the students to read each statement in advance and to place a check in the Before column if they agree with it. After they read, students are asked to return to the guide and put a check in the After column for each statement they still support.

Before	After	
_____	_____	1. The word *hurricane* comes from the name of an evil god.
_____	_____	2. People who live away from the coast are safe from hurricanes.
_____	_____	3. A hurricane is a cyclone.
_____	_____	4. The greatest threat of a tropical storm is high winds.
_____	_____	5. A "super typhoon" can never strike Florida.
_____	_____	6. A hurricane could strike the United States on Thanksgiving Day.
_____	_____	7. It is very violent inside the eye of a hurricane.

Constructing a Reading Guide

Our discussion of various formats for reading guides should in no way limit your thinking about how to construct them. In fact, there is no real limit to the number of formats possible, and Wood et al. (1992) provide an excellent resource for additional blueprints for developing guides. The reading selection itself should always be the major factor in developing a guide. Rather than use one of these formats, you may wish to improvise a unique format. You can use any of the purpose-setting devices discussed in Chapter 7—including questions, charts, graphic organizers, problems, and the like—to develop a guide. These hybrid guides are ideally suited to the reading selections they cover. The key to constructing them is to be familiar with a wide variety of purpose-setting techniques.

Figure 8.2 is actually a hybrid, containing several types of purpose-setting techniques. They include literal, inferential, and critical questions to answer, a chart to complete, true/false statements to judge, checklists to evaluate, and a list to compile. We might have combined techniques still further by merging Figures 8.2 and 8.5. That is, we might have begun with an anticipation-reaction guide and then proceeded to cover the selection! Constructing a good guide is a truly creative process.

We offer the following suggestions for constructing a reading guide that will effectively focus attention and enhance comprehension as students read. The first four suggestions come from Earle (1969) in an early discussion of study guides.

1. *Analyze the material.* Read the selection carefully to decide which information to emphasize. Ask yourself what thought processes students will need to use as they read. For example, will they need to classify information into categories? If so, the completion of a chart may be an effective format for a guide. Will they need to understand the relationships among clusters of concepts? In this case, the completion or construction of a graphic organizer may be warranted. Do they need to be able to recall detailed factual information? Guided notes may be indicated. Do they need to arrive at inferences based on the factual information presented? Here, question clusters proceeding from literal to inferential thinking would be ideal.

2. *Don't overcrowd the print.* A page teeming with type may overwhelm some students, particularly weaker readers. Effective guides contain plenty of white space, inviting the students to make notes. The best guides are friendly aids, not laborious appendages that simply add to the total reading assignment.

3. *Make the guide interesting.* There is no reason a guide should not motivate as well as assist. Use clear and considerate wordings. Rely on your own background knowledge to add an occasional (though brief) interesting tidbit or sidelight. From time to time, you might also include a little cheerleading ("We're about to wrap this up," "You're doing great—only two more sections," etc.).

4. *Review your own purposes.* When you have finished the guide, read it over to ensure that it captures your own instructional objectives. Ask yourself whether students who successfully complete the guide will have the knowledge and skills that the reading and writing activities should give them. Be prepared to modify the guide whenever you are not satisfied.

5. *Use word processing to prepare the guide.* Like any writing product, the best reading guides are not first drafts. Word processing tends to make revisions relatively painless. Because some of your best ideas for revision will come as a result of actually using the guide with students, it is important to keep your thoughts about a guide as fluid as possible so that changes can easily be made long after the guide is initially printed. Using a word processor helps to keep your thinking flexible.

6. *Include page numbers or subheads.* Students must know how each part of a guide relates to the reading selection. You can make this relationship clear by indicating the page numbers or subsections to which questions, charts, and so forth refer. Providing this information helps ensure that students will read and complete each section of a guide as they encounter the corresponding portion of the selection rather than read the entire guide in advance.

7. *Label the thinking skills students will need.* When a guide consists of questions, consider labeling them according to the level of comprehension they require (literal, inferential, and so forth). In other cases, make sure to emphasize the skill in the instructions to the student. You might precede a chart with instructions like these: "In this section, be on the lookout for ways in which igneous, sedimentary, and metamorphic rocks are different. Classify them by putting a check mark in the chart when you find one of the characteristics listed."

8. *Include comprehension aids.* Some of the formats we've discussed, such as the selective reading guide, incorporate help with possible comprehension problems. We suggest that the best guides anticipate possible difficulties. That is, they should do more than set purposes; they should also assist students through potential pitfalls so they can actually accomplish the purposes. This assistance might include the following:

- Quick definitions or synonyms for key terms
- Bridging comments (for example, "This is like the example we read about in Chapter 2")
- Clarifying comments that might paraphrase or summarize difficult passages
- Indications of material that is extremely important
- Indications of material that may be skipped or skimmed

9. *Include questions that encourage students to think carefully about the content.* Fordham (2006) suggests that teachers must learn to distinguish between questions that merely assess comprehension and those that help students think through content. For example, a question might prompt a student to link an idea expressed in one paragraph to one that was expressed in a previous paragraph. Such questions are ideally placed *during* rather than *after* reading, and a guide can position them at just the right spot.

Computerizing Reading Guides and Units

In Chapter 5, we introduced the idea of hypermedia, a nonlinear arrangement of reading materials and other media ideally suited to computer presentation. Dillner (1993–1994) describes how an American history teacher constructed a hypermedia unit for the Bill of Rights to complement the textbook treatment of the same topic. Dillner's pioneering work can be replicated far more easily today with authoring software such as Inspiration and Kidspiration.

This application of hypermedia to content materials suggests a wide range of possible applications. For example, the text itself might be incorporated into the computerized unit. If this were done, the students might toggle back and forth between the guide and the material. The textbook content might also be interwoven with other selections, allowing students to explore subtopics in more detail, explore other writers' perspectives, or access simplified treatments. Involving students in the development of units as a postreading activity is another possibility of proven effectiveness (Reinking & Watkins, 2000). The creativity of the teacher is apparently the only limit on what can be achieved.

Using Reading Guides

There is more to using a reading guide than simply distributing it—construction is only half the job. Begin with a final check of its adequacy by filling one out yourself. This exercise may alert you to important aspects of a selection that the guide may have ignored. It will also provide you with a convenient reference when conducting the postreading discussion. If you have produced the guide on a word processor, you can easily correct those sections where too much or too little space is available.

Guides and Comprehension Monitoring

An ample body of research informs us that good readers constantly monitor their own comprehension as they read (Paris, Wasik, & Turner, 1991). When a sentence or paragraph does not make sense, they reread to discover the source of the difficulty. When textual information jars their prior understanding of a topic, they consciously reason the matter through. When their purposes for reading are not being met, they ask why and seek ways of meeting these purposes.

Reading guides facilitate the process of comprehension monitoring. Because they require written responses, students cannot proceed until they have fashioned an acceptable response to each task the guide presents—or at least until they *realize* they have been unable to do so. In this sense, guides model for students the very processes that mature readers use to check their understanding as they read. Teachers must make this fact clear to students. They must inform them that this is the manner in which effective reading should work and that students should endeavor to check their understanding whenever they read.

Using Guides from Day to Day

Once students become familiar with reading guides, do not assume that no introduction is necessary. Always take a few moments to walk the students through a new guide. You might undertake this as part of a chapter walk-through, as discussed in Chapter 5. When the time for discussion comes, ask the students to place the completed guide on their desks and to refer to it as necessary when responding. By using the guide as a blueprint for your postreading discussion, you will reinforce for your students the expectation that completing it has benefits. Once the discussion is over, encourage students to keep the guide as an aid to review. You can reinforce this suggestion by basing examinations, in whole or in part, on the content of completed guides. Other ways to encourage students to complete guides include (1) assigning grades occasionally to the guides themselves and (2) administering tests during which the guides may be used (open-note tests).

Finally, be reflective. During class discussions be attentive to possible deficiencies, or "bugs," in your guides. Look on each discussion as a field test of the reading guide, and be prepared to revise it when you discover problems. Having the guide on a word processor simplifies the procedure.

> To the list of basic purpose-setting devices presented in Chapter 7, we can now add another: assigning students the task of constructing a reading guide or of modifying, refining, or critiquing one that you provide. To do so, they would of course need to be fairly familiar with guides of various types.

Guides and Cooperative Learning

Cooperative learning involves placing students in groups that work collaboratively to achieve common goals. An underlying idea is that cooperation is healthier and more productive than the competition that individual work may foster. Research on cooperative learning has been encouraging with respect both to students' achievement and to their growth in social skills and attitudes (Slavin, 1988, 1989–1990). However, content area teachers in the secondary grades are often reluctant to experiment with the approach, perhaps because it differs so markedly from the lecture-oriented instruction they find more familiar.

Reading guides provide an excellent way of introducing cooperative learning in a limited, structured way. A good approach for teachers to begin with is the Jigsaw technique (Aronson, Stephan, Sikes, Blaney, & Snapp, 1978). Freely adapted for use with literacy guides, the Jigsaw technique involves these steps:

1. Choose a reading selection that can be divided into relatively independent sections. For example, a biology chapter on mammals might contain sections on physical characteristics, different types of mammals, their geographic distribution, and so on. The idea is that each section could be comprehended adequately without first having read other sections. (This type of reading selection is necessary because each student will read only one section.)
2. Partition your reading guides into sections corresponding to the sections of the reading assignment.
3. Develop an objective quiz over the entire selection.
4. Assign students to groups of about four. The groups should represent the ability distribution of your class. For a heterogeneous class, a mix of one above-average student, one below-average student, and two average students is recommended.
5. Build background for the reading selection in the usual manner, using techniques described in Chapters 5 and 6.
6. Give each student a portion of the reading guide. Each group will have one person responsible for reading and completing a specific portion of the partitioned guide.
7. Give each student an opportunity to teach the other group members the material that was assigned.
8. Administer the quiz to all students.

The knowledge that they must eventually pass a test on the material motivates the students to do well on their assigned work. Peer pressure is brought to bear in an unusual way: Students expect other group members to do well, since their own grades depend on it.

Tierney and Readence (2005) list several potential problems with Jigsaw, including (1) the effect of student absences when the activity lasts more than one day, (2) the possibility that team members may not get along, and (3) the chance that a predominance of slow learners may prohibit the effectiveness of groups. These problems are not without solution, however, and our experience is that Jigsaw is well worth the effort. A useful variation of the technique involves letting each team work collaboratively on completing an assigned section of the reading guide. Each group then teaches its section to the rest of the class.

SUMMARY

Reading guides provide students with a variety of writing tasks as they read. They offer teachers and students a number of powerful advantages. Such guides focus the attention of students on important information and ideas as students encounter them in print. Guides make reading an active process during which students are involved in specific thinking tasks. In this way they provide an excellent means of integrating reading and writing. Completed literacy guides serve as review aids and as a prompt during class discussions.

Authorities differ on the subject of when to use reading guides and with which students. We discussed evidence suggesting that guides can improve comprehension of virtually any reading selection and that better students may profit from them as much as or more than students experiencing reading difficulties. These are strong arguments for the use of guides at all times.

Numerous types of guides have been developed and researched. Hierarchical guides use questions to move students from the literal to higher levels of comprehension. Three-level hierarchical guides pose all literal questions first, then progress to inferential questions, and so forth, while cluster guides repeatedly move from literal to inferential or critical with each new subtopic. Nonhierarchical guides present questions in the order in which the material is organized, without regard to the question levels. Guided notes are composed simply of subheads, suggestions as to important points students must work toward with regard to each, and plenty of blank space in which to write. Selective guides assist students by indicating sections of greater or lesser importance and suggesting appropriate reading speeds. Point-of-view guides present questions in interview form, requiring the students to adopt the role of a specified individual. Anticipation guides survey the prior beliefs and expectations of students in the hope of alerting them to issues on which their thinking may change as they read. All of these types of guides have been the subject of numerous research studies. Some now seem to be more effective than others. In particular, the anticipation guide and the traditional three-level guide are currently somewhat suspect.

While no magic formula can produce perfect guides every time, a few simple suggestions will help. Teachers should begin by analyzing reading selections to determine what they actually expect students to derive from them. The guide itself should be unintimidating and should offer plenty of white space in which to write and should be in a format as interesting as possible. Teachers should review their own purposes in an effort to ensure that the guide reflects the purposes. Word processing makes revisions reasonably easy. For lengthier selections, subheads or page numbers provide students with landmarks that enable them to correlate the guide with the selection. It is a good idea to label the thinking skills or levels associated with each writing task and to provide comprehension assistance—definitions, synonyms, restatements, and so on—wherever needed.

Prior to actual use, the teacher should complete the finished guide with expected responses, both as a final check for "bugs" and as a means of providing a discussion aid. The teacher should walk students through the guide rather than simply hand it out. It is important to familiarize students with the nature of reading guides early on. Describing the content literacy inventory as the first in a series of guides can be highly effective. Presenting guides to cooperative learning groups can be another effective way to engage students in completing guides. Teachers must use reading guides reflectively, remaining alert to problems and be willing to revise them whenever deficiencies become evident.

Getting Involved

1. Take a few minutes to contrast the two guides presented in Figures 8.1 and 8.2. Their content is identical, but the hierarchical guide (Figure 8.1) presents the student first with all of the literal questions and tasks, then all of the inferential, and finally all of the critical. The nonhierarchical guide (Figure 8.2) intermingles these tasks in the order of the text. Which do you think would be more effective?

2. If you are currently teaching, prepare a reading guide for a selection you will assign in the near future. When the time comes, try an action research experiment in which you compare the discussion that follows a reading selection that made use of the guide with the discussion of a comparable reading selection for which no guide was developed. Do the results convince you?

3. If you are not currently teaching, develop a reading guide for a stand-alone selection that you may assign regardless of the official text or curriculum from which you may eventually teach. (We hope you have chosen such a selection already, as part of Getting Involved activities in previous chapters.) It could be a magazine article, short story, essay, or poem. Follow the construction guidelines provided in this chapter as closely as you can. If you lack students with whom to field-test your guide, exchange guides with a colleague in the same subject area and provide one another with feedback.

Providing Time to Read: When, Where, and How?

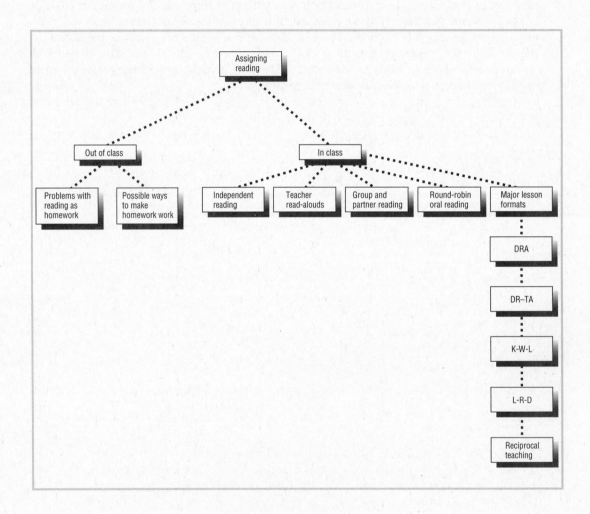

There are favorable hours for reading a book, as for writing it.

—Longfellow

Take a moment to consider when and where you are reading this chapter. We suspect you're at home or at some other location outside the college classroom. It is rare (indeed, almost unheard of) for college instructors to allow students time in class for reading text materials.

Typically, students are expected to read assignments between sessions and to come to each class prepared to discuss them. This may be a realistic expectation in the large majority of cases because college students have usually developed adequate skills and strategies to read most of their assignments independently. But is this a realistic assumption for middle and secondary school students? Do they possess the maturity and self-discipline needed to undertake reading assignments independently? And what about those who are problem readers? Are they likely even to attempt such assignments?

Unfortunately, the prospect that many students may not complete out-of-class reading assignments raises additional issues when we consider the possibility of allotting time *during* class sessions for this purpose. The chief problem is that such a practice would mean less time for the introduction of new content. Many teachers may regard this as too high a price to pay for content literacy, and their sympathies may well be with the science teacher, discussed in Chapter 1, who suggested abandoning printed materials entirely (see Getting Involved, No. 1). If this were to happen, the textbook would become little more than a curriculum guide and a source of questions, exercises, and graphics. This chapter confronts these issues head-on and offers realistic approaches that make reading an important component of content learning.

Objectives

When you finish this chapter, you should be able to take effective steps to ensure that your students read the material you assign. You should be able to

1. organize a unit so that at least some of the reading is done in class;
2. describe read-alouds and their advantages;
3. link read-alouds to chapter walk-throughs;
4. describe effective teacher practices to use during silent reading;
5. describe team and partner approaches to reading and describe their strengths and limitations;
6. list the difficulties inherent in round-robin oral reading as a means of "covering" assigned material; and
7. outline the five major lesson formats.

Reading Assignments as Homework

Assigning materials to be read at home has the natural appeal of conserving class time for other activities. For example, a teacher might devote Monday to prereading activities for a given selection, asking students to read the selection Monday evening, and on Tuesday conduct a discussion and begin postreading activities. But is it realistic to expect students to actually undertake the reading at home? Some students will complete the reading as hoped, but others typically will not. In some cases a lack of self-discipline and parental support may be to blame, while in others the reading may be too difficult despite the use of prereading activities and literacy guides.

This is a bleak picture, but there are ways that might prove effective in ensuring that out-of-class reading assignments prove successful. One approach is to treat the guide as if it were an exercise and grade it like any other student product. The fact that the guide can be completed only in conjunction with reading the assignment will serve as a strong inducement to read. A problem with such a policy is that the content literacy guide becomes a kind of reading "test," and poor readers will inevitably be penalized because of their low ability. Facilitating poor readers at a distance is never easy. Audiotapes (suggested in Chapter 5) could be sent home with the poorest readers. Parents could be encouraged to lend their children assistance when necessary. Forming a working liaison with the reading specialist in your school may give some students support during the school day (Bean, Grumet, & Bulazo, 1999; Bonk, 1998; Jaeger, 1996; Tancock, 1995). These options may not be very realistic, however, at least in all instances.

At the same time, it is important to stress that in some classroom settings assigning reading as homework is a reasonable policy. Classroom assessments, such as those described in Chapter 3, will provide a quick index of the proportion of problem readers. If this proportion is not too high, reading as homework could be tried on an experimental basis.

Structuring Units to Allow Reading in Class

If a portion of class time were allotted for silent reading of assigned material, the teacher would be in a position to offer assistance to students experiencing difficulties. By actively monitoring students as they read and complete their reading guides, a teacher could provide the kind of support not typically available at home, where parents often lack the time and expertise to give adequate assistance (Hoover-Dempsey, Bassler, & Burrow, 1995). Moreover, the use of class time would help ensure that students actually attempted the material assigned.

Some experienced teachers would argue that these advantages are offset by the loss of direct instructional time. They may even feel that in affording their students time to read in class, they are somehow abrogating their own responsibility as teachers. As we hope to make clear, however, there is much to be gained by making assigned reading a regular part of classroom activity. This is not to say that homework will not be assigned, but if reading is to be a part of the unit, then it may make more sense to expect that some of the follow-up activities be completed as homework and that part or all of the reading be undertaken in class. In that way, the reading is supported by the teacher while follow-up activities assigned as homework are undertaken on the basis of more extensive student preparation.

To illustrate, let's consider a hypothetical five-day unit involving one textbook chapter as assigned reading. Figure 9.1 illustrates how such a unit might be planned conventionally, so that the reading is done out of class. The expectation that the reading will be completed in class, however, leads to several possible alternatives for arranging the components.

Figure 9.2 presents one such possibility, in which the first day of the unit is devoted to in-class prereading activities, the second day of the unit to in-class reading, and the third, fourth, and fifth days to discussion and postreading activities. Figure 9.3 depicts another option, in which the assigned material is tackled in smaller, "bite-size" segments—perhaps the sections of a chapter. The first day is devoted to prereading activities, just as in Figure 9.2. During the second day, however, the first segment is read in class, followed by postreading activities for that segment only. Days 3 and 4 are organized in a similar way. Day 5 is devoted to postreading activities covering the entire unit.

In each of these alternatives, homework assignments are associated with postreading activities of some kind and not with initial reading of the assigned materials. The timing of such homework assignments should suit the nature of the unit and its objectives. For certain units, daily assignments would be appropriate, with the expectation that they be completed each evening. For other units, a single assignment, due at the end of the unit, might be more suitable.

Homework completion rates are a problem in middle and secondary schools, and even programs designed deliberately to improve them do not always succeed. For this reason it seems more logical to use homework for tasks that extend and reinforce content knowledge (tasks that

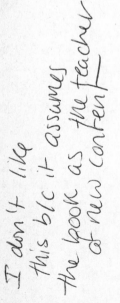

(handwritten margin note: I don't like this b/c it assumes the book as the teacher of new content)

FIGURE 9.1

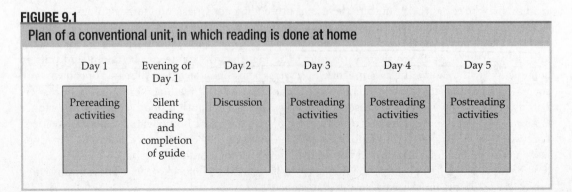

Plan of a conventional unit, in which reading is done at home

Day 1	Evening of Day 1	Day 2	Day 3	Day 4	Day 5
Prereading activities	Silent reading and completion of guide	Discussion	Postreading activities	Postreading activities	Postreading activities

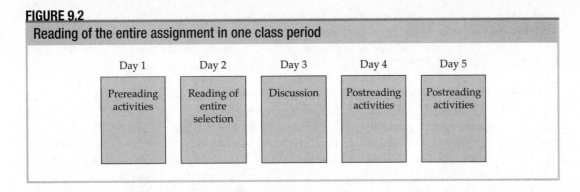

FIGURE 9.2

Reading of the entire assignment in one class period

Day 1	Day 2	Day 3	Day 4	Day 5
Prereading activities	Reading of entire selection	Discussion	Postreading activities	Postreading activities

FIGURE 9.3

Reading distributed across several class periods

Day 1	Day 2	Day 3	Day 4	Day 5
Prereading activities	Reading of section 1 of selection plus discussion	Reading of section 2 of selection plus discussion	Reading of section 3 of selection plus discussion	Postreading activities

will be explored in Chapter 11) rather than for the initial exposure of students to new content through reading.

Making the Reading Assignment

In a broad sense, all of the prereading activities discussed in Chapters 5 through 8 can be thought of as "assigning" the material to be read—from assessing and building background knowledge to introducing technical vocabulary to conducting chapter walk-throughs and, finally, to setting purposes for reading by means of reading guides. All of these components prepare the student for efficient, focused, and purposeful reading.

Figures 9.2 and 9.3 suggest that there is more than one way to incorporate assigned reading into class sessions. In particular, a teacher must decide whether the selection will be divided into parts or read in its entirety. We recommend breaking down lengthy selections into segments for three reasons:

1. Shorter assignments are less likely to turn off your students, to cause fatigue, or to exceed their attention spans.
2. Each section helps build prior knowledge for the next so that comprehension is aided over time.
3. Differences in reading speed among your students are less problematic for shorter assignments.

For all of these reasons, we encourage you to consider Figure 9.3 as a planning guide for assigning longer selections.

Deciding How Reading Will Be Done

It might surprise you to learn that there are several possibilities for asking your students to read. Each approach has its advocates, but some are clearly more productive than others. We will now explore the four most common methods.

Independent Silent Reading. This is perhaps the most "natural" alternative. Each child works individually in the allotted time to read the material and complete the reading guide. Some students may work under special conditions, as with taped versions of the material or a text containing marginalia. The teacher's role meanwhile should not be passive. Active monitoring is appropriate,

The best thing about textbooks is, they don't break when you drop them.

NIKKI, FIFTH GRADER, VIDALIA, GEORGIA

during which the teacher circulates and occasionally stops in order to provide help, hints, or praise. If students are completing guides as they work, the teacher has a visible sign of where they are and how well they have comprehended to that point. It is advisable to visit good and poor readers alike so that no stigma is attached to the stops.

Teacher Read-Alouds. For students not used to learning from text, an effective way of modeling what is expected is for the teacher to read a portion of the material aloud (Albright & Ariail, 2005). It also provides an opportunity to interject commentary and explanations where needed. Our experience in classrooms suggests that students in the upper elementary grades may benefit from such modeling. These students are typically still moving from what Chall (1983/1996) has called the fluency stage of development (see Chapter 2) to the point at which reading to learn is efficient and familiar.

It is important to consider carefully how much of the material to read aloud. For some classes, entire chapters may need to be approached this way—at least for a while. Breaking up the reading is also important and gives the students time to process what they have heard. Because they will have guides, an effective way to extend the modeling still further is for the teacher to complete the guide in the process of the read-aloud. Transparencies can be useful and can be completed with plenty of commentary about where the responses are coming from.

Reading textbook material aloud to students is closely connected with the organizational walk-through, described in Chapter 5. You will remember that walk-throughs involve commenting on headings to give students an overview of how the material is organized. A teacher who reads the material aloud will be in a position to comment on the organizational pattern as each heading is reached. (This does not mean that a start-to-finish walk-through cannot *also* be done before the read-aloud begins.)

Reading in Groups. Some teachers prefer having their students work in groups as they read assigned materials. Cooperative learning formats can be employed and the reading guide used as the focus of group activity. A difficulty with this approach is that students read at different rates and with varying degrees of fluency. The least able member of a group would be ignored or else constantly hold the others back. In addition, there is some evidence that better students resent carrying a disproportionate share of the load in cooperative settings (Turley, 1994). Our view is that group work is best left until the postreading phase of the unit.

A variation on cooperative grouping is to arrange students in pairs so that they can take turns reading the material aloud to one another. This system of partner, or "buddy," reading may have some advantages in keeping students actively engaged and in giving the teachers some opportunities to creatively pair certain students. However, the approach has been used chiefly in the primary grades as a way of increasing the time children spend reading so that they can attain fluency (e.g., Stahl, Heubach, & Cramond, in press).

The thing I don't like about textbooks is that they have too many pages.

JOSHUA, FIFTH GRADER, VIDALIA, GEORGIA

Round-Robin Oral Reading. The age-old practice of having students read the text aloud in ordered turns is alive and well in many content area classrooms. This is unfortunate because the practice has little to recommend it (Eldredge et al., 1996; Kelly, 1995; Wolf, 1998). As Ruddell (1993) puts it, round-robin oral reading "is unfair to everyone: It's deadly dull for good readers and a source of immediate, abject terror for those students whose oral reading skills are not so good. It really does not belong in the classroom" (p. 50).

We might add further drawbacks as well. The practice encourages inattentiveness (unless one's turn is approaching!). It either delays the completion of content literacy guides or makes their completion awkward. Further, it taxes the comprehension of the student reading aloud, whose efforts are understandably directed at accuracy. In short, it is a practice fraught with problems, and we suggest that any of the three alternatives just introduced will produce better results.

Major Lesson Formats

Successfully guiding students as they read assigned materials requires planning. Several options are available, and they allow teachers to create a lesson that accounts for the nature of the material, student background knowledge, and instructional objectives. We will introduce five lesson formats, which vary widely in design and which offer great flexibility to teachers as they plan.

The Directed Reading Activity (DRA)

Description: A five-step plan based on a particular reading assignment. The goal is to improve comprehension by preparing students for the assigned reading and by following up with discussion and other activities.

Steps:
1. Develop readiness for the reading activity.
2. Set purposes for reading.
3. Arrange for students to read silently.
4. Discuss what has been read.
5. Extend students' understanding of the material.

Uses: Works with any reading material that may be challenging

Advantages: Flexible in terms of time devoted to each step
Useful with any assigned reading
Purposeful, as it assumes teacher will determine purposes for reading

Drawbacks: Risk of being overly teacher directive
Risk of overrelying on teacher-supplied purposes

The Directed Reading Activity (DRA)

The Directed Reading Activity (DRA) has long been a staple of elementary teachers (Betts, 1946; Tierney & Readence, 2005) and remains the format of choice in organizing basal reader lessons. However, its great flexibility and breadth of application make it an effective plan for content area teachers as well. The DRA is appropriate whenever a reading assignment is to be a focal point of instruction. The assignment of a textbook chapter by a biology teacher, of a poem or short story by a literature teacher, and a historical novel by a social studies teacher are all occasions suitable to a DRA.

The chief assumption of the DRA is that the comprehension of students can be increased by building their background knowledge in advance and by giving them specific purposes for which to read. Once they complete the reading, the students engage in class discussion and then in activities designed to extend their understanding still further. The DRA therefore has components that come before and after reading. A five-step process is usually recommended, and in the following description we follow the outline provided by Robinson and Good (1987), though with slight modifications for the content area setting.

Step 1: Develop readiness for the reading activity.
   a. Develop the background needed for good comprehension. Begin by introducing the new topic and relating it to what students have already studied and, where pertinent, to their personal experiences. An effort may also be made to stimulate student questioning and to set an appropriate mood or tone for what is to be read. Writing activities may be initiated at this point.
   b. Develop special reading abilities if they are needed. If the selection contains unusual features that might cause difficulties, review them with students in advance. Such features might include charts, maps, diagrams, and the organizational pattern employed.
   c. Develop vocabulary introduced in the material to be read. Present technical terms and the names of people and relevant places. The discussion should link the new terms with those previously introduced.

Step 2: Set purposes for reading.
   a. Determine the objectives for reading. Decide what knowledge, impressions, and understandings you want students to come away with. If the selection is lengthy and/or contains subdivisions, analyze each section separately.
   b. Convey the purposes to the students. Tell students what you expect of them. Outline questions to be answered, information to be obtained, and so on. One means of accomplishing this goal is the content literacy guide, which is discussed in Chapter 8.

Step 3: Arrange for students to read silently.

Decide how much class time and how much out-of-class time will be apportioned for silent reading. Set clear expectations that the material will be read, not necessarily word for word, but with sufficient care to accomplish the purposes set forth in Step 2.

Step 4: Discuss what has been read.

    a. Respond to the purposes set prior to reading. Lead a class discussion, using as a blueprint the purpose set forth to students in advance. The text (or whatever the students have read) should be used as a resource during the discussion. Portions may be reread orally to review or underscore certain points.

    b. Develop oral reading for a purpose. In certain classes, though not in all, the teacher may wish to encourage oral reading. In the study of literature, for example, students may be asked to read a poem aloud for rhetorical effect or to read aloud the dialogue of characters in a conversation-rich short story in a classroom version of reader's theater.

Step 5: Extend students' understanding of the material.

    a. Use collateral materials where appropriate. Select additional sources that may be used to stretch your students' grasp of what has been read. These might include library materials, reference books, treatments of the same topic by different authors, and other works by the same author.

    b. Stimulate student thinking through writing activities. Select an activity well matched to the initial purposes for reading. Such activities can vary widely in nature, from writing out a step-by-step problem-solving process in an algebra class to writing a personal response to a poem read as a literature assignment.

A basic strength of the DRA is that it is easily adapted to a wide range of content reading situations. The DRA can be thought of as a framework within which the content teacher determines the specific details of what is to be taught. It should be emphasized that the DRA does not dictate what is to be included in a particular lesson but only how to organize the instruction.

The Directed Reading–Thinking Activity (DR–TA)

The Directed Reading–Thinking Activity (DR–TA) is a popular variation of the Directed Reading Activity. First suggested by Stauffer (1969, 1980), the DR–TA is designed to help readers determine their own purposes for reading a selection and then to decide on the most appropriate strategies for achieving these purposes. A strength of the DR–TA is the emphasis placed on reading as a thinking activity and on the need for students to determine their own purposes for reading.

The teacher accomplishes this by asking them to make predictions. If the selection is narrative, the predictions involve what will happen next. If the material is expository, the predictions focus on factual information. The students pause at key points to discuss whether predictions were correct. They then generate new predictions. Their predictions are general at first but grow increasingly specific as the students make their way through the material.

The following steps outline the strategy and are based on Stauffer's revised (1980) format:

Step 1: Assist students in developing purposes for reading.

    a. Determine students' background related to the material to be read. Ask questions that assess the knowledge of students to determine whether their prior understanding will be equal to the demands of the reading. In reality, past experiences with a group of students will often provide a teacher with a fair appraisal of whether their existing knowledge is adequate.

    b. Provide appropriate teaching, when needed, to address any lack of information or misconceptions about the reading. Many of the activities to be presented in later chapters are appropriate here.

    c. Discuss new vocabulary relative to the reading material. This process is likely to be an essential part of background building.

The Directed Reading–Thinking Activity (DR–TA)

Description: A three-step plan designed to assist readers in setting their own purposes for reading. The teacher's role is to help students make predictions about a selection and later to help them test their predictions.

Steps:
1. Assist students in developing purposes for reading.
2. Facilitate reasoning as students read.
3. Help students test their predictions.

Uses: Works best with narrative materials and with topics that are already fairly familiar to students

Advantages: Stresses the need to think actively while reading
Emphasizes the need to set one's own purposes

Drawback: Not well suited to unfamiliar or new topics

d. Help students set purposes for reading the material. As we have mentioned, this is largely a predictive process. Ask the students what they *suspect* will be presented in the material to be read. Encourage class members to critique one another's projections in an effort to explore a variety of possibilities and, in many cases, to get competing predictions into the open simultaneously.

Step 2: Facilitate reasoning as students read.

a. Circulate as students read, offering assistance where needed. Respond to specific questions about vocabulary first, by encouraging students to make use of context, glossaries, and other aids available to them.

b. Break down longer assignments into manageable segments. Predictions can be checked at the end of each section and new ones formed. (See Step 3.)

Step 3: Help students test their predictions.

a. After students have read a selection (or a specified section of an entire selection), remind them of their predictions; have the students examine the predictions to decide whether they were supported by what was encountered in print.

b. Require proof based on the reading. Ask students to locate and share aloud supporting material. When predictions are not borne out, require students to cite information that refutes their original assumptions.

We have suggested that the DR–TA offers an important alternative to guiding students through certain kinds of reading materials. Stauffer (1980) has argued that the plan will work for any reading selection, but this is true only if the idea of prediction is broadly assumed to mean any speculation about what the material contains and not the usual time-related notion of "what happens next."

K-W-L

The DR–TA is arguably more student centered than the DRA because students, by making repeated predictions, take an active part in setting their own purposes for reading. K-W-L (Ogle, 1986) is perhaps still more student centered by allowing them even wider latitude in deciding what information they will seek.

Ogle's strategy involves three steps: (1) a discussion designed to determine what students already know prior to reading, (2) group and individual decisions about what they would like to learn from the material, and (3) a postreading appraisal of what they did in fact learn. From these three steps—what the students already *know,* what they *want* to learn, and what they have *learned*—comes the acronym K-W-L. Let's examine these steps in greater detail.

Step 1: Determine what students already know (K).

a. Begin by leading a brainstorming session with the students about the topic to be addressed by the reading. Use a word or brief phrase to sum up the principal topic—crustaceans, sonnets, the legislative branch, and so on. Be as specific as possible. (If a social studies chapter deals with the legislative branch of government, don't say the topic is government.) Ask what students know about the topic. If you draw a blank with your topic label, try to be a little more general. For example, you might ask what they know about the branches of government. Write responses on the board or use the overhead projector. Be receptive to student input without close regard to its appropriateness. As you write, abbreviate and condense where necessary.

b. With the students' help, identify categories that can be used to group the information you've listed. You may need to model this process until students become familiar with K-W-L. For legislature, for example, you may note that several items supplied by students have to do with passing bills into law. You would suggest this as a category, write it on the board as a heading, and list the items below it.

Step 2: Help students determine what they *want* to learn (W).

a. As you proceed through Step 1, gaps and uncertainties in students' preexisting knowledge will begin to become clear. Your goal is to translate these into reasons for reading. Ask students what they wish to learn from the material, and in the ensuing discussion attempt to steer them toward their deficiencies. Attempt to arouse their curiosity about these points by asking questions (e.g., "I wonder, what happens if the vote on a bill is a tie?").

b. Ask students to decide on purpose questions individually. They should write these out. Expect overlap in the questions but some divergence as well. Tolerate individual interests, but shepherd students toward obvious shortcomings in their knowledge base.

Step 3: Assess what students have *learned* (L).

a. Request that students jot down, at least in abbreviated form, the answers to their questions as they read. Caution them in advance that they might not find the answers to all the questions.

b. Conduct a discussion comparing what students wished to learn with what they actually gained from the reading. Stress points at which the selection did not address their needs, pointing out that what an author chooses to include is not the beginning and end of a topic. Indicate other sources where students might have their questions answered, and provide opportunities for using them.

Although K-W-L is relatively specific about the activities to be included, there are many points at which a teacher can insert literacy activities designed to facilitate learning. For example, the process of categorizing student input in Step 1 can be accomplished through the use of a

---

K-W-L

Description:	A three-step plan in which the teacher helps the students first to locate gaps in their existing knowledge of the topics covered by a selection and then to turn these gaps into purposes for reading.
Steps:	1. Determine what students already *know* (K).
	2. Help students determine what they *want* to learn (W).
	3. Assess what students have *learned* (L).
Uses:	Designed primarily for expository materials, such as textbooks
Advantages:	Stresses the need to link old learning with new
	Provides for the activation of prior knowledge
	Lends itself well to the goal of acquiring knowledge
Drawbacks:	May not be sufficiently teacher centered for some
	Does not work well with highly unfamiliar material
	Limited research base

FIGURE 9.4

A K-W-L chart on the topic of Pluto, partially completed prior to reading

K	W	L
It's a planet. Farthest planet It's cold.	Does it have a moon? Could there be life? How did it get its name? Has a spaceship gone there?	

graphic organizer or semantic map, techniques we explore in Chapter 6. Carr and Ogle (1987) recommended this modification in what they termed K-W-L Plus. This variation, however, is just one additional example of how K-W-L can serve as a global start-to-finish structure for organizing many activities.

An effective way to organize a K-W-L lesson is to use a three-column chart like the one represented in Figure 9.4. Use a transparency to record student input about what they already know and what they would like to learn. After the students have read the selection, again place the chart on the overhead projector and complete the final column with the help of your students. A K-W-L chart helps organize the lesson and ties before-and-after activities together in a meaningful way.

Listen-Read-Discuss (L-R-D)

Originally devised for learning-disabled children, Listen-Read-Discuss (Manzo & Casale, 1985) can be applied successfully with any population. Like the DRA, DR-TA, and K-W-L, Listen-Read-Discuss (L-R-D) has a prereading phase, but it is quite different. Manzo and Casale correctly assume that the chief problem faced by students in the upper elementary and middle grades is lack of prior knowledge. They may know so little about a topic that learning about it through reading is a daunting task. Rather than attempt to build prior knowledge by supplying a few important facts and introducing new terms, the teacher goes much further before the students are asked to read the selection.

In L-R-D, the background step of the DRA is expanded to the point that the content of the selection is fully presented through lecture. In a sense, then, when the students begin to read, the experience is more like a review than an encounter with fresh material.

The idea behind L-R-D may seem self-defeating. After all, if the content has been completely presented prior to reading, a student might well conclude that reading is unnecessary. In a study with high school students, however, Watkins and her colleagues (Watkins, McKenna, Manzo, & Manzo, 1994) found that students were actually *more* likely to read the assigned material, presumably because the content has been made more accessible. Compared with a more traditional DRA, L-R-D resulted in higher levels of content learning, particularly for low-ability students. When interviewed as to their preferences, Watkin's students definitely believed L-R-D to be the more effective approach.

In classes where low reading ability is a widespread problem, L-R-D offers a preemptive way of dealing with difficulties. In essence, the teacher attempts to *fully develop in advance* the ideas presented in the text so that reading becomes a process of confirming and reinforcing. If only a few students are encountering significant problems, however, L-R-D may be too tedious for the majority and might best be reserved for more difficult assignments.

Reciprocal Teaching

Many of the struggling readers in the upper-elementary and middle grades have developed adequate decoding skills. What they lack are strategies for comprehending nonfiction material.

Listen-Read-Discuss (L-R-D)

Description: A three-part plan designed to make assigned reading easier for low-ability readers by presenting virtually all of the text content through lecture prior to reading.

Steps:
1. Present complete text content through lecture and demonstration.
2. Give students a chance to read the material silently.
3. Conduct a discussion of the selection.

Uses: Can be used with virtually any nonfiction selection

Advantages: Is effective with low-ability readers
Does not appear to discourage actual reading

Drawbacks: Highly teacher directed
May encourage overreliance on teacher for direction
May be poorly suited to high-ability students

Reciprocal teaching, described by Palincsar and Brown in 1984 and 1986, is an instructional technique in which students work in small groups and apply comprehension strategies together to a new reading selection. These strategies include predicting, clarifying, questioning, and summarizing. In order for reciprocal teaching to work, the teacher must spend some time explaining these four strategies so that students can apply them to new material. Research suggests that this is time well spent (Hacker & Tenent, 2002; Palincsar & Herrenkohl, 2002; Slater & Horstman, 2002; Smith & Elder, 2001). Let's briefly examine each of them.

Comprehension Strategies.   The students begin by examining the reading selection and *predicting* what it seems likely to be about. To do so they consider subtitles, pictures, boldface terminology, and graphic aids. Some students may not be used to predicting, so starting with simple examples, such as pictures and picture books, may be necessary (Smith & Elder, 2001).

New content material may well contain concepts and ideas that are not entirely clear after students are finished reading. In *clarifying*, they focus on words, ideas, and even pronunciations that may require further explanation. Others in the group may be able to help, as can the teacher. The important thing is that they realize where problems lie.

Students are asked to engage in *questioning* once they have read each portion of a selection. They are encouraged to ask questions at a variety of comprehension levels. Other members of the collaborative group will attempt to answer these questions as they are asked. (Refer back to Chapter 7 for a discussion of question types.)

Once the students are finished asking and answering their own questions, they begin *summarizing* what they have read and discussed. One option is to have students coauthor a written summary, but other possibilities include producing an informal outline of new material, creating a semantic map, or simply identifying the most important ideas and terminology introduced in the selection.

These four strategies are used by proficient readers whenever they encounter new content material. Such readers form predictions about what the test will be about, though these predictions may not always be formally worded. Then, as they read, they attempt to clarify the meanings of new terms and reflect on difficult ideas before moving on. They often form questions as they read and do their best to answer them. When they finish a selection, they consider the major points it has taught them and the overall significance they may have. All of these strategies are applied internally, within the mind of the proficient reader. They form a kind of dialogue through which good readers attempt to monitor their own comprehension in order to ensure understanding. Struggling readers frequently lack this internal "conversation," and their comprehension suffers as a result.

Preparing Students for Reciprocal Teaching.   It is important to take nothing for granted in getting students ready for reciprocal teaching experiences. Palincsar and Brown (1986) have suggested several steps for accomplishing this goal.

Reciprocal Teaching

Description: A collaborative approach in which students work in groups as they read assigned material. Together they apply comprehension strategies, including predicting, questioning, clarifying, and summarizing.

Steps:
1. Teacher thoroughly acquaints students with how reciprocal teaching works.
2. Teacher introduces the selection and appoints a "teacher" in each group to keep them on task.
3. Students make predictions about the first section.
4. One student in each group reads the section aloud.
5. Students question one another and seek clarifications.
6. One student summarizes the section.
7. Steps 3 through 6 are repeated.

Uses: Useful primarily with nonfiction

Advantages: Extensive research base
Tends to be highly engaging

Drawbacks: Potentially time consuming
Students exhibiting behavior problems may need to be excluded.

1. *Instruction.* Each of the strategies must be carefully explained and defined.

2. *Modeling.* On the basis of selections familiar to the students, the teacher must illustrate how the strategies are applied. The students are encouraged to contribute to the teacher-led examples by generating questions and predictions of their own and also contributing to summaries.

3. *Guided Practice.* As new selections are introduced, the teacher gradually shifts the responsibility for applying the strategies to the students. They are called upon in the course of the dialogue to play an increasing role in making predictions, seeking clarifications, asking questions, and creating summaries. The teacher monitors the students' efforts, providing feedback and praise where needed.

Introducing students to these strategies does not require time that is set aside from content instruction. The reading selections are the teacher's own materials and represent the curriculum of the content subject.

Once the students have had some experience in applying the four strategies in guided settings, it is time to conduct a reciprocal teaching lesson from start to finish. In describing a typical lesson, we'll draw on the experience of Claire Smith and Joanne Pelton, seventh-grade teachers at Winder-Barrow Middle School in Georgia. These two colleagues have refined the technique of reciprocal teaching with their struggling seventh-grade readers and report phenomenal success in improving both comprehension ability and content learning (Smith & Elder, 2001).

Students should be assigned to groups of four to six without regard to reading proficiency. Students with behavioral problems may need to be separated from one another or even given different assignments during reciprocal teaching time. The selection to be read is introduced to the students in much the same manner as any reading assignment. The teacher builds background by briefly introducing the topic and linking it to previous content. The teacher stops short, however, of introducing the material in great detail (as might be the case in L-R-D, for example) because the students will be assisting one another during the processes of questioning and clarifying.

A reminder of the steps in the reciprocal teaching process is posted so that the students can refer to it as necessary. Figure 9.5 shows how Joanne Pelton outlines her expectations for each of the strategies that the students will undertake during reciprocal teaching. Within each group, one of the students serves as "teacher" and is responsible for keeping the group on task as it moves from one strategy to the next and from one page to the next. This does not mean that the "teacher" conducts instruction, however. The role of the teacher is rotated among the group

FIGURE 9.5

Steps in a reciprocal teaching lesson*

Predict

Use clues from pictures, the title, and subtitles.

Each student makes a prediction.

Read Aloud

One paragraph per student until you have finished a page.

Go on to the next step.

Clarify

Focus on an idea, word, or pronunciation you need help on.

Make sure everyone in the group understands before going on.

Question

Ask questions that can be answered from the page you just read.

Ask questions that may require inferring.

Ask questions that may require evaluation.

Summarize

When you are finished clarifying and questioning, summarize the page. You may do this by out-lining, making a word web, or listing the most important points.

* Worded as Joanne Pelton posted the steps for her seventh graders.

members from one reciprocal teaching lesson to the next. The composition of the groups remains relatively stable over time unless in the teacher's judgment (the classroom teacher, that is!) a better mix can be established by transferring one or more students.

The teacher's expectations for a particular reciprocal teaching lesson are made clear at the beginning by placing them on a transparency or on the board and checking to be sure that the students clearly understand what is required. Figure 9.6 contains an example of how Joanne Pelton set purposes for a lesson on dolphins based on an issue of *Current Science*. Notice that she pointed students toward a culminating activity, in this case the creation of a poster that allowed them an opportunity to apply what they learned from the selection.

After the students begin, the teacher monitors their activity by "hobnobbing" from one group to another. It may be necessary to provide prompts, ask questions, suggest clarifications, or take other actions in order to keep a group on task. As the lesson proceeds, Claire Smith describes what she calls "The Wave." The groups will naturally reach different strategies at different times, and one group may be relatively quiet (for instance, during the reading phase), while others are engaged in active discussion. This constructive noise then moves on to another group.

Reciprocal teaching not only accomplishes its purpose of fostering strategic reading on the part of struggling readers, it is highly motivational and appropriately based on social interaction. Claire Smith and Joanne Pelton have even used reciprocal teaching as a reward. It is clearly an instructional approach worthy of regular use.

FIGURE 9.6

Sample directions for a reciprocal teaching lesson

1. Reciprocal-teach the article on pages 4, 5, 6, and 7.

2. As a group, design a poster that you, as Beach Rangers, would post at a beach to educate the public about dolphins. Use the blank sheet of paper I'll give you to get your ideas together, and then have your "teacher" pick up the markers and poster board from Mrs. Pelton.

(Hint: List or illustrate characteristics of dolphins that the public may need to know. But remember, you are out of a job if people are not warned *or* if they are scared off.)

NET Worth

Materials on the Web

New York Times. Presents a daily article from the *New York Times,* complete with classroom activities, plus This Date in History, a crossword puzzle, and a current-events quiz. Also offers online software and e-mail access to reporters.

www.nytimes.com/learning

The Children's Literature Web Guide. An attempt to gather together and categorize the growing number of Internet resources related to books for children and young adults. Much of the information that you can find through these pages is provided by others: fans, schools, libraries, and commercial enterprises involved in the book world.

www.ucalgary.ca/~dkbrown

Education World: American Fidelity Educational Services. This site features a searchable database of 56,000+ sites. Links include: Lesson Planning, News/Eye on School, Curriculum, Books in Education, Administrators, Education Site Reviews, Financial Planning.

www.education-world.com

SUMMARY

The way in which reading is incorporated into units is an important consideration during planning. Assigning reading as homework is not usually advisable, especially for poor readers, but under certain circumstances it may work. Holding students accountable for completed guides could help, as could encouraging parental assistance, sending home audiotapes, and forming working liaisons with remedial teachers.

The policy of allotting class time for reading assigned materials is a more viable option. Doing so allows the teacher to monitor student progress without giving up significant amounts of time, especially when homework is used for postreading activities. There are many ways to build in-class reading into a unit. For example, lengthier selections might be broken into sections to be read over several days.

Several options are available for the way in which in-class reading is done. Some of these alternatives are more viable than others. Independent silent reading while students complete a literacy guide allows the teacher to monitor progress actively. The teacher might also read portions of the material aloud, interjecting commentary and completing the guide publicly. Less viable is the practice of having students read in pairs or groups. Such interaction is better left to the postreading phase. Finally, round-robin oral reading, while still popular, has many problems. These include tedium, frustration, inattentiveness, and reduced opportunity for students to complete content literacy guides.

Five major lesson formats were introduced. The Directed Reading Activity (DRA) comprises five steps: (1) establishing readiness for reading, (2) setting purposes for reading, (3) reading assigned materials silently, (4) discussing what has been read, and (5) doing activities designed to extend and reinforce what has been learned. The Directed Reading–Thinking Activity (DR–TA) is a major modification of the DRA based largely on the use of prediction as a means of setting purposes for reading. Its three steps include (1) assisting students to set their own purposes for reading based on what they expect the selection to contain, (2) assisting students to reason as they read, and (3) helping students to test their predictions following reading. The DRA tends to be more teacher directed than the DR–TA largely because the teacher, rather than the students, is responsible for setting the purposes. Consequently, the postreading discussion in a DRA is also more teacher directed because it centers around teacher-determined purposes rather than those set by individual students. An advantage of the DRA is its applicability to virtually all reading materials, while the DR–TA tends to be better suited to narrative than to expository selections and to topics that are relatively familiar to students so that predictions can be reasonably made.

Pause a moment to think about your reactions to the five major lesson formats presented. Does one of them seem more "like you" than the others? You may have made your judgment based on visualizing yourself as a student in each of the four settings. In Chapter 1, we discussed this tendency, and we encourage you now to keep an open mind as we explore how each plan might be used to achieve different purposes.

A third lesson format is K-W-L. This plan begins with the teacher helping students survey what they already *know* (K) about a topic. The teacher then assists students in determining what they *want* (W) to know by helping them turn gaps in their knowledge into reasons for reading. Finally, the teacher follows the reading of the selection with a discussion of what the students have actually *learned* (L).

A fourth format is Listen-Read-Discuss (L-R-D). Here, the teacher thoroughly presents the entire content of the selection before the students read. Doing so helps contend with severe deficits in background knowledge.

The final format is reciprocal teaching. Once the teacher introduces the selection, students make their way through it page by page or section by section, working in small groups. They begin by making predictions about what the next page or section will contain. They then read aloud and proceed to question each other, seek clarifications, and summarize before moving to the next section.

Getting Involved

1. Select a veteran teacher in your own subject area. Ask the teacher about homework policy and whether reading assigned materials at home plays any part (or ever did). If the teacher has succeeded in using homework as an approach to assigned reading, ask how problem readers are accommodated. If students are not asked to read at home, how is reading integrated into class time, if at all?

2. We have suggested five ways of incorporating reading into classroom activities (not all of which we endorse). Our list was not meant to be exhaustive. Can you suggest other approaches?

3. Figure 9.7 presents a chart comparing the five global formats described in this chapter. On the left side are characteristics that may or may not apply to each format. Test your understanding by writing a plus (+) if a format possesses a characteristic, or a zero (0) if it lacks it. Refer to the discussion to check your judgments, but note that not all of the characteristics have been specifically addressed. You will need to infer some of your conclusions, and even then some may involve an element of discretion.

FIGURE 9.7

An exercise in contrasting the major lesson formats

For each of the characteristics listed, place a plus (+) under the heading of each of the plans to which it applies. Place a zero (o) where the characteristic does not apply. Write an "S" if the characteristic sometimes applies.

Characteristic	DRA	DR–TA	K-W-L	L-R-D	Reciprocal Teaching
Highly teacher directed					
Students set purposes for reading					
Useful with unfamiliar topics					
Students make predictions					

4. Locate a brief reading selection that has future potential for use with your students. A stand-alone selection (an article, essay, short story, poem, etc.) is better for this task than a textbook chapter because you will be able to incorporate it into your instruction regardless of the text that is in use. Choose either DRA, DR–TA, or K-W-L, and outline a lesson plan for your selection. Make notes about what you would generally do to guide students at each step, but do not be overly detailed in your planning because these formats allow for many additional "tactical" devices to be incorporated. These devices are discussed in Chapters 5 through 10, and you will be asked to implement some of them in your plan. So choose well! We'll revisit this selection in the future.

Postreading Strategies

Content area teachers must follow up the reading material they assign before going on to other topics for at least three reasons. One is the need to monitor how well students have comprehended. Another is to give them opportunities to practice applying the knowledge they have gained. A third is to extend that knowledge beyond what the text has provided. The two chapters in this section offer techniques for accomplishing these aims.

Chapter 10 discusses postreading questioning techniques. We suggest a distinction between true discussion and mere recitation and recommend a compromise position. We provide advice on how to plan, and we discuss such issues as deciding which students to call on, using time prudently, responding to unacceptable answers, and responding to acceptable ones. Chapter 10 also addresses alternatives to traditional teacher-led discussions, such as techniques that link questioning and writing.

Chapter 11 looks beyond postreading discussion to examine methods of reinforcing and extending students' knowledge of what they have read. We revisit some of the techniques for introducing vocabulary (see Chapter 6), this time as postreading reinforcement activities. We consider more extensive writing projects to further develop student understanding. We also describe activities that have game formats. Last, we describe how previous content can be reinforced while new content is introduced by using such techniques as review and bridging.

CHAPTER 10

Effective Questioning

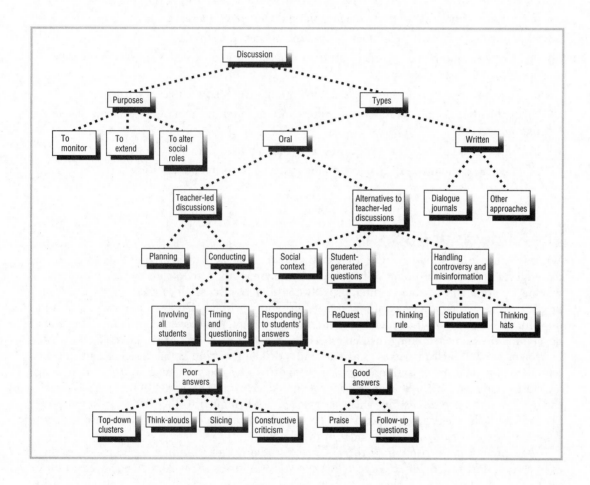

The first key to wisdom is this—constant and frequent questions,
for by doubting we are led to arrive at the truth.

—Pierre Abelard (c. 1120)

Think back to the last classroom discussion in which you participated *as a student*. Did the experience focus on literal-level questions posed by the teacher—questions that required the recitation of clipped, parroted facts from the material covered? Now consider the last time you worked with friends in a study group or joined in an after-class conversation about the content of the presentation. Was the experience something more than a mere bandying of facts? Was it conducive to inferences and judgments? Was it dependent for direction on all the participants rather than a single individual?

This contrast is somewhat exaggerated and represents extreme positions concerning the proper purpose of questioning and discussion. Your own views of these purposes will do much to determine the kind of questioner, and the kind of discussion leader, you become. It is important for you to think through the issues involved and to develop a coherent philosophy of how questioning can best serve your students.

Objectives

When you have read this chapter on questioning, you should be able to

1. plan an effective discussion based on your instructional purpose or objectives;
2. identify the principles of effective questioning documented by research;
3. explain and apply such techniques as question clusters and think-alouds;
4. describe the importance of student-generated questions and explain methods for encouraging such questioning;
5. describe how the social context of a discussion influences how students participate;
6. suggest methods of taking the social context into account in encouraging student participation;
7. link discussion to the literacy processes of writing and reading; and
8. suggest classroom methods of encouraging students to formulate questions.

The Purposes of Discussion

No one is without knowledge except the one who asks no questions.

WEST AFRICAN
PROVERB

While we discuss questioning in the context of a postreading activity geared to the content of the material read, most of the points to be made in this chapter apply to *any* instructional discussion, whether or not it is related to reading. Broadly considered, discussion can serve a variety of purposes, three of which are especially useful in classroom settings. Discussion allows teachers to monitor the extent to which students understand content. Moreover, it provides a means of developing their understanding further, especially when inadequacies are discovered (Worthy & Hoffman, 1999). Finally, it serves as a vehicle for social interaction among teacher and students, who extend their learning and modify their perspectives by using language to share knowledge and ideas (Giorgis, 1999). Some authorities (e.g., Alvermann, Dillon, & O'Brien, 1987) prefer the term *recitation* to *discussion* whenever the activity is limited to the first of these purposes. Because we believe all three purposes can be served during the same activity, we use the more general term *discussion* in the remainder of the chapter.

Questioning used to monitor the extent of student understanding is the most common application. Research on effective teaching certainly confirms the need to keep abreast of how well students have comprehended new material, whether introduced by reading or other means (e.g., Klingner & Vaughn, 1999). And yet a discussion that consists entirely of low-level monitoring questions (the first type of experience we asked you to recall in the opening paragraph) seems overly tedious and not very likely to enhance students' interest or deepen their understanding. Mehan (1979) coined the acronym IRE to describe this model: teacher *i*niative, student *r*esponse, teacher *e*valuation. Cazden (1988) described IRE as the "'default' position—what happens unless deliberate action is taken to achieve an alternative" (p. 53). Nevertheless, such questioning has its place, as in the course of short, intensive review sessions. Literal questions can also serve the goal of monitoring effectively when embedded in the context of broader, meaning-extended questioning. This is the sort of discussion we argue for as one of several alternatives to IRE.

When used to develop understanding further, to push students beyond facts toward an appreciation of their significance, questioning is an equally worthwhile goal of discussion. A classic example of questioning used for this purpose is that of Socrates helping a student reach a mathematical inference (see page 153). Note, however, that several of Socrates' questions called for everyday factual information. He asked these questions both to bring out the facts his student needed to arrive at the inference about the square root of 2 (the real point of the discussion) and to assure himself that the boy was actually in possession of these facts. If the student did not possess this knowledge, Socrates could have helped him acquire the necessary information before continuing toward the objective. The same process can guide students to the formation of defensible critical judgments. As with inferences, the formula is the same: *facts first, conclusions afterward.*

The use of questioning to take advantage of social dimensions inherent in the classroom structure is just beginning to be understood. We do know that students and teacher alike adopt social roles as they discuss content and that these roles have important implications for the nature and the extent of students' thinking. A teacher cannot afford to pursue the first two purposes mentioned above and ignore the third, for social factors can reduce the effectiveness of a discussion if they are not considered.

Discussion as a Language Process

You may have noted that when discussion is used for the second of these purposes—to extend and clarify understanding—its role is similar to that of the literacy processes of reading and writing. Indeed, discussion involves the oral counterparts of these processes: listening and speaking. We have already seen that writing and reading are *constructive* activities, for through them students build an internal, mental representation of content. In this respect, speaking and listening are no different from one another. In asking a question, the teacher places the students in the position of thinking through what they know in order to *construct* their responses. This construction does not simply evaporate once a response has been given. The act of having thought through the response affects a student's conceptualization of the topic. There are thus knowledge-building forces at work in a good classroom discussion—the same forces that lead to knowledge acquisition in reading and writing. Even when the teacher has posed key questions in advance (by means of a literacy guide, for example) so that students have thought through their responses before the discussion begins, the prudent teacher pushes, nudges, suggests, and encourages. Follow-up questions, not previously posed, extend the student's understanding as do the input of peers and the commentary of the teacher.

The only interesting answers are those which destroy the questions.
SUSAN SONTAG

The Rarity of True Discussion

Classroom observational research, most notably that by Dillon (1984) and Good and Brophy (2002), has shown that the actual use of discussion by teachers is rare. What is frequently referred to as discussion is in reality student recitation under the direct control and authority of the teacher. Student responses consist almost entirely of repeating information encountered in text or presented by the teacher through lecture. True discussion, during which there is a sharing of opinions and ideas by both teacher and students in an atmosphere of mutual trust and respect, simply does not happen in many content classes.

Alvermann et al. (1987) have suggested the following three criteria for a true discussion:

1. the discussants must present multiple points of view and then be ready to change their minds after hearing convincing counterarguments;
2. the students must interact with one another as well as with the teacher; and
3. a majority of the verbal interactions, especially those resulting from questions that solicit student opinion, must be longer than the typical two- or three-word phrases found in recitations. (p. 3)

Note that these criteria do not preclude incorporating lower-level questions that are used to monitor and reinforce. Figures 10.1 and 10.2 are examples we offer to aid in distinguishing recitation from discussion. They may be best seen as extremes on a continuum, however. Our view is that intermediate approaches are possible, in which monitoring coexists with the open exchange of ideas. As noted earlier, we use the word *discussion* to refer to such approaches.

FIGURE 10.1

An example of recitation*

Setting Students in Ms. Arroyo's eighth-grade health class have read a portion of a chapter on marijuana and its effects on the body.

Arroyo: All right, Gail, can you tell us another name for marijuana?

Gail: Cannibus.

Arroyo: Right! Ben, can you describe its effects?

Ben: Well, you have this mellow feeling and your judgment is changed.

Arroyo: Roger, do you agree?

Roger: Yes.

Arroyo: OK, let's start a list. [She writes "Effects" on the board and "altered judgment" beneath.] Would you add anything, Roger?

Roger: Memory problems?

Arroyo: Yes. [She adds this to the list.] Anything else? Latrelle?

Latrelle: You're not as coordinated.

Arroyo: True. [She continues the list.] What about long-term effects? Paulo?

Paulo: Coughing. [Ms. Arroyo writes.]

Arroyo: Any more? Ruth Ann?

Ruth Ann: It said maybe your immune system gets messed up.

Arroyo: Right! [She continues her list.]

*Note: The fictional exchange is based on information obtained at the National Institute on Drug Abuse (National Institutes of Health) (www.nida.nih.gov).

As you continue in this chapter, consider carefully the following points in the development and the encouragement of effective discussion in your own content classes:

1. What do you perceive to be the proper role of the teacher in classroom discussion?
2. Will you allow students to contribute new information and ideas to the class discussion?
3. What are your chief purposes for conducting discussions?

FIGURE 10.2

An example of discussion

Setting Students in Mr. Wagner's eighth-grade health class have read the same chapter on marijuana as Ms. Arroyo's students.

Wagner: OK, Rick, now that you've studied what marijuana can do to you, do you think it should be legalized?

Rick: Well, no.

Carlo: I do. Why not give people the choice? I mean it's supposed to be a free country.

Maria: 'Cause I don't want those people on the road.

Tisha: But you don't have to ban it. Just pass a law. You can't be under the influence when you're driving.

Rick: Man, I don't know. It'd be weird going into a convenience store and seein' weed on the shelf.

Tisha: [Laughing] You'd get used to it!

Tom: Didn't they ban alcohol once?

Wagner: Yes, years ago.

Tom: Right, and it didn't work because people wanted to drink it.

Maria: But liquor's different than grass.

Vintage Questioning

Socrates and Meno's Boy

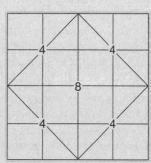

Soc.: Tell me, boy, do you know that a figure like this is a square?

Boy: I do.

Soc.: And do you know that a square figure has these four lines equal?

Boy: Certainly.

Soc.: And these lines which I have drawn through the middle of the square are also equal?

Boy: Yes.

Soc.: A square may be of any size?

Boy: Certainly.

Soc.: And if one side of the figure be of two feet, and the other side be of two feet, how much will the whole be? Let me explain: If in one direction the space was of two feet, and in the other direction of one foot, the whole would be of two feet taken once?

Boy: Yes.

Soc.: But since this side is also of two feet, there are twice two feet?

Boy: There are.

Soc.: Then the square is of twice two feet?

Boy: Yes.

Soc.: And how many are twice two feet? Count and tell me.

Boy: Four, Socrates.

Soc.: And might there not be another square twice as large as this, and having like this the line equal?

Boy: Yes.

Soc.: And of how many feet will that be?

Boy: Of eight feet.

Soc.: And now try and tell me the length of the line which forms the side of that double square: this is two feet—what will that be?

Boy: Clearly, Socrates, it will be double.

Soc.: Do you observe, Meno, that I am not teaching the boy anything, but only asking him questions; and now he fancies that he knows how long a line is necessary in order to produce a figure of eight square feet; does he not?

Men.: Yes.

Soc.: And does he really know?

Men.: Certainly not.

Soc.: He only guesses that because the square is double, the line is double.

Source: From *Dialogues of Plato* (pp. 41–42) trans. by B. Jewett, 1892, New York: Macmillan.

4. Do your students know how to participate in a discussion?
5. Are you willing to allow students to address one another during the discussion, or do you believe all student input must be directed to the teacher?

Planning a Discussion

Good discussions don't just happen. They are the result of teachers' first deciding what they wish to accomplish and then planning to bring it about. We have described three general purposes for discussion, but more specific objectives are needed when a discussion is actually planned.

In the case of postreading discussions, the reading guide provides a blueprint of the key points to be covered. In effect, the teacher plans the discussion before the reading assignment is made, that is, while constructing the guide. Using the guide to determine the general course of the discussion is a major help, and it develops in students an expectation that discussions will be organized around guides. There is more to do, however. We offer a few suggestions for thinking through a discussion from start to finish, though we will see in the next section that not everything can be anticipated in advance.

1. *Decide how to introduce the discussion.* Like all instructional activities, discussions must be introduced in such a way that students are prepared for what is to come. Just as you now know to activate prior knowledge and set purposes before a reading assignment, you should plan similar measures for the beginning of a discussion. Reminding students of the key topics and telling them succinctly what you hope to accomplish are ways to start. You may occasionally vary this approach by asking a rhetorical question, offering a provocative quotation, or employing some other attention-getting device.

2. *Decide where to depart from the guide.* A discussion that merely "covers" the guide risks becoming as tedious as a discussion that comprises only literal-level questions. Even if the guide contains higher-order questions, you have asked the students to think through them in advance, so that sticking rigidly to the guide may have a deadening effect. Examine the guide for points where you wish to extend the knowledge and understanding of the topics a little further than the text. Think about how an effective departure question might be framed or what additional facts or examples you might wish to add. Students should come to expect these departures and may, with numerous chances, begin to anticipate them.

A very effective departure is to ask *why* the facts are as they are (Menke & Pressley, 1994). That is, the guide should provide the students with the factual basis of the content, but discussion can push understanding by causing them to elaborate on it. Doing so assists factual learning.

3. *Decide whom to ask.* In the next section, we describe the importance of involving every student in every discussion. This does not mean that certain students should not be matched with specific questions. If you are trying to develop certain insights or comprehension skills in a particular student, then you might wish to earmark key questions. If you do not want a smoothly progressing discussion to bog down at a critical point, you might select in advance a capable student to handle an especially difficult question at that juncture.

4. *Decide on an effective closure.* Good discussions don't simply trickle away with the last question. They end, like all well-planned instructional episodes, with a summing up, an effective closure, in which important facts and conclusions are summarized in brief review. Students should develop an expectation that discussions will routinely end in this manner. You may involve them in this process by calling on them to offer key summary statements themselves. This is an excellent exercise in deciding which ideas and concepts are the most important.

Conducting a Discussion

Even though you have planned your discussion, conducting it is more than a matter of simply proceeding step-by-step through your plan. Unforeseen situations will inevitably arise. Being able to think on your feet and apply what is now known about effective questioning is the mark of the expert teacher. The guidelines we present in this section are powerful techniques that should become second nature.

Ensuring Student Involvement

Not long ago, the first author observed a middle school teacher as she videotaped a class discussion. Her class consisted of equal numbers of boys and girls and an equal proportion of blacks and whites. During the discussion, the teacher addressed 90 percent of her questions to white females. When asked afterward why this had been her practice, she denied that she had done it. It was not until she reviewed the videotape that she became convinced of the fact! Her case is similar to that of many teachers who *think* they are distributing questions equitably but instead tend to direct them to a small subset of the class, usually abler students, who are most likely to respond appropriately.

Asking questions of students who can answer them creates the illusion of effective teaching. It may soothe our egos and deceive us into believing that widespread learning is occurring, but we are in fact denying ourselves the opportunity to monitor all students and to remediate difficulties when, through such monitoring, we discover them. On the other hand, using the content literacy guide as the blueprint of a discussion is one way to create reassuring expectations for all students about what the discussion will entail. Another way is to give students five minutes prior to the beginning of the discussion in which to *write* a response to a single higher-level question based on the selection. Gaskins and her colleagues (Gaskins, Satlow, Hyson, Ostertag, & Six, 1994) found that this exercise caused all of the students to think through an issue and gave them "something to say" when the time came.

Effective questioners are systematic. They ensure broad student involvement by keeping track of which students have participated and which have not. Some studies have shown that even an obvious system can be effective, such as proceeding up one row, down the next, and so on. A difficulty with this approach is that it is predictable and may lose some students once their turn has passed. In addition, it does not mesh well with our advice about earmarking key questions in advance for certain students. A system that ensures involvement of students, while preserving some spontaneity and flexibility, is that of placing check marks next to students' names once they have responded. You can tell at a glance who has yet to participate (see Figure 10.3). Two suggestions may make this approach especially effective. One is to use a plus (+) or minus (–) instead of a check mark to denote whether a question was successfully answered. You can then return to unsuccessful students to give them additional opportunities. The second suggestion is to make it a point to call on some students more than once even before everyone has had a chance. This policy prevents the notion that it is safe to drift off as soon as an answer is given (a problem with the up-one-row-down-the-next approach). In short, you can keep attentiveness relatively high by not being too predictable.

Effective questioners are also good listeners (Barton, 1995). They do not assume that all students must come to think exactly like the teacher. Instead, they encourage and reward efforts to think about content in novel ways, and they ask themselves why a given student might have responded in an unexpected way.

Timing and Questioning

How questions are timed is an issue of great interest to classroom researchers. Four recurrent findings are noteworthy.

First, student attentiveness tends to increase when the teacher occasionally poses the question prior to naming a particular student to answer it. A teacher might say, for example, "In a moment, I'm going to ask someone to define *photosynthesis*." This approach should not be the primary one used but should serve instead as a way of introducing variety and enhancing interest.

FIGURE 10.3

The class roll can be used to chart student responses

Student	Oct. 3
Adams, Bill	– – +
Cane, Brenda	+
Douglas, Rich	–
Elkins, Maxine	

. . .

Note: A plus (+) indicates a correct or defensible response. A minus (–) indicates a wrong answer or one that lacks a reasonable basis in fact.

Second, it is a good idea to wait a few seconds following an incorrect answer or a failure to respond at all. This "wait time" provides the student a chance to think further, which is especially important in the case of higher-level questions. When a response is incomplete, incorrect, or otherwise inappropriate, wait time subtly conveys the message that more is expected. If you have never practiced wait time before, do not be surprised if it seems a little uncomfortable at first. Society conditions us to avoid "dead air"—periods of silence during conversation—but these are vital if thinking and talking are to occur together. (They don't always, as you know!)

Third, a subtle device useful on occasion (though not frequently) is to wait a few seconds after an appropriate response to an inferential or critical question. The wordless message that you expect more will often prompt students to elaborate on what they have already said.

Fourth, regardless of whether an answer is correct or incorrect, appropriate or inappropriate, the student needs prompt feedback. This knowledge may come from the teacher, from another student, or from printed materials referenced during the discussion, but it must come quickly. A recent comprehensive review of research on the timing of feedback can be summarized in four words: the sooner the better (Kulik & Kulik, 1988).

Responding to Incorrect or Inadequate Answers

We have been making a distinction between answers that are plainly wrong and those that are somehow inappropriate or inadequate. Our distinction concerns the *level* of the question. Literal questions, with clear-cut "Christopher Columbus" answers, can be answered incorrectly. But when questions require students to arrive at inferences or critical judgments, the situation is more complex. With every critical judgment and many inferences, the issue is not correctness but defensibility, as in the example of Mr. Williams and his student Harold on page 157. Has the student reasoned appropriately on a foundation of fact? This distinction—between questions with clear, factual answers and questions that require reasoning and judgment—is important in deciding how to react when a student has responded unacceptably.

Prompting. For literal questions, a useful technique is prompting. This is the process of providing the student with additional information, hints, and clues that might elicit a correct response. Good prompts progress from subtle nudges to heavy-handed pushes in the right direction. For example, during a recent observation we heard a middle grades social studies teacher ask a particular student to tell who had contributed the land for the United Nations headquarters. When the student could not answer, the teacher hinted that it was a famous New York family. When even this didn't work, she said, "It starts with an R!" Prompting isn't always successful, to be sure, but it is a skill worth developing and applying.

Top-Down Question Clusters. For higher-level questions, prompting is less appropriate. Because such questions call for students to reason on the basis of facts, the problem is more often a matter of selecting and using facts than of recalling them. A useful strategy in these instances is the top-down question cluster. You will recall from Chapter 8 that cluster guides endeavor to lead students to appropriate inferences and judgments by taking them first through a series of relevant literal questions. This bottom-up approach can be reversed whenever a student stumbles on a higher-level question. A *top-down cluster* begins with an inferential or critical question that a student answers inappropriately. It then proceeds to one or more literal questions, the answers to which should provide the basis of the reasoning required by the initial question. The teacher therefore drops to the literal level until the relevant facts are introduced into the discussion. The focus then returns to the original question. The example of Socrates and Meno's boy might have involved a top-down cluster if Socrates had begun by asking the boy to infer whether the square root of 2 is a real number. You can see that the top-down cluster is akin to prompting because the teacher is not content to give up on the students but wishes to urge them to reason out an appropriate response. Top-down clusters are not possible, of course, when the initial question is itself at the literal level: You are already at the level of explicitly stated factual information.

Vintage Questioning

Mr. Williams and Harold

Not long ago, the first author observed the following interaction between an eleventh-grade student, Harold, and Mr. Williams, an American history teacher. The class had just finished reading a textbook chapter on the American Revolution and were about to begin a discussion. Mr. Williams led off with what he apparently thought was a rhetorical question.

"The Revolution," he said, "is the best thing that ever happened to this country. I think you'd all agree with that, wouldn't you?"

Toward the back of the room, one student raised his hand. Mr. Williams's expression wilted, just a little, as though he was afraid of what was to come. "Harold?" he said.

The boy lowered his hand, "I'm afraid I disagree," he said. "I know most people don't think so, but I think the Revolution was the worst thing that ever happened, not the best."

Mr. Williams at that moment faced a classic dilemma. He had asked a critical-level question and was met with a response that he felt was inconsistent with the facts. His decision was to drop to the literal level and challenge Harold to back up his judgment. "That's a pretty radical view," he said. "How did you arrive at it? Give us a few facts."

"Well," Harold began, "in the first place, we'd have avoided a lot of casualties on both sides. Surely that's worth something." He paused briefly and half smiled at Mr. Williams. "Plus, I've read ahead a little," he went on. "I learned that all the other colonies in Britain's empire were simply given their independence without a war. If we'd bided our time, that would probably have happened to us. We might have had a parliament instead of a congress, and a prime minister instead of a president, but so what?"

Mr. Williams looked thoughtful. "Anything else?"

"There's one thing," said Harold. "Britain abolished slavery in the 1820s. This affected all its colonies. But of course we were no longer in the empire so it didn't affect us. If we had been, we'd have been spared forty years of slavery and probably the Civil War, too."

"The Civil War?" someone asked.

"Sure. The South couldn't have fought the North plus Britain in the 1820s. They'd have had to give in."

By now even I was nodding my head. Harold had brought some "extra" facts into the discussion in order to defend an unpopular position in a novel way. To his credit, Mr. Williams acknowledged Harold's resourcefulness (though a little grudgingly, it seemed to me). When we ask critical questions, the results can sometimes challenge even our firmest judgments. So be prepared to model what you expect of your students!

Think-Alouds. An excellent method of demonstrating how thinking ought to occur in responding to higher-level questions is the think-aloud (Oster, 2001; Tierney & Readence, 2005; Wilhelm, 2001). The teacher "makes thinking public" by talking through the process of arriving at an inference or critical judgment. Cullum (1998) suggested ways in which teachers might use think-alouds to gradually build comprehension ability (see also Kucan & Beck, 1997). However, think-alouds are also useful in content classrooms when students experience difficulty with higher-level thinking. That is, it is not necessary to make thinking skills a specific focus of your teaching in order to employ think-alouds. They are quite helpful as a troubleshooting device, one in which the teacher briefly models proper thinking (without making an issue of it) and then moves on to other matters. Consider the following exchange, based on "The Worst Bank Robbers" (page 159):

Teacher: Maria, do you think the bank robbers might have been better off to abandon their plan after they left the first time?

Maria: Considering how it all turned out, yes.

Teacher: But what about before they made the second attempt? Did they have good reason to just give up and go home?

Maria: I'm not sure I know what you mean.

Teacher: Well, let's think about that first episode. You'll recall they got caught in the revolving doors.

Maria: Yes.

Teacher: The staff had to help them out. Now I don't suppose people got stuck in the doors very often, so it was all quite a spectacle. Think about it: three grown men caught in those doors. Everyone's attention was drawn to them, people who might later be witnesses who could identify them. And, of course, they would need to pass through those very doors again to get away with the money. I'm not sure I'd trust myself to do that if I'd had trouble the first time. Would you?

Maria: No. If they'd really thought about it, they might have considered a different bank.

Teacher: Yes, or a different line of work!

Think-alouds offer several powerful advantages. They provide an effective means of modeling a complex process. They tend to be quick and are therefore useful when available time is short or when a discussion is proceeding smoothly and you do not wish it to bog down. Moreover, there is now good research evidence that think-alouds do work as a method of improving comprehension (e.g., Duffy et al., 1987). Wade (1990) has suggested an interesting twist: asking students to share their own think-alouds. The teacher can then assess the thought processes a particular student is employing.

Slicing. A second device sometimes useful when students balk at a higher-order question is slicing (Otto, 1991; Pearson & Johnson, 1978; Readence & Moore, 1980). *Slicing* involves reducing the scope of a question without altering what it essentially asks. Consider a social studies teacher who asks a student to project the possible consequences of a given piece of legislation. When the student selected does not respond, the teacher might "slice" the question: "Can you suggest just one possible result?"

Slicing is also useful with literal questions whenever they ask students to recall a large amount of information. A history teacher might be frustrated when students cannot recite the three principal causes of the Civil War, even though they were clearly delineated in the text. A science teacher may throw up her hands when a top student cannot recall the steps of the scientific method—steps that were plainly enumerated in a key figure. These questions call for an extensive response, however, and even good students might be reluctant to begin something they may not be able to finish with success. One solution is to slice the question. "All right," the history teacher might continue, "who can remember *one* of the causes?" Likewise, the science teacher might proceed by paring the question down to size: "Let's start with the *first* step. Do you recall that?"

*A word is dead
When it is said
Some say.*

*I say it just
Begins to live
That day.*

EMILY DICKINSON

Constructive Criticism. The techniques we have been describing—prompting top-down clustering, think-alouds, and slicing—have the effect not only of facilitating good comprehension, but of positively reinforcing self-esteem as well. Because such techniques leave the student with a feeling of success, they have a face-saving effect that is important in promoting productive attitudes toward learning. Any technique useful in providing negative feedback (that is, in telling a student that an answer is inaccurate or inappropriate) is a means of constructive criticism. The message is not pleasant, to be sure, but it must be conveyed if learning is to continue. However, there is no reason for the message to be punitive, sarcastic, or perceived as an attack on the student's self-worth.

In addition to the devices already introduced, we suggest the following guidelines for becoming a constructive critic.

1. *Never equate the student with the response.* Through your comments, try to make clear that it is the answer that is incorrect, inadequate, or unacceptable—not the student. This may seem like a trivial distinction, but it can speak volumes to the pupil who lacks self-assurance and breadth of knowledge.

2. *Find something positive to stress.* Accentuating some positive aspect of a wrong answer can be reassuring and encouraging. It is a technique you should probably reserve for occasions when the need for such encouragement seems substantial, however. Making positive comments

about every unacceptable response may convey an undesirable message to students. When circumstances warrant, however, several approaches are useful. One involves identifying some portion of the answer that is acceptable. When a student responds correctly to half of a two-part question, you should acknowledge the correct portion. Likewise, when the response is in some way near the mark, the teacher should underscore the closeness, as in the following example:

> **Teacher:** John, can you name a nineteenth-century president?
> **John:** Franklin Roosevelt.
> **Teacher:** Well, he was *born* in the nineteenth century.

Another method of responding to an incorrect answer made in good faith is to suggest a question that would fit the answer. For example:

> **Teacher:** Mary, what's the chemical symbol for carbon?
> **Mary:** Ca?
> **Teacher:** Close. If I'd said calcium, you'd be right on!

This approach can be overdone but occasionally provides an alternative means of accentuating some positive aspect of an incorrect response.

3. *Try focusing on the thinking process.* When the product (the answer itself) is wrong, there may be something praiseworthy in the process (the thinking that led to the answer). Asking students to recount how they arrived at an answer can be an effective way to lay the thought process bare and find something positive to say, such as "You were on the right track to this point."

Responding to Correct and Appropriate Answers

What happens when there is no discernible problem with an answer? In some respects, this question may seem too simple to take seriously. After all, if there's no problem for the student, there's none for the teacher, right? Actually, there are decisions to make even when all goes well.

Praise.   One issue is whether to praise the response. By praise we do not mean feedback that the answer is correct or acceptable. Such feedback is a necessary part of any exchange. By praise we mean verbal reinforcers that go beyond mere feedback and communicate that the response was exemplary in nature. It might seem natural to suggest that there can never be enough praise—that if some is good, then more is better. Research suggests otherwise, however. Effective teachers tend to be stingy with praise, applying it to as few as 10 percent of the correct answers that occur in discussions (e.g., Brophy, 1986). Praise, it would appear, is like money: The more of it there is in circulation, the less any of it is worth!

The Worst Bank Robbers

In August 1975 three men were on their way in to rob the Royal Bank of Scotland at Rothesay, when they got stuck in the revolving doors. They had to be helped free by the staff and, after thanking everyone, sheepishly left the building.

A few minutes later they returned and announced their intention of robbing the bank, but none of the staff believed them. When, at first, they demanded £5,000 the head cashier laughed at them, convinced that it was a practical joke.

Considerably disheartened by this, the gang leader reduced his demand first to £500, then to £50 and ultimately to 50 pence. By this stage the cashier could barely control herself for laughter.

Then one of the men jumped over the counter and fell awkwardly on the floor, clutching at his ankle. The other two made their getaway, but got trapped in the revolving doors for a second time, desperately pushing the wrong way.

Source: From *The Book of Failures* by Stephen J. Pyle.

To be most effective, praise must be more than sparing. It must be *specific*. Students must know what it is that makes a response praiseworthy if they are to be able to produce similar responses in the future (which is the point of praise). Rather than say, "That's a good answer," it is more effective to say, "That's a good answer because . . . " Praise must also be *varied*. For students who hear the same congratulatory word or phrase repeatedly, the expression soon rings hollow. For teachers who concentrate on making their praise specific, however, variety ordinarily takes care of itself.

Follow-Up Questions.   Another decision is whether to follow a correct or appropriate answer with additional questions. There are at least three reasons for doing so. One involves inferences and critical judgments that may be difficult for some class members. By asking the student how an appropriate conclusion was reached, the thought process is revealed for all to hear. Another reason is to extend the student's thinking a bit. Even though the answer was appropriate, a teacher might press for additional development of a line of thought. Finally, a student may need to clarify some aspect of a response. For example, a word or expression that is familiar to the teacher may require explanation for some students.

Alternatives to Teacher-Led Discussions

Traditional instruction gives the teacher a central role in planning and conducting a discussion. More recent thinking urges a reduced role, at least at times, in an effort to develop within students the capacity to formulate their own questions and to see material from more than a single perspective en route to becoming independent learners. Traditionalists often view this notion skeptically, but it is easy enough to take a few short steps in the direction of student-led discussions. Getting one's feet wet by encouraging students to produce their own questions and to don various roles during a discussion may convince you of the utility of instructional options in which the normal roles of teacher and student are occasionally reversed.

The Social Context of Discussion

Because discussion requires two or more people, we must also consider its social aspects. The discussants assume certain roles with respect to one another, and these roles affect both how the experience proceeds and what is gained from it. In the teacher-directed discussions we have been describing, the teacher can assume a variety of roles, from recorder to coach to critic. The student's role is generally the traditional one of an inferior progressing toward equality with the teacher in content understanding. Both teacher and student assume, without ever saying so, that such equality will not occur, at least not during the course of instruction. The relationship is similar to that between master and apprentice. The former, through discussion, monitors, corrects, and extends the performance of the latter. Not surprisingly, this difference in status leads to observable differences in the way both students and teachers take part in discussions. In his review of research, Carlsen (1991) noted findings that students react differently to teacher questions than to questions posed by their peers (usually giving shorter, more declarative answers to teachers) and that teachers tend to wrest control of the discussion away from students who ask questions, often by responding with another question.

Social relationships also exist among students. Some of those relationships involve inevitable comparisons in terms of content mastery. The roles of "brain" and "failure," with various degrees in between, are inescapably clear to students. Other social relationships exist, many of which may be invisible to the teacher. These may involve friendship, role modeling, romance, rivalry, or antagonism. They involve perceptions of broad socioeconomic class membership and ethnic identity as well as membership in school circles and cliques. Whenever a teacher calls on a student to answer a question (or participate in any other activity), the response depends in part on the effect the student believes it will have on others.

Most important, each student is involved in social relationships that extend outside the classroom, to parents, peers, and siblings. These relationships exert powerful influences on the thoughts and attitudes of students and cause school (and any course taught in school) to be viewed in the context of these forces. For some students the forces are quite positive and compel them to become active learners; for many, they are negative and inhibit participation to the extent a teacher may desire.

One way of breaking the hold of negative social forces on classroom learning is to deliberately alter the roles played by teachers and students. The result can be students who, caught temporarily off balance, must think in new ways from novel perspectives. (We look next at several methods of altering social roles for this purpose.) Another way of dissolving negative social forces is to bring the students into the planning process by giving them a say in how the discussion will proceed and what ground rules will be followed (Calfee, Dunlap, & Wat, 1994). Yet another is to hold discussions frequently, so that students get used to the idea of participating and a sense of classroom community can develop (Alvermann et al., 1995).

Student-Generated Questions

Placing students in the role of questioner upsets the normal order of a classroom, and the results can be productive. Researchers have looked rather closely at student questioning over the past two decades, and the results are encouraging. Gillespie (1990–1991), in her comprehensive review of research, came to these conclusions:

- All students can be taught to generate questions, but some direct instruction in how to do so is usually necessary.
- A good place to begin is by teaching the types of questions possible.
- The poorest readers tend to benefit the most from producing questions.
- Asking questions tends to improve both comprehension and motivation to read.
- Student-produced questions probably work because they focus attention during reading and compel the student to seek to understand before a good question can be formulated.

These findings are encouraging but also make it clear that some preparation is necessary (Ciardiello, 1998; Crapse, 1995; Ortiz, 1996; Sampson, 1995; Taboada & Guthrie, 2006; Tower, 2000). Students should know before reading that questions will be required, so that this expectation can become an added purpose for reading. They must also understand basic question types (literal, inferential, and critical, in particular) if the questions they produce are to comprise anything beyond the literal. You will recall that we have already recommended direct instruction in these types while you familiarize students with reading guides.

K-W-L is a good means of encouraging students to formulate questions. The W step (what students *want* to learn) is a natural opportunity to pose questions about an upcoming reading selection. Tower (2000) warns that the questions students generate during a K-W-L lesson tend to be exclusively factual in nature, however. They must be nudged toward including higher-level questions as well. Teachers must be careful not to take over the K-W-L process, of course, by imposing higher-order questions of their own that they feel their students *should* have asked.

Ciardiello (1998) stressed the need to train students in the difference between convergent and divergent questions. Convergent questions constrain thinking toward a single answer. They are literal in nature or involve straight-forward inferences. Divergent questions invite a range of answers and are critical in nature or else entail speculative inferences. Ciardiello warned that the natural tendency among students is to generate divergent questions, which are clear-cut and simple to ask and answer. Students must be instructed in how to ask divergent questions, and plenty of teacher modeling is essential.

Student-generated questions are therefore not an unreachable goal that requires prohibitive preparation. We now look at one of the best-known approaches to making them work.

ReQuest

*Reciprocal quest*ioning (ReQuest) is a technique developed by Manzo (1968, 1969) for giving students the dual roles of questioner and respondent in the same discussion. A belief underlying ReQuest is that the task of formulating a question requires a student to think actively about the content of the material (Tierney & Readence, 2005).

Manzo originally viewed the technique as a global lesson plan in which the teacher begins by introducing the reading selection, as in the DRA and DR–TA. Teacher and student then read a portion of the selection silently. When they finish, the student asks questions of the teacher. The teacher responds, with book closed, and may reinforce good questioning technique on the part of the student. The student is free to ask as many questions as desired. The roles are then reversed, and the teacher attempts to move the discussion to a point at which the student can make reasonable predictions about what is to come. After completing the selection, the two reconsider the student's prediction and may also engage in other follow-up activities (Manzo & Manzo, 1995).

A limitation of ReQuest as a global lesson plan is that it assumes a tutorial situation (one student only), or at most the presence of only a small group. It also has many of the features of a DRA or a DR–TA. Not surprisingly, many teachers have modified the technique to make it work in larger groups and in the context of other global lesson designs. One modification, reciprocal teaching, places students together in the role of teacher and requires that they conduct short lessons on the material in addition to questioning (Palincsar & Brown, 1984).

Another modification, suggested by Tierney and Readence (2005), involves an exchange of roles after each question. This format allows for any number of students to become involved in the discussion as questioners. It also works well as a postreading device. That is, the teacher can delay reciprocal questioning until the students have finished the selection. While ReQuest can work as an "unannounced" alternative to a traditional discussion, a teacher can also prepare students for the experience. Asking students to read with the idea of forming good questions to be used later in a give-and-take round of questioning is an excellent way of setting purposes. You should add it to the strategies introduced in Chapter 7. However, this particular approach to purpose setting does not mean that reading guides cannot be used. In fact, question formation can be built deliberately into various portions of a guide.

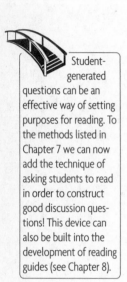

Student-generated questions can be an effective way of setting purposes for reading. To the methods listed in Chapter 7 we can now add the technique of asking students to read in order to construct good discussion questions! This device can also be built into the development of reading guides (see Chapter 8).

Cooperative Learning Revisited

You will recall that the Jigsaw technique, described in Chapter 8, also involved students in the act of teaching. Each student was made responsible for a section of the reading material and used a corresponding content literacy guide to plan and deliver a lesson to other group members. Jigsaw provides one means of encouraging student-generated questions by placing students in the role of teachers. Our experience, however, has been that most students need to be reminded that questioning should be a part of instruction. Otherwise, there is an alarmingly strong tendency to resort to a questionless lecture approach to teaching. Nevertheless, cooperative learning provides an excellent circumstance for discussion, since the groups are small and since each student has specific responsibilities that might give rise to talk (Slavin, 1999; Stearns, 1999).

Strategies for Controversy and Misinformation

You may suspect that controversial issues enliven discussion and promote the kind of active engagement that enhances learning. The actual result can be quite different, however. When students encounter material that conflicts with their existing beliefs and values, learning and retention often suffer.

Two situations are important to consider. In one, the new material is in conflict with a student's values and past critical judgments. In the other, new information is at odds with "facts" the student had previously believed to be true and that may prove difficult to supplant (Dole & Niederhauser, 1990). In both cases, the introduction of the new material creates what Festinger (1957) called "cognitive dissonance." The student can, on the one hand, reject or somehow discount the new information. ("That can't be true," "I don't believe it," "That's not always the case," the student may respond.) On the other hand, the student can accept the new information—but only at the cost of modifying prior notions. You will recall from Chapter 2 that Piaget (1952) described this process as accommodation. It is not always easy and may involve discomfort, soul searching, and self-criticism. As Lynch and McKenna (1990) put it:

> Changing schemata may be difficult because doing so requires that students recognize why their prior notions were incorrect or indefensible. If the controversial topic engages their emotions, it is often more comfortable for the students to reject the teacher or the text

rather than reexamine their erroneous beliefs. (Teachers who deal with controversial issues often notice that students take challenges of their ideas as a personal attack on their self-worth and react defensively.) (p. 317)

Misinformation and controversy are frequent factors in classroom discussions and deserve conscious attention from teachers. You should begin by realizing that these factors can inhibit learning even while they arouse your students. Beyond this realization, the following strategies may be useful.

The Thinking Rule.   A teacher must make clear the guidelines for discussing sensitive issues. When, on occasion, some students become abusive, Berman (1987) has suggested the *thinking rule*. When enacted by the teacher, the rule requires that the next five minutes of discussion be devoted to producing ideas in support of the person whose views have just been attacked. The thinking rule causes students to view matters from perspectives very different from those they prefer. It subtly conveys the message that other perspectives are possible.

Stipulation.   Heated discussions can sometimes end abruptly when one student makes a sweeping pronouncement, phrased as a fact, but without documentation. Statements like these can cause a discussion to die prematurely: "With all the cars and factories it's impossible to save the environment, so why talk about it?" Newmann and Oliver (1970) have recommended the use of *stipulation* at such points—a technique that involves the temporary invention of facts or assumptions to restart the discussion. Here is an example of a teacher employing stipulation to lead a discussion out of a dead end:

Tom: Hardened criminals should be executed because the prisons aren't making them any better anyway.

Mary: You don't know that! How many criminals do you know?

Teacher: Let's stipulate a fact here—let's assume that prisons could be changed from their current form to some other form that did indeed rehabilitate criminals. If that were true, Tom, what would you think of the death penalty? (Lynch & McKenna, 1990, p. 318)

Note that the word *stipulate* does not mean that an actual fact is necessary. The teacher simply imposes a "fact" that the students assume is true *for the sake of argument*.

Thinking Hats.   DeBono (1999) has offered a novel suggestion for encouraging students to adopt perspectives different from those they normally have. The teacher assigns various students to wear one of six color-coded "thinking hats" to designate a range of viewpoints. The colors are suggestive of the perspective they represent and add a definite sense of imagery to the discussion. The colors are these:

white	=	objective, fact-oriented thinking
red	=	emotional, intuitive thinking
black	=	critical, fault-finding, judgmental thinking
yellow	=	optimistic, positively focused thinking
green	=	creative, innovative thinking
blue	=	overseeing, managerial thinking

The hats probably do not need to exist in reality, but we believe it is better to acquire six hats (or make paper ones!) and physically distribute them at the beginning of a discussion. The student donning a particular hat will be more likely to keep in mind the responsibility it entails, while other students will have visual reminders of which students have assumed each of the roles.

Assignment of the hats should vary from one discussion to the next; you could even have students exchange hats in the midst of a lengthy discussion. You can use knowledge of your students to make assignments that encourage them occasionally to alter their perspectives. A typically argumentative, fault-finding student might profit from wearing the yellow hat on occasion. A student who tends to react emotionally and impulsively to situations that require critical thinking would do well to don the white hat at times.

Discussion and Recitation: A Second Look

In this chapter, we have maintained that recitation, in which a teacher simply monitors content acquisition, and discussion, in which a teacher encourages open exchanges of comments, questions, and reactions, can coexist in the same activity. Now that your background includes some of the issues and research findings that touch on the problem, it is time to reconsider our suggestion.

We now know that social relationships in the classroom, especially those between teacher and student, influence the ways in which students participate. Teacher questions, for example, can have the effect of inhibiting true, invitational discussion by provoking short, factual answers without elaboration (Boggs, 1972; Dillon, 1985). How does a teacher balance the need to monitor with the need to stimulate shared thinking?

Several answers are warranted. First, not all classes are alike. You may find that a given group participates fully and freely in teacher-led discussions during which some questions serve a monitoring function. Second, your reliance on inferential and critical questions as mainstays should do much to prevent terse, lower-level responses since they are inappropriate to such questions. Third, building discussions around content literacy guides that both rely on such questions and give students ample opportunity to formulate answers should help still further.

If even these measures fail to foster open and uninhibited discussion, try partitioning the discussion into phases. Herber (1978) recommended laying the groundwork for the literal first, then the inferential, and finally the critical. As we mentioned in Chapter 8, we believe this approach is a little disjointed, because relevant factual information is widely separated from related inferences and judgments. It seems more productive to complete the discussion according to the guide's organization and then to open things up to more freewheeling commentary. This suggestion implies a two-stage discussion. During the first stage, a range of questions issues largely from the teacher, who monitors, while at the same time encouraging and modeling, higher cognition. During the second stage, the teacher relinquishes control and with a minimum of intervention allows students to take the conversation where they will. Alpert (1987) found that students tended to participate actively in such discussions when teachers observed the following guidelines:

1. Ask questions that are personal or critical, not factual. Avoid inferential, as well as literal, questions.
2. Do not evaluate student responses. Do not pass judgment. Accept and encourage instead.
3. Do not decide who shall speak. That is, do not call on students. Let the discussion take its course.

It is up to you to gauge the need for such measures in your own classes. Techniques for accomplishing a variety of purposes through discussion are now clearly available. You must decide your own purposes, assess whether they are being met, and then select among the techniques accordingly.

Discussion and Writing

There is no subject so old that something new cannot be said about it.
FYODOR
DOSTOEVSKY

Imagine a discussion in *written* form, in which teacher and students exchange comments and questions after writing them out. Most of the advantages of an oral discussion would still apply, such as monitoring students' understanding of content and correcting and extending that understanding. Some of the features would be absent, of course, including the speed, spontaneity, and give-and-take of a productive classroom dialogue. Nor would feedback from the teacher be immediate.

On the other hand, there are compensating strengths to make written dialogue well worth considering. It limits the negative effect of social forces exerted by peers. It gives students ample time to consider replies to higher-order questions. It permits the exchange of sensitive comments in private. It can combine replies with other activities. (For example, a teacher might write, "I think this will be clearer when we've finished Chapter 6. Let's come back to it then.") Perhaps most important, written interchanges take full advantage of writing as a learning tool, a function we discussed in Chapters 1 and 2.

In the remainder of this chapter we describe a number of techniques for converting discussion (or parts of discussion, such as question generation) to written form. We do not intend these as alternatives to oral discussion but as supplements that offer additional benefits.

Dialogue Journals

Staton's (1980) original intent in using the term *dialogue journal* was to denote a correspondence focused on students' understanding of and responses to literature. The technique has clear applications to other content areas. Of all the possible writing-based approaches to discussion, it is closest in form to oral discussion because of the progressive nature of the interchange: from teacher to student, back to teacher, and so forth. As we shall see, this alternating form is not necessary to writing adaptations.

Hall and Robinson (1995) have stressed the need for affective considerations in teacher contributions to dialogue journals. These include accentuating positive aspects of what the student has written, responding at the same time with sincerity and meaning, and protecting the feelings of each student. Such guidelines not only make sense but are largely congruent with those associated with oral questioning listed earlier in this chapter (Nistler, 1998).

Dialogue journals have much to offer, but they also have several drawbacks. First, they may not be effective with some students, especially those with poor verbal skills and those whose feelings are not readily expressed. Second, they become tedious if overused or used mechanically or with indifference. Baskin (1994) found that after even six months of use dialogue journals did not always provide teachers with adequate information about student understanding. Third, they tend to be time-consuming if meaningful teacher input is to be a part of the exchange.

You may have noted a similarity between the dialogue journal and a reading guide. A crucial difference is that students respond to all of the guide's tasks before receiving *any* response from the teacher. In the journal, the exchange of comments and questions after each entry means that the "discussion" may assume a direction of its own as entries build on and react to one another.

The ideal place for dialogue journals in content classrooms may well be *after* students have completed reading guides and *after* oral classroom discussion. Content knowledge of present topics will by then be adequate for the kind of extension, refinement, and individual pursuit journals afford.

Clearly, dialogue journals offer an opportunity for students to pursue lines of thinking with the input and guidance of an expert (Cohen, 2007; Tierney & Readence, 2005; Werderich, 2006). Edwards (1991–1992) has suggested that teachers can sometimes involve students in a "dialectical" thinking process, in which, by raising tactful counterpoints to a student's statements, the teacher encourages an evolution in the student's viewpoint. Applications like these argue against any attempt to correct the mechanics of writing, as attempts to do so would probably dampen student participation. As Strackbein and Tillman (1987) noted, "The journal is for a private audience—not a critical public" (p. 29). This no-red-pencil policy not only encourages student involvement but also makes the demands on teachers realistic by focusing on meaning.

> Dialogue journals also provide another means of assessing content learning (Paris & Oyres, 1994). Their entries can provide running supplements to the content literacy inventory (discussed in Chapter 3).

Other Approaches to Written Discussion

There are few limits to the variations possible on written interchanges with students. We offer here just a few.

Anonymous Questions. You may have viewed talk shows during which the host responds humorously to questions written in advance by members of the audience. This technique can work in classroom settings. The teacher asks students to submit questions following a class discussion. They can be collected in a "question box" (like a suggestion box). Students who still fail to understand certain aspects of new material even after the discussion may be too embarrassed to continue asking questions in class. The question box approach allows students to ask questions anonymously.

Questions to Outsiders. Students can involve others besides the teacher in written discussion by writing letters that include questions and observations (see Figure 10.4). Students who share a particular interest might undertake this project as a group. You will need to provide specific

> *Talking is a hydrant in the yard and writing is a faucet upstairs in the house. Opening the first takes all the pressure off the second.*
>
> ROBERT FROST

FIGURE 10.4

A class letter, drafted as a collaborative project, and the unexpected reply it received

Office of the Mayor
Post Radium
Northwest Territories
CANADA

Dear Sir or Madam:

Our sixth grade class has been studying the geography of North America. Our teacher often uses a large rolled map that pulls down like a blind. Several of us noticed your town, located on the shore of Great Bear Lake. There do not appear to be any cities anywhere near to you. There also seem to be no roads leading in or out. Some of us think your town is there because of mining. This would explain its name. It is so far north, we think it must be snowed in much of the year. Are we right? What can you tell us about your town? Thank you for any information you can give us.

Sincerely,

(Signed by 27 class members)

Handwritten note on the envelope, which was returned unopened:

Dear Sender—

Town no longer exists.

—Postmaster
Yellowknife
Northwest Territories
CANADA

suggestions in terms of where they should send their inquiries. The beginnings of such a list might include the following:

- Governmental agencies (the Freedom of Information Act requires that they respond!)
- Organizations associated with a topic
- Textbook authors
- Nearby university professors in the field being studied
- Local individuals with expertise in the area

Writing when properly managed, is but a different name for conversion.
LAURENCE STERNE

Student Self-Questioning.   Try asking students to compose dialogues in which they both pose and respond to questions (Poindexter, 1995; Rich & Blake, 1995; Williamson, 1996). These Socratic "exchanges" will encourage students to form their own questions as they encounter new material. Your responses to the dialogues should be directed not only at the accuracy and defensibility of answers but at the appropriateness and insights of the questions as well. A specific application requires each student to select an individual (real or generalized) and then write both sides of an interview conducted with that individual. This technique takes Wood's (1988) point-of-view guide (discussed in Chapter 8) a step farther by asking students to formulate their own interview questions (Commeyras & Sumner, 1995).

SUMMARY

Questioning serves many purposes in content classrooms. It enables a teacher to monitor learning. It provides an opportunity to further develop students' understanding. It also takes advantage of social relationships that inevitably exist among teacher and students.

Discussion that amounts to more than student recitation of factual material is rare. This is unfortunate, because discussion that invites students to share ideas and think aloud in a nonthreatening environment takes advantage of the fact that answering questions is a constructive process. Students refine and clarify knowledge through the process of responding. In this respect, responding is analogous to writing.

Planning a good discussion begins with the reading guide, but there is more to it. The teacher must decide how to introduce the discussion, at what points to depart from the guide, which students to call on, and how to close the discussion effectively.

Recent research has shed light on the issue of how to conduct a good discussion. Teachers must ensure that every student is involved. They must attend to the way questions and feedback are timed. They must react to wrong or inappropriate answers in productive ways, such as using prompting, top-down clusters, think-alouds, slicing, and constructive criticism. They must be equally attentive to how they react to acceptable answers. Praise must be sparing, specific, and varied. Follow-up questions should occasionally be used to extend thinking.

Alternatives to teacher-led discussion grow increasingly popular. They involve manipulating the social relationships that exist among teacher and students. An important technique is to place the student in the role of questioner. One such approach is reciprocal questioning (ReQuest), in which the teacher and students take turns asking and answering questions. Other techniques are useful when topics involve controversy or misunderstanding. The thinking rule compels students to support the victim of verbal attacks. Stipulation involves the teacher's statement of an assumption in order to get past an impasse. DeBono's (1999) "thinking hats" technique allows students to play a variety of predefined roles during the course of a discussion.

Many of the benefits of an oral discussion are available by conducting it in written form. Dialogue journals, which incorporate a written exchange between an individual student and the teacher, are closest in form to an oral discussion. Other techniques use anonymous student questions, questions sent to outsiders, and question-and-answer dialogues composed entirely by students.

Getting Involved

1. Identify a prominent teacher and ask permission to observe a class discussion. Be sure to obtain in advance a copy of any materials the students will have read. As the discussion proceeds, keep track of the number of literal, inferential, and critical questions the teacher asks. Make notes on specific classroom incidents that involve techniques such as top-down clustering, slicing, constructive criticism, and think-alouds. Afterward, discuss these incidents with the teacher.

2. Practice student-generated questioning by applying it to this course. Compose a few inferential and critical questions over the material to be discussed during your next class meeting. Then attempt to interject them at appropriate points into the discussion. Study the instructor's reaction. Was the teacher receptive to such questions? Did certain questions "work" better than others? If so, which ones and why?

3. Using a concept, fact, or principle from your field of expertise, compose your own Socratic dialogue in which you use questions to guide a hypothetical child to a particular conclusion or insight. Write both the teacher's and the student's contributions to the exchange. Where the latter is concerned, try to predict how a typical student might respond. Next, look for an opportunity to try out the dialogue on a real student. Did the student respond as you predicted? If not, were you able to recover and adjust, and ultimately reach the goal of your dialogue?

Reinforcing and Extending Content Knowledge

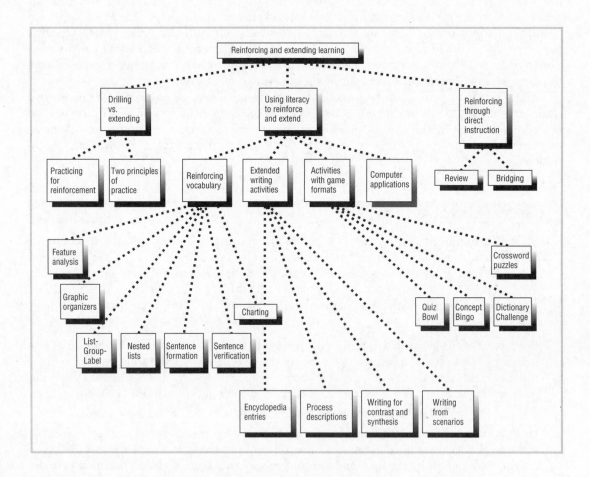

Practice is the best of all instructors.

—Publilius Syrus (first century B.C.)

We begin this chapter with a thought experiment. Imagine a list of twenty technical terms associated with a particular content subject. You must teach these new terms to three classes of seventh graders. You decide to try different techniques with each class and compare the results. You begin by introducing the terms in the same way to all three classes, using some of the approaches you learned about in Chapter 6. When you've finished, you're convinced that most of the students in all three classes have a working knowledge of the word meanings. For the first class, you move on to other topics and do not revisit the twenty terms. For the second class, you place the list of terms on an overhead projector and conduct a quick review once every two weeks. For the third class, you periodically relate one or more of the terms to new topics the class is studying. You remind the third class of the meanings of these words and make a deliberate connection with new content. At the end of the year, you give all three classes the same quiz over the twenty terms. Which class do you predict would do the best? Which do you think would do the worst?

As you might suspect, similar comparisons have long been a focus of educational research, and we can predict the results of our three scenarios with confidence. The second condition leads to better retention than the first, while the third condition is better still. Put differently, rote drill is more effective than no drill, but repeated meaningful involvement is even more effective.

Objectives

How does our example relate to teaching through text? In the remainder of this chapter, you will learn to

1. differentiate rote drill from higher-level practice activities;
2. state two essential rules governing the impact of practice;
3. describe and implement various methods of reinforcing content vocabulary;
4. describe and implement various activities for using extended writing to reinforce and deepen content understanding;
5. adapt a variety of reinforcing game formats for use in your own teaching specialty; and
6. explain how bridging and review offer opportunities to reinforce earlier material while introducing new material.

Drilling versus Extending

How does a teacher tell when a particular segment of content—a unit, a lesson, a concept—has been "covered"? Does the fact that students appear to *understand* the content make it safe to move on to new topics? There is often substantial pressure to do so, but unless the teacher makes provision to reinforce the content, the students' situation will be little different from this chapter's opening scenario, in which a new fact was encountered, understood, and then abandoned. Learning is reinforced whenever our experiences bring it to mind in meaningful ways.

Practicing for Reinforcement

One way of bringing content repeatedly to mind is through rote drill. In the second scenario, for example, the learner repeatedly reviews the same factual information until it is easily recalled. There are several drawbacks to this kind of drill. It tends to be tedious. It emphasizes low-level cognitive skills, such as quick recall. Most important, it fails to recognize the interconnectedness of the content.

On the other hand, drill does work as a means of enhancing the retention of information. A crucial question for teachers is whether it is possible to derive the benefits of drill without incurring its negative side effects. The answer is yes. By designing activities in which the recall of information is integrated with its application at higher levels, teachers can ensure the repetition needed for retention while deepening understanding through higher-level thought. By *higher level* we mean activities that stress relationships between and among concepts and that require students to make inferences and reach defensible critical judgments.

Two Principles of Practice

Can such activities effectively incorporate lower-level drill? Again, the answer is yes. The two basic principles of effective practice, now thoroughly documented by research, apply not only to rote drill but to higher-order activities as well.

The grand result of schooling is a mind with just vision to discern, with free force to do: the grand schoolmaster is Practice.

THOMAS CARLYLE

1. *Guided practice precedes independent practice.* After the introduction of new materials and skills, a teacher should provide opportunities for practice. Whether such practice includes the mere repetition of simple tasks or more advanced cognitive activities that *require* such tasks, practice opportunities must progress from a teacher-assisted situation to one in which learners undertake the tasks without help (e.g., Rosenshine, 1986). At two key points, the teacher must judge whether the students are ready to go on. One of these is the point between initial, direct instruction and guided practice. The second is between guided practice and independent practice. Proceeding to the next phase before readiness is achieved in the current phase will impair learning.

2. *Massed practice precedes distributed practice.* Practice opportunities should be especially frequent just after the introduction of new material. Extremely frequent practice opportunities are said to be *massed* and coincide roughly with the guided practice phase. As students become better prepared to undertake practice activities on their own, not only does the teacher's role diminish but the frequency of the activities declines as well. At this point, the activities are said to be *distributed*. That is, they occur periodically, after intervals during which newer content is introduced.

Using Literacy to Reinforce and Extend

What can teachers do to strengthen and deepen their students' understanding of content? While most teachers recognize the clear need to do so, they also feel frustration over curricular demands. There is always, it seems, another chapter to cover, another concept to introduce. The following suggestions can help.

1. *Distribute practice.* Remember that the frequency of activities does not need to be great once the students have initially grasped the content and have had some success in recalling and applying it.

2. *Give comprehensive exams.* Examinations that hold students accountable repeatedly for the same material compel them to distribute their review.

3. *Provide activities that link new content with old.* You can greatly increase the efficiency of practice by designing activities in which content previously taught is used with new material. This is usually not difficult because of the interconnectedness of the concepts.

4. *Provide activities that require higher-level skills.* When practice opportunities require students to apply and think about content, drill of individual facts will occur in meaningful contexts. The result will be learning that students not only recall but transfer, adapt, and apply as well.

Reading and writing are useful ways to implement the last two of these suggestions. The activities that follow use literacy to provide quality practice and extension in a manner that stresses conceptual linkages and causes information to be brought to mind repeatedly, though not in rote fashion. The notion of distributing practice in content so that students encounter it in higher and higher contexts is called the *spiral curriculum* (Bruner, 1960). That is, repeatedly meeting the same facts and concepts makes the curriculum circular, in a sense, but meeting them at higher levels converts the circle into a spiral. This powerful idea underlies all the techniques presented in this chapter. We begin by reexamining three of the approaches to vocabulary that were introduced in Chapter 6.

Reinforcing Vocabulary

In designing reinforcement activities for newly introduced terms, teachers can easily incorporate some of the terms previously studied. The interconnectedness of content—the fact that new information and ideas build on an existing knowledge base—facilitates this practice. Teachers may object that precious time is wasted by rehashing old material. The rule of distributed practice suggests that the time is well spent, however, for integrating new and old vocabulary into the same activity makes the effort a time-effective one. Some of the approaches described earlier as ways of *introducing* vocabulary also have great potential for *reinforcing* it.

Feature Analysis.   You will recall that feature analysis involves charts that list category members in the left-most column and specify differentiating features as headings of the other columns. Students can use the charts to compare and contrast concepts that belong to the same category. Compiling such a chart and then using it to make comparisons requires repeated attention to word meanings. The benefits of rote drill are evident without the tedium. Students review the concepts en route to higher-level accomplishments.

Feature analysis charts can contain previously introduced terms as well as new ones. In many cases, a chart completed earlier can serve as the basis of a new activity. Students first add the new category members, then chart their characteristics, and finally contrast them with the terms entered earlier. Charts used in this way underscore the *continuity* of content, that is, its natural tendency to build on itself.

Figure 11.1 demonstrates how a teacher might return to the same feature analysis chart used in an earlier lesson to characterize governmental checks and balances. Initially, the chart addressed only those used by the judicial and the executive branches. The expanded form includes devices used by the legislative branch as well. Note that the teacher has had to tell students to add a new column at the right of the original chart. This addition broadens the chart's scope to encompass the three branches.

Graphic Organizers.   Like feature analysis charts, graphic organizers stress the interrelatedness of terms by presenting them in closely connected clusters (Fisher & Blachowicz, 2007;

FIGURE 11.1

Example of a feature analysis chart (a) expanded to accommodate new content (b)

(a)   Initial form of the chart:

Checks and balances	Aimed at judiciary	Aimed at executive
Override vote	o	+
Confirmation	s	+
Impeachment trial	+	+

(b)   The chart's expanded form:

Checks and balances	Aimed at judiciary	Aimed at executive	Aimed at legislature
Override vote	o	+	o
Confirmation	s	+	o
Impeachment trial	+	+	o
Veto	o	o	+
Construction	o	o	+
Appointment	+	o	o

Note: A plus (+) indicates a positive relationship; a zero (o) indicates a negative relationship; an **s** indicates a relationship that sometimes exits.

McKenna, 2004; Robinson, 1998). The diagrams highlight the most important relationship connecting the terms: time, place, subconcepts, and so on. Teachers can return to past organizers in the way we've described for feature analysis. Students begin with a previously completed diagram and a list of carefully selected new terms. Their task is to integrate the new words into the existing diagram.

Figure 11.2 provides a before-and-after example of how this process works with a tree diagram. Expanding old diagrams in this way causes students to reconsider previous material (the intent of distributed practice) but does so in a manner that underscores meaning and aids the student in getting the "big picture" of how knowledge in a given content area is organized.

Sometimes the introduction of a new topic will make using a previous organizer seem irrelevant or unfeasible. The solution can lie in higher-level connections that link the topics and show students how seemingly unrelated prior material is in fact integrally connected. As an example, a biology teacher has used the graphic organizer depicted in Figure 11.3(a) to describe the hierarchical organization of the class Insecta. She later employs a different diagram—Figure 11.3(b)—to present the organization of another class, Arachnida. By means of a bridging activity, she and the class combine the two organizers by adding a connecting higher-order concept. This is possible because both classes belong to the same phylum, Arthropoda. (This is only one sort of bridging device. We explain this topic in more detail later in the chapter.) The result is Figure 11.3(c).

FIGURE 11.2

Example of a tree diagram (a) expanded to include new content (b)

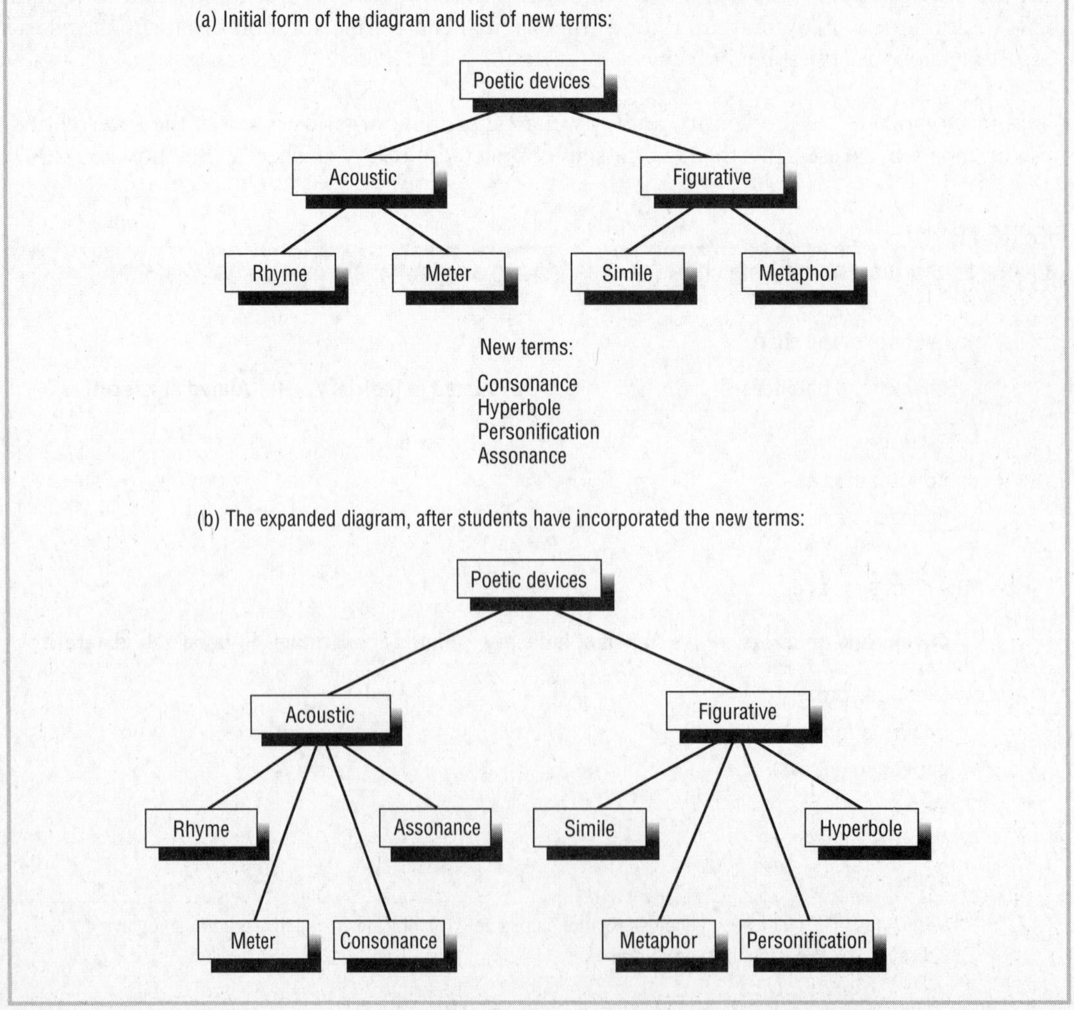

FIGURE 11.3

Linking two graphic organizers with a higher-order concept

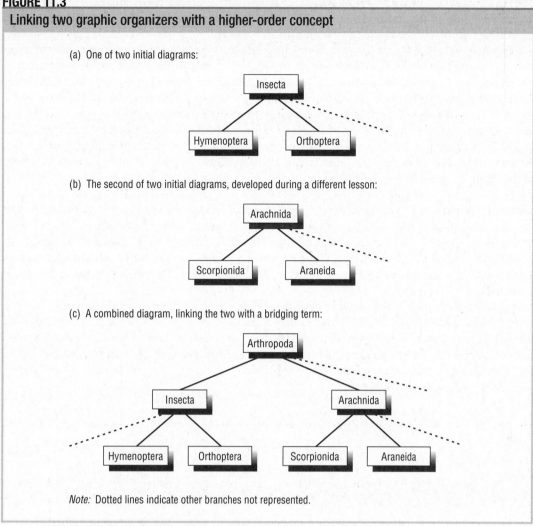

(a) One of two initial diagrams:

(b) The second of two initial diagrams, developed during a different lesson:

(c) A combined diagram, linking the two with a bridging term:

Note: Dotted lines indicate other branches not represented.

List-Group-Label. Taba (1967) introduced a vocabulary method that may have its greatest utility in reviewing and activating word knowledge. For this reason, the technique is useful *after* new reading has been completed, as a means of refining and extending knowledge (Tierney & Readence, 2005). On the other hand, it does not work well as a prereading activity when the students know little about a topic and cannot be expected to "list" very much.

The teacher begins by suggesting to the class a major topic they have been studying. In the List stage, the teacher asks the students to brainstorm all the words they have learned in association with the topic. The teacher records these words on the board or transparency until twenty-five or thirty have been accumulated. In the Group stage, the students work together to rearrange the words into categories. Finally, in the Label stage, each category of words is given an appropriate designation. Occasionally, some of the words may be left over without clear-cut category membership. The teacher should encourage students not to worry about these cases but to suggest instead category labels for each leftover term.

List-Group-Label has several notable strengths. It stresses the interrelationships that exist among technical vocabulary words. It provides an environment for actively engaging students with the content (and is especially well suited to collaborative activities). It provides a good method of linking the new with the familiar.

Nested Lists. A natural offshoot of List-Group-Label is a newer technique introduced by Kirsch and Mosenthal (1990). Their notion of *nesting* (embedding lists within one another) requires that students seek out instances in which some categories are actually subsets of others. This might well occur as an additional step in a List-Group-Label activity when a number of student-generated categories are plainly visible on the chalkboard.

In Figure 11.4, students can combine three categories into a single system of nested categories by noting how they are interrelated. A teacher cannot always expect three such ready-made categories to occur so conveniently, however. Teachers must encourage students to ferret out nested relationships and then combine (or nest) the original lists accordingly.

You may have noted that nested lists bear a close similarity to graphic organizers. In fact, they represent an alternative way of conveying the information contained in a tree diagram. Figure 11.5 illustrates how the nested lists of our example can be translated into graphic form. Pointing out this relationship to students and affording them opportunities to convert one form to the other is a good idea.

Sentence Formation.   Another way to stress interconnections among content vocabulary is to provide students with sets of two or more terms and require that they be combined in a sentence or paragraph that focuses on their relationship. This technique, called *sentence formation,* is an excellent means of (1) reviewing previous vocabulary while emphasizing links with new terms and (2) taking advantage of writing as a means of refining and elaborating each student's content knowledge.

Sentence formation tasks can vary considerably in sophistication, depending on which terms are included in a given set and how many terms are used. Figure 11.6 illustrates how progressive the difficulty and complexity can become. This is a good reason to start simply, providing only two terms and requiring a single sentence. You will need to prepare students for more complex tasks involving three or more terms. These tasks also present good opportunities for collaborative efforts among students.

FIGURE 11.4

Example of nesting (b) used as an extension of List-Group-Label (a)

(a)   In this example, students complete List-Group-Label with the following lists (among others) appearing on the board:

Types of Government	*Democracies*	*Kingdoms*
Democracy	United States	Saudi Arabia
Kingdom	France	Jordan
	Great Britain	
	Germany	
	Japan	

(b)   The students continue by nesting these lists into the following list:

Types of Government

DEMOCRACY

United States

France

Great Britain

Germany

Japan

KINGDOM

Saudi Arabia

Jordan

FIGURE 11.5

Nested categories represented in a tree diagram (see Figure 11.4)

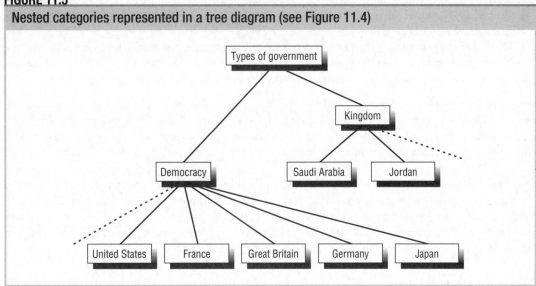

Sentence Verification. The opposite of the sentence formation exercise, sentence verification, involves providing students with ready-made sentences that express relationships among two or more of the concepts being studied. Royer, Greene, and Sinatra (1987) have suggested this as a method of assessing comprehension (see also Royer, 2001). In their approach, students must classify each sentence as "old" (representing material from the text) or "new" (involving inferences based on text material).

Sentence verification also offers an excellent opportunity to reinforce content learning. We suggest a modification of the original technique for use in reinforcement activities.

1. Begin by listing key vocabulary from the current unit.
2. Add closely related terms from earlier units.
3. Select a number of sentences that contain the new terms from the reading material.
4. Rewrite some of the sentences, expressing the same meaning in a different way.

FIGURE 11.6

Examples of sentence formation tasks

1. Example of using two terms:
    real numbers
    rational numbers
       Possible response: Every rational number is a real number.
2. Example of using three terms:
    real numbers
    rational numbers
    integers
       Possible response: All integers are both rational and real numbers.
3. Example of using four terms:
    real numbers
    rational numbers
    integers
    prime numbers
       Possible response: All prime numbers are integers, which in turn are always both rational
                            and real numbers.

5. Rewrite others so that their meaning is no longer true.
6. Write some original sentences that link the new and old terms in meaningful ways. Include a few false statements.
7. Write original sentences that express inferences about the content. The inferences may be altogether certain or merely probable. Again, include some that are false.
8. Ask students to classify each sentence as true, possibly true, or false.

This is an open-book exercise and should encourage students to look for more than the literal match to the sentences. Verbatim sentences are included, to be sure, but along with inferences, paraphrases, and logical links with previous material. Figure 11.7 provides examples of each type of sentence verification exercise, based on the Pluto selection in Figure 7.2.

Possible Sentences.   Remember that the postreading discussion is the proper time to revisit the "possible sentences" you might have asked students to generate prior to reading (see Chapter 7). Students will now be in a position to evaluate whether or not each sentence is correct. Group processing of the sentences should lead to (1) accepting a sentence as accurate, (2) modifying the sentence if it is feasible to do so, or (3) abandoning the sentence.

Charting New Territory

Forgive the pun, but charting is one of the simplest and most effective ways of helping students learn from nonfiction text. A *chart* is any arrangement of information in rows and columns. Feature analysis is only one of many kinds. When students engage in charting, they first locate information in a print source, decide where it belongs in the chart, and place it there. Research clearly shows that activities that cause students to translate information from one form to another help them better understand the content (Blachowicz & Fisher, 2004; Pearson & Fielding, 1991). Charting is such an activity.

Advantages of Charting.   Charting permits flexibility in planning. It can be used as a purpose-setting activity *prior* to reading, or it can become a *post*reading activity. It lends itself to collaborative interaction among students, and it can provide the basis of class discussions as the contents are reviewed as a group. It also leaves students with something succinct to study as they prepare for tests. Best of all (at least from the perspective of most students), charts require very little writing. They're long on thinking and short on tedium. The basic thinking skill entailed in charting is *categorization,* one of the most important cognitive processes in any subject area. Charting has a hidden benefit as well. It helps students understand how charts work, and this understanding aids them in interpreting charts and even in creating their own as they write.

FIGURE 11.7

Examples of sentence verification

Exact sentence (from the Pluto selection in Figure 7.2):
   Pluto's most recent close approach to the Sun was in 1989.
Paraphrased version:
   The last time Pluto came close to the Sun was in 1989.
False version:
   In 1989, Pluto was at its farthest point from the Sun.
Original sentence linking old and new terms:
   Pluto's most recent close approach to the Sun was in 1989, but it was still farther from the Sun than the Earth.
Original sentence, expressing an inference:
   Pluto's most recent close approach to the Sun was in 1989, and its next close approach will not occur for many years.

Many kinds of charts are possible. As long as it has rows and columns, it's a chart! You needn't be concerned about whether you're using a particular type of chart. The only important consideration is whether the chart makes sense to students—whether it helps them think through the content of a reading selection. Here are a few types that might help get you started. Keep in mind, however, that often the best plan is to fashion your own chart based on the nature of the content.

T-Charts. This is probably the simplest type of chart. It resembles a large, lowercase *t* and requires students to categorize information into either of two columns. It's great for stressing comparisons and contrasts. It's also a good way to begin charting with your students. With T-charts, you provide the two column headings. The students do the rest. In Figure 7.7, we saw an example of a T-chart used to set purposes.

Tables. A table is a chart in which most of the information is in the form of numbers. Tables are useful in virtually all subject areas. Being able to interpret tabular data is an essential literacy skill, and constructing simple tables from nonfiction selections is a good starting point. An example of a table appears in Figure 5.3. Tables are common in science materials.

Two-Column Charts. A very simple chart is one that arranges information in two columns. The first provides a topic, the second a corresponding fact or figure. Part of a two-column chart on Florida, for example, might look like this:

Population	about 15 million
Area	about 60,000 square miles
State flower	orange blossom
State bird	mockingbird

(Notice how a chart can combine numbers with verbal information.)

Multiple-Column Charts. Simply by adding columns, you can dramatically increase the amount and variety of information a chart contains. Be sure your students are ready for more complex charts, however. Start simple.

Instructional Tips for Charting. Here are some suggestions for integrating charts more effectively into your instruction.

- Look for examples of charts in reading selections and make them the basis of discussion.
- Pose questions that require students to locate information in a published chart. Almanacs are an excellent source of charts. Another is *USA Today*.
- Start your students on the road to constructing their own charts by using simple ones. Progress gradually to more complex charts.
- Fill in part of the chart yourself as an example of what the chart requires the students to do.
- Make a transparency of the chart and display it during a class discussion. Complete it with a marker as you call on individual students for input.

Extended Writing Activities

A recurrent theme of this book is that providing students with opportunities to write about content will deepen and refine their understanding. Postdiscussion writing activities are ideally positioned to make this happen; they come *after* the initial direct instruction in new material and *after* some of the students' difficulties with the material have been remedied by discussion. Here and in Chapter 10 we have already described some of the brief writing activities students might undertake, such as composing questions and constructing sentences that link technical terms. Extended writing serves the same goal of deepening understanding but on a larger scale. Here, students have the chance to draw on many aspects of what they know—including knowledge from other content areas—in creating a written product that represents how they have mentally constructed their content knowledge. Research has demonstrated the value of such activities (Vacca & Linek, 1992). See the following examples.

To read means to borrow; to create out of one's readings is paying off one's debts.

GEORGE
CHRISTOPHER
LICHTENBERG

Encyclopedia Entries.   Give students a concept (a key word or phrase) and ask them to compose an encyclopedia entry for that term. Be careful to specify what you expect such an entry to contain. Examples of real entries can be helpful in providing students with an idea of the format and content of this type of writing. Do not use entries that cover the term itself, however. The students must decide what information to include and how to convey it succinctly to an encyclopedia user, who is typically in search of a rapid introduction to the topic.

Writing encyclopedia entries is an excellent collaborative activity. One student might serve as editor, assigning subsections and expediting their completion. Another student could construct figures, tables, and diagrams, while still others could compose the subsections.

Process Descriptions.   Studying processes allows students to summarize them step by step; this activity helps the students crystallize their conceptualization of how the processes occur. Applications arise in many subject areas. They abound in the physical sciences (e.g., evaporation, digestion, erosion, life cycles, solar formation, the scientific method itself) but also occur in such widely diverse areas as language arts (e.g., the writing process and library research procedures), mathematics (steps to follow in solving a particular type of problem, proving a theorem, creating a geometric construction, etc.), and social studies (how a bill becomes a law, naturalization, colonization, election procedures, etc.).

An especially good way to present the task of process writing is to show students a diagram of the process. A timeline, especially a flowchart, is suitable for this purpose. Ask students to convert the diagram to words—to describe in prose what the diagram denotes. A hidden benefit of this activity is that it underscores for students how graphic organizers work.

Writing for Contrast and Synthesis.   There is much to be gained from writing about, or in response to, a single source, such as a textbook selection, book, essay, or article. In many subjects, however, it is important to expose students to multiple sources and to ask that they either contrast them or integrate them into a single, coherent statement on a given topic. Both tasks require (1) access to multiple sources, (2) the ability to read each source critically and with a specific purpose in mind, and (3) the capacity to quote or paraphrase selectively to achieve the purpose of this method.

Students should begin with a limited number of sources. If they are unfamiliar with this sort of writing, the teacher might actually prescribe the specific sources. However, those selected by students themselves are apt to be more meaningful and motivating.

Students just beginning to write for such purposes will need plenty of help. Synthesis or contrast writing is a high-level cognitive task and should be modeled like any other. Showing students finished examples of writing can be effective, of course, but it is not enough. You must demonstrate the process as well as the *product*. Begin by selecting a topic together with two or more sources that treat the topic. Tell how you found the sources. Introduce the students to each source. (They will not necessarily need to read each one in detail.) Point out information in the sources that is related to your purpose. For example, if your goal is to contrast conservative and liberal approaches to the environment, proceed through each source until you reach suggested actions and their justification. A good method is to make transparencies of the source material, highlighting points with a marker as you move through it with the class. Next, discuss how you would plan the organization of your essay.

Constructing an informal outline, perhaps with student input, can be beneficial. Finally, distribute copies of the actual written product, allowing students to read and emulate it.

At all times, stress that the procedure is general and independent of a specific topic. The danger in using just one example is that students may overgeneralize its elements. Therefore, use more than one. Start fresh with a new—and, ideally, quite different—illustration. When students possess both written products, point out their similarities (resulting from the same basic writing/thinking process) and their differences (resulting from the specific nature of the two topics).

By selecting topics with immediate relevance to course material, you can ensure that modeling this process will do double duty, not only showing students how to proceed but also instructing them in the content contained in the examples themselves! Once they begin their own projects, this activity is well suited to meaningful review of facts and concepts in the context of a higher-level task.

Writing from Scenarios. You can encourage students to view content from novel perspectives and to apply it to realistic situations by suggesting a set of circumstances, or a scenario, together with a specific writing task. Here are some examples from a variety of content areas:

■ *Business*. Give students a warranty and a hypothetical case involving a defective product. They are to become dissatisfied consumers. Ask them to compose a letter to the dealer asking for a replacement or a refund. Insist that they cite the warranty appropriately.

■ *Social studies*. Place students in the role of the current president and ask that they write a State of the Union address. Numerous sources should be used. Note that in real life this speech is produced by a coordinated team, not by the president acting alone. A collaborative activity may be appropriate.

■ *Science*. Ask students to play the role of scientist by predicting the results of an experiment of their own design. Have them write a proposal that includes background information (what they currently know), their hypothesis, and the proposed method. Having them perform their experiment at school may not be feasible. However, they could send the proposal to an industry scientist or to a professor in the appropriate field and ask for a projection of what would happen. The cover letter communicating their request would constitute yet another writing opportunity!

■ *Mathematics*. Ask students to become "math reporters" who research and report on real-world math applications. They can begin with the *Reader's Guide to Periodical Literature* in the school library and use "mathematics" as a descriptor. What they discover will probably surprise them and may help solve a thorny problem for math teachers: convincing apathetic students that mathematics has relevance to their lives.

■ *Literature*. Ask students to select an author they have studied, preferably on more than one occasion, and then to "become" that author by composing an original work that imitates their chosen author's style.

■ *Art*. Ask students first to choose both a noted artist and one painting by that artist and then to role-play the artist by assuming that a fine arts magazine editor has asked for an "explanation" of the painting. The editor has touched on such questions as why certain colors were selected, why the objects in the painting are arranged as they are, and so on.

■ *Physical education*. Ask each student to select a strategy, play, or formation associated with a given sport. The students' task is to describe and defend their selections, contrasting them favorably with alternatives.

■ *Music*. Suggest that each student select a popular song and then write out the lyrics. This process will require them to give ample attention to rhyme schemes, refrains, and other literary elements, since the lyrics are essentially a form of poetry (see McKenna, 1977b). They are then to describe how the musical elements of the song (pitch, speed, rhythm, instrumentation, etc.) reinforce the message conveyed by the lyrics.

Activities with Game Formats

Our experience is that many content teachers tend to be skeptical about activities that resemble games. A common objection is that they represent a waste of time. Ensuring that practice with skills and concepts is an integral part of the activities should counter such an objection, however. Another complaint is that the competition inherent in all games tends to reinforce differences between the academic haves and have-nots—differences that may already be painfully apparent to the latter students. To reduce this tendency teachers should (1) use games sparingly, as a means of introducing variety into instruction; (2) use formats that involve elements of chance as well as skill; (3) make certain that a variety of skill levels is represented in the game, making success possible for all students; and (4) employ formats that encourage team play so that individuals are not readily isolated as deficient. The formats that follow meet all four of these criteria.

Quiz Bowl. In Quiz Bowl, teams of four students vie in responding to factual questions. An electronic buzzer system that identifies the first player to "buzz in" is helpful, though not essential. (Production of such a system is cheap and makes a good science project, which you might suggest to a colleague.) The format used for years by NBC's weekly *G.E. College Bowl* program entails toss-up questions, worth ten points, and bonus questions, worth varying numbers of points. Toss-ups are clear-cut, single-answer queries. The student who buzzes in must answer the question without the help of teammates. A student may interrupt the teacher-moderator if the rest of the question is inferred, but there is a five-point penalty if, after interrupting, the student gives a wrong answer. The question is then repeated in its entirety for the other team. When the student is wrong but has not interrupted, no penalty is assessed. The other team does receive a chance to respond, however. When a toss-up is correctly answered, that student's team receives a chance to answer a bonus question. The team works together to answer these questions, which, while factual, may involve lists, have multiple parts, or comprise a sequence of clues (the more clues the team needs, the fewer the points awarded). The team routes answers to bonus questions through a captain, who is the official spokesperson for the team and must quickly decide differences of opinion among team members.

Quiz Bowl can easily promote motivational practice in content. Some suggestions for enhancing its effectiveness include the following:

1. Make certain that each team has a balance of students in terms of ability. Strive for parity.
2. Ask students to write questions (an interesting writing activity) for later use in Quiz Bowl. Use these questions (perhaps with a little editing) along with those you write yourself. Asking students to write their names on the questions ensures that a particular item is used only when its author is not a member of one of the teams.
3. Determine whether an organized Quiz Bowl system exists on an interschool basis. If so, your class sessions might be linked to qualification trials for interschool competition. Note that the format we described above is for the original NBC version. It may differ from local adaptations.

Concept Bingo.   Based on the ordinary bingo format, Concept Bingo begins with a list of twenty-five new terms written on the board. The teacher instructs students to create a 5×5 grid and to write the words, one by one in any order, in each of the grid's squares. Prior to the game, the teacher should have written each word and its definition on an index card. The teacher shuffles the cards and reads aloud one definition at a time (but not the word!). Students find the word that matches the definition and cover it with a small scrap of paper, paper clip, or anything handy. Winning occurs as it does in regular bingo. Note that every student will have a play for every definition the teacher reads. The difference is in the random arrangement originally chosen by the student. This element of luck is important, for it helps disguise the fact that some students may be learning the word meanings at a slower rate than others. They will not be embarrassed, because all the students realize that there is a large chance factor involved.

Dictionary Challenge.   With Dictionary Challenge, not only do you review selected vocabulary, but in passing you also expose students to a host of other terms. You can use an ordinary dictionary, but it is preferable to locate a dictionary specific to your teaching specialty. The game involves a small group of students, so that several games may be going on at once in the same classroom if all students are to participate. Provide students with a lengthy list of content terms. Include previous terms and, if you wish, even terms they have yet to encounter. You may place the list on the board, on a transparency, or on paper so that students can refer to it during the game.

Each round begins with one student secretly choosing a term from the list, looking it up in the dictionary, and then reading (1) the definition given or (2) the definition of another term from the dictionary. Afterward the other students must decide whether the definition read aloud is true or false and then simultaneously signal their responses. The reader receives one point for each response by a student who was fooled. The book then passes from one student to the next around the circle. When it has made one full round, the game is over. It is important to devise a system that compels students to signal their beliefs simultaneously so that some are not tempted to wait and see how a superior student responds.

This game does more than provide an entertaining review. It also exposes students in a non-threatening way to a multitude of content-specific terms. Imagine how many definitions a student may browse through while looking for a distractor to read aloud.

Crossword Puzzles. A game that works well as a reinforcement activity is the traditional crossword puzzle. This format stresses word meanings as an individual activity that can be completed outside of class. All students are likely to be familiar with the format, so that little explanation is necessary. Crosswords also provide an excellent method of reinforcing old and current vocabulary in the same exercise.

A few additional suggestions will add variety to the games you produce. You can spice up a puzzle by adding a few extra words that are relevant to your class (e.g., students' names, the school mascot, etc.). Also, do not feel constrained to use only formal definitions as clues. Use related facts and details occasionally that suggest some of the words without actually defining them.

A drawback to the creation of crossword puzzles is the time required on the part of the teacher. Two recommendations can help. First, use computer software to generate puzzles. If you're not familiar with how such programs work, you'll be amazed at how quick and convenient they can be. Figure 11.8 presents an example of a puzzle created with Crossword Creator, using some of the

FIGURE 11.8

Example of a computer-generated crossword puzzle

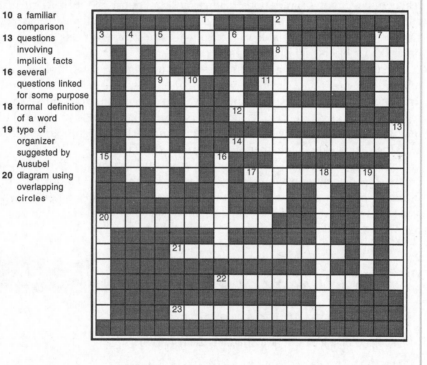

ACROSS

3 building bridges from the new to the known
8 diagram showing social relationships
9 type of global lesson plan
11 type of organizer using diagram
12 interesting story about content
14 guide that gets at prior assumptions
15 reducing the scope of a question
17 text that accounts for reader knowledge
20 criticism that saves face
21 guide organized by comprehension levels
22 too limited to be true discussion
23 assumption made for the sake of argument

10 a familiar comparison
13 questions involving implicit facts
16 several questions linked for some purpose
18 formal definition of a word
19 type of organizer suggested by Ausubel
20 diagram using overlapping circles

DOWN

1 diagram using overlapping circles
2 reading level best for textbooks
3 test using deleted words
4 notes made on edges of pages
5 difficulty level of materials
6 all one knows about a concept
7 list, group, and then...

terms introduced in this book thus far. Our second suggestion is nontechnological: Create a square grid for use as a master and, once you've decided on the arrangement of words, darken the unused squares with a felt-tip marker. This method is not nearly so quick as using a computer, but it eliminates using a ruler to construct each puzzle from scratch (see answer key on page 188).

Using Technology to Extend Content Understanding

Computers make possible new ways for students to refine and extend their understanding of content. These applications also provide opportunities for social collaboration that can make limited hardware go a long way! A few suggestions follow.

Let Simulations Make Content Come Alive.   Simulations create the illusion that some process or scenario is actually happening. Thus, they involve an element of unpredictability that builds interest and even suspense. Because simulations are interactive—calling on students to make decisions at crucial points—they naturally encourage student involvement in active learning.

Because simulations are so much a part of present-day industry (think of flight simulators, economic forecasting models, engineering design software, and the like), it is tempting to dismiss simulations as too technical and scientific for most classroom uses. It is certainly true that science teachers have many simulations from which to choose. Numerous chemistry programs allow chemicals to be realistically mixed and processed without danger or expense. But educational simulations are now available in virtually all other content fields as well. A few examples from other core subjects will illustrate their range.

Imagine yourself on a Conestoga wagon heading west with other pioneers. Your very life might depend on the decisions you make concerning food supply, route, and so on. The Oregon Trail, now published by Riverdeep, has evolved through the years into a sophisticated and engaging simulation. According to its developers, the program helps students "build real-life decision-making and problem-solving skills as they choose their wagon party and supplies, read maps, plan their route, and guide their team through the wilderness." We agree.

SimCity, published by Maxis, permits students in the upper-elementary and middle grades to create their own cities from scratch, converting an untouched landscape into a thriving metropolis over a period of many hours. In the process, the students experience the challenge of building and maintaining these complex systems. Students learn vocabulary and gain a better understanding of how a modern city functions and grows.

NET Worth

Sources of Online Interactive Units

Intersect Digital Library. **http://intersect.uoregon.edu**

Diary of Opal Whiteley. **http://intersect.uoregon.edu/opal**

National Geographic Society. **www.nationalgeographic.com**

National Oceanic and Atmospheric Administration. **www.noaa.gov**

U.S. Geological Survey. **www.usgs.gov**

National Park Service (WebRangers). **www.nps.gov**

U.S. Mint (h.i.p. Pocket Change). **www.usmint.gov**

National Aeronautics and Space Administration. **www.nasa.gov**

Smithsonian Institution. **www.si.edu**

U.S. Department of Agriculture. **www.ars.usda.gov/is/kids**

National Institutes of Health. **www.nih.gov**

NET Worth

Online References

Wikipedia. Free online encyclopedia. (See an example in Figure 11.9.)

http://en.wikipedia.org/wiki

Merriam-Webster Dictionary and Thesaurus. It's free and thorough. Make it a favorite.

www.merriam-webster.com

Bibliomania. Lots of online books that are in the public domain.

www.bibliomania.com

Jolly Roger. Lots of teen classics online, chat room available for students to chat about books they have read.

www.jollyroger.com

State Information. Gives information about all fifty states, including a bio and picture of the governor, the state flower, the state capital, links, and so on. Just replace "ga" in this address with the two-letter postal abbreviation of the state you wish to research.

www.state.ga.us

Ask.com. Pose any factual question and this site will look up the answer. This site is linked to several major search engines. It provides not only the answer, but lots of related information. Results can be a bit complex, but upper-elementary students should be able to sift through them.

www.ask.com

Word Central. Offers a student dictionary, a "Build Your Own Dictionary" option, and the "Daily Buzzword." Operated by Merriam-Webster. The Daily Buzzword gives an in-depth definition and a non-threatening multiple-choice question.

www.wordcentral.com

CIA World Fact Book. This site offers extensive information (maps, facts, figures) about countries around the world. This is not really a kid site, but some will find it intriguing because of the CIA connection, which is quite real. An excellent database for strategic reading.

www.cia.gov/library/publications/the-world-factbook/index.html

Online Interactive Units. An ever-increasing number of online units are available to teachers. The first task is to locate them. The next is to navigate them yourself and decide whether to integrate them into your instruction and, if so, how. Some of these units are beautifully constructed and offer students a rich hypermedia experience. An excellent example, constructed by Lynne Anderson-Inman and her colleagues, is *The Diary of Opal Whiteley,* written by "a young girl growing up in the woods and farming community of western Oregon." This unit is part of the University of Oregon's Intersect Digital Library, which offers other social studies units as well.

One way to locate interactive units is to visit the home pages of organizations associated with content subjects. In Net Worth, we list some key organizations that feature interactive units and activities. (We have drawn on some of these resources for examples in this book, such as Figures 5.3 and 7.2.)

Writing with Technology. The way students write has changed considerably over the past two decades. A sweeping transformation occurred when word processing software became available on most classroom and home computers. Students can now produce written responses, reports, and journals that are superior in quality to handwritten work.

Word processing has a number of qualities that contribute to its success. It emphasizes the interconnectedness of reading and writing (Shaver & Wise, 1991). It leads to a neatly printed, pride-inspiring final product (Wepner, 1990–1991). It permits students to publish their own "books," which can be a highly motivating undertaking, especially in the middle grades (Stratton & Grindler, 1992). It encourages revision, because changes do not require extensive recopying. It offers assistance with mechanics (especially spelling) and even with matters of style and expression. Finally, it reflects the way most students will eventually write in workplace environments—a fact that virtually behooves teachers to use word processing in the classroom.

A second transformation involves the use of the Internet as a resource for writing. This treasure trove of information can be both boon and bane, however. For example, a student asked to write a report on the planet Pluto might locate the Wikipedia entry displayed in Figure 11.9. The fluid nature of digital text permits the student to copy and paste sections of the article into an "original" report. When teachers become suspicious that this has happened, they sometimes type a sentence or two into a search engine, making sure to surround the sample with quotation marks. If an online match exists, it easily can be found in this way.

FIGURE 11.9

Wikipedia entry for Pluto

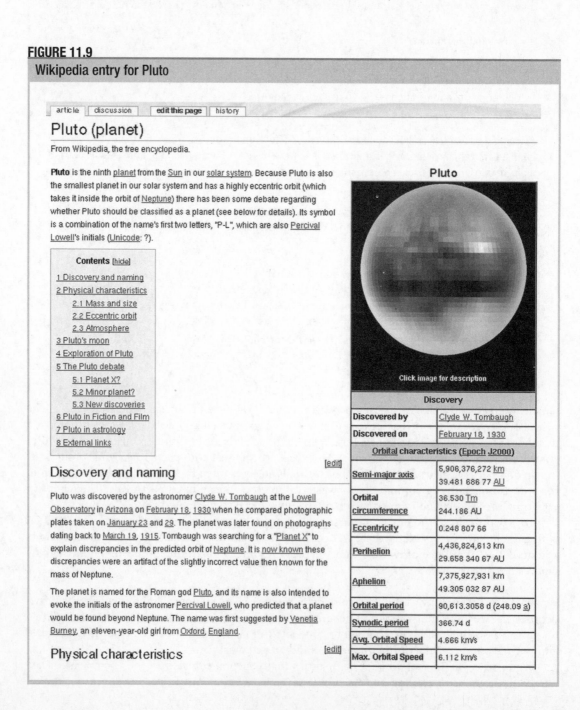

FIGURE 11.9 *(continued)*

Wikipedia entry for Pluto

Mass and size [edit]

Pluto is not only much smaller and less massive than every other planet, it is also smaller and less massive than seven moons of other planets: Ganymede, Titan, Callisto, Io, Earth's Moon, Europa and Triton. However, Pluto is larger than any minor planet in the main asteroid belt, or any minor planet so far discovered in the trans-Neptunian Kuiper belt. See List of solar system objects by mass and List of solar system objects by radius.

Pluto's mass and diameter were unknown for many decades after its discovery and could only be estimated. The discovery of its satellite Charon permitted determining the mass for the Pluto-Charon system by simple application of Newton's formulation of Kepler's third law. Meanwhile, its diameter is now known since telescopes using adaptive optics can resolve its disk.

Eccentric orbit [edit]

Pluto's highly eccentric orbit makes it the eighth-most distant planet from the Sun for part of each orbit; this most recently occurred from February 7, 1979 through February 11, 1999. Pluto orbits in a 3:2 orbital resonance with Neptune. When Neptune approaches Pluto from behind their gravity start to pull on each other slightly, resulting in an interaction between their positions in orbit of the same sort that produces Trojan points. Since the orbits are eccentric, the 3:2 periodic ratio is favoured because this means Neptune always passes Pluto when they're almost farthest apart. Half a Pluto orbit later, when Pluto is nearing its closest approach, it initially seems as if Neptune's about to catch up to Pluto. But Pluto speeds up due to the gravitational acceleration from the Sun, stays ahead of Neptune, and pulls ahead until they meet again on the other side of Pluto's orbit.

Because of its small size and eccentric orbit, there has been some debate over whether it truly should be classified as a planet. There is mounting evidence that Pluto may in fact be a member of the Kuiper belt, only one of a large number of distant icy bodies. A subclass of such objects have been dubbed plutinos, after Pluto.

Atmosphere [edit]

Pluto has an atmosphere when it is close to perihelion; the atmosphere may freeze out as Pluto moves farther from the Sun. It is thought by some that Pluto shares its atmosphere with its moon. Pluto was determined to have an atmosphere from an occultation observation in 1988. When a planet or asteroid occults a star, if it has no atmosphere, the star abruptly disappears. In the case of Pluto, the star dimmed out gradually. From the rate of dimming, the atmosphere was determined to have a pressure of 1.5 microbars. This thin atmosphere is most likely nitrogen and carbon monoxide, in equilibrium with solid nitrogen and carbon monoxide ices on the surface.

Min. Orbital Speed	3.676 km/s
Inclination	17.141 75° (11.88° to Sun's equator)
Longitude of the ascending node	110.303 47°
Argument of the perihelion	113.763 29°
Number of satellites	1
Physical characteristics	
Diameter	2390 km (0.180 Earths)
Surface area	1.795×10^7 km² (0.033 Earths)
Volume	7.15×10^9 km³ (0.0066 Earths)
Mass	1.25×10^{22} kg (0.0021 Earths)
Mean density	1.750 g/cm³
Equatorial gravity	0.58 m/s² (0.059 gee)
Escape velocity	1.2 km/s
Rotation period	6.387 d (6 d 9 h 17.6 min)
Rotation velocity	47.18 km/h (at the equator)
Axial tilt	119.61°
Right ascension of North pole	313.02° (20 h 52 min 5 s)
Declination	9.09°
Albedo	0.30
Surface temp.	min mean max 33 K 44 K 55 K
Atmospheric characteristics	
Atmospheric pressure	0.15-0.30 Pascal
Composition	Nitrogen, Methane

A third transformation involves the very way we define *writing*. We no longer limit ourselves to sentence after sentence of linear text. Software now permits us to embed other media, including still pictures, graphics, animation, movie clips, audio, and art. Of course, writing coherent prose will always have its place, but there are now far more colors on the writer's palette. In a project involving fourth and fifth graders, for example, Reinking and Watkins (2000) described how the students learned to create multimedia alternatives to the age-old (and potentially deadly!) book report. The students added audio and graphics, and they became highly engaged in the activity.

Another example is Alisha Hilson's middle school class in Gibson, Georgia. These students demonstrate their science knowledge by working in pairs to construct PowerPoint presentations. They find ample opportunity to be creative by searching the Internet for pictures and incorporating a variety of colors and designs. A sample slide appears in Figure 11.10. These examples may not seem like "writing" on first consideration, but they serve the same function and represent the expanded view of communication that has become part of the modern workplace.

FIGURE 11.10

Student-constructed PowerPoint slide

Gastropods

Members of gastropods include snails, conchs, abalone, whelks, sea slugs, and garden slugs.

Characteristics: Gastropods have a single shell. Many have a pair of tentacles with eyes at the tips.

Obtain Food: Gastropods use a radula, a tongue-like organ with rows of teeth to obtain food. The radula works like a file to scrape and tear food.

How they Move: They move by rhythmic contractions of the muscular foot. Glands in the foot secrete a layer of mucus instead, so they must live in moist places.

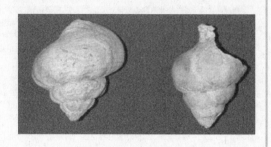

Reinforcing through Direct Instruction

One of the most efficient ways to reinforce content that has been covered is to refer to it again while introducing new material. Among many teachers, there is an unfortunate tendency to compartmentalize content into segments that are all but abandoned on completion. In other words, teachers assume that once a unit is over, it's time to move on. This may be a consequence of planning in units, but it is not unavoidable.

Two important techniques useful in referring to previous material while conducting instruction in new material are review and bridging. Let's look at each.

Review

We introduced the idea of review in Chapter 5 as a means of building the background students will need for a particular reading assignment. The role of initial review can be broader, however, and is not limited to lessons that center around assigned reading. Review is effective in the readiness phase of any lesson. Reviewing underscores the connectedness of content and encourages students to learn new content by integrating it with their existing knowledge. It also allows a lesson to begin with a feeling of student success and recollection, a warm-up for the actual agenda.

Bridging

Bridging is the act of specifying logical connections between new and previous material. Review provides one opportunity for a teacher to bridge, by linking new ideas and concepts with those recently studied. Bridging need not be a part of review, however. It can occur during the direct instruction phase or at any other appropriate juncture. Bridging is effective when a logical connection with *any e*arlier material (not just the material that has been most recently covered) becomes possible. Unlike review, which is an appropriate way to begin almost any lesson, bridging must wait until an adequate foundation of content knowledge has been established. That is, there must be something to which to bridge.

Bridging can take many forms, but two seem especially useful. One involves the teacher's use of earlier content to make a comparison. For example, a history teacher in the midst of discussing World War II will have numerous opportunities to compare the circumstances with those of World War I (covered earlier in the course). These comparisons not only strengthen the students' conceptual framework for World War II but provide a quick, distributed review of the earlier material as well.

The second means of bridging goes a step beyond mere comparison. Where appropriate, the teacher offers an overarching fact or principle that links the elements being compared. Our history teacher might begin by comparing the Allied forces and Axis powers of World War II with the Allied forces and Central Powers of World War I. One of the similarities—that Britain and

Reviewing the old while introducing the new may bring to mind the distinction between recitation and discussion explained in Chapter 10. That idea is similar to reinforcement, in that discussions that include some factual questions provide for review and extension during the same lesson.

the United States were allied in both causes—might form the basis of a transcendent fact: that these two countries have been allied for well over a century in what Churchill called the "Grand Alliance." Stating this bridging fact before covering World War II would have less impact because it would lack that very powerful example. Similar occasions arise in the sciences, as when numerous experiments or subprocesses can finally be linked by more general principles. The big picture becomes clear.

This is not to say that bridging cannot occur in advance as a way of setting the stage for what is to come. Mention of the Grand Alliance during a discussion of World War I might well serve to enhance students' appreciation of events in that war. Bridging, however, is retrospective. Even if the Alliance were mentioned before, it should be reintroduced later.

Bridging is a relatively new target for researchers, but the investigations conducted to date have provided evidence of its effectiveness in developing comprehension at higher levels (e.g., Thompson & Taymans, 1994; White, Hayes, & Pate, 1991).

SUMMARY

Practice is an essential ingredient of content learning. To be effective, practice need not consist of rote drill of factual information. Providing students with opportunities to use content knowledge in meaningful ways—ways that often involve literacy—serves to reinforce basic facts. Practice should progress from a guided to an independent condition and from an intensive, massed schedule to a distributed, periodic one.

Some of the vocabulary techniques useful in introducing new terms can also serve to reinforce them. These include feature analysis and graphic organizers. List-Group-Label is an excellent means of helping students organize vocabulary knowledge following a reading selection, and it can be extended with nested lists. Other activities entailing brief written exercises include charting, sentence formation, and its opposite, sentence verification. More extensive writing activities are also appropriate, and many are possible. We examined here activities that engage students in the writing of encyclopedia entries, process descriptions, contrasts and syntheses of material from multiple sources, and compositions based on various scenarios. This chapter also explored the limited use of game formats for reinforcement and extension, though several cautions and criteria were noted. We described examples that met all the criteria.

The postreading phase of a content literacy unit also presents good opportunities for using computers to extend the content understanding of students. Simulations are now available in most subject areas and have the potential to enliven content and provide opportunities for realistic thinking. Databases allow students to research their own hypotheses about the topics they study and to pick up additional information incidentally. Word-processing software encourages thoughtful revision and allows teachers to prompt responses. Other software applications, such as PowerPoint, allow students to "write" in multimedia formats that afford rich new opportunities for expression.

Finally, we introduced two methods of reinforcing previous content in the midst of direct teaching of new material. These were (1) reviewing just prior to the new instruction and (2) bridging, which entails making logical connections between previous and current facts and concepts.

Getting Involved

1. Build a unit for teaching students to write for the purpose of synthesizing or contrasting sources (choose one skill or the other). Begin by selecting two topics, for your goal will be the creation of two examples. For each topic, select two sources (for simplicity's sake), making sure the sources are relatively easy to comprehend. Avoid sources and topics that will soon be dated, such as current events, so that the unit will be useful regardless of when you teach it or which textbook you may be using. Last, construct the written examples themselves, making certain to target appropriate levels of difficulty and prior knowledge. In other words, aim for considerate writing.

2. Choose a topic that will not be readily outdated and that is apt to be included in any text-book used in your teaching specialty. Compile a list of closely related terms associated with the topic you've chosen. Then compose sentences that express relationships among the terms. These relationships should be altogether true, probably true, or false. Your sentences can form the basis of a sentence verification exercise for eventual use with your students. Your list of words, of course, will be useful in the opposite activity, sentence construction.

3. Create a PowerPoint presentation that introduces the terms you chose in the preceding activity. Incorporate graphics, pictures, clip art, and possibly audio and video clips. When you've finished, ask yourself what grade Ms. Hilson might have given you!

4. As a review of what you've read to this point in the book, try completing the crossword puzzle presented in Figure 11.8. The program that produced the puzzle, Crossword Creator, also generates an answer key. Figure 11.11 provides the key for our example, just as it was automatically generated by the computer. Consult it if you need help!

FIGURE 11.11

Answers to content literacy crossword puzzle presented in Figure 11.8 (note that the answer key was also produced by the computer—automatically)

More Ways to Facilitate Learning through Text

In the final two chapters, we introduce new ideas and approaches and explore the need to create coherent content literacy units.

Chapter 12 introduces the topic of study skills, focusing on those skills and strategies that are (1) most useful to content literacy and (2) most easily addressed by content specialists in the course of subject matter instruction. The four areas that meet our two requirements are note taking, review and homework, test taking, and strategies for helping students with independent reading.

Chapter 13 examines one of the most neglected areas in content literacy: student attitudes. We begin by providing an understanding of motivation (in a way that may be useful in other contexts) and examine a quick method of determining specific areas of student interest within your subject specialty. We then turn to methods of improving student attitudes toward content literacy.

CHAPTER 12

Study Skills: Encouraging Independence in Content Literacy

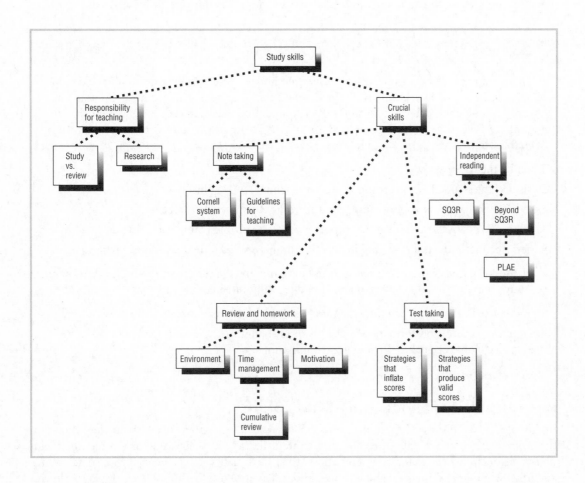

Children have to be educated, but they have also to be left to educate themselves.

—Ernest Dimnet

As a successful college student, you are undoubtedly able to apply a variety of skills in learning whatever your courses may require. These skills include the ability to take notes during lectures, to read certain assignments without benefit of an introduction, to review for tests, and to take tests with an awareness of how they are typically designed. Odds are that no one directly taught you these skills. You probably acquired most of them through trial and error, refining them through application in secondary classrooms. Your success in developing good study techniques on your own may have led you to a common assumption that such techniques do not need to be taught, that they are somehow self-evident. For various reasons, however, many students fail to acquire adequate study skills. Some students are so constrained by limited decoding ability that the notion of productive study is only a distant goal. For others, the trial-and-error process may never have produced the right formulas for success. Still others are unwilling to try different approaches and are locked by habit into ineffective methods.

In this chapter, we strive for a balance between two conflicting demands. One is the need to convey content knowledge and understanding. The time required to do so leaves little extra time for lessons in how to learn. At odds with this demand is the reality that, unless they receive guidance in effective study, many students will not acquire the intended content. This amounts to a paradox—a catch-22—that we address and, hopefully, resolve.

Objectives

The main goal of this chapter is to present methods of integrating study skill instruction into content teaching. In this way, the demand for extra time is minimized and students can see how the skills should be used with actual course material. To accomplish this goal we focus on several objectives. Specifically, your reading of this chapter should enable you to

1. define the term *study*;
2. discuss the issue of who is responsible for teaching study skills;
3. identify the study skills most important in content coursework in general;
4. further identify those skills most important in your own teaching specialty; and
5. describe methods of integrating instruction in these skills into content instruction.

In addition, this chapter is rather unusual in that it gives you a chance to judge your own study techniques as a college student. Reading it should enable you to

6. undertake independent reading assignments more effectively; and
7. improve your test performance by means of (a) better methods of review and (b) more knowledgeable approaches to taking examinations.

Responsibility for Teaching Study Skills

In Chapter 1, we discussed the objections usually voiced by content teachers to the suggestion that they play an active role in developing content literacy in their students. Three important objections included the inability to contend with student deficiencies, the suspicion that literacy activities will demand too much class time, and a denial of any real need for instruction in this area. These objections are likely to be even stronger in the matter of study skills, which are often viewed as naturally developing without direct instruction.

If you have not yet taught, we can probably do little to convince you that such skills do not automatically accrue as students pass upward through the secondary grades. You will need to experience the situation for yourself firsthand. What we *can* do is to equip you with a knowledge of the most important skills and with methods of instilling them that do not greatly intrude on instructional time. We begin by considering exactly what it means to study.

Study versus Review

By *study* we mean "the process of learning the content of printed materials without direct assistance" (Miller & McKenna, 1989, p. 281). This definition is intentionally broad and exceeds the common view that study is the same as review (as in "studying" for a test or "studying" a list of facts until you remember them). Our definition applies to any activity in which the student must learn without help. One such activity is review, to be sure, but there are others. They include (1) reading materials that have not been introduced and for which a student may lack adequate background, (2) taking notes that capture the organization and content of lectures, and (3) taking tests intelligently by avoiding unnecessary pitfalls. We could extend this list considerably, but our aim is to focus on skills that are central to success in content subjects. Even these few examples, however, suggest that study is far more than review. It entails a set of skills for learning independently.

What the Research Suggests

It is probably natural for teachers, who tend to be good students and who have rarely received instruction in how to study, to assume that their students do not need direct instruction in study skills (Brozo & Simpson, 1999; Harvey & Chickie-Wolfe, 2007; Richardson & Morgan, 2003). Not surprisingly, teachers rarely teach these skills, particularly as they relate to the effective study of textbook material. Durkin (1978–1979) spent over 7000 minutes observing reading and content lessons in the intermediate grades and witnessed no instruction in study skills at all.

The realization that teachers must teach study skills comes at a time when the psychology of learning suggests that students must be actively engaged with content in order to learn it. As Gall et al. (1990) put it, "Educators are seeing more clearly than ever that the student is not a passive recipient of the teacher's instruction, but an active participant in it" (p. 6). Study skills, by their very nature, require active participation.

You may suspect that a reasonable way of instilling good study skills is to teach them as part of a reading or language arts course. Indeed, this is the approach used most often with deficient college freshmen. Although it can be effective, there are drawbacks, especially with less mature and less academically able students in the middle and secondary grades. One problem is that it is up to the student to transfer study strategies learned in an abstract form, independent of any specific content subject, to day-to-day classroom situations. This transfer may be difficult because of differences in the materials used and in the requirements of individual courses. Perhaps the most effective approaches to study are those best matched to the criteria that a particular teacher would use to assess performance. For example, a student might be ill advised to concentrate on mnemonic strategies for detailed facts when the instructor will administer essay examinations. A student enrolled in a study skills class may therefore learn too many techniques, or the wrong techniques, to be able to apply them appropriately to a specific course. Only one educator is in an ideal position to develop the right skills in the right place at the right time: the content teacher.

When the content teacher selects a set of study skills to emphasize, it is possible to ensure that those skills are geared to the requirements the teacher has established for the students. And there is a second, equally powerful advantage. By showing how the skills work with actual course material (not "canned" commercial material), the teacher further ensures that the students will be able to apply the skills in the context of *that* course. True, the students may acquire the skills in the abstract so that they can apply them elsewhere or on other occasions, but this is a by-product. The primary concern of the content teacher is met—students can apply the skills to the task at hand.

For example, Stoodt and Balbo (1979) found that when content teachers took a little time to teach appropriate study skills, using their own materials as the basis, their students demonstrated significantly better comprehension and learning. However, it is not enough to insist that teachers provide instruction in how to study. Showing them how to provide that instruction is just as important. It is to that goal that we devote the remainder of this chapter.

Note Taking

Good students concur in their belief that note taking is worthwhile (Igo & Kiewra, 2007; Irvin & Rose, 1995; Zapprich, 1997). Recent studies have shown that even young students can be effectively taught to develop and improve their note-taking skills (Irvin & Rose, 1995). Psychologists differ, however, as to exactly how notes help us learn. One view is that the *process* of taking notes (selecting, condensing, organizing, paraphrasing, and so forth) assists us in integrating the new material into memory. Another view holds that it is in the *product*—the written notes themselves as an aid to later review—that the real value lies.

Anderson and Armbruster (1991), in examining research into the matter, found mixed evidence for the process view but strong and consistent support for the product theory. We suspect that, under the right conditions, both factors play a role in effective note taking. Students can take notes on lectures or written materials. Because we have already discussed ways to guide students in writing while reading (see Chapter 8), we focus here on note taking during lectures. Let's begin by inspecting one of the most popular techniques yet developed.

The Cornell System

Walter Pauk, of the Cornell University Reading Research Center, has developed over the course of several years a system of note taking that incorporates a number of sensible ideas (Pauk, 2004). With the Cornell system, students use ruled paper with an especially wide left margin (2 inches or so). If they begin with ordinary notebook paper with a 1-inch margin, Pauk encourages them to draw a new vertical line and to use this as the margin. During class, the students take notes only to the right of the line. Soon after class, while memory is fresh, they rewrite their notes onto paper that is similarly ruled. This is the time to improve legibility, rephrase certain points, add remembered details, insert punctuation, number subpoints, and so forth. When the revision is complete, the wide left-hand margin comes into play. Here the students write headings, symbols, questions, short phrases, and other cues that might help them categorize and remember the material to the right of the line. Thinking of these cues, of course, is a good way to arrive at an understanding of how the content is organized. Later review consists of covering the right-hand portion of each page while using the left-hand cues to help recall the material. Research suggests that the Cornell system is effective (Anderson & Armbruster, 1991; Jacobsen, 1989).

Teaching Note Taking

Norm Stahl and his colleagues (Stahl, King, & Henk, 1991) advocate the explicit teaching model for showing students how to take notes. This approach first involves modeling the technique for students and then allowing them to practice it while the teacher monitors and reinforces. Deliberately devoting a lesson to note-taking instruction may sound inappropriate to a content classroom, but two advantages make the idea appealing. First, note taking need not be the sole objective. You can teach whatever material you normally would while using it as a vehicle to convey note-taking skills. Second, there is no need for students to transfer a set of skills learned elsewhere (in a reading class, perhaps) to the content setting. Stahl et al. (1991) warn of the reluctance of some students to risk trying a new technique when grades are at stake. Encouraging that technique yourself, while modeling it with your own materials, can help overcome this reluctance.

Modeling good note-taking skills can begin with a brief introduction to the Cornell system or an adaptation of it. Teaching note taking yourself is efficient because every example then comes from current content. By using the chalkboard or overhead projector as you lecture, you show students precisely how the notes should look at each point. During the important last step of filling in the left margin with cues, you can soon begin to seek input from students.

Using the Cornell system as a means of organizing the notes overall is a good beginning. However, you must make additional points and use other techniques if you hope to change the habits of your students significantly. The following recommendations come from two recent sources in which teams of investigators have looked carefully at research:

1. Take stock of your students' note-taking abilities early by collecting notebooks and examining their written products (Anderson & Armbruster, 1991).

2. Lecture at a reasonable rate for novice note takers and construct model notes over important content on the chalkboard or overhead projector as you speak (Anderson & Armbruster, 1991).

3. Pause frequently to allow students to process what you've said more fully as they write (Anderson & Armbruster, 1991).

4. Encourage students to be alert for definitions and examples as they listen (Gall et al., 1990).

5. Teach useful abbreviations, including not only standard ones (such as *w/o* for *without*) but those that students should "coin" on the spot (such as *phot.* for *photosynthesis*) (Gall et al., 1990).

6. Encourage students to paraphrase rather than strive for verbatim transcriptions (Gall et al., 1990).

7. Stress the need to look for cues the teacher provides that certain material is important. "Examples of such signals are emphasis words (e.g., 'the chief cause was . . .'), transitions (e.g., 'now let's look at . . .'), enumerations (e.g., 'there are five characteristics of . . .'), repetitions ('let me remind you that . . .'), as well as nonverbal movements and gestures" (Gall et al., 1990, p. 97).

To these suggestions we add three more.

8. Encourage students to use an informal outline format in which they indent to show subpoints and examples. Indention is an age-old trick of note taking for it provides a good visual organizer without the need to write anything additional. Figure 12.1 presents examples of notes actually taken by an A student and a C student during the same lecture in a seventh-grade social studies class. Note the organizing use of indention that is beginning to develop in the notes of the superior student.

9. Consider giving grades on the notes themselves as an added inducement to students to take them effectively.

10. As you monitor and reinforce students' efforts to practice their note taking, make transparencies of selected student notes to use as examples (anonymously, of course) with the class as a whole.

One of the best methods of encouraging good note taking is to administer tests that have a reasonable basis in the notes taken (Anderson & Armbruster, 1991). This policy leads to better review habits and to better performance on tests. We now look at each of these two study skills in turn.

Review and Homework

Note taking and review are naturally linked. You will recall that an important way notes help students is as an aid during review. Not surprisingly, Hartley and Davies (1978) observed that teaching note taking is most effective when notes make review easier. The guidelines suggested in the previous section are a first step, but teachers must attend to the review habits of students and be ready to provide direct instruction when necessary.

Environment

A traditional suggestion is to study in the same place each time and to use that place for nothing else. The rationale is that conditioning will cause the student to anticipate studying on arrival at the designated place. There are difficulties with this suggestion, however. To begin with, a long history of research does not support the practice (Risko, Alvarez, & Fairbanks, 1991). Moreover, the suggestion is often unattainable for disadvantaged individuals. It is better to advise students to seek out a place that is as free from distractions as possible. According to most studies, music and television qualify as distractions under most circumstances (Risko et al., 1991). This finding does not mean that students must envelop themselves in cryptlike silence to be successful. It does mean reducing distractions as much as possible, including friends, media, and the temptation of pastimes. Where cramped quarters and the sounds of television and

Memory is a net; one finds it full of fish when he takes it from the brook; but a dozen miles of water have run through it without sticking.

OLIVER WENDELL HOLMES, SR.

FIGURE 12.1

Sample lecture notes produced by two seventh graders during the same material presentation

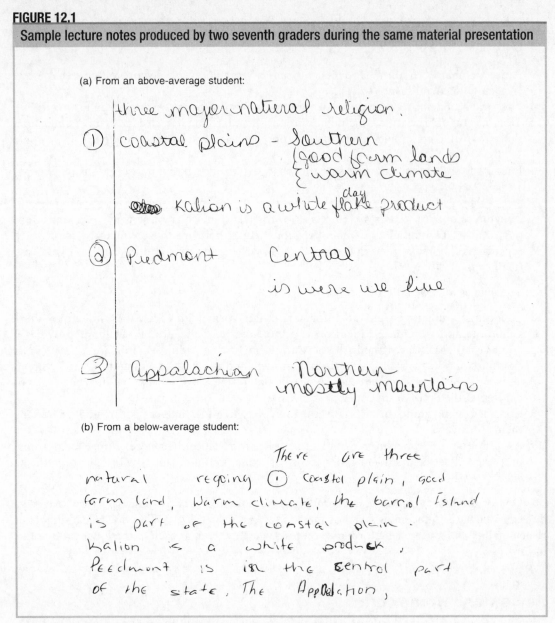

(a) From an above-average student:

(b) From a below-average student:

Source: Courtesy Andrea Matthews, Henry County Junior High School, Georgia.

siblings cannot be entirely escaped, a student can still largely avoid them by the use of earplugs or a headset tuned to white noise.

Time Management

In terms of habit formation, it is probably more effective to begin at the same time each night rather than reserve an exclusive place. To avoid fatigue, students might try dividing time allocated for review and homework—after school and before bed, for example (not just after dinner). Gall and his colleagues (Gall et al., 1990) recommend dividing complex tasks, such as writing a report, into manageable components (gathering information, making an outline, etc.).

Research argues against advising students to maintain a rigorous schedule (Risko et al., 1991). More effective is advising them to set priorities for each session in advance—deciding what it is reasonable to try to accomplish (Gall et al., 1990). Where deadlines are the same, it may be wise to begin with the most difficult subject first, when the student is freshest. This policy is contrary to human nature, however, and must be consciously instilled. Another helpful suggestion is to think ahead to predictable distractions and to schedule easier subjects for these times. A student who must study in the same bedroom with her sister, whose boyfriend calls dutifully each night at nine, would do well to schedule routine tasks for that time. The more difficult the reading, the more susceptible we are to distractions. Perhaps the important point is this: Parents of school-age students can do a great deal to help with developing and maintaining an effective time management plan for the home and teachers must make every effort to mobilize parents.

I took a speedreading course and read War and Peace *in two minutes. It's about Russia.*
WOODY ALLEN

Cumulative Review.   One of the most important aspects of time management is the need for periodic review (e.g., Gall et al., 1990). In Chapter 11, we stressed the effectiveness of distributing practice. Our focus was on lesson planning that leads to distribution, but the same principle applies to review. Consider the actual case of Bill, an average student who entered a twelfth-grade botany class and was elated to discover that there would be no textbook. Tests would be based on notes alone. By the end of the first fifty-minute period, however, Bill's elation had turned to dismay. He had taken five pages of notes. Afraid to allow his notebook to accumulate untouched until the first exam (Bill's usual modus operandi), he reviewed that day's notes after school. The next day, burdened with an additional five pages, Bill thought it prudent to review again. This time, however, instead of reviewing only the second day's installment, he began with the previous day's notes. Each day, he repeated this cumulative process, always starting with the very beginning of his notebook. His initial suspicion that this practice would soon require inordinate amounts of time was quickly dispelled. He found that he zipped rapidly through earlier material, which had become quite familiar to him. Bill's botany teacher used a combination of short quizzes and lengthy exams that together totaled 1200 points by the end of the course. Bill, who had been a B-minus student, missed only 10 points!

Motivation

A teacher cannot guarantee that students will review independently, regardless of what steps may be taken to do so. And, after all, independent study is essentially a matter of self-discipline and maturity (Dreher, 1999; Guthrie & Wigfield, 1999; Schraw & Bruning, 1999). On the other hand, teachers may be able to marshal two sources of motivation that are present even when the teacher is not: the student and the parents.

Encourage students to set short-term goals for a study session and to reward themselves when they accomplish those goals. Zimmerman and Pons (1986) observed that high-achieving high school students tended to apply self-administered rewards and punishments far more frequently than low achievers. For example, a student may wish to watch a favorite sitcom at 8:30 and may use this as an incentive for finishing a given segment of homework by this time. Failure to do so means missing the show.

Enlisting the aid of parents, while occasionally difficult, is often worth the effort. Many cooperative parents are unaware of specific ways they may be able to contribute to the development of good study habits in their children. Gall et al. (1990) suggest that parents arrange a regular study time, monitor their children as they study, and provide praise and encouragement.

Test Taking

Is it advisable to teach students how to take tests? Millman, Bishop, and Ebel (1965) defined *test wiseness* as the "capacity to utilize the characteristics and formats of the test and/or the test taking situation to receive a high score. Test wiseness is logically independent of an examinee's knowledge of the subject matter" (p. 707). Deliberately setting out to instill test wiseness in one's students has long been decried as bad practice (e.g., Hoffman, 1962). Millman et al. (1965), however, argue that test wiseness actually reduces measurement error. The logic here is that if students are equally test wise, so that no one has an unfair advantage, differences in performance must be attributable to varying degrees of content understanding. Accordingly, present-day authorities often recommend teaching students to be test wise (e.g., Wark & Flippo, 1991).

Our position is more moderate. We suggest that there are two major strategies for helping students take tests. One type increases the student's chance to respond correctly when the answer is not known. An example is the suggestion that true-false items containing an absolute term (such as *always* or *never*) are generally false. An answer of "false" to these items will often be correct. The second type of strategy allows the student to make a better score by being more efficient and logical. For example, skipping harder questions the first time through a test is an effective strategy for managing time and reducing anxiety; however, it does not reward ignorance.

We recommend that teachers adopt a three-part policy. First, they should teach students strategies that promise to make their test taking more efficient and to display their achievement to best advantage. Second, they should become aware of techniques calculated to improve scores in the absence of achievement. Finally, they should not teach these strategies but should instead construct tests that are impervious to their use. Let's look at each type of strategy more closely.

Strategies That Inflate Scores

Objective tests present many pitfalls for the novice test writer. Even professional test developers frequently fall victim to them, as witnessed by studies in which students given only the questions (not

Assisting Students with Special Needs

Classroom Testing

Written tests represent a common form of evaluation in content classrooms. Unfortunately, many poor readers and other mildly handicapped students perform poorly on written tests. Basic skill deficits and poor self-management skills confound their efforts to demonstrate what they have learned. According to Wood and Miederhoff (1988), such students often know the correct answers to test questions, but they either do not understand the directions or fail to comprehend the questions. In such cases, poor test performance is a sign of poor reading ability rather than poor content learning.

What can be done to make testing reflect what these students have learned? Wood and Miederhoff suggest that effective test construction begins with *clear directions* for taking the test. They offer the following suggestions:

1. Provide an example of how the student is to respond. (Follow the lead of standardized tests in this regard.)
2. Keep the directions simple.
3. Have directions written on the test and read them orally.
4. Place the directions at the beginning of each separate test section.
5. Make sure students clearly understand the directions. As students begin to take the test, circulate around the room and check the first few responses made by students.

In addition, numerous test modifications allow special-needs students to take the same test as their classmates regardless of each student's particular disability. Vogel and Sattler (1981) and Lazarus (1989) list the following modifications:

1. Allow for untimed tests.
2. Allow an oral reader for objective exams.
3. Allow the students to take the test alone with a proctor and to give oral responses.
4. Provide clarification and oral rephrasing of questions to bypass vocabulary, syntactic, and comprehension deficits.
5. Allow students to use calculators, dictionaries, and other resource books during exams.
6. Provide scratch paper and ruled paper to aid students who have poor handwriting skills.
7. Provide alternatives to computer-scored answer sheets (e.g., allow students to circle or underline the correct answer).
8. Give the test page by page over a longer period of time.
9. Enlarge the print and shorten the number of lines on the test.

the passages) from standardized reading comprehension tests do significantly better than chance (e.g., see Tuinman, 1971). Our listing of some of the more common errors is by no means complete, but it should help you become aware of numerous traps. Remember, we offer these guidelines for *constructing* tests and not as a curriculum for students who will be *taking* them. The idea, of course, is that even students familiar with the techniques will be unable to apply them.

1. *Avoid using two multiple-choice options with essentially the same meaning.* Test-wise students know that neither can be correct. Yet it is tempting, after constructing two good distractors, to concoct a third by paraphrasing one of the other two (Wark & Flippo, 1991).

2. *Avoid creating two options with opposite meanings.* Logic tells the testwise student, who may know nothing of the idea being tested, that one of the two options must be wrong.

3. *Avoid options that are absurdly false.* One justification for the occasional use of this practice is that it may relieve anxiety through humor. On the other hand it increases the odds of a correct response through sheer guessing and should be employed sparingly.

4. *Avoid options that disagree grammatically with their stem.* Two errors are especially common: (a) subject-verb disagreement and (b) inappropriate presence of *a* or *an* (see Figure 12.2).

5. *Avoid "hiding" the correct option in the b or c position.* Instructors often suspect that when the correct option is either first or last (in the *a* or *d* position), it is overly "exposed" (Wark & Flippo, 1991). Test-wise students exploit this practice, however, by guessing *b* or *c* far more frequently than *a* or *d*.

6. *Avoid using the absolutes* always *and* never *in false statements.* If, on the other hand, you can use them in true statements, all the better.

Strategies That Produce Valid Scores

When students employ test-taking strategies that are inefficient or illogical, their poor performance may be the result of their defective technique, which may in turn mask their real ability. Creating *positive test wiseness* by instilling strategies that enable students to show what they know is not difficult. It requires briefly but repeatedly discussing the strategies before tests. It requires discussing them again when you distribute the corrected exams for review. That's it. The strategies are simple enough that little time need be set aside for direct instruction. These techniques are good examples of the content area teacher 's being the right person for the job, because no transfer is required. The following are some strategies that underlie positive test wiseness*:

1. Encourage students to read all multiple-choice options before responding.
2. Encourage students to skip harder items and return to them later.

FIGURE 12.2

Sample test items containing grammatical clues

(a) Option *a* cannot be right because of a subject–verb disagreement. Teachers should avoid multiple choice options that
   a. is absurdly true.
   b. have opposite meanings.
   c. grammatically agree with their stem.
   d. are only a few words long.

(b) Option *b* cannot be right because its first word cannot follow the article *an*. In writing multiple-choice tests, teachers should avoid an
   a. option that is absurdly false.
   b. distractor that is too short.
   c. item with only one correct answer.
   d. answer that may relieve anxiety through humor.

---

*The first three suggestions are based on McClain's (1983) observation that better students employ them much more often than average students.

3. Encourage students to use the process of elimination in responding to different multiple-choice items.

4. Teach students to be alert for "Type K" multiple-choice items (those that contain options involving other options—for example, "all of the above," "none of the above," "*a* and *c* above"). The best strategy for responding to such items is to realize that the options must be treated as individual true-false items. The student must first determine the truth of each stand-alone option (that is, each option that does not refer to any others) and then consider the alternatives that do refer to other options.

5. Encourage students to change their answers on reconsideration whenever closer inspection suggests a change. The widespread notion that one's first impression is best is a myth that runs counter to a large and consistent body of research (see Lynch & Smith, 1975; Wark & Flippo, 1991).

6. Stress the importance of time management. Students should note the time regularly and adjust their pace as needed. One usually thinks of running short of time as the inevitable result of poor management, but in reality the opposite is often true, especially for poor students, who find testing unpleasant and rush through, squandering precious time (Gall et al., 1990).

7. Regarding essay tests, Gall et al. (1990) have crystallized a number of studies into four succinct suggestions: "(a) Read the question carefully; (b) jot key words and phrases next to the question and use them to outline the answer; (c) make the answer appropriate in length; and (d) review the answer for clarity, grammar, and spelling" (p. 188).

8. Readence, Bean, and Baldwin (1981) offer an additional suggestion for approaching essay questions: Pay close attention to the verb. This word invariably suggests how a student should organize a response.

We suspect that even the most strident opponent of teaching test wiseness could live with these two sets of suggestions for (1) making tests immune to negative test-wise strategies while (2) helping students demonstrate their understanding by better managing their time and thought processes. It is certainly clear that teachers cannot afford scrupulously to avoid discussing tests. Convincing research has long told us that learning improves when students know how they will be measured (Anderson & Armbruster, 1991). Such knowledge helps them take the right kind of notes and review in appropriate ways. It makes good sense to confront the issue of testing proactively, equipping students with test-taking skills and preparing them thoroughly for each exam by means of in-class review and a written study guide. The story related in Figure 12.3 suggests how convincing a little positive experience can be.

FIGURE 12.3

A tale of "accidental" review

There's a good story about a guy who planned to cheat on a history test. He decided to write all the main ideas and dates down on a sheet of paper and hide it in his inside jacket pocket. When he had finished writing it all down, he realized the paper was way too big to go in his pocket, so he got a smaller piece. This time he used many abbreviations and he skipped information that he realized he already knew. Boy, was he disgusted when he found he still had a paper so big it would be obvious he was concealing something. This time he used a really small piece and abbreviated everything—skipping lots of stuff that by now he knew.

The next day he tucked the paper in his jacket, and went off to school. During the morning he put his jacket in his locker to be sure nothing happened to it. Unfortunately, just before history class he was talking to a girl and forgot to get his jacket. His teacher would not let him leave.

Scared, he looked at the test, and to his astonishment it didn't look too hard. He answered all he could and passed with a respectable C+. Why? His repeated writing and reviewing as he prepared his cheat materials was the ideal way to study.

Cheating is cheating. There is no way that it is right. In the long run you will get caught and you will be the one hurt. Don't do it.

Source: From *I Hate School: How to Hang In and When to Drop Out* (p. 92) by C. G. Wirths and M. Bowman-Kruhm. Copyright © 1987, New York: Harper & Row.

Strategies for Independent Reading

We have organized this text around the vital need to prepare students for reading assignments, to provide guidance during reading, and to extend comprehension following reading. In short, comprehension is better when certain activities occur before, during, and after reading. When a teacher gives the same assignment to an entire class, these activities are organized on a classwide basis. For example, the same background-building techniques or the same content literacy guide would precede a textbook chapter to be read by all students. But what about reading selections that students select individually? Because a teacher cannot possibly provide background, set purposes, and so on for such reading, the student must do without the benefits of a DRA, DR–TA, K-W-L, or relevant explicit instruction. The student who encounters an encyclopedia entry while doing a report, selects a book as part of a project, or reads a magazine article while researching a term paper must rely on strategies previously learned for approaching these tasks. Unfortunately, many students fail to attain the goal of *strategic reading*—selecting and using strategies depending on the reader's purposes and the material to be read. In the remainder of this chapter, we will explore some ways of moving students toward this goal.

I read part of it all the way through.
SAMUEL GOLDWYN

SQ3R

Robinson (1946) offered an effective technique to help readers approach reading assignments without assistance. SQ3R consists of five steps:

1. *Survey*. The reader looks over the entire selection before reading, noting subheads, diagrams, captions, and possibly, the summary.
2. *Question*. The reader converts each subhead into a question, perhaps by marking on the text.
3. *Read*. The reader approaches each section by noting the question fashioned from the subhead. The question provides a focus for reading the section.
4. *Recite*. Before proceeding to the next section, the reader again considers the question and inwardly "recites" the answer. If the reader is unable to construct a reasonable answer, selective rereading may be needed.
5. *Review*. After completing the entire selection, the reader reflects on the questions again and also considers main ideas learned from the reading.

The similarity between SQ3R and the DRA is apparent. Because a teacher is unavailable to provide background, students acquire it through surveying the selection. They develop questions from subheads in lieu of a content literacy guide. In place of discussion, they both ask and answer these questions. To be sure, these devices are no substitute for expert guidance, but they go far toward enhancing comprehension. Figure 12.4 illustrates the relationship between SQ3R and the first four steps of the DRA.

A limitation of SQ3R is that it requires direct teaching and extensive practice. Research has shown that simply mentioning the steps and hoping for the best is not enough to assure that students will acquire a reading strategy of this kind (Caverly & Orlando, 1991). On the other hand, teachers can do much to provide extensive practice opportunities with SQ3R by relating it to textbook assignments (Scott, 1994). Once students have become familiar with reading guides, teachers can

FIGURE 12.4

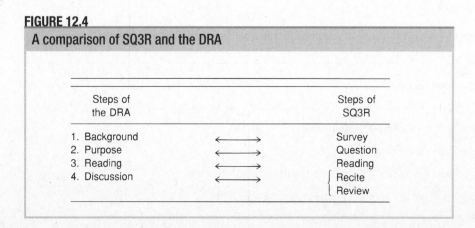

A comparison of SQ3R and the DRA

Steps of the DRA		Steps of SQ3R
1. Background	⟷	Survey
2. Purpose	⟷	Question
3. Reading	⟷	Reading
4. Discussion	⟷	Recite Review

introduce a new type of guide based on SQ3R. After introducing the five steps together with an example based on the chapter the students have just read, the teacher distributes an SQ3R worksheet. Like other literacy guides, the worksheet compels the student to interact with the text and to write information and responses. The chief difference is that the worksheet requires students to generate questions from subheads. Figure 12.5 presents an example of an SQ3R worksheet.

FIGURE 12.5

Example of an SQ3R worksheet

SURVEY the section beginning on p. 188.

What is the title of the section? _____

What does the chart describe on p. 196? _____

Notice the boldface terms. Do any of them look familiar?

What are the 3 subheadings in this section?

_____

_____

_____

Where are the study questions located? p. _____

QUESTION   Turn the title of this section into a question:

_____

Now turn each of the 3 subheadings into a question.

1. _____

2. _____

3. _____

READ each subsection. Before you go on to the next subsection, answer the question you wrote for it.

1. _____

_____

_____

2. _____

_____

_____

3. _____

_____

_____

Now go back to the question you wrote for the whole section. Write your answer.

_____

_____

_____

REVIEW the section. Do the following:

1.   Skim back through it.

2.   Check whether you know the meanings of boldface terms.

3.   See if you can answer the section review questions on p. 198.

Beyond SQ3R

When it was introduced in 1946, SQ3R represented a novel approach to strategic reading. More recently, its usefulness in some situations has led educators to regret its limitations in others. For example, the approach does not work with material that lacks subheads. Moreover, the subheads may at times fail to address a student's purposes in reading. It is not surprising that SQ3R led to a spate of adaptations. By 1982, Walker (1982) was able to list 39 (each known by an acronym)!

PLAE. It would appear that, to be effective, students must be able to apply a variety of techniques, depending on their purposes and the nature of the material. Simpson and Nist (1984), responding to the inability of any single strategy to be effective on all occasions, suggested a method for making students consciously select the strategies they use. In PLAE (preplan, list, activate, evaluate), the student begins by examining the task at hand to determine what must be accomplished. The student then mentally lists strategies that may be useful and uses (activates) one or more that seem best suited to accomplishing the desired purposes. Finally, the student evaluates whether the purpose has in fact been achieved and, if not, what other strategies might be used to achieve it. Not surprisingly, research has shown that PLAE works, at least for older students (Nist & Simpson, 2000).

At the heart of the technique is the notion that superior students have a variety of strategies at their command and are capable of selecting those that are best suited to a given situation. Content teachers can move their students toward this point first by seizing opportunities to build their ability to take notes, review, take tests, and read independently and second by encouraging them to become cognizant of how and when to employ these skills.

SUMMARY

Study involves learning independently the content of printed materials. Although numerous skills are involved, some are best taught by content teachers, who are in a position to demonstrate their use with course materials. Centrally important are the abilities to take notes, to review, to take tests, and to read independently using purposeful strategies. These abilities receive little attention from teachers, who often assume that students will develop them naturally. Research, however, suggests that teachers must directly instruct students in the use of these skills.

Note-taking aids learning by the mental involvement needed in taking the notes and also by their use during review. Content teachers can develop note-taking skills in their students by modeling them during content lectures. The Cornell system provides a good basis from which to begin teaching, but other guidelines are also important. These include (1) assessing students' note-taking abilities, (2) speaking at a slow rate, (3) pausing often, (4) stressing definitions and examples, (5) teaching abbreviations, (6) encouraging the use of paraphrase, (7) helping students focus on cues the teacher provides, (8) recommending indention as a means of organizing, (9) giving grades on notes, and (10) preparing transparencies from actual examples of students' notes.

When reviewing or doing homework assignments, superior students seek a relatively quiet environment. They also manage their time by setting priorities, avoiding early fatigue, and motivating themselves. Cumulative review can be an especially effective way to ensure long-term retention.

Whether to teach test wiseness is a controversial issue. Our suggestion is to teach those techniques that contribute to valid test scores and to construct tests that are immune to techniques that tend to inflate scores. Teachers should avoid (1) distractors with similar meanings, (2) options with opposite meanings, (3) absurdly false options, (4) options that disagree grammatically with their stem, (5) hidden placement of the correct choice in the b or c position, and (6) absolutes in true-false items. At the same time, they should teach students (1) to read all options before responding, (2) to skip harder items till last, (3) to use the process of elimination, (4) to use true-false strategies with "Type K" items, (5) to change answers when it seems warranted, (6) to manage their time, (7) to read essay questions carefully, jotting down key words and producing an answer of appropriate length and clarity, and (8) to pay special attention to the verb in an essay question.

Numerous strategies for independent reading are available. Most are adaptations of SQ3R (survey, question, read, recite, review), which provides some of the benefits of a DRA in the absence of a teacher. SQ3R is limited, however, and superior students must be able to call on other strategies when their purposes or the material requires them.

Getting Involved

1. Use yourself as a guinea pig. Select one or more of the note-taking and review techniques discussed here that you do not already use in your own approach to college course-work. Try out each technique and judge for yourself whether you want to encourage your students to employ it. We suggest you keep an informal log as you begin to use the method you've chosen. Record any problems you may experience in getting used to it, any modifications you may develop, and, of course, any evidence you may gather of its effectiveness in helping you retain course material.

2. Compare a sample of your own lecture notes with the guidelines recommended in the Cornell system. Which of the guidelines do you follow? With which ones is your own system at odds? In these cases, can you give reasons (other than habit) in defense of your approach over the Cornell system?

3. Here's an action research project to try with your students. Select a unit that contains factual information for students to remember. If you teach two sections of the same course, use a carefully distributed review schedule with one of the classes. We suggest ten minutes, one day a month, for five months. The last ten-minute review should occur just prior to a quiz on the unit. On the day that this class undertakes its last ten-minute review, conduct a fifty-minute review with the other class. (This will be the only review this class will receive.) Both classes will have participated in the same total amount of review when you administer the quiz. Judge for yourself whether distributing the review had an effect on the class average for the quiz. If you do not teach two sections of the same course concurrently, you can still perform the experiment by comparing the results of using one of the methods with your current class and the other method with students who will take the course the next time you teach it. In either case, you'll need to use classes that in your judgment are of relatively comparable ability.

CHAPTER 13

Student Attitudes: Encouraging Content Literacy

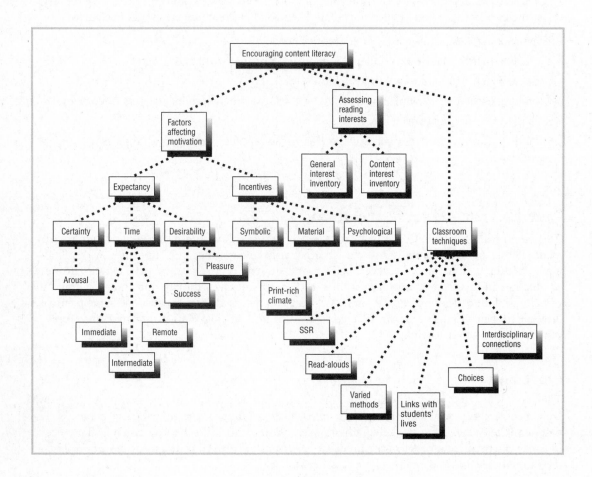

Knowledge which is acquired under compulsion obtains no hold on the mind.

—Plato

As you begin this chapter, pause for a moment to consider *why* you are reading it. Is it because we have aroused your curiosity to the point that you want to learn more in general about content literacy? Could it be that you have specific instructional questions that you think might be addressed in this chapter? Or is it that your instructor will hold you accountable for the chapter on an exam? Perhaps you've read an account of the topic by other authors and wish to contrast their views with ours. Or finally, and perhaps most important, you are a person who enjoys reading and you want to share your experiences with your students (Otto, 1995). Whatever the case, you are reading this chapter, and this is evidence that some factor or set of factors is causing you to do so. Had they not existed, you would at this moment be doing something other than reading Chapter 13.

Effective teachers know something about how these factors operate and are able to translate them into instructional practice. The result is improved learning for good and poor readers alike (Clary, 1991) and, in addition, better attitudes toward the subject matter and toward literacy activities related to it.

Objectives

This chapter describes the basic principles of motivation and suggests ways of making those principles work for you in the classroom. When you have read it, you should be able to

1. describe the basic factors that affect motivation;
2. create a literate classroom climate conducive to positive attitudes;
3. implement a program of voluntary reading related to your subject area;
4. undertake thematic planning as a means of stressing the interconnectedness of content;
5. suggest alternatives to traditional book reports; and
6. modify your teaching in other ways to encourage reading, writing, and thinking about content.

Factors That Affect Motivation

All human behavior is the result of factors that operate both within us and within our environment. These are often complex and may interact with one another in complicated ways. Knowing something about them, however, helps make student behavior more predictable and more productive. In this section, our discussion is rather general, even though our aim is to apply the principles of motivation to content literacy. Our treatment is general because the same principles underlie *all* behavior, not just that related to reading and writing. This means that they apply to other aspects of your teaching.

Expectancy

The probability that we will behave in a particular way depends to a large extent on the results we expect. Expectancies have three characteristics that influence how they affect behavior. The first characteristic is *certainty*—the individual's notion of how likely an outcome is. The second is *time*—the prediction of when the outcome will occur. The third characteristic is *desirability*—the estimation of how appealing the outcome will be.

Certainty. A student begins any task with an idea of what will happen in the process. Sometimes the student is virtually certain of what will occur, as when, upon opening the book, the pages are filled with print. At other times, a student may be far less certain, such as during the first class session with a new teacher. When actual events are similar to what the student expects, the level of *arousal*, or alertness, is apt to be low. When, however, expectancies are vague to begin with (during the first day with a new teacher, for example) or when real occurrences are different from the student's expectancies, arousal increases.

When a teacher skillfully arranges for student expectancies to be slightly thwarted, the result can be heightened arousal, attentiveness, and curiosity. Changes in classroom routine, variations in methods of instruction, and the occasional use of novel approaches and topics are ways of ensuring that student expectancies are not always confirmed.

Time. Students also have some notion of when outcomes will occur. Whether they expect a given event to happen soon may have a great effect on the role that event will play in their decision making. For the sake of convenience, we can describe expectancies in relation to time as immediate, intermediate, and remote. *Immediate expectancies* involve outcomes in the near future. As a result of reading this chapter, for example, you may expect to do well on a test. *Intermediate expectancies* concern outcomes that are slightly more distant. Because you believe that reading the chapter will help you on the test, you also expect to do well in the course. In other words, you recognize that there is a link between your reading now and the letter grade you will ultimately receive, even though those two events may not occur in quick succession. *Remote expectancies* involve outcomes that we project for the relatively distant future. You have probably thought, for example, how passing this course will contribute to earning a degree or certificate, which in turn may mean a job, salary schedule advancement, and so forth. Without necessarily verbalizing these outcomes, you are nevertheless able to relate remote results to the reading of this chapter.

The effect of intermediate and remote expectancies on behavior depends in part on the maturity and foresight of the student. Because these outcomes do not occur quickly, they lack the reinforcing power of immediate results. For this reason it is more effective (with some students) to remind them of an upcoming test than to warn them they may not get into college without an understanding of a given unit, lesson, or concept.

Immediate expectancies are sometimes at odds with intermediate and remote ones. You may be tempted by a chocolate sundae because of your immediate expectancies concerning how it will taste. However, the intermediate expectancy of gaining weight and the remote expectancy of health risks due to fat and cholesterol may be enough to inhibit you. Whenever there is a mixture of desirable and undesirable expectancies, an *approach/avoidance* situation occurs. When the pluses and minuses are nearly equal, temporary indecision and even anxiety may result. Usually, however, the scales quickly tip one way or the other. One of the most effective approaches to motivation is to add positive expectancies when the thinking of students is dominated by undesirable predictions. How to do so is the principal aim of this chapter.

Desirability. Another useful way of classifying expectancies is to distinguish between the *expectancy of success* and the *expectancy of pleasure*. Psychologists generally refer to the latter as *valence*, which is roughly equivalent to "appeal." Expectancy of success and valence are related but they are not the same. It is easy to imagine wishing to do something even though we suspect we may fail (high valence, low expectancy of success). You can also name an endless assortment of tasks you could easily accomplish but have little desire to do (low valence, high expectancy of success). Figure 13.1 depicts the four combinations of high and low valence and expectancy of success. A teacher's goal must be high levels of each. When this situation occurs, students will be likely to engage in the behavior. We have devoted most of

FIGURE 13.1

The relationship of valence to expectancy of success

		Valence	
		High	*Low*
Expectancy of success	*High*	The student wants to succeed and expects to.	The student knows that he or she can succeed but does not care.
	Low	The student wants to succeed but does not expect to.	The student doubts that he or she can succeed but does not care.

this book to methods of increasing a student's expectancy of success. We turn now to ways of increasing valence.

Incentives

The well-meaning people who talk about education as if it were a substance distributable by coupon in large or small quantities never exhibit any understanding of the truth that you cannot teach anybody anything that he does not want to learn.
GEORGE SAMPSON

An incentive is any inducement or reward used to encourage a particular behavior. It can be *symbolic* in nature (the honor roll, letter grades, etc.), *material* (food, privileges, etc.), or *psychological* (praise, teacher approval, self-satisfaction, etc.). By using incentives, the teacher acknowledges that an academic task has little valence for students. The incentive presents a desirable expectancy to counterbalance the undesirable outcome students may project, such as boredom, frustration, or fatigue.

Though incentives can be very effective, their use is somewhat controversial (Baumann, 1995; Kohn, 1999; Sax & Kohn, 1996). Some educators equate incentives (especially the material kind) with bribes that cause students to learn for the wrong reasons. Defenders of incentives counter that if a learning task has intrinsic appeal, students will eventually come to recognize that appeal. The challenge lies in giving students enough experience to make a judgment. Incentives can help persuade them to participate (Gambrell, 1996; McQuillan, 1997; Sweet & Guthrie, 1997).

Using incentives requires no special talent, but a few simple guidelines can make them more effective.

1. *Use a variety of incentives.* Try to match the incentive with the required task. Avoid overuse of the same incentive. Brainstorming a list like the one in Figure 13.2 is a good first step.

2. *Individualize incentives.* Not all incentives work equally well with all students. Some may shun public praise, for example, while others thrive on it. Be alert to the effects an incentive has.

3. *Don't use incentives when they're not needed.* When motivation is already adequate, it is pointless to use incentives. In fact, it can even be counterproductive by creating an expectation of external rewards that did not exist before.

4. *Provide the incentive as soon as possible after the desired behavior.* Reinforcement by incentives works best when the reward quickly follows the targeted behavior. Even major incentives like a party or a field trip should follow soon after the attainment of the goal.

FIGURE 13.2

A partial list of incentives available to classroom teachers

Material
> food
> privileges
> field trips
> reading (SSR)
> being read to (read-alouds)

Symbolic
> grades
> distinctions
> awards

Psychological
> oral praise
> written praise
> nonverbal positives (smiles, gestures, etc.)
> calls or letters to parents

Assessing Reading Interests

Many students harbor negative attitudes toward content assignments and schooling in general. The reasons are many and include a history of frustration due to poor reading ability, a failure to perceive the relevance of content, and poorly designed instruction (Dreher, 1999; Robb, 1998; Worthy, Moorman, & Turner, 1999). The total of a student's past experiences contributes to an overall attitude toward the subject area in general (Bean & Readence, 1994). In discussing preferences, a student may state an interest in social studies, a dislike for math, indifference to science, and so forth. In other words, students have an overall attitude toward content subjects, and it is easy to assume that that attitude may extend to any content task related to the subject. McKenna (1986) asked middle-grade and secondary students with reading problems to rate each of the core content areas as possible reading interests. These topics were interspersed among a total of forty-four varied reading interests. Not surprisingly, the students rated the traditional subjects quite low. Science, for example, was ranked forty-fourth out of forty-four choices!

We suggest, however, that it would be a mistake to conclude that the attitude of these students toward reading within the field of science was uniformly negative regardless of the specific subtopic. There may well be areas *within* science that they viewed much more favorably. In psychological terms, these areas may have had a higher valence than the subject area as a whole. Discovering these existing interest areas within a field of study is therefore a first step toward encouraging more content reading. When such interests exist, incentives are unnecessary (Campbell, Kapinus, & Beatty, 1995; Pinnell, Pikulski, Wilson, Campbell, Gough, & Beatty, 1995).

Teachers can rapidly assess interests by means of an inventory. Two types are in common use. A *general interest inventory* presents a wide range of topics not confined to a given content area. General interest inventories may be of interest to language arts teachers, who often wish to encourage reading by offering an array of subjects. A *content interest inventory* also presents a list of topics, but all of them derive from the same subject area. The content interest inventory gets past a student's general attitude toward the subject by breaking it down into subtopics. The students in McKenna's (1986) study might have rated the following science-related subtopics much higher than their overall rating of science per se:

- Mysteries science cannot explain
- Viking's trip to Mars: pictures and account
- Evolution versus creationism
- The Manhattan project: building the first atomic bomb

The content interest inventory treats a subject like science not as one topic but as many. By using it teachers recognize that a student's interest may not be uniform across an entire subject. Identifying possible interests within the broader subject is an activity that is highly worthwhile.

Constructing a Content Interest Inventory

To produce a good content interest inventory, you must possess an adequate working knowledge of your subject together with an idea of what reading materials are available to students within that subject. The following guidelines can help.

1. *Make a list of interesting subtopics.* The key word is *interesting.* You must attempt to outguess your students by predicting aspects of your subject matter that may have built-in appeal. One finding of the McKenna (1986) study may offer some help. He observed that the unusual or strange aspects of virtually any subject tend to give it appeal. Be on the lookout for the unusual aspects of your own subject area—aspects that many content teachers ironically avoid.

2. *Identify materials for each area.* Make sure you can deliver the goods! There is little reason to assess the extent of a student's interest in a given area if you cannot place in that student's hand corresponding materials. These can include books (fiction and nonfiction), magazine articles, newspaper articles you have collected, and so forth.

3. *Add a few blanks at the end of the inventory*. In many respects, a content interest inventory is like an election ballot. You are asking students to vote for their preferences. Like any ballot, an inventory should provide for write-ins. Inspecting what students may write on these blanks can give you an idea of topics you may not have thought of when you constructed the inventory. In fact, students' suggestions may cause you to revise the inventory before using it again.

4. *Word-process the inventory*. Revisions are easy when you produce the instrument on a computer. You can quickly remove unpopular topics and add write-ins that appear often. With repeated use you can see your inventory evolve into a well-designed opinion poll.

5. *Decide how students will respond*. The simplest format is a checklist. Students simply check the topics they prefer and make no marks next to those they aren't interested in. Unfortunately, this system is too crude to provide much information about how strong an interest may be. We recommend a rating scale format in which students respond to each topic by indicating their *degree* of interest. One possibility is to have them assign "letter grades" to each of the inventory's topics. A grade of A indicates strong interest, a B moderate interest, a C relative indifference, a D dislike, and an F strong dislike.

Administering a Content Interest Inventory

Giving the inventory is simple and requires little time. At the beginning of a term, it provides an excellent opportunity to discuss the subject area in general and apprise students of some of its more interesting dimensions. When you give your inventory, keep the following guidelines in mind.

1. *Make your purpose clear*. Tell students that the inventory is not a test and that there are no right or wrong answers. Point out that there is not even a way of tallying the results to produce a score. Make it plain that you do not care how they respond as long as they answer sincerely. You might suggest that you would be rather surprised if anyone were to rate all the categories highly. Most important, communicate the true purpose of the inventory, which is to enable you to suggest materials corresponding to those topics the students rate favorably.

2. *Read the inventory aloud as students respond*. This practice ensures that even poor decoders can respond sincerely, provided they can follow along while you read. It also affords an opportunity to elaborate informally on certain topics and to suggest an example or two of what you have in mind.

Interpreting the Results

Topics receiving a grade of A are pure gold. In them you have managed to uncover a potential source of subject matter curiosity and excitement. For some students, of course, A's will be few in number or nonexistent. You will have to rely on grades of B or below in these cases. In other words, where there is no primary interest area, one that is strong relative to the other areas is the best you can hope for. Be prepared to recommend materials that correspond to the strengths you have identified. Later in this chapter we will discuss methods for providing students with the opportunity to read such materials.

There is also a way to quantify the results of the inventory and to produce a single score that represents overall interest in reading about the content area. Even though the letter grades cannot be directly summed, they can be converted to numerical values in the same way that grade point averages are determined. An F would receive zero points, a D one point, a C two points, and so forth. By adding these numbers for all topics and dividing by the number of topics, you can produce a student's average rating based on the same scale used to compute grade point averages. An average could in fact be interpreted in roughly the same way, with values above three indicating a strong general attitude and a healthy breadth of interests. Although these averages are of little diagnostic value, you can use them to gauge your own success in fostering an interest in your subject area. By averaging these scores for an entire class, and by giving the inventory again at the end of the term, you will be in a position to make a pre/post comparison.

Promoting Content Literacy in Your Classroom

The remainder of this chapter presents a variety of techniques for fostering positive attitudes toward literacy activities—reading in particular related to your subject area. Some of the techniques involve activities, whereas others amount to no more than slight modifications in your style of teaching. Together they represent an extensive array of possibilities. One word of caution, however: Although there are many techniques, there are no guarantees. We would invite you to read, sample, and implement with your own students. See for yourself which of these approaches produces the best result *for you*.

Create a Print-Rich Environment

A subtle way to promote literacy is to immerse your students in surroundings that are rich in print. Perhaps the best way is to bring books related to your subjects into the classroom. These books might include some that belong to you personally as well as school library books. Consider establishing a "branch" library in your classroom—a system in which the books are officially checked out to you but are then subchecked out to individual students or simply used within the classroom. Keep in mind that paperbacks are far more inviting than hardbound editions. They are less intimidating to students, less like textbooks in appearance, and often smaller and embellished with cover art. Fader and Shaevitz (1966), in their classic *Hooked on Books,* suggest displaying the books so that the covers are visible. An old wire rack from a drugstore is ideal for this purpose, but other methods are equally acceptable. You can, for example, simply place the books on a shelf so that they lean against the back wall, their covers in full view. Fader and Shaevitz compared booksellers, who display books in this manner, with librarians, who, in an effort to conserve space, typically shelve books so that only the spines are visible. Booksellers, whose livelihood depends on attracting readers, tend to have greater success than librarians in luring consumers to their product.

Even the walls of your classroom can encourage content literacy. Line them with dust jackets, posters, mounted articles, and selected student work. An appealing extra touch is the display of quotations related to your area. A thought-provoking "quote of the day," written in a conspicuous spot at the front of the room, can serve as an interest-grabbing sponge activity as students file into class. With a little foresight, you can often find quotations that bear on the day's lesson. Any book of quotes can become a content literacy resource, as the examples in Figure 13.3 show. Quotations have two characteristics that arouse interest: They are brief and they are carefully crafted to convey an insight. You can test the value of our suggestion to use them by asking yourself whether your own reading of this text hasn't been drawn irresistibly toward the quotable nuggets we've deliberately buried throughout it for effect! Our point is that there are many ways to create what Clary (1991) has called "an atmosphere that shouts the importance of reading" (p. 343).

> In Chapter 6, we suggested using quotations that had the form of false definitions as a means of introducing new vocabulary. Our suggestion here is much more general: Display quotations to enliven content.

Give Students a Chance to Read

You cannot expect students to become content literate unless you give them opportunities to explore the subject area through print. Textbook assignments are not enough. Students occasionally need time to browse wherever their inclinations lead them and to do so in an atmosphere free of accountability and restraint (Meyers, 1998; Schiavone, 1999; Virgil, 1995).

Content Area SSR. A systematic way of providing exploratory reading time is *sustained silent reading* (SSR). Hunt (1967) originally intended the technique as a means for building *general* reading interest and for providing additional practice in *general* reading skills. But SSR holds immense potential for content literacy. By defining acceptable materials as any that relate to your area, you can ensure that SSR will broaden students' encounters with the discipline.

The advantages of content area SSR are persuasive. It extends understanding by offering new contexts for some of the very concepts students are studying. Its timing is flexible, so that teachers can use it without observing rigid time demands. It uses choice as a motivator, for even though the selections are limited to the confines of a subject area, the options are still plentiful. It is appealing, because the teacher does not hold students accountable for what they

FIGURE 13.3

Examples of brief, provocative, content-specific quotations

Science

In science, all facts, no matter how trivial or banal, enjoy democratic equality.

—Mary McCarthy

The physicists have known sin; and this is a knowledge which they cannot lose.

—J. Robert Oppenheimer

Children are the only true scientists.

—R. Buckminster Fuller

Mathematics

There is no royal road to geometry.

—Euclid

A man has one hundred dollars and you leave him with two dollars, that's subtraction.

—Mae West

They say there is divinity in odd numbers, either in nativity, chance, or death.

—Shakespeare

Language Arts

Literature is the art of writing something that will be read twice; journalism what will be grasped at once.

—Cyril Connolly

Prose,—words in their best order; poetry,—the best words in their best order.

—Samuel Taylor Coleridge

All books are either dreams or swords.

—Amy Lowell

Social Studies

Half a truth is better than no politics.

—G. K. Chesterton

The worst thing in this world, next to anarchy, is government.

—Henry Ward Beecher

Ballots are the rightful and peaceful successors to bullets.

—Abraham Lincoln

read. This policy conveys the powerful lesson that there are times when reading—even content area reading—is done for pleasure. Finally, SSR offers a subtle but effective reward that teachers can use in good conscience to reinforce achievement and encourage reading at the same time. Imagine the effect of telling students that if they complete an assignment successfully and efficiently, they may participate in SSR for the final ten minutes of class. The thought of students working industriously for the privilege of reading further in the same general area is greatly satisfying.

SSR is not a highly structured technique. Teachers can adapt it easily to meet their needs, particularly in content settings. A few basic guidelines, however, can mean the difference between an effective program and a relative waste of time.

1. *Make the purposes of SSR clear.* Describe the procedure before you begin. Emphasize that the point is to give the students an opportunity to pursue their own interests within the subject area. Make it plain that there will be no reports to write, no questions to answer, no follow-up of any kind. The idea is to explore, sample, and browse.

2. *Define acceptable materials.* Making an assortment of content-related reading materials available in your classroom is a good first step toward defining what is acceptable and what is

not. However, do not limit students to these materials alone. Invite them to explore the field on their own. Such an invitation will mean spelling out what you will permit, and you'll need to think through this issue relative to your own instructional philosophy.

3. *Encourage students to select materials in advance.* You cannot depend on every student's having appropriate materials prior to each SSR session, even when you have announced the session in advance. One of the many benefits of stockpiling reading matter in your classroom is that it becomes a convenient SSR resource for these students. Begin a session by allowing one minute to find something to read if necessary. Trips to the library or locker will not be needed.

4. *Announce the time limit.* Tell students at the beginning of each session how much time you have set aside for SSR. Start with five minutes or so until students become comfortable with the routine. You may later wish to increase the length of sessions gradually. Some teachers use a spring-driven kitchen-type timer, but a wall clock will do. On those occasions when SSR is the last activity of the class period, the bell serves as a signal to stop.

5. *Prohibit studying.* SSR is not a study hall. Its success depends on making time available for free reading within your subject area. Using the time to complete assignments defeats this purpose.

6. *Enforce silence.* A quiet environment is essential if SSR is to work. Deal with disruptions by ending the session and returning to more structured activities. The culprits will soon get the message.

7. *Participate in SSR yourself.* If reading is really worth doing, model it by using the SSR session to extend your own content reading. If you subscribe to a professional journal, this may be a good time to look through the latest issue. If you're currently engrossed in a new book in your area, bring it with you to school and bring it out of hiding for SSR.

8. *Avoid accountability.* One of SSR's most appealing traits is that students are not required to report on, discuss, or be tested on what they read. Don't spoil this positive feature by asking them to do any of these.

9. *Link SSR to the content interest inventory.* Try to ensure the availability of materials that correspond to each of the subtopics on your content interest inventory. Use the inventory results to make suggestions to students who seem indifferent or hesitant to choose. Do not be overly prescriptive, however. Suggest, but don't push.

Read Aloud to Your Students

Researchers have amply documented the value of reading aloud to young children. But what about students in middle-grade and secondary content classes? Can teachers justify the time needed to read selections aloud in class? The answer, we believe, is a qualified yes (Ivey & Broaddus, 2000). When selections are relatively brief and when they are carefully chosen to emphasize current topics, they can add variety, stimulate enthusiasm, and model the importance of literacy without diverting excessive time away from direct instruction.

Read-alouds often conjure thoughts of short stories and novels, but nonfiction can be just as viable. Consider a few examples.

- A newspaper article on cancer research appears the week before a teacher begins a health unit on the subject of cancer. She reads selected portions at the beginning of the unit.
- An article in *Sports Illustrated* details how modern advances in protective gear now reduce the chances of football injuries. A coach reads it aloud to his team just before equipment is distributed during late summer practices.
- A mathematics teacher, looking for a fresh approach to teaching percentages to a "practical math" class, brings the sports page of the morning paper and reads the win-loss records of various teams, asking students to compute their winning percentages.
- A history teacher reads the accounts of President Zachary Taylor's exhumation. The articles lead naturally into a unit on the Civil War.

- A sociology teacher leads off a discussion of marriage with recent selections from "Dear Abby."
- A civics teacher reads aloud two recent syndicated columns that take opposite sides on a current issue.

This does not mean that fiction has no place in content classrooms. Our history teacher might have read selections from *Gone with the Wind,* and our sociology teacher might have read aloud from Isaac Asimov's "robot" novels, detailing how different social systems arose on various fictitious planets and why.

Read-alouds offer a valuable flexibility in planning for stimulating instruction. They afford an excellent way to introduce an objective by focusing students' attention and thoughts. They can emphasize the contemporary import of content whenever the sources are news reports and current articles. You can even use read-alouds to fill up an odd moment pleasantly or to reward students for their efforts in class assignments. (Here is yet another way of using reading as a reward!)

The most effective read-alouds are interactive (Fisher et al., 2004). They encourage discussion at strategic points. It is important to plan them carefully, and it is a mistake to assume that all one needs to do is open the book and begin reading. We offer here some suggestions for planning and conducting a read-aloud tied to a content subject.

Planning a Read-Aloud.   Planning is a bit different depending on whether the book is fiction or nonfiction, but these differences are noted in the following steps.

1. Read the material carefully beforehand, identifying:
   a. Key vocabulary likely to be unfamiliar to the students (excluding terminology that is actually defined in a nonfiction book);
   b. Background information the author assumes readers possess but that your students may lack;
   c. Points at which reasonable predictions may be appropriate; and
   d. Points where there are good visual descriptions contained in the text.

Try attaching stickies at the points you identify so that you can find them easily later on.

2. Make a plan for building and activating background knowledge prior to the read-aloud. Consider:
   a. Relating content to students' past experiences ("Have you ever . . . ?");
   b. Jotting down the information you need to provide the students before you begin and the most effective way of doing so;
   c. Planning a brief overview of the material to be read ("This is a story about . . ." or "This book tells us about . . .").
3. Mentally segment the book by thinking ahead about points where you will pause. For chapter books or nonfiction trade books, mark good stopping points using a pencil or stickies. For picture books, each two-page spread will usually work, though in some cases you may want to go further before pausing.
4. For each reading segment decide on a focusing technique. You might, for example:
   a. Pose a question ("As I read, see if you can find out . . ."); or
   b. Ask for a prediction, using pictures if available ("What do you think will happen? . . . Let's find out.").

Keep in mind that not all text segments lend themselves to predictions. Limit this technique to segments where reasonable predictions can be made by the students.

Conducting a Read-Aloud.   Now that you've planned, you're ready to conduct the Strategic Read-Aloud. Before you begin, write key words and, if appropriate, graphic organizers on the marker board or on chart paper. These should be available during the read-aloud so that you can quickly refer to them as you progress through the selection. They will provide the students with a visual version of important terms. Beck and McKeown (2001) recommend taking stock of words that may already be on display on word walls or charts.

Begin by providing the background you've decided is important. Make an effort to fully engage students in this process so that the appropriate prior knowledge is developed and activated.

Wait to show pictures until you've read their context. Some teachers attempt to hold the book so that is visible to the students as the teacher reads. Research indicates, however, that youngsters' attention is drawn to the illustrations and that they may not adequately attend to the text (Beck & McKeown, 2001). We suspect it's true of older students as well.

Ask some questions before revealing the illustrations as well. Doing so compels the students to answer on the basis of the language they have heard rather than the pictures. Make sure that some of the questions cannot be answered solely on the basis of prior knowledge. Tie them directly to the story line. Children have a tendency to overrely on their own background (Beck & McKeown, 2001).

While reading each segment, use rewordings and quick asides when you think they will help the students comprehend. These may amount to simple rephrasings or synonym substitutions. This practice will help LEP students and native English speakers as well. Here are two examples from *The Wretched Stone* by Chris Van Allsburg.

Example 1

"'Slightly before sunset we spotted an island. I have consulted my charts'—ocean maps, that is—'but do not see it recorded.'"

Example 2

"'I have decided to scuttle the *Rita Anne*.' That means he wants to sink it on purpose."

Be sure to vary your voice a bit when making these "editorial comments." This will help the students understand that you are making slight alterations as you read. Make sure that these changes are not overly intrusive, however. They must not be too frequent and they must not detract from the coherence of the material or from its appeal. When you arrive at one of those points where you think a comprehension problem might occur, use a Think-Aloud in order to model "fix-up" strategies that proficient readers use. You'll recall that these include:

1. Rereading to ensure that you did not make a mistake;
2. Reflecting, in an attempt to resolve the problem; or
3. Reading ahead, in the hope that the author will provide some clarification.

Occasionally remind the students of what a good reader would do in a troublesome situation.

Example 3

"'After I pounded at the door of the forward hatch, it finally swung open. But it was not a man who opened the door, it was an ape.'" The teacher pauses here and says, "Hmm, now how could that be? There were no apes on the whole ship! A good reader would try to make this make sense, right? But how? Well, I think a *really* good reader might keep reading to see if the author explains." The teacher continues and, sure enough: "'The whole crew has turned into hairy beasts.' I guess that explains it!"

When you arrive at the marks or stickies for points where predictions or visual imaging are appropriate, take the time to lead students through these activities. You will always need to monitor the time, however, and you may need to recap before going on.

NET Worth

CyberGuides. These are activities and lesson plans centered around popular children's literature, grades K–12. Prepared through S.C.O.R.E. (Schools of California Online Resources in Education).

www.sdcoe.k12.ca.us/score/cyberguide.html

When you reach the end of the read-aloud, ask students to help you summarize what you have read to them. You might divide this task into the beginning, middle, and end of a story or into subtopics in a nonfiction selection. Try to get the students to provide main ideas only. A few suggestions for getting at this elusive skill are:

1. Suggesting an alternative title or subtitle for the selection;
2. Limiting the number of words (e.g., "Tell me all you can in ten words.");
3. Asking the children to "tell a friend" about the book if they ran into the friend in the hall and had only a moment to spend.

Finally, do some self-reflecting about how well the read-aloud went. What might you change that would lead to a better experience next time?

Vary Your Teaching Methods

We have discussed how creating slight differences between what students expect to happen and what actually happens tends to increase arousal. The key word is *slight*. Major unannounced departures from classroom routine can be disruptive and even anxiety provoking. When the routine is constantly varied in small ways, however, students are apt to become more attentive because of the uncertainty of their expectancies (Mathison, 1989).

An important way to create small deviations is by varying the methods you employ. This is one reason we have deliberately introduced a variety of techniques for building background knowledge (Chapter 5), for introducing technical vocabulary (Chapter 6), and so on. By adding these techniques to your teaching repertoire, you are in a much better position to select for variety. If you used a graphic organizer to introduce terms for the previous unit, use a feature analysis chart for the next one. If you feel you've fallen into a rut with the DRA, try K-W-L for a change.

In Chapter 1, we referred to the movie *Teachers*, which contains a number of insights into the instructional issues educators face. An amusing example of what can happen when variety is all but eliminated involves a teacher nicknamed "Mr. Ditto." You will note in Figure 13.4 that the nickname is an apt one.

Look for Links with the Lives of Students

No barrier of the senses shuts me out from the sweet, gracious discourse of my book friends. They talk to me without embarrassment or awkwardness.

HELEN KELLER

Researchers have observed that the most successful teachers consistently point out to students how new material relates to their lives (e.g., Bean, 2000; Hunter, 1993; Rosenshine, 1986). This is not always an easy task. When the topic in health class is pregnancy or when the introduction of the electoral process in civics coincides with student council elections, the linkage is natural. (You should point it out, however, no matter how obvious it seems!) But when the topic in algebra is the quadratic formula, the task of relating your objective to students' perceptions of relevance is more demanding. Resourcefulness and creativity are occasionally required.

When you can see no persuasive connection, two suggestions might help. One is to remind students of an in-school, short-term, academic purpose, such as an upcoming exam. A statement like "Today's lesson will be very important for Friday's quiz" will at least have a motivational effect on students who are achievement conscious. The second suggestion is to ask students why they think a particular objective is important to them. Some teachers find this strategy risky, because it may invite negative responses, but if students do announce that they see no utility in a given lesson, they are merely saying aloud what they already think. If, however, even one student can suggest something positive, it may well have a ripple effect among the other class members and give you an idea for an effective purpose statement the *next time* you teach the same lesson.

Provide Choices Wherever Possible

We have discussed the fact that any proposed task has an inherent valence, or appeal. This quality will differ from one student to the next and is usually difficult to predict with certainty.

FIGURE 13.4
The story of Mr. Ditto

"Mr. Ditto" had perfected his classroom routine to the point at which students knew precisely what to do at all times. As they entered the classroom, they took a copy of the day's assignment from one tray and worked on it independently until the bell signaled the end of the period. They then dropped it into an adjacent tray on their way out of the room.

Mr. Ditto meanwhile sat at his desk in the back of the room while his students worked away, their backs toward him. Mr. Ditto never spoke, nor was there need to. Every student knew the general routine, and the details were self-explanatory. Mr. Ditto would occasionally nod off, but who wouldn't now and then after engineering such a beautiful system?

One day tragedy struck. Mr. Ditto succumbed to a heart attack. He had been dutifully manning his post at the rear of the room when it happened. It was several hours later, however, before anyone noticed he was dead!

Affording a choice of assignments will permit students to select the option with the highest personal valence. The key is to extend choices that *all* lead to the objectives you have targeted. A math teacher may feel comfortable asking students to compute any ten of the thirty problems at the end of a chapter, even in the knowledge that many will select those that seem easiest to them. If, on the other hand, the problems do not uniformly reflect the content of the chapter, the teacher might still be able to make choices available without compromising the objectives. For example, the teacher might ask students to "work any five of the first ten problems and any five of the last twenty," or to "work number seven and any nine of the remaining ones."

There are two additional benefits of choice that are more difficult to quantify. One is that power transfers from the teacher to the student whenever alternatives are offered. By being empowered to choose, students may develop a more positive outlook toward the climate of a class and may consequently take greater responsibility for their own learning. The second benefit is equally subtle. By offering choices, the teacher compels students to make those choices. This urges their active engagement with the content as they weigh, consider, and ultimately select. The math teacher who tells students to select any ten of thirty problems virtually assures that they will *read* all thirty!

Look for Interdisciplinary Connections

When students can see how content in one area relates to the concepts and ideas of other areas, their understanding is broadened and, equally important, they are more likely to perceive its significance. Indicating connections across content areas is therefore an additional way of demonstrating the purpose for learning it. These connections can be very motivational.

In middle schools, *thematic planning* by teams of teachers aims at showing students how content actually transcends the boundaries of traditional subject areas (Cooter & Griffith, 1989). The team might, for example, coordinate the start of a unit on percentages in math with the calculation of election results in social studies and calories in health. A short story studied in language arts might have references germane to a science or history unit, so that these teachers can refer to the story in their own lessons while the language arts teacher references the links with history and science as the story is discussed. Such connections allow an additional (and extremely effective) means of reinforcing content: reciprocation.

What about circumstances in which team planning is not the norm? Even if you plan and teach in relative isolation, interdisciplinary links are still possible. For example, you can examine what is required in language arts and look for connections with your own units. You can suggest titles of fiction that are especially relevant to the topics in your course. You can use literature as a change of pace whenever you find a good link. Finally, you can form your own "team" by identifying even one colleague in another area with whom you can compare curricula in a quest for cross-references.

That which any one has been long learning unwillingly, he unlearns with proportionable eagerness and haste.

WILLIAM HAZLITT

Organize Idea Circles

Literature discussion groups bring students together to discuss *fiction* they have all read. Guthrie and McCann (1996) discovered that using *nonfiction* as the basis of these discussions can be highly motivating as well. Best of all, students need not have read the same selection. Rather, the common element is the topic. Guthrie and McCann define an idea circle as a "peer-led, small-group discussion of concepts fueled by multiple text sources" (p. 88). In an idea circle, everyone has something unique to contribute to the discussion by virtue of having read different sources.

You can differentiate these assignments deftly, ensuring that abler readers undertake more challenging materials. You may need to take precautions, however, to guard against one or two students taking over the discussion and eclipsing others. Spelling out some simple ground rules in advance can foster balanced discussions. For example, the discussion might begin with each student sharing one fact that he or she discovered. A moderator might also be appointed, with the duty to solicit input from all participants.

Plan Activities That Challenge Your Students

Samuel Miller's work (2003) with upper-elementary classrooms documents this striking fact: Even poor readers are motivated by activities that are creative and challenging, and they generally rise to the occasion when the opportunity presents itself. What clearly does not motivate them, on the other hand, is a steady diet of worksheet gruel. They can learn the routines and complete the assigned material, but their motivation to read is anything but improved.

A high-challenge language arts activity has these characteristics:

- It lasts more than a single day.
- It involves writing one or more paragraphs aimed at higher-order thinking (e.g., character analysis, science research, letters to real people, etc.).
- Students work collaboratively to share ideas and give one another feedback.
- Teachers monitor closely and provide support where needed.

Tasks having these features bolster children's ability to regulate their own efforts and to work collaboratively in social settings.

Just as important is what a high-challenge activity lacks. It will not include tasks found in many worksheets, such as matching, underlining, and bubbling in answers. Nor will it target low-level word recognition and grammatical skills.

Miller found that all of the students he studied (high and low achievers alike) preferred the high-challenge activities, although low achievers lacked self-confidence *unless* such assignments were frequent. He also found that none of the teachers with whom he worked experienced a decline in achievement test scores after committing to this approach. In fact, the scores of several teachers rose significantly.

Assign Projects

Research demonstrates that students in the middle grades are motivated by interdisciplinary projects that incorporate reading and writing. These projects promote group inquiry and social interaction rather than passive listening. They center around concrete, relevant questions rather than seemingly insignificant abstractions. Elizabeth Moje and her colleagues (2000) list four features of effective projects:

1. They are centered around "driving questions that encompass worthwhile or meaningful content anchored in real-world problems."
2. They include "investigations and artifact creation [for example, posters, pictures, documents, or models] that allow students to learn concepts, apply information, and represent knowledge."
3. They provide the opportunity for "collaboration among students, teachers, and others in the community."
4. They often make "use of technological tools."

A science teacher, for instance, might devise a project concerning pollution levels in a nearby river. Students could begin the project by reading a variety of sources, including their textbook, newspaper articles, magazines, Internet documents, and so forth. Not all of the students would necessarily read all of the sources. They might then work in groups to discuss and pool their background information and to pose questions about the river. A biologist might be persuaded to speak to the class and even to attend a field trip to the river, during which samples could be drawn. Results of these samples could be discussed by the collaborative groups, each of which might then choose a culminating activity. Such activities might include writing a letter to the editor of the local paper, drafting a letter to one or more legislators, preparing and teaching a lesson aimed at elementary-age children, or creating awareness posters to be placed in local grocery stores (or at the sites of the school's other business partners).

Teach for Engagement

John Guthrie and his colleagues (2003) have argued that the transition from elementary to middle school leaves many struggling readers alienated, unenthused, uncertain of themselves, and disengaged. They are faced with far more formidable textbooks, larger and more impersonal classes, a growing lack of self-confidence in their abilities, social marginalization, and less reading-related support from their teachers.

As bleak a picture as this may be, there is hope. Guthrie and Davis (2003) used their extensive work at the National Reading Research Center to distill several guidelines for planning instructional activities that will motivate struggling readers in the middle grades. Use them as a checklist in evaluating your own typical lessons and in planning new ones.

1. *Activities should stress knowledge goals rather than performance (grades, etc.).* Such activities include self-questioning, using background knowledge, monitoring their own comprehension, searching for information, and synthesizing multiple sources.

2. *Activities should include real-world interactions.* This means going beyond the text to provide students with experiences that bring them into contact with the physical world—things they can see, hear, or touch, even smell and taste. Such experiences might include manipulatives, video clips, models, experiments, simulations (computer and otherwise), reenactments, plants, animals, and artifacts.

3. *Activities should include many interesting texts.* Teachers must become collectors of appealing sources and make them available for students to read. These might include trade books, magazines, laminated newspaper articles, Internet printouts, and other documents. It is important to become familiar with sources available in a given subject area. *Current Science*, for example, is a natural for supplementing textbook treatments of many science-related topics.

4. *Activities should involve choices and student control.* Involving students in the choice of which questions to investigate, for instance, which sources to read, or which projects to undertake will give them a motivating sense of empowerment. Ironically, student choice and control tend to diminish in the upper grades. Effective teachers must look for ways to reinstate these qualities.

5. *Activities should incorporate instruction in effective comprehension strategies.* Teachers should carefully model the strategies that will assist students as they tackle assignments. These strategies are not taught in isolation but are directly connected with the assignment. For example, the teacher might show students how to complete a reading guide, how to make an inference between two statements, or how to construct a timeline. The teacher would then return to these same strategies in later assignments, expecting students to shoulder more of the responsibility for applying them.

6. *Activities should include collaboration.* Working with other students on projects; engaging in reciprocal teaching; taking part in debates, simulations, or dramatizations; contributing to discussions; and participating in peer tutoring are among the many collaborative strategies that tend to break through social barriers and lead to greater motivation.

Guthrie and Davis point out that many lessons possess several of these features but not all. Ask yourself how you can design lessons that incorporate all six.

More Ideas

Mathison (1989) has listed some of the most frequently recommended ideas for stimulating interest in content area reading. We have discussed nearly all of these at various points in this text, but now is an ideal time to review them. Mathison's list includes the following techniques that are discussed in our text:

1. Using analogies (Chapter 5)
2. Relating personal anecdotes (Chapter 5)
3. Disrupting students' expectancies (Chapter 13)
4. Challenging students to resolve a paradox (Chapter 10)
5. Introducing novel and conflicting information or situations (Chapter 10)

SUMMARY

Several factors influence whether students will be motivated to undertake literacy tasks. One is their expectancies about the nature of these tasks. An important aspect of these expectancies is the degree of certainty in students' minds. Relative uncertainty can lead to heightened arousal and is a useful motivator. A second aspect involves the time at which students expect outcomes to occur. Immediate expectancies usually have greater motivational power than intermediate or remote expectancies. Desirability is a third characteristic of expectancies and is termed *valence*. One method of motivating students to undertake tasks with low valence is to use incentives, or rewards. Symbolic, material, and psychological incentives couple, in the student's mind, a desirable expectancy with one that is less desirable (performing the task itself). Teachers should vary and individualize incentives. They should avoid using them when they are not needed, and when they do use them they should try to apply them as soon as possible after the desired behavior.

Content teachers should attempt to identify areas within their subject that may hold strong appeal (valence) for students. A content interest inventory is an assessment tool that asks students to rate subtopics that might be appealing. A teacher can construct such an inventory by first listing potentially interesting subtopics and then identifying available reading materials associated with each. Some blanks for "write-in" suggestions make a nice addition. Teachers who word-process the inventory find revising it convenient. Students can respond in numerous ways, but one of the best is by indicating letter "grades." Reading the inventory aloud while students mark their responses helps ensure that reading problems do not interfere. Topics awarded a grade of A are useful to know in recommending materials for further reading.

Various teaching techniques can improve student attitudes toward content literacy. Creating a classroom environment rich in print is a good start. Providing time on occasion to read further within the subject area without accountability is helpful, and sustained silent reading (SSR) is a proven structure for developing such a program. Reading aloud to students is also remarkably effective and can be done quite flexibly. Varying instructional methods is another means of arousing interest and requires no departure from direct instruction time. Motivational teachers also look for links between content and its impact on the lives of students. Making these links clear to students can be quite effective. Giving students choices, especially where reinforcement activities are concerned, is another subtle means of motivation and can usually be done without compromising instructional objectives. Looking for interdisciplinary connections is one more way of stressing the importance of content. Emphasizing these connections invites collaborative planning and can lead to mutual reinforcement of colleagues' instructional objectives.

Getting Involved

1. Construct a content interest inventory. You will need to examine your teaching specialty closely, noting aspects that are likely to have special appeal for students. Remember to look

for the unusual aspects of your area. That is, do not merely break down the general subject area into its typical components. Try to identify intriguing subtopics that students will not be likely to know about themselves.

2. Compile a list of fiction related to your area. Your school library's media specialist can help. Aim for appropriate difficulty levels and lengths. Then assemble the books, whether you check them out, order them with school funds, or acquire your own copies. Finally, read them yourself, however quickly, so that you can make informal recommendations for SSR and so that you can reference appropriate titles as you teach.

3. Identify periodicals that relate to your area. Student-oriented magazines are available in most subjects, and it is worthwhile to learn about those related to your own area. Find out which of these are available in the school library, and investigate the possibility of moving all but the most recent issues into your room. These periodicals will make an excellent resource for content area SSR. Olson, Gee, and Forester (1989) offer many other practical suggestions for incorporating content-specific magazines into classroom instruction.

References

Adams, M.J. (1990). *Beginning to read: Thinking and learning about print.* Cambridge, MA: MIT Press.

Ainslie, D. (2001). Word detectives. *The Reading Teacher, 54,* 360–362.

Albright, L., & Ariail, M. (2005). Tapping the potential of teacher read-alouds in middle schools. *Journal of Adolescent and Adult Literacy, 48,* 582–591.

Allen, J. (2002). "I am Thorgood, King of the Orgies": The reading challenge of content vocabulary. *Voices from the Middle, 9,* 22–27.

Alpert, B.R. (1987). Active, silent and controlled discussion: Explaining variations in classroom conversations. *Teaching and Teacher Education, 3,* 29–40.

Alvermann, D.E., & Boothby, P.R. (1983). A preliminary investigation of the differences in children's retention of "inconsiderate" text. *Reading Psychology, 4,* 237–246.

Alvermann, D.E., Dillon, D.R., & O'Brien, D.G. (1987). *Using discussion to promote reading comprehension.* Newark, DE: International Reading Association.

Alvermann, D.E., & Phelps, S.F. (2004). *Content reading and literacy: Succeeding in today's diverse classrooms* (4th ed.). Boston: Allyn & Bacon.

Alvermann, D. E., & Swafford, J. (1989). Do content area strategies have a research base? *Journal of Reading, 32,* 388–394.

Alvermann, D.E., Weaver, D., Hinchman, K.A., Moore, D.W., Phelps, S.F., Thrash, E.C., & Zalewski, P. (1995). *Middle- and high-school students' perceptions of how they experience text-based discussions: A multicase study* (Reading Research Rep. No. 36). Athens, GA, and College Park, MD: National Reading Research Center.

Ambe, E.B. (2007). Inviting reluctant adolescent readers into the literacy club: Some comprehension strategies to tutor individuals or small groups of reluctant readers. *Journal of Adolescent and Adult Literacy, 50,* 632–639.

Anders, P.L., & Bos, C.S. (1986). Semantic feature analysis: An interactive strategy for vocabulary development and text comprehension. *Journal of Reading, 29,* 610–616.

Anderson, T.H., & Armbruster, B.B. (1991). The value of taking notes during lectures. In R.F. Flippo & D.C. Caverly (Eds.), *Teaching reading and study strategies at the college level* (pp. 166–194). Newark, DE: International Reading Association.

Armbruster, B.B. (1984). The problem of inconsiderate text. In G. Duffy, L. Roehler, & J. Mason (Eds.). *Comprehension instruction: Perspectives and suggestions* (p. 203). White Plains, NY: Longman.

Armstrong, D.P., Patberg, J.P., & Dewitz, P. (1988). Reading guides: Helping students understand. *Journal of Reading, 31,* 532–541.

Armstrong, D.P., Patberg, J.P., & Dewitz, P. (1989). Using reading guides to improve comprehension in literature classes. *English Quarterly, 21,* 233–246.

Aronson, E., Stephan, C., Sikes, J., Blaney, N., & Snapp, M. (1978). *The Jigsaw classroom.* Beverly Hills: Sage.

Ash, G.E. (1998). Literacy is a human endeavor: Literacy definition and delineations from the JLR Editorial Board. In T. Shanahan & F.V. Rodriguez-Brown (Eds.), *Forty-seventh yearbook of the National Reading Conference* (pp. 451–460). Chicago: National Reading Conference.

Au, K.H. (1993). *Literacy instruction in multicultural settings.* Orlando, FL: Harcourt Brace & Company.

Au, K.H., & Jordan, K. (1981). Teaching reading to Hawaiian children: Finding a culturally appropriate solution. In H. Trueba, G.P. Guthrie, and K. Au (Eds.), *Culture in the bilingual classroom: Studies in classroom ethnography* (pp. 139–162). Rowley, MA: Newberry House.

Aulls, M.W. (2003). The influence of reading and writing curriculum on transfer learning across subjects and grades. *Reading Psychology, 24,* 177–215.

Ausubel, D. (1960). The use of advance organizers in the learning and retention of meaningful verbal material. *Journal of Educational Psychology, 51,* 267–272.

Avery, P.G., Baker, J., & Gross, S. (1996). "Mapping" learning at the secondary level. *Social Studies, 87,* 217–223.

Avery, P.G., et al. (1997). "Mapping" learning at the secondary level. *Clearing House, 70,* 279–285.

Barrett, T.C. (1972). Taxonomy of reading comprehension. In *Reading 360 Monograph.* Lexington, MA: Ginn.

Barron, R.F. (1969). The use of vocabulary as an advance organizer. In H.L. Herber & P.L. Sanders (Eds.), *Research on reading in the content areas: First-year report.* Syracuse, NY: Syracuse University, Reading and Language Arts Center.

Barton, J. (1995). Conducting effective classroom discussions. *Journal of Reading, 38,* 346–350.

Basche, P., Trabasso, T., Risden, K., Yuhtsuen, T., & van den Broek, P. (2001). Inferential questioning: Effects on comprehension of narrative texts on as a function of grade and timing. *Journal of Educational Psychology, 93,* 521–529.

Baskin, R.S. (1994). *Student feedback on dialogue journals.* (ERIC Document Reproduction Service No. ED 375 627)

Baumann, J.F. (1984). Implications for reading instruction from the research on teacher and school effectiveness. *Journal of Reading, 28,* 109–115.

Baumann, N.L. (1995). Reading millionaires—It works! *The Reading Teacher, 48,* 730.

Baxendell, B.W. (2003). Consistent, coherent, creative: The 3 C's of graphic organizers. *Teaching Exceptional Children, 35,* 46–53.

Bean, R.M., Grumet, J.V., & Bulazo, J. (1999). Learning from each other: Collaboration between classroom teachers and reading specialists interns. *Reading Research and Instruction, 38,* 273–287.

Bean, T. W. (2000). Reading in the content areas: Social constructivist dimensions. In M. L. Kamil, P. B. Mosenthal, P. D. Pearson, & R. Barr (Eds.), *Handbook of reading research* (Vol. 3, pp. 629–644). Mahwah, NJ: Lawrence Erlbaum.

Bean, T.W., & Readence, J.E. (1994, December). *A comparative study of content area literacy students' attitudes toward reading through autobiography case study analysis.* Paper presented at the meeting of the National Reading Conference, San Diego.

Bean, T.W., & Steenwyk, F.L. (1984). The effect of three forms of summarization instruction on sixth graders' summary writing and comprehension. *Journal of Reading Behavior, 16,* 297–306.

Beaudin, B.P. (1993). *Kodak skills enhancement program: U.S. Department of Education national workplace literacy project final report.* Fort Collins: Colorado State University.

Beck, I.L., & McKeown, M.G. (2001). Text talk: Capturing the benefits of read-aloud experiences for young children. *The Reading Teacher, 55,* 10–19.

Beck, I.L., McKeown, M.G., & Kucan, L. (2002). *Bringing words to life: Robust vocabulary instruction.* New York: Guilford.

Benito, Y.M., Foley, C., Lewis, C.D., & Prescott, P. (1993). The effect of instruction in question-answer relationships and metacognition on social studies comprehension. *Journal of Research in Reading, 16,* 20–29.

Berman, S. (1987, Summer). Beyond critical thinking: Teaching for synthesis. *Educators for Social Responsibility: Forum 6,* 1–2.

Bernhardt, E.B. (2006). Real and imagined roles for technology in acquiring second-language literacy. In M.C. McKenna, L.D. Labbo, R. Kieffer, & D. Reinking (Eds.), *International handbook of literacy and technology* (Vol. 2). Hillsdale, NJ: Lawrence Erlbaum.

Betts, E.A. (1946). *Foundations of reading instruction.* New York: American Book Company.

Binkley, M.R. (1988). New ways of assessing text difficulty. In B.L. Zakaluk & S.J. Samuels (Eds.), *Readability: Its past, present, and future* (pp. 98–120). Newark, DE: International Reading Association.

Blachowicz, C.L.Z., & Fisher, P. (2004). Building vocabulary in remedial settings: Focus on word relatedness. *Perspectives, 30*(1), 24–31.

Blanchard, J.S. (1996). Issues in technology and literacy education. In R.D. Robinson, M.C. McKenna, & J.M. Wedman (Eds.), *Issues and trends in literacy education* (pp. 316–331). Boston: Allyn and Bacon.

Boggs, S.T. (1972). The meaning of questions and narratives to Hawaiian children. In C.B. Cazden, V.P. John, & D. Hymes (Eds.), *Functions of language in the classroom* (pp. 299–327). Prospect Heights, IL: Waveland.

Bonk, R.M. (1998). *The effects of a reading specialist in a K–4 school.* (ERIC Document Reproduction Service No. ED 417 384)

Bormuth, J.R. (1967). Comparable cloze and multiple-choice comprehension test scores. *Journal of Reading, 10,* 291–299.

Bos, C.S., & Anders, P.L. (1990). Effects of interactive vocabulary instruction on the vocabulary learning and reading comprehension of junior-high learning disabled students. *Learning Disability Quarterly, 13,* 31–42.

Britton, J.B., Burgess, T., Martin, N., McLeod, A., & Rosen, H. (1975). *The development of writing abilities.* London: Macmillan.

Bromley, K. (2007). Nine things every teacher should know about words and vocabulary instruction. *Journal of Adolescent and Adult Literacy, 50,* 528–537.

Brophy, J. (1986). Principles for conducting first grade reading group instruction. In J.V. Hoffman (Ed.), *Effective teaching of reading: Research and practice* (pp. 53–84). Newark, DE: International Reading Association.

Brown, K.J., et al. (1996). Exploring the potential of analogy instruction to support students' spelling development. *Elementary School Journal, 97,* 81–99.

Brozo, W.G., & Simpson, M.L. (1999). *Readers, teachers, learners.* Upper Saddle River, NJ: Merrill.

Bruner, J. (1960). *The process of education.* Cambridge, MA: Harvard University Press.

Brunn, M. (2002). The four-square strategy. *The Reading Teacher, 55,* 522–525.

Cairney, T.H. (2000). The construction of literacy and literacy learners. *Language Arts, 77,* 496–503.

Calfee, R.C., Dunlap, K.L., & Wat, A.Y. (1994). Authentic discussion of texts in middle grade schooling: An analytic-narrative approach. *Journal of Reading, 37,* 546–556.

Campbell, J.R., Kapinus, B.A., & Beatty, A.S. (1995). *Interviewing children about their literacy experiences: Data from NAEP's integrated reading performance record (IRPR) at grade 4.* Princeton, NJ: Educational Testing Service. (ERIC Document Reproduction Service No. ED 378 549)

Carlsen, W.S. (1991). Questioning in classrooms: A sociolinguistic perspective. *Review of Educational Research, 61,* 157–178.

Carr, E., & Ogle, D. (1987). K-W-L Plus: A strategy for comprehension and summarization. *Journal of Reading, 30,* 626–631.

Caselton, G. (2002). Workplace literacy as a contested site of educational activity. *Journal of Adolescent & Adult Literacy, 45,* 556–566.

Caverly, D.C., & Orlando, V.P. (1991). Textbook study strategies. In R.F. Flippo & D.C. Caverly (Eds.), *Teaching reading and study strategies at the college level* (pp. 86–165). Newark, DE: International Reading Association.

Cazden, C.B. (1988). *Classroom discourse: The language of teaching and learning.* Portsmouth, NH: Heinemann.

Chall, J. (1983/1996). *Stages of reading development.* New York: McGraw-Hill.

Ciardiello, A.V. (1998). Did you ask a good question today? Alternative cognitive and metacognitive strategies. *Journal of Adolescent and Adult Literacy, 42,* 210–219.

Clariana, R.B. (1991). A computer administered cloze placement test and a standardized reading test. *Journal of Computers in Mathematics and Science Teaching, 10,* 107–113.

Clary, L.M. (1991). Getting adolescents to read. *Journal of Reading, 34,* 340–345.

Cochran-Smith, M. (1991). Word processing and writing in elementary classrooms: A critical review of related literature. *Review of Educational Research, 61,* 107–155.

Coffman, G.A. (1994). The influence of question and story variations on sixth graders' summarization behaviors. *Reading Research and Instruction, 34,* 19–38.

Cohen, J. (2007). A case study of a high school English-language learner and his reading. *Journal of Adolescent and Adult Literacy, 51,* 164–175.

Come, B.G., McKenna, M.C., & Robinson, R.D. (1996). Coursework requirements for middle and high school content area teachers: An American survey. *Journal of Adolescent and Adult Literacy, 40,* 194–198.

Commeyras, M., & Sumner, G. (1995). *Student-posed questions for literature-based discussion.* Instructional Resource No. 6. Athens, GA, and College Park, MD: National Reading Research Center.

Connolly, P. (1989). Writing and the ecology of learning. In P. Connolly & T. Vilardi (Eds.), *Writing to learn mathematics and science* (pp. 1–14). New York: Teachers College Press.

Conway, B.J., Browning, L.J., & Purdum-Cassidy, B. (2007). Teacher candidates' changing perceptions of urban schools: Results of a 4-year study. *Action in Teacher Education, 29,* 29–31.

Cooter, R.B., Jr., & Griffith, R. (1989). Thematic units for middle school: An honorable seduction. *Journal of Reading, 32,* 676–681.

Craig, J.C. (2001). The missing link between school and work: Knowing the demands of the workplace. *English Journal, 91,* 46–50.

Crapse, L. (1995). Helping students construct meaning through their own questions. *Journal of Reading, 38,* 389–390.

Cullum, L. (1998). *Encouraging the reluctant reader: Using a think-aloud protocol to discover strategies for reading success.* (ERIC Document Reproduction Service No. ED 420 837)

Cunningham, D., & Shablak, S.L. (1975). Selective reading guide-o-rama: The content teacher's best friend. *Journal of Reading, 18,* 380–382.

Cunningham, J.W. (1982). Generating interactions between schemata and text. In J.A. Niles & L.A. Harris (Eds.), *New inquiries in reading research and instruction: Thirty-first yearbook of the National Reading Conference* (pp. 42–47). Washington, DC: National Reading Conference.

Dahlberg, L.A. (1990). Teaching for the information age. *Journal of Reading, 34,* 12–18.

Dalle, T., & Inglis, M. (1990). *ITA "teacher talk": Discourse markers as guideposts to learning.* (ERIC Document Reproduction Service No. ED 353 827)

Damico, J., & Baildon, M. (2007). Examining ways readers engage with websites during think-aloud sessions. *Journal of Adolescent and Adult Literacy, 51,* 254–263.

Darch, C.B., Carnine, D.W., & Kameenui, E.J. (1986). The role of graphic organizers and social structure in content area instruction. *Journal of Reading Behavior, 18,* 275–295.

Darvin, J. (2001). Beyond filing out forms: A more powerful version of workplace literacy. *English Journal, 91,* 35–40.

deBono, E. (1999). *Six thinking hats.* Boston: Little, Brown.

Delpit, L. (1988). The silenced dialogue. *Harvard Educational Review, 58,* 280–298.

Delpit, L. (1995). *Other people's children: Cultural conflict in the classroom.* New York: The New Press.

Deshler, D.D., & Graham, S. (1980). Tape recording educational materials for secondary handicapped students. *Teaching Exceptional Children, 12,* 52–54.

DiCecco, V.M., & Gleason, M.M. (2002). Using graphic organizers to attain relational knowledge from expository text. *Journal of Learning Disabilities, 35,* 306–320.

Dillner, M. (1993–1994). Using hypermedia to enhance content area instruction. *Journal of Reading, 37,* 260–270.

Dillon, J.T. (1984). Research on questioning and discussion. *Educational Leadership, 42,* 50–56.

Dillon, J.T. (1985). Using questions to foil discussion. *Teaching and Teacher Education, 1,* 109–121.

Dinnel, D., & Glover, J.H. (1985). Advance organizers: Encoding manipulations. *Journal of Educational Psychology, 77,* 514–521.

Dole, J.A., & Niederhauser, D.S. (1990). Students' level of commitment to their naive conceptions and their conceptual change learning from texts. In J. Zutell & S. McCormick (Eds.), *Literacy theory and research: Analyses from multiple paradigms: Thirty-ninth year-*

book of the National Reading Conference (pp. 303–310). Chicago: National Reading Conference.

Dreher, M.J. (1999). Motivating children to read more nonfiction. *The Reading Teacher, 52,* 414–417.

Duffelmeyer, F. A. (1994). Effective anticipation guide statements for learning from expository prose. *Journal of Reading, 37,* 452–457.

Duffy, G.G., Roehler, L.R., Sivan, E., Rackliffe, G., Book, C., Meloth, M.S., Vavrus, L.G., Wesselman, R., Putnam, J., & Bassiri, D. (1987). Effects of explaining the reasoning associated with using reading strategies. *Reading Research Quarterly, 22,* 347–368.

Duke, N.K. (2003). Reading to learn from the very beginning: Information books in early childhood. *Young Children, 38,* 14–20.

Dunston, P.J. (1992). A critique of graphic organizer research. *Reading Research and Instruction, 31,* 57–65.

Durkin, D. (1978–1979). What classroom observations reveal about reading comprehension instruction. *Reading Research Quarterly, 14,* 481–533.

Earle, R.A. (1969). Developing and using study guides. In H.L. Herber & P.L. Sanders (Eds.), *Research in reading in the content areas: First year report* (pp. 71–92). Syracuse, NY: Syracuse University.

Edwards, P.R. (1991–1992). Using dialectical journals to teach thinking skills. *Journal of Reading, 35,* 312–316.

Ehri, L.C., & Wilce, L.S. (1985). Movement into reading: Is the first stage of printed word learning visual or phonetic? *Reading Research Quarterly, 20,* 163–179.

Eldredge, J.L., et al. (1996). Comparing the effectiveness of two oral reading practices: Round-robin reading and the shared book experience. *Journal of Literacy Research, 28,* 201–225.

Ezell, H.K. (1992). Use of peer-assisted procedures to teach QAR reading comprehension strategies to third-grade children. *Education and Treatment of Children, 15,* 205–227.

Fader, D.N., & Shaevitz, M.H. (1966). *Hooked on books.* New York: Berkley Publishing.

Farris, P.J., Fuhler, C.J., & Walther, M.P. (2004). *Teaching reading: A balanced approach for today's classroom.* Boston: McGraw-Hill.

Ferguson, R.F. (2007). Become more sophisticated about diversity. *Journal of Staff Development, 28,* 33–34.

Fernandez, M. (1998). *Reading/writing connection.* (ERIC Document Reproduction Service No. ED 418 391)

Festinger, L. (1957). *A theory of cognitive dissonance.* New York: Harper & Row.

Fiderer, A. (1998). *35 rubrics and checklists to assess reading and writing: Time-saving reproduction forms for meaningful literacy assessment.* (ERIC Document Reproduction Service No. ED 423 522)

Fisher, C.H. (1990). *Speech of students during the performance of a task.* (ERIC Document Reproduction Service No. ED 353 487)

Fisher, D., Flood, J., Lapp, D., & Frey, N. (2004). Interactive read-alouds: Is there a common set of implementation practices? *The Reading Teacher, 58,* 8–17.

Fisher, P., & Blachowicz, C. (2007). Teaching how to think about words. *Voices From the Middle, 15,* 6–12.

Flanigan, K., & Greenwood, S.C. (2007). Effective content vocabulary instruction in the middle: Matching students, purposes, words, and strategies. *Journal of Adolescent and Adult Literacy, 51,* 226–238.

Flood, J., Lapp, D., & Wood, K. (1998). Viewing: The neglected communication process or "When what you see isn't what you get." *The Reading Teacher, 52,* 300–304.

Fly, P.K. (1994, April). *Constructing meaning in a classroom context.* Paper presented at the meeting of the American Educational Research Association, New Orleans.

Fordham, N.W. (2006). Crafting questions that address comprehension strategies in content reading. *Journal of Adolescent and Adult Literacy, 49,* 390–396.

Frager, A.M. (1984). How good are content teachers' judgments of the reading abilities of secondary school students? *Journal of Reading, 27,* 402–406.

Freedman, L., & Carver, C. (2007). Preservice teacher understandings of adolescent literacy development: Naïve wonder to dawning realization to intellectual rigor. *Journal of Adolescent and Adult Literacy, 50,* 654–665.

Fry, E. (1981). Graphical literacy. *Journal of Reading, 24,* 383–390.

Fry, E. (1989). Reading formulas: Maligned but valid. *Journal of Reading, 32,* 292–297.

Fry, E. (1998). *The legal aspects of readability.* (ERIC Reproduction Service No. ED 416 466)

Fry, E. (2002). Readability versus leveling. *The Reading Teacher, 56,* 286–291.

Fuhler, C.J. (2003). Joining theory and best practice to drive classroom instruction. *Middle School Journal, 34,* 23–30.

Furr, D. (2003). Struggling readers get hooked on writing. *The Reading Teacher, 56,* 518–525.

Gall, M.D., Gall, J.P., Jacobsen, D.R., & Bullock, T.L. (1990). *Tools for learning: A guide to teaching study skills.* Alexandria, VA: ASCD.

Gambrell, L. (1996). Creating classroom cultures that foster reading motivation. *The Reading Teacher, 50,* 14–25.

Gardner, M.K., & Smith, M.M. (1987). Does perspective taking ability contribute to reading comprehension? *Journal of Reading, 30,* 333–336.

Gaskins, I.W., Satlow, E., Hyson, D., Ostertag, J., & Six, L. (1994). Classroom talk about text: Learning in science class. *Journal of Reading, 37,* 558–565.

Gay, G. (2000). *Culturally responsive teaching: Theory, research, and practice.* New York: Teachers College Press.

Gillespie, C. (1990–1991). Questions about student-generated questions. *Journal of Reading, 34,* 250–257.

Giorgis, C. (1999). The power of reading picture books aloud to secondary students. *Clearing House, 73,* 51–53.

Glynn, S. (1989). The teaching with analogies model. In K.D. Muth (Ed.), *Children's comprehension of text: Research into practice* (pp. 185–204). Newark, DE: IRA.

Glynn, S. (1995). Conceptual bridges: Using analogies to explain scientific concepts. *The Science Teacher, 62*(9), 25–27.

Glynn, S. (1996). Teaching with analogies: Building on the science textbook. *The Reading Teacher, 49,* 490–492.

Glynn, S.M., Aultman, L.P., & Owens, A.M. (2005). Motivation to learn in general education programs. *Journal of General Education, 54,* 150–170.

Good, T., & Brophy, J. (2002). *Looking in classrooms* (9th ed.). New York: HarperCollins.

Governor's Cabinet Council on Human Investment. (1988). *Countdown 2000: Michigan's action plan for a competitive workplace.* Lansing, MI: Author.

Graham, L. (2003). Writing journals: An investigation. *Reading, Literacy and Language, 37,* 39–42.

Gray, W.S. (1969). *The teaching of reading and writing: An international survey.* Paris: United Nations Educational, Scientific, and Cultural Organization.

Gunning, T. G. (2007). *Creating literacy instruction for all students.* Boston: Allyn & Bacon.

Guthrie, J.T. (1983). Equilibrium of literacy. *Journal of Reading, 26,* 668–670.

Guthrie, J.T., & Davis, M.H. (2003). Motivating struggling readers in middle school through an engagement model of classroom practice. *Reading and Writing Quarterly, 19,* 59–85.

Guthrie, J.T., and McCann, A.D. (1996). Idea circles: Peer collaborations for conceptual learning. In L.B. Gambrell and J.F. Almasi (Eds.), *Lively discussions! Fostering engaged reading* (pp. 87–105). Newark, DE: International Reading Association.

Guthrie, J.T., & Wigfield, A. (1999). How motivation fits into a science of reading. *Scientific Studies of Reading, 3,* 199–205.

Guzzetti, B.J., Hynd, C.R., Skeels, S.A., & Williams, W.O. (1995). Improving physics texts: Students speak out. *Journal of Reading, 38,* 656–663.

Hacker, D.J., & Tenent, A. (2002). Implementing reciprocal teaching in the classroom: Overcoming obstacles and making modifications. *Journal of Educational Psychology, 94,* 699–718.

Hadaway, N.L., & Young, T.A. (1994). Content literacy and language learning: Instructional decisions. *The Reading Teacher, 47,* 522–527.

Hall, N., & Robinson, A. (1995). *Keeping in touch: Using interactive writing with young children.* Portsmouth, NH: Heinemann.

Hartley, J. (2007). Reading, writing, speaking and listening: Perspectives in applied linguistics. *Applied linguistics, 28,* 316–320.

Hartley, J., & Davies, S.K. (1978). Note-taking: A critical review. *Programmed Learning and Educational Technology, 15,* 207–224.

Harvey, S., & Goudvis, A. (2007). *Strategies that work: Teaching comprehension for understanding and engagement.* Portland, ME: Stenhouse.

Harvey, V.S., & Chickie-Wolfe, L.A. (2007). *Fostering independent learning: Practical strategies to promote student success.* New York: Guilford Press.

Hayakawa, S.I. (1939). *Language in thought and action.* New York: Harcourt Brace Jovanovich.

Hayes, D., & Tierney, R. (1982). Developing readers' knowledge through analogy. *Reading Research Quarterly, 17,* 256–280.

He, M.F. (2003). *A river forever flowing: Cross-cultural lives and identities in the multicultural landscape.* Greenwich, CT: Information Age.

He, M.F., & McKenna, M.C. (2005). Culturally responsive approaches to reading in the multicultural classroom. In R. Hoosain & F. Salili (Eds.), *Language in multicultural education.* Greenwich, CT: Information Age Publishing.

Heath, S.B. (1983). *Ways with words: Language, life, and work in communities and classrooms.* Cambridge, UK: Cambridge University Press.

Heath, S.B. (2000). Linguistics in the study of language in education. *Harvard Educational Review, 70,* 49–59.

Heffernan, N. (2003). Helping students read better: The use of background knowledge. *English Teacher, 6,* 62–65.

Hemming, H., Symons, S., & Langille, L. (2002). Bridging the gap: Workforce literacy for an electronic age. *English Quarterly, 34,* 16–23.

Henk, W.A. (1981). Effects of modified deletion strategies and scoring procedures on cloze test performance. *Journal of Reading Behavior, 13,* 347–357.

Henk, W.A., & Selders, M.L. (1984). A test of synonymic scoring of cloze passages. *The Reading Teacher, 38,* 282–287.

Herber, H.L. (1978). *Teaching reading in content areas* (2nd ed.). Englewood Cliffs, NJ: Prentice-Hall.

Hernandez, A. (2003). Making content instruction accessible for English language learners. In G.G. Garcia (Ed.), *English learners: Reaching the highest level of English literacy* (pp. 125–151). Newark, DE: International Reading Association.

Hill, M. (1991). Writing summaries promotes thinking and learning across the curriculum—but why are they so difficult to write? *Journal of Reading, 34,* 536–539.

Hobbs, R. (2001). Improving reading comprehension by using media literacy activities. *Voices from the Middle, 8,* 44–50.

Hoffman, B. (1962). *The tyranny of testing.* New York: Collier.

Hoke, B.L. (1999). *Comparison of recreational reading book levels using the Fry readability graph and the Flesch-Kincaid grade level.* (ERIC Reproduction Service No. ED 42833)

Holbrook, H.T. (1984). Prereading in the content areas. *Journal of Reading, 27,* 368–370.

Holmes, B.C., & Roser, N.L. (1987). Five ways to assess readers' prior knowledge. *The Reading Teacher, 40,* 646–649.

Holt-Reynolds, D. (1991, December). *Directed reading strategies and how preservice teachers decide they are unnecessary: Exploring the effects of personal histories.* Paper presented at the meeting of the National Reading Conference, Palm Springs, CA.

Holt-Reynolds, D. (1992). Personal history-based beliefs as relevant prior knowledge in course work. *American Educational Research Journal, 29,* 325–349.

Hoover-Dempsey, K.V., Bassler, O.C., & Burrow, R. (1995). Parents' reported involvement in students' homework: Strategies and practices. *Elementary School Journal, 95,* 435–450.

Horton, S.V., & Lovitt, T.C. (1989). Construction and implementation of graphic organizers for academically handicapped and regular secondary students. *Academic Therapy, 24,* 625–640.

Howie, S.H. (1990). Adult literacy in a multiliterate society. *Journal of Reading, 33,* 260–263.

Hunt, L.C., Jr. (1967). Evaluation through teacher-pupil conferences. In T.C. Barrett (Ed.), *The evaluation of children's reading achievement.* Newark, DE: International Reading Association.

Hunter, M. (1993). *Enhancing teaching.* Upper Saddle River, NJ: Prentice Hall.

Igo, L., & Kiewra, K. (2007). How do high-achieving students approach web-based, copy and paste note taking?: Selective pasting and related learning outcomes. *Journal of Advanced Academics, 18,* 512–529.

Irvin, J.L., & Connors, N.A. (1989). Reading instruction in middle level schools: Results of a U.S. survey. *Journal of Reading, 32,* 306–311.

Irvin, J.L., & Rose, E.O. (1995). *Starting early with study skills: A week-by-week guide for elementary students.* Boston: Allyn & Bacon.

Ives, B., & Hoy, C. (2003). Graphic organizers applied to higher-level secondary mathematics. *Learning Disabilities: Research & Practice, 18,* 36–51.

Ivey, G., & Broaddus, K. (2000). Tailoring the fit: Reading instruction and middle school readers. *The Reading Teacher, 54,* 68–78.

Ivey, G., & Fisher, D. (2006). *Creating literacy-rich schools for adolescents.* Alexandria, VA: ASCD.

Jacobsen, D.R. (1989). *The effects of taking class notes using the Cornell method on students' test performance in note-taking quality.* Unpublished doctoral dissertation, University of Oregon, Eugene.

Jaeger, E.L. (1996). The reading specialist as collaborative consultant. *The Reading Teacher, 49,* 622–629.

Janzen, J. (2003). Developing strategic readers. *Reading Psychology, 24,* 25–55.

Johnson, D.W., & Johnson, R.T. (1984). *Cooperation and competition: Theory and Research.* Edina, MN: Interaction Book Company.

Johnson, D.D., & Pearson, P.D. (1984). *Teaching reading vocabulary* (2nd ed.). New York: Holt, Rinehart, & Winston.

Johnson, D., & Steele, V. (1996). So many words, so little time: Helping ESL learners acquire vocabulary-building strategies. *Journal of Adolescent & Adult Learning, 39,* 348–357.

Kaestle, C.F., Campbell, A., Finn, J.D., Johnson, S.T., & Mikulecky, L.J. (2001). *Adult literacy and education in America: Four studies based on the National Adult Literacy Survey.* Washington, DC: National Center For Educational Statistics.

Kelly, P.R. (1995). Considering alternative instructional practices that make more sense. *Reading Horizons, 36,* 99–115.

Kinney, M.A., & Harry, A.L. (1991). An informal inventory for adolescents that assesses the reader, the text, and the task. *Journal of Reading, 34,* 643–647.

Kintsch, W., & van Dijk, T.A. (1978). Toward a model of text comprehension and production. *Psychological Review, 85,* 363–394.

Kirkman, G., & Shaw, E.L. (1997). *Effects of an oral advance organizer on immediate and delayed retention.* (ERIC Document Reproduction Service No. ED 425 263)

Kirsch, I.S., & Mosenthal, P.B. (1990). Understanding documents: Nested lists. *Journal of Reading, 33,* 294–297.

Klare, G.R. (1988). The formative years. In B.L. Zakaluk & S.J. Samuels (Eds.), *Readability: Its past, present, and future* (pp. 14–34). Newark, DE: International Reading Association.

Klingner, J.K., & Vaughn, S. (1999). Promoting reading comprehension, content learning, and English acquisition through collaborative strategic reading (CSR). *The Reading Teacher, 52,* 738–747.

Kneale, P.E. (1998). Note taking for geography students. *Journal of Geography in Higher Education, 22,* 427–433.

Kohn, A. (1999). *Punished by rewards: The trouble with gold stars, incentive plans, A's, praise, and other bribes.* Boston: Houghton Mifflin.

Kolic-Vehovec, S., & Bajsanski, I. (2007). Comprehension monitoring and reading comprehension in bilingual students. *Journal of Research in Reading, 30,* 198–211.

Kucan, L., & Beck, I.L. (1997). Thinking aloud and reading comprehension: Inquiry, instruction, and social interaction. *Review of Educational Research, 67,* 271–299.

Kucer, S.B., & Tuten, J. (2003). Revisiting and rethinking the reading process. *Language Arts, 80,* 284–290.

Kulik, J.A., & Kulik, C.C. (1988). Timing of feedback and verbal learning. *Review of Educational Research, 58,* 79–97.

Kuse, L.S., & Kuse, H.R. (1986). Using analogies to study social studies texts. *Social Education, 50,* 24–25.

Labov, W. (1971). Stages in the acquisition of Standard English. In H.B. Allen & G.N. Underwood (Eds.), *Readings in American dialectology* (pp. 473–499). New York: Appleton-Century-Crofts.

Ladson-Billings, G. (1992). Liberatory consequences of literacy: A case of culturally relevant instruction for African American students. *Journal of Negro Education, 61*(3), 378–391.

Ladson-Billings, G. (1994). *The dream keepers: Successful teachers of African American children.* San Francisco: Jossey-Bass.

Ladson-Billings, G. (1995). Challenging customs, canons, and content: Developing relevant curriculum for diversity. In C.A. Grant Boston (Ed.), *Educating for diversity: An anthology of multicultural voices* (pp. 327–340). Boston: Allyn & Bacon.

Ladson-Billings, G. (2001). *Crossing over to Caanen: The journey of new teachers in diverse classrooms.* New York: Jossey-Bass.

Langer, J.A. (1981). From theory to practice: A prereading plan. *Journal of Reading, 25,* 152–156.

Langer, J.A., Bartolome, L., & Vasqueze, T.M. (1988). *Meaning construction in school reading tasks: A study of Mexican-American students.* ERIC Document Reproduction Service No. ED 295 133.

Lazarus, B.D. (1988). Using guided notes to aid learning disabled students in secondary mainstream settings. *The Pointer, 33,* 32–36.

Lazarus, B.D. (1989). Serving learning disabled students in postsecondary settings. *Journal of Developmental Education, 12*(3), 2–7.

Lazarus, B.D. (1991). Guided notes, review, and achievement of learning disabled adolescents in secondary mainstream settings. *Education and Treatment of Children, 14,* 112–128.

Lazarus, B.D. (1993). Guided notes: Effects with secondary and postsecondary students with mild disabilities. *Education and Treatment of Children, 16,* 272–289.

Lazarus, B.D. (1996). Flexible skeletons: Guided notes for adolescents with mild disabilities. *Teaching Exceptional Children, 28*(3), 36–40.

Lazarus, B.D., & McKenna, M.C. (1991, April). *Guided notes: Review and achievement of mainstreamed LD students.* Paper presented at the meeting of the Council for Exceptional Children, Atlanta.

Leach, J.T., Konick, R.D., & Shapiro, B.L. (1992). *The ideas used by British and North American school children to interpret the phenomenon of decay: A cross-cultural study.* (ERIC Document Reproduction Service No. ED 354 156)

LeNoir, W.D. (1993). Teacher questions and schema activation. *Clearing House, 66,* 349–352.

Lieven, E., Behrens, H., Speares, J., & Tomasello, M. (2003). Early syntactic creativity: A usage-based approach. *Journal of Child Language, 30,* 333–370.

Linderholm, T., & van den Broek, P. (2002). The effects of reading purpose and working memory capacity on the processing of expository text. *Journal of Educational Psychology, 94,* 778–784.

Lipson, M. (1995). The effect of semantic mapping instruction on prose comprehension of below-level college readers. *Reading Research and Instruction, 34,* 367–378.

Lipson, M.Y., & Wixson, K.K. (2003). *Assessment and instruction of reading and writing difficulty* (3rd ed.). Boston: Allyn & Bacon.

Luckner, J., Bowen, S., & Carter, K. (2001). Visual teaching strategies for students who are deaf and hard of hearing. *Teaching Exceptional Children, 33,* 38–44.

Lynch, D., & Smith, B. (1975). Item response changes: Effects on test scores. *Measurement and Evaluation in Guidance, 7*(4), 220–224.

Lynch, D.J., & McKenna, M.C. (1990). Teaching controversial material: New issues for teachers. *Social Education, 54,* 317–319.

Maclachlan, K., & Cloonan, M. (2003). Three dimensional change? The relationship between theory, policy and adults' understanding of literacies. *Research in Post-Compulsory Education, 8,* 123–126.

Manzo, A.V. (1968). *Improving reading comprehension through reciprocal questioning.* Unpublished doctoral dissertation, Syracuse University.

Manzo, A.V. (1969). The ReQuest procedure. *Journal of Reading, 2,* 123–126.

Manzo, A.V., & Casale, U.P. (1985). Listen-Read-Discuss: A content reading heuristic. *Journal of Reading, 28,* 732–734.

Manzo, A.V., & Manzo, U.C. (1995). *Teaching children to be literate: A reflective approach.* Orlando, FL: Harcourt Brace.

Margolis, J. (1990, June 25). Jimmy! This is cricket? Coming to terms with a confusing foreign game. *Chicago Tribune,* Sec. 3, p. 7.

Marshall, N. (1989). The students: Who are they and how do I reach them? In D. Lapp, J. Flood, & N. Farnan (Eds.), *Content area reading and learning: Instructional strategies* (pp. 59–69). Englewood Cliffs, NJ: Prentice-Hall.

Mathison, C. (1989). Activating student interest in content area reading. *Journal of Reading, 33,* 170–176.

McCarthey, S.J., Dressman, M., Smolkin, L., McGill-Franzen, A., & Harris, V.J. (2000). How will diversity affect literacy in the next millennium? *Reading Research Quarterly, 35,* 548–552.

McClain, L. (1983). Behavior during examinations: A comparison of A, C, and F students. *Teaching of Psychology, 10*(2), 69–71.

McCormick, M. (2006). *Text comprehensibility and graphic organizers: Influences on reading to learn in sixth-grade social studies.* Unpublished doctoral dissertation, University of Virginia.

McKenna, M.C. (1976). Synonymic versus verbatim scoring of the cloze procedure. *Journal of Reading, 20,* 141–143.

McKenna, M.C. (1977a). Searching for roots—of words. *Teacher, 95*(2), 93, 96, 99–101.

McKenna, M.C. (1977b). Songs for language study. *Audiovisual Instruction, 22*(4), 42.

McKenna, M.C. (1978). Portmanteau words in reading instruction. *Language Arts, 55,* 315–317.

McKenna, M.C. (1983). *The Stein and Day dictionary of definitive quotations.* New York: Stein & Day.

McKenna, M.C. (1986). Reading interests of remedial secondary school students. *Journal of Reading, 29,* 346–351.

McKenna, M.C. (2002). Hypertext. In B.J. Guzzetti (Ed.), *Literacy in America: An encyclopedia of history, theory, and practice* (pp. 233–237). Santa Barbara, CA: ABC-CLIO.

McKenna, M.C. (2004). Teaching vocabulary to struggling older readers. *Perspectives, 30*(1), 13–16.

McKenna, M.C., Davis, L.W., & Franks, S. (2003). Using reading guides with struggling readers in grades 3 and above. In R.L. McCormack & J.R. Paratore (Eds.), *After early intervention, then what? Teaching struggling readers in grades 3 and beyond* (pp. 208–216). Newark, DE: International Reading Association.

McKenna, M.C., & Layton, K. (1990). Concurrent validity of cloze as a measure of intersentential comprehension. *Journal of Educational Psychology, 82,* 372–377.

McKenna, M.C., & Robinson, R.D. (1980). *An introduction to the cloze procedure: An annotated bibliography* (2nd ed.). Newark, DE: International Reading Association.

McKenna, M.C., & Robinson, R.D. (1990). Content literacy: A definition and implications. *Journal of Reading, 34,* 184–186.

McKenna, M.C., & Stahl, S.A. (2003). *Assessment for reading instruction.* New York: Guilford.

McKenzie, G.R., & Danielson, E. (2003). Improving comprehension through mural lessons. *The Reading Teacher, 56,* 738–742.

McQuillan, J. (1997). The effects of incentives on reading. *Reading Research and Instruction, 36,* 111–125.

McTigue, E.M. (2006). *Graphical support in science text: The contributions of design and text directives.* Unpublished doctoral dissertation, University of Virginia.

Mehan, H. (1979). *Learning lessons.* Cambridge, MA: Harvard University Press.

Menke, D.J., & Davey, B. (1994). Teachers' views of textbooks and text reading instruction: Experience matters. *Journal of Reading, 37,* 464–470.

Menke, D.J., & Pressley, M. (1994). Elaborative interrogation: Using "why" questions to enhance learning from text. *Journal of Reading, 37,* 642–645.

Merkley, D.M., & Jefferies, D. (2001). Guidelines for implementing a graphic organizer. *The Reading Teacher, 54,* 350–357.

Meyers, R. (1998). *Uninterrupted sustained silent reading.* (ERIC Document Reproduction Service No. ED 418 379)

Mikulecky, L., & Kirkley, J.R. (1998). Literacy interpretation for the 21st-century workplace. *Peabody Journal of Education, 73,* 290–316.

Miller, G.R., & Coleman, E.B. (1967). A set of 36 prose passages calibrated for complexity. *Journal of Verbal Learning and Verbal Behavior, 6,* 851–854.

Miller, J.W., & McKenna, M.C. (1989). *Teaching reading in the elementary school.* Scottsdale, AZ: Gorsuch Scarisbrick.

Miller, S.D. (2003). How high- and low-challenge tasks affect motivation and learning: Implications for struggling learners. *Reading and Writing Quarterly, 19,* 39–57.

Millman, J.C., Bishop, C.H., & Ebel, R. (1965). An analysis of test wiseness. *Educational and Psychological Measurement, 25,* 707–727.

Millstone, D.H. (1997). Transforming children into story tellers. *NAMTA Journal, 22,* 82–117.

Moje, E.B. (1993, December). *Life experiences and teacher knowledge: How a content teacher decides to use literacy strategies.* Paper presented at the meeting of the National Reading Conference, Charleston, SC.

Moje, E.B., Young, J.P., Readence, J.E., & Moore, D.W. (2000). Reinventing adolescent literacy for new times: Perennial and millennial issues. *Journal of Adolescent and Adult Literacy, 43,* 400–410.

Moore, D.W., & Moore, S.A. (1986). Possible sentences. In E.K. Dishner, T.W. Bean, J.E. Readence, & D.W. Moore (Eds.), *Reading in the content areas: Improving classroom instruction* (2nd ed., pp. 174–179). Dubuque, IA: Kendall/Hunt.

Moore, D.W., & Readence, J.E. (1980). A meta-analysis of the effect of graphic organizers on learning from text. In M.L. Kamil & A.J. Moe (Eds.), *Perspectives on reading research and instruction: Twenty-ninth yearbook of the National Reading Conference* (pp. 213–218). Washington, DC: National Reading Conference.

Moore, M.T. (2004). Issues and trends in writing instruction. In R.D. Robinson, M.C. McKenna, & J.M. Wedman (Eds.), *Issues and trends in literacy education* (3rd ed.). Boston: Allyn & Bacon.

Morris, D., Bloodgood, J.W., Lomax, R.G., & Perry, J. (2003). Developmental steps in learning to read: A longitudinal study in kindergarten and first grade. *Reading Research Quarterly, 38,* 302–338.

Moyer, P.S., & Bolyard, J.J. (2003). Classify and capture: Using Venn diagrams and tangrams to develop abilities in mathematical reasoning and proof. *Mathematics Teaching in the Middle School, 8,* 325–330.

Muller, A., & Murtagh, T. (2002). Literacy—The 877 million left behind. *Education Today, 2,* 4–7.

Myers, J.W. (1984). *Writing to learn across the curriculum.* Bloomington, IN: Phi Delta Kappa.

Nagy, W.E., & Anderson, R.C. (1984). How many words are there in printed school English? *Reading Research Quarterly, 21,* 304–330.

Nagy, W.E., & Herman, P.A. (1984). *Limitations of vocabulary instruction* (Tech. Rep. No. 326). Urbana, IL: Center for the Study of Reading, University of Illinois. (ERIC Document Reproduction Service No. ED 24898)

Nagy, W.E., & Herman, P.A. (1985). Incidental vs. instructional approaches to increasing reading vocabulary. *Educational Perspectives, 23,* 16–21.

National Reading Panel. (2000). *Report of the National Reading Panel: Reports of the subgroups.* Washington, DC: NICHD. Available http://www.nationalreadingpanel.org

Ness, M. (2007). Reading comprehension strategies in secondary content-area classrooms. *Phi Delta Kappan, 89,* 229–231.

Newmann, F.M., & Oliver, D.W. (1970). *Clarifying public controversy: An approach to teaching social studies.* Boston: Little, Brown.

Nieto, S. (2000). *Affirming diversity: The sociopolitical context of multicultural education.* New York: Longman.

Nist, S.L., & Simpson, M.L. (1989). PLAE, a validated study strategy. *Journal of Reading, 33,* 182–186.

Nist, S.L., & Simpson, S.L. (2000). College studying. In M.L. Kamil, P.B. Mosenthal, P.D. Pearson, & R. Barr (Eds.), *Handbook of reading research* (Vol. 3, pp. 645–666). Mahwah, NJ: Erlbaum.

Nistler, R.J. (1998). Preservice teachers, sixth graders and instructors use dialogue journals to extend their classroom communities. *Reading Horizons, 38,* 203–216.

Norton, T.L., & Anfin, C.S. (1997). Brush up your booktalks: Promoting literature-based reading: Part II. *School Library Media Activities Monthly, 14,* 27–29, 32, 34.

Ogle, D. (1986). K-W-L: A teaching model that develops active reading of expository text. *The Reading Teacher, 39,* 564–570.

Olson, M.W., Gee, T.C., & Forester, N. (1989). Magazines in the classroom: Beyond recreational reading. *Journal of Reading, 32,* 708–713.

Orr, E.W. (1987). *Twice as less: Black English and the performance of black students in mathematics and science.* New York: Norton.

Ortiz, R.K. (1996). Awareness of inner dialogues can alter reading behaviors (Open to suggestion). *Journal of Adolescent and Adult Literacy, 39,* 494–495.

Oster, L. (2001). Using the think-aloud for reading instruction. *The Reading Teacher, 55,* 64–69.

Otto, W. (1991). Dining on mince and slices of quinces (Research). *Journal of Reading, 34,* 482–485.

Otto, W. (1995). The smell of paint. *Journal of Reading, 38,* 392–395.

Padak, N. (1997). *Trade book teaching ideas from the OLRC Reading Group.* Teacher to Teacher Series. (ERIC Document Reproduction Service No. ED 423410)

Palincsar, A.S., & Brown, A.L. (1984). Reciprocal teaching of comprehension-fostering and comprehension-monitoring activities. *Cognition and Instruction, 2,* 117–175.

Palincsar, A.S., & Brown, A.L. (1986). Interactive teaching to promote independent learning from text. *The Reading Teacher, 39,* 771–777.

Palincsar, A.S., & Herrenkohl, L.R. (2002). Designing collaborative learning contexts. *Theory Into Practice, 41,* 26–32.

Paris, S.G., & Oyres, L.R. (1994). *Becoming reflective students and teachers with portfolios and authentic assessment.* Washington, DC: American Psychological Association.

Paris, S.G., Wasik, B.A., & Turner, J.C. (1991). The development of strategic readers. In R. Barr, M.L. Kamil, P.B. Mosenthal, & P.D. Pearson (Eds.), *Handbook of reading research* (Vol. 2, pp. 609–640). White Plains, NY: Longman.

Parker, R., Guillemard, M.S., Goetz, E., & Galarza, A. (1996). Using semantic map tests to assess subject matter comprehension. *Diagnostique, 22,* 39–62.

Parker, W.C., & Jarolimek, J. (1997). *Social studies in elementary education* (10th ed.). Upper Saddle River, NJ: Prentice-Hall.

Parkinson, W. (2000). Language whys. A reevaluation of the rationale for language education in today's world. *Babel, 34,* 12–15.

Pauk, W. (2004). *How to study in college* (8th ed.). Boston: Houghton Mifflin.

Payne, J. (2002). *Basic skills in the workplace: A research review*. London: Learning and Skills Development Agency, Regency Arcade House.

Pearson, P.D., & Fielding, L. (1991). Comprehension instruction. In R. Barr, M.L. Kamil, P.B. Mosenthal, & P.D. Pearson (Eds.), *Handbook of reading research* (Vol. 2, pp. 815–860). White Plains, NY: Longman.

Pearson, P.D., & Johnson, D.D. (1978). *Teaching reading comprehension*. New York: Holt, Rinehart, & Winston.

Perfetti, C.A. (2003). The universal grammar of reading. *Scientific Studies of Reading, 7,* 3–24.

Perry, N.E., Norby, C.J., & VandeKamp, K.O. (2003). Promoting self-regulated reading and writing at home and school. *Elementary School Journal, 103,* 317–338.

Petersen, D., & VanDerWege, C. (2002). Guiding children to be strategic readers. *Phi Delta Kappan, 83,* 437–439.

Peterson, J., & Carroll, M. (1974). The cloze procedure as an indicator of the instructional level for disabled readers. In P.L. Nacke (Ed.), *Interaction: Research and practice in college-adult reading: Twenty-third yearbook of the National Reading Conference* (pp. 153–157). Clemson, SC: National Reading Conference.

Peterson, J., Paradis, E., & Peters, N. (1973). Revalidation of the cloze procedure as a measure of the instructional level for high school students. In P.L. Nacke (Ed.), *Diversity in mature reading: Theory and research: Twenty-second yearbook of the National Reading Conference* (Vol. 1, pp. 144–149). Boone, NC: National Reading Conference.

Peterson, J., Peters, N., & Paradis, E. (1972). Validation of the cloze procedure as a measure of readability with high school, trade school, and college populations. In F.P. Greene (Ed.), *Investigations relating to mature reading: Twenty-first yearbook of the National Reading Conference* (Vol. 1, pp. 45–50). Milwaukee: National Reading Conference.

Piaget, J. (1952). *The origins of intelligence in children*. New York: International University Press.

Pinnell, G.S., Pikulski, J.J., Wilson, K.K., Campbell, J.R., Gough, P.B., & Beatty, A.S. (1995). *Listening to children read aloud: Data from NAEP's integrated reading performance record (IRPR) at grade 4*. Princeton, NJ: Educational Testing Service. (ERIC Reproduction Service No. ED 378 550).

Poindexter, C. (1995). Applying effective reading techniques in content area classes. *Reading Horizons, 35,* 244–249.

Prentice, L., & Cousin, P.T. (1993). Moving beyond the textbook to teach students with learning disabilities. *Teaching Exceptional Children, 26,* 14–17.

Prince, A.T. (1987). Enriching comprehension: A schema altered basal reading lesson. *Reading Research and Instruction, 27,* 45–53.

Radencich, M.C. (1998). Multicultural education for literacy in the year 2000: Traversing comfort zones and transforming knowledge and action. *Peabody Journal of Education, 73* (3&4), 178–201.

Rafferty, C.D. (1992, December). *What will it take to ensure implementation? A content literacy dilemma*. Paper presented at the meeting of the National Reading Conference, San Antonio.

Rankin, E.F., & Culhane, J. (1969). Comparable cloze and multiple-choice comprehension test scores. *Journal of Reading, 13,* 193–198.

Raphael, T.E. (1984). Teaching learners about sources of information for answering comprehension questions. *Journal of Reading, 27,* 303–311.

Raphael, T.E., Highfield, K., & Au, K.H. (2006). *QAR Now: Question answer relationships: A powerful and practical framework that develops comprehension and higher-level thinking in all students*. New York: Scholastic.

Raygor, A.L. (1977). The Raygor readability estimate: A quick and easy way to determine difficulty. In P.D. Pearson (Ed.), *Reading: Theory, research, and practice: Twenty-sixth yearbook of the National Reading Conference* (pp. 259–263). Clemson, SC: National Reading Conference.

Readence, J.E., Bean, T.W., & Baldwin, R.S. (1981). *Content area reading: An integrated approach*. Dubuque, IA: Kendall/Hunt.

Readence, J.E., & Moore, D. (1980). Differentiating text assignments in content areas: Slicing the task. *Reading Horizons, 20,* 112–117.

Readence, J. E., Moore, D.W., & Rickleman, R. J. (2000). *Prereading activities for content area reading and learning* (3rd ed.). Newark, DE: IRA.

Reinking, D. (1986). Integrating graphic aids into content area instruction: The graphic information lesson. *The Reading Teacher, 30,* 146–151.

Reinking, D., & Watkins, J. (2000). A formative experiment investigating the use of multimedia book reviews to increase elementary students' independent reading. *Reading Research Quarterly, 35,* 384–419.

Rice, G.E. (1994). Need for explanations in graphic organizer research. *Reading Psychology, 15,* 39–67.

Rich, R.A., & Blake, S. (1995). Collaborative questioning: Fostering the self-regulated learner. *LD Forum, 20,* 38–40.

Richards, J.C., & McKenna, M.C. (2003). Integrating multiple literacies in K–8 classrooms. Mahwah, NJ: Lawrence Erlbaum.

Richardson, J.S., & Morgan, R.F. (2003). *Reading to learn in the content areas* (5th ed.). Belmont, CA: Wadsworth.

Richgels, D.J., & Hansen, R. (1984). Gloss: Helping students apply both skills and strategies in reading content texts. *Journal of Reading, 27,* 312–317.

Rinehart, S.D., Stahl, S.A., & Erickson, L.G. (1986). Some effects of summarization training on reading and studying. *Reading Research Quarterly, 21,* 422–438.

Risko, V.J., Alvarez, M.C., & Fairbanks, M.M. (1991). External factors that influence study. In R.F. Flippo & D.C. Caverly (Eds.), *Teaching reading and study strategies at the college level* (pp. 195–236). Newark, DE: International Reading Association.

Rivers, L.E. (1980). Use a tape recorder to teach basic skills. *Social Studies, 71*(4), 171–174.

Robb, L. (1998). Helping reluctant readers discover books. *Book Links, 7,* 51–53.

Robinson, D.H. (1998). Graphic organizers as aids to text learning. *Reading Research and Instruction, 37,* 85–105.

Robinson, F.P. (1946). *Effective study*. New York: Harper & Row.

Robinson, R.D., & Good, T.L. (1987). *Becoming an effective reading teacher*. New York: Harper & Row.

Rose, B. (1989). Writing and mathematics: Theory and practice. In P. Connolly & T. Vilardi (Eds.), *Writing to learn mathematics and science*. New York: Teachers College Press.

Rosenbaum, C. (2001). A word map for middle school: A tool for effective vocabulary instruction. *Journal of Adolescent & Adult Literacy, 45,* 44–49.

Rosenshine, B.V. (1986). Synthesis of research on explicit teaching. *Educational Leadership, 43,* 60–69.

Roskos, K.A., & Christie, J.F. (2002). Knowing in the doing—Observing literacy learning in play. *Young Children, 57,* 46–54.

Roskos, K.A., Christie, J.F., & Richgels, D.J. (2003). The essentials of early literacy instruction. *Young Children, 58,* 52–60.

Rowsell, J., & Pahl, K. (2007). Sedimented identities in texts: Instances of practice. *Reading Research Quarterly, 42,* 388–404.

Royer, J. M. (2001). Developing reading and listening comprehension tests based on the sentence verification technique (SVT). *Journal of Adolescent and Adult Literacy, 45,* 30–41.

Royer, J.M., Greene, B.A., & Sinatra, G.M. (1987). The Sentence Verification Technique: A practical procedure for testing comprehension. *Journal of Reading, 30,* 414–422.

Ruddell, M.R. (1993). *Teaching content reading and writing*. Boston: Allyn & Bacon.

Ruddell, R.B., & Ruddell, M.R. (1995). *Teaching children to read and write*. Boston: Allyn & Bacon.

Sampson, M.B. (1995). Circle of questions. *The Reading Teacher, 48,* 364–365.

Savage, J.F. (1983). Reading guides: Effective tools for teaching the gifted. *Roeper Review, 5*(3), 9–11.

Sax, R., & Kohn, A. (1996). Should we pay kids to learn? *Learning, 24,* 6–7.

Schiavone, J.P. (1999). *An old practice in an ESL context.* (ERIC Document Reproduction Service No. ED 434 534).

Schmoker, M. (2007). Reading, writing, and thinking for all. *Educational Leadership, 64,* 63–66.

Scholtz, S., & Prinsloo, M. (2001). New workplaces, new literacies, new identities. *Journal of Adolescent & Adult Literacy, 44,* 710–713.

Schraw, G., & Bruning, R. (1999). How implicit models of reading affect motivation to read and reading engagement. *Scientific Studies of Reading, 3,* 281–302.

Schumaker, J.B., Deshler, D.D., & Denton, P.H. (1982). *An integrated system for providing content to LD adolescents using an audio-taped format* (Research Rep. No. 66). Lawrence: University of Kansas Institute for Research in Learning Disabilities.

Schwartz, R.M. (1988). Learning to learn vocabulary in content area textbooks. *Journal of Reading, 32,* 108–118.

Schwartz, R.M., & Raphael, T.E. (1985). Concept of definition: A key to improving students' vocabulary. *The Reading Teacher, 39,* 198–205.

Scott, J.E. (1994). Teaching nonfiction with the shared book experience. *The Reading Teacher, 47,* 676–678.

Shaver, J.C., & Wise, B.S. (1991). Literacy: The impact of technology on early reading. In B.L. Hayes & K. Camperell (Eds.), *Literacy: International, national, state, and local: Eleventh yearbook of the American Reading Forum* (pp. 139–145). Logan: Utah State University.

Shiveley, J.M., & van Fossen, P.J. (2000). Using the Internet to create primary source teaching packets. *Social Studies, 91,* 244–252.

Simonini, R.C., Jr. (1966). Word-making in present-day English. *English Journal, 55,* 752–757.

Simpson, M.L., & Nist, S.L. (1984). PLAE: A model for planning successful independent learning. *Journal of Reading, 28,* 218–223.

Singer, H. (1975). The SEER technique: A non-computational procedure for quickly estimating readability level. *Journal of Reading Behavior, 7,* 255–267.

Skinner, B.F. (1981). How to discover what you have to say: A talk to students. *The Behavior Analyst, 4,* 1–7.

Slater, W.H., & Horstman, F.R. (2002). Teaching reading and writing to struggling middle school and high school students: The case for reciprocal teaching. *Preventing School Failure, 46,* 163–166.

Slavin, R.E. (1988). Cooperative learning and student achievement. *Educational Leadership, 45,* 31–33.

Slavin, R.E. (1989–1990). Research on cooperative learning: Consensus and controversy. *Educational Leadership, 47,* 52–54.

Slavin, R.E. (1999). Comprehensive approaches to cooperative learning. *Theory into Practice, 38,* 74–79.

Smith, C., & Elder, T. (2001, April). *A reading game plan to assist struggling readers in grades 4–8: New twists on old methods.* Paper presented at the meeting of the International Reading Association, New Orleans.

Smith, F. (2004). *Understanding reading: A psycholinguistic analysis of reading and learning to read* (6th ed.). Hillsdale, NJ: Lawrence Erlbaum.

Sommers, C.H. (2000). *The war against boys: How misguided feminism is harming our young men.* New York: Simon & Schuster.

Spear-Swerling, L., & Sternberg, R.J. (1996). *Off track: When poor readers become learning disabled.* Westview Press.

Spiro, R.J. (1991, December). *Integrative reconciliation of paradigm conflict in reading: Joining multiple perspectives in reading research, in learning to read, and in preparing reading teachers for practice.* Paper presented at the meeting of the National Reading Conference, Palm Springs, CA.

Squire, J.R. (1983). Composing and comprehending: Two sides of the same basic process. *Language Arts, 60,* 581–589.

Stahl, N.A., King, J.R., & Henk, W.A. (1991). Enhancing students' notetaking through training and evaluation. *Journal of Reading, 34,* 614–622.

Stahl, S.A. (1999). *Vocabulary development: From research to practice* (vol. 2). Cambridge, MA: Brookline Books.

Stahl, S.A. (2004). Scaly? Audacious? Debris? Salubrious? Vocabulary learning and the child with learning disabilities. *Perspectives, 30*(1), 5–12.

Stahl, S.A., Heubach, K., & Cramond, B. (2005). Fluency-oriented reading instruction. *Journal of Literacy Research*.

Stahl, S.A., & Kapinus, B.A. (1991). Possible sentences: Predicting word meanings to teach content area vocabulary. *The Reading Teacher, 45*, 36–45.

Stahl, S.A., & Nagy, W.E. (2006). *Teaching word meanings*. Mahwah, NJ: Lawrence Erlbaum.

Stahl, S.A., & Vancil, S.J. (1986). Discussion is what makes semantic maps work in vocabulary instruction. *The Reading Teacher, 40*, 62–67.

Stanovich, K.E. (2000). *Progress in understanding reading*. New York: Guilford.

Staton, J. (1980). Writing and counseling: Using a dialogue journal. *Language Arts, 57*, 514–518.

Stauffer, R. (1969). *Directing reading maturity as a cognitive process*. New York: Harper & Row.

Stauffer, R. (1980). *The language experience approach to the teaching of reading* (2nd ed.). New York: Harper & Row.

Stearns, C.J. (1999). A middle school venture into cooperative learning: Successes and dilemmas. *Theory into Practice, 38*, 100–104.

Stephens, E.C., & Brown, J.E. (2000). *A handbook of content literacy strategies: 75 practical reading and writing ideas*. Norwood, MA: Christopher-Gordon.

Stewart, R.A., & O'Brien, D.G. (1989). Resistance to content area reading: A focus on pre-service teachers. *Journal of Reading, 32*, 396–401.

Sticht, G. (2002). Adult basic skills: How many need it? How many want it? *Basic Skills, 12*, 26–29.

Stoodt, B.D., & Balbo, E. (1979). Integrating study skills instruction with content in a secondary classroom. *Reading World, 18*, 247–252.

Strackbein, D., & Tillman, M. (1987). The joy of journals—with reservations. *Journal of Reading, 31*, 28–31.

Stratton, B.D., & Grindler, M.C. (1992). Discovering oneself: An important attribute in the middle school. *Middle School Journal, 24*, 42–43.

Strong, G.E. (1998). A life in literacy. *American Libraries, 29*, 36–39.

Sukow, W.W. (1990). Physical science workshops for teachers using interactive science exhibits. *School Science and Mathematics, 90*, 42–47.

Sweet, A.P., & Guthrie, J.T. (1997). How children's motivations relate to literacy development and instruction. *The Reading Teacher, 49*, 660–662.

Taba, H. (1967). *Teacher's handbook for elementary social studies*. Reading, MA: Addison-Wesley.

Taboada, A., & Guthrie, J.T. (2006). Contributions of student questioning and prior knowledge to construction of knowledge from reading informational text. *Journal of Literacy Research, 38*, 1–35.

Tancock, S.M. (1995). Classroom teachers and reading specialists examine their Chapter 1 reading programs. *Journal of Reading Behavior, 27*, 315–335.

Thompkins, A.C., & Binder, K.S. (2003). A comparison of the factors affecting reading performance of functionally illiterate adults and children matched by reading level. *Reading Research Quarterly, 38*, 236–258.

Thompson, K.L., & Taymans, J.M. (1994). Development of a reading strategies program: Bridging the gaps among decoding, literature, and thinking skills. *Intervention in School and Clinic, 30*, 17–27.

Thorp, C. (2002). Reading and writing in the content areas. *Educational Leadership, 60*, 96.

Tierney, R.J., & Readence, J.E. (2005). *Reading strategies and practices: A compendium* (6th ed.). Boston: Allyn & Bacon.

Tobias, S. (1982). When do instructional methods make a difference? *Educational Researcher, 11*, 4–9.

Tompkins, G.E. (1998). *Literacy strategies. Step by step*. Upper Saddle River, NJ: Prentice-Hall.

Tompkins, G.E. (2003). *Literacy for the 21st century* (3rd ed.). Upper Saddle River, NJ: Merrill/Prentice Hall.

Torgesen, J.K., & Kail, R.J. (1985). Memory processes in exceptional children. In B.K. Keogh (Ed.), *Advances in special education: Basic constructs and theoretical orientations*. Greenwich, CT: JAI Press.

Tower, C. (2000). Questions that matter: Preparing elementary students for the inquiry process. *The Reading Teacher, 53*, 550–557.

Trueba, H.T., Guthrie, G.P., & Au, K.H.P. (1981). *Culture and the bilingual classroom: Studies in classroom ethnography*. Rowley, MA: Newbury House.

Tuinman, J.J. (1971). Asking reading dependent questions. *Journal of Reading, 14*, 289–292, 336.

Turley, S. (1994, April). *"The way teachers teach is, like, totally whacked": The student voice on classroom practice*. Paper presented at the meeting of the American Educational Research Association, New Orleans.

UNESCO. (2003). *Education in a multilingual world*. France: UNESCO Publishing.

United States Census Bureau. (2002). *United States Census 2000*. Washington, DC: U.S. Government Printing Office.

Vacca, R.T., & Linek, W.M. (1992). Writing to learn. In J.W. Irwin & M.A. Doyle (Eds.), *Reading/writing connections: Learning from research* (pp. 145–159). Newark, DE: International Reading Association.

Vacca, R.T., & Vacca, J.L. (2004). *Content area reading: Literacy and learning across the curriculum* (8th ed.). New York: Longman.

Valdés, G. (2001). *Learning and not learning English: Latino students in American schools*. New York: Teachers College Press.

Vasilyev, Y. (2003). The network of concepts and facts: Forming a system of conclusions through refection. *Thinking Classroom, 4*, 29–33.

Vaughan, J.L., Jr. (1982). Use the ConStruct procedure to foster active reading and learning. *Journal of Reading, 25*, 412–422.

Venezky, R. (1995). Literacy. In T. Harris & R. Hodges (Eds.), *The literacy dictionary* (p. 142). Newark, DE: International Reading Association.

Villegas, A.M., & Lucas, T. (2007). The culturally responsive teacher. *Educational Leadership, 64*, 28–33.

Virgil, S. (1995). More time and choices overcome students' resistance to reading. *Clearing House, 68*, 52–54.

Vogel, S., & Sattler, J. (1981). *The college student with a learning disability: A handbook for college and university admission officers, faculty, and administration*. N.p.: Illinois Council for Learning Disabilities.

Wade, S.E. (1990). Using think-alouds to assess comprehension. *The Reading Teacher, 43*, 442–451.

Wade, S.E., Trathen, W., & Schraw, G. (1990). An analysis of spontaneous study strategies, *Reading Research Quarterly, 25*, 147–166.

Walley, C., & Kommer, D. (2000). Writing as part of the team. *Clearing House, 73*, 232–234.

Walker, J.E. (1982). Study strategies: Too many, too few or just right? In D.R. Fleming (Ed.), *Proceedings of the Fifteenth Annual Conference of the Western College Reading Association*.

Walpole, S. (1998–1999). Changing texts, changing thinking: Comprehension demands of new science textbooks. *The Reading Teacher, 52*, 358–369.

Walsh, K. (2003). Basal readers: The lost opportunity to build the knowledge that propels comprehension. *American Education, 27*, 24–27.

Wark, D.M., & Flippo, R.F. (1991). Preparing for and taking tests. In R.F. Flippo & D.C. Caverly (Eds.), *Teaching reading and study strategies at the college level* (pp. 294–338). Newark, DE: International Reading Association.

Watkins, J.H., McKenna, M.C., Manzo, A.V., & Manzo, U.C. (1994, April). *The effects of the Listen-Read-Discuss procedure on the content learning of high school students*. Paper presented at the meeting of the American Educational Research Association, New Orleans.

Webster, J.P. (1998). Semantic maps. *TESOL Journal, 7,* 42–43.

Wedman, J., & Robinson, R.D. (1990). Workplace literacy: A proposed model. *Adult Literacy and Basic Education, 14,* 45–53.

Wepner, S.B. (1990–1991). Computers, reading software, and at-risk eighth graders. *Journal of Reading, 34,* 264–268.

Werderich, D. (2006). The teacher's response process to dialogue journals. *Reading Horizons, 47,* 47–54.

White, C.S., Hayes, D.A., & Pate, P.E. (1991). Bridging across instances of a concept in science instruction. In J. Zutell & S. McCormick (Eds.), *Learner factors/teacher factors: Issues in literacy research and instruction: Fortieth yearbook of the National Reading Conference* (pp. 263–268). Chicago: National Reading Conference.

Wilhelm, J.D. (2001). Think-alouds: Boost reading comprehension. *Instructor, 11,* 26–28.

Williams, B.T. (2007). Action heroes and literate sidekicks: Literacy and identity in popular culture. *Journal of Adolescent and Adult Literacy, 50,* 680–685.

Williams, S.M., & Callins, T. (2007). Creating culturally responsive literacy programs in inclusive classrooms. *Intervention in School and Clinic, 42,* 195–197.

Williamson, R.A. (1996). Self-questioning—An aid to metacognition. *Reading Horizons, 37,* 30–47.

Wolf, S.A. (1998). The flight of reading: Shifts in instruction, orchestration, and attitudes through classroom theatre. *Reading Research Quarterly, 33,* 382–415.

Wood, J.W., & Miederhoff, J.W. (1988). A model for adapting the teacher-made test. *The Pointer, 33,* 7–11.

Wood, K.D. (1988). Guiding students through informational text. *The Reading Teacher, 41,* 912–920.

Wood, K.D., Lapp, D., & Flood, J. (1992). *Guiding readers through text: A review of study guides.* Newark, DE: International Reading Association.

Worthy, J., & Hoffman, J.V. (1999). Critical questions. *The Reading Teacher, 52,* 520–521.

Worthy, J., Moorman, M., & Turner, M. (1999). What Johnny likes to read is hard to find at school. *Reading Research Quarterly, 34,* 12–27.

Yopp, H.K., & Yopp, R.H. (1996). *Literature-based reading activities* (2nd ed.). Des Moines: Allyn & Bacon.

Zakaluk, B.L., & Samuels, S.J. (1988). Toward a new approach to predicting text comprehensibility. In B.L. Zakaluk & S.J. Samuels (Eds.), *Readability: Its past, present, and future* (pp. 121–144). Newark, DE: International Reading Association.

Zapprich, M.A. (1997). Web-making: An easy but critical first step to better writing. *Reading and Writing Quarterly: Overcoming Learning Difficulties, 13,* 391–395.

Zimmerman, B.J., & Pons, M.M. (1986). Development of a structured interview for assessing student use of self-regulated learning strategies. *American Educational Research Journal, 23,* 614–628.

Name Index

Abelard, P., 149
Adams, M. J., 21
Ainslie, D., 84
Albright, L., 136
Allen, A., 197
Allen, J., 84
Alpert, B. R., 164
Alvarez, M. C., 195, 196
Alvermann, D. E., 9, 68, 150
Ambe, E. B., 65
Anders, P. L., 96
Anderson, R. C., 81
Anderson, T. H., 194
Anderson-Inman, L., 183
Anfin, C. S., 73
Antisthenes, 78
Aquinas, T., 104
Ariail, M., 136
Aristotle, 10, 82
Armbruster, B. B., 61, 194, 195, 200
Armstrong, D. P., 119
Aronson, E., 129
Ash, G. E., 5
Au, K., 51, 109
Aulls, M. W., 7, 15
Aultman, L. P., 74
Ausubel, D., 69, 83
Avery, P. G., 93

Baildon, M., 102
Bajsanski, I., 34
Balbo, E., 193
Baldwin, R. S., 126, 200
Balfour, A., 102
Barrett, T. C., 103
Barron, R. F., 83, 85
Bartolome, L., 96
Baskin, R. S., 165
Bassiri, D., 158
Bassler, O. C., 134
Baumann, J. F., 208
Baxendell, B. W., 83
Bean, R. M., 133
Bean, T. W., 113–114, 126, 200, 209, 216
Beatty, A. S., 209
Beck, I. L., 81, 157, 214, 215

Beecher, H. W., 96
Behrens, H., 18
Benito, Y. M., 109
Berman, S., 163
Betts, E. A., 137
Bierce, A., 96
Binder, K. S., 5
Binkley, M. R., 33
Bishop, C. H., 197
Blachowicz, C. L. Z., 79, 171
Blake, S., 166
Blaney, N., 129
Bloodgood, J. W., 5, 6
Boggs, S. T., 164
Bolyard, J. J., 85
Bonk, R. M., 133
Book, C., 158
Bormuth, J. R., 36
Bos, C. S., 96
Bowen, S., 83
Bowman-Kruhm, M., 200
Britton, J. B., 22
Broaddus, K., 213
Bromley, K., 79
Brophy, J., 151, 159
Brown, A. L., 142, 162
Brown, J. E., 4
Brown, K. J., 73
Browning, L. J., 47
Brozo, W. G., 193
Bruner, J., 170
Bruning, R., 197
Brunn, M., 83
Bulazo, J., 133
Bullock, T. L., 193, 195, 196, 197, 200
Burgess, T., 22
Burrow, R., 134
Byron, G. G., 96

Cairney, T. H., 5
Calfee, R. C., 161
Callins, T., 51
Campbell, A., 4
Campbell, J. R., 209
Camus, A., 22, 62
Carlsen, W. S., 160
Carlyle, T., 170

Carnine, D. W., 94
Carr, E., 141
Carroll, L., 80
Carroll, M., 36
Carson, R., 66
Carter, K., 83
Carver, C., 16
Casale, U. P., 141
Caverly, D. C., 201
Cazden, C. B., 150
Chall, J., 16, 119, 136
Chickie-Wolfe, L. A., 193
Christie, J. F., 5
Ciardiello, A. V., 161
Clariana, R. B., 36
Clary, L. M., 206, 211
Cloonan, M., 4
Cochran-Smith, M., 23
Coffman, G. A., 113
Cohen, J., 165
Coleman, E. B., 36
Come, B. G., 8
Commeyras, M., 166
Connolly, P., 21
Connors, N. A., 9
Conway, B. J., 47
Cooter, R. B., Jr., 217
Cousin, P. T., 9
Craig, J. C., 6
Cramond, B., 136
Crapse, L., 161
Culhane, J., 36
Cullum, L., 157
Cunningham, D., 123
Cunningham, J. W., 113

Dahlberg, L. A., 112, 113
Dalle, T., 76
Damico, J., 102
Danielson, E., 18, 65
Darch, C. B., 94
Darvin, J., 6
Davey, B., 27
Davies, S. K., 195
Davis, L. W., 119
Davis, M. H., 219
Day, C., 61
DeBono, E., 163

Subject Index